'Much more than an introduction, John Morecroft's *Strategic M[odelling and Business] Dynamics* uses interactive "mini-simulators and microworlds" [to create a vivid] and effective learning environment in which readers, whatever [their background] develop their intuition about complex dynamic systems. The e[xamples, ranging from] manufacturing operations to competitive strategy, corporate growth and environmental sustainability, provide a rich test-bed for the development of the systems thinking and modelling skills needed to design effective policies for the strategic challenges faced by senior managers throughout the economy today.'
John Sterman, Jay W. Forrester Professor of Management, MIT Sloan School of Management

'We are living in a world revolutionised by six decades of exponential growth in computing speed, where powerful computers have become consumer electronics and simulation has become virtual reality. Business modelling has come of age. This book, with its vivid examples and simulators, is helping to bring modelling, system dynamics and simulation into the mainstream of management education where they now belong.'
John A. Quelch, Professor of Marketing, Harvard Business School, Former Dean of London Business School

'John Morecroft's book is an ideal text for students interested in system modelling and its application to a range of real-world problems. The book covers all that is necessary to develop expertise in system dynamics modelling and through the range of applications makes a persuasive case for the power and scope of SD modelling. As such, it will appeal to practitioners as well as students. At Warwick we have a range of undergraduate, masters and MBA courses in simulation, business modelling and strategic development/planning and the text would provide valuable support to those courses.'
Robert Dyson, Emeritus Professor, Operational Research and Management Sciences Group, Warwick Business School

'Illustrated by examples from everyday life, business and policy, John Morecroft expertly demonstrates how systems thinking aided by system dynamics can improve our understanding of the world around us. Indeed, such thinking provides the basis for improving our world, from making everyday decisions to leading key strategic and policy initiatives. Anyone who is interested in understanding the world and making better choices should read this book.'
Stewart Robinson, Associate Dean Research, President of the Operational Research Society, Professor of Management Science, School of Business and Economics, Loughborough University

'This text fills the gap between texts focusing on the purely descriptive systems approach and the more technical system dynamics ones. I consider it particularly well suited to the more mature student (MBA, EMBA, Executive courses) due to the focus on conceptualisation and the understanding of complex dynamics.'
Ann van Ackere, Professor of Decision Sciences, HEC Lausanne, Université de Lausanne

'In today's complex business world company leaders are repeatedly challenged to rethink dominant strategic logics, and if necessary to adapt their firms to cope with turbulence and change. Strategic modelling based on system dynamics is a powerful tool that helps to better understand the feedback structures underlying the dynamics of change. The author demonstrates the appeal and power of business modelling to make sense of strategic initiatives and to anticipate their impacts through simulation. The book offers various simulators that allow readers to conduct their own policy experiments.'
Dr Erich Zahn, Professor for Strategic Management, University of Stuttgart

Strategic Modelling and Business Dynamics

A Feedback Systems Approach

Second Edition

John D.W. Morecroft

Library of Congress Cataloging-in-Publication Data is available.

Morecroft, John D.W. (John Douglas William)
  Strategic modelling and business dynamics : a feedback systems approach /
John D.W. Morecroft. – Second edition.
    pages cm
  Includes bibliographical references and index.
  ISBN 978-1-118-84468-7 (paper) 1. Decision making–Simulation methods.
2. Business–Simulation methods. 3. Social systems–Simulation methods.
4. System analysis. 5. Computer simulation. I. Title.
  HD30.23.M663 2015
  001.4'34–dc23   201501

A catalogue record for this book is available from the British Library.

ISBN 978-1-118-84468-7 (pbk)
ISBN 978-1-118-99481-8 (ebk)   ISBN 978-1-118-84470-0 (ebk)

Cover image: © Getty Images/Stockbyte
Cover design: Wiley
Set in 10/13pt ITCGaramond by Aptara Inc., New Delhi, India

To Jay Forrester, academic pioneer

Brief Contents

Contents

x ■ Contents

About the Author

John Morecroft is Senior Fellow in Management Science and Operations at London Business School where he has taught system dynamics, problem structuring and strategy in MBA, PhD and Executive Education programmes. He served as Associate Dean of the School's Executive MBA and co-designed EMBA-Global, a dual degree programme with New York's Columbia Business School. He is a leading expert in system dynamics and strategic modelling. His publications include numerous journal articles and three co-edited books. He is a recipient of the Jay Wright Forrester Award of the System Dynamics Society for his work on bounded rationality, information feedback and behavioural decision making in models of the firm. He is a Past President of the Society and one of its Founding Members. His research interests include the dynamics of firm performance and the use of models and simulation in strategy development. He has led applied research projects for international organisations including Royal Dutch/Shell, AT&T, BBC World Service, Cummins Engine Company, Ford of Europe, Harley-Davidson, Ericsson, McKinsey & Co and Mars. Before joining London Business School he was on the faculty of MIT's Sloan School of Management where he received his PhD. He also holds degrees in Operational Research from Imperial College, London and in Physics from Bristol University.

Foreword by Peter Checkland

When I was a manager in the synthetic fibre industry in the 1950s and 60s, there was a recognised but problematical pattern of activity in the textile industry. A small increase in demand for textile products would induce big ups and downs back in yarn and fabric production. This arose as a result of the structure of the production-to-retail chain, a sequence from fibre to yarn to fabric to products, these being stages in the hands of different companies between which were time delays. This recurring pattern of response to demand change was one which no one stakeholder could command and control.

Many areas of human activity reveal dynamics of this type, with several classic patterns of behaviour: exponential growth or decline; oscillation; S-shaped growth; growth followed by collapse, etc.

John Morecroft's textbook is a brilliantly clear guide to elucidating and modelling such patterns of behaviour. The modelling is normally a team effort based on both real-world experience of the area and the principles of system dynamics. Such modelling seeks to reveal enduring feedback structures (both balancing and reinforcing) which are real characteristics of the situation in question but are normally hidden. Once developed, such models are 'instruments for investigation, clarification and discovery', and can be used to feed better evidence into discussion of strategy than does the reliance on experience and gut feel, which is the common mode of managing.

These pictures of dynamic behaviour may be relevant within an organisation (public or private) or may be characteristic of an industry. A particularly interesting example in the book is the one which in the end affects us all – the dynamics of the oil industry. Here is complexity stemming from an oil market which tries to meet demand, a fluctuating price for oil, an organisation of some producers (OPEC) which sets quotas for production and suppliers consisting of independents, opportunists and a 'swing producer' (Saudi Arabia), which produces just enough to defend OPEC's intended price. The build-up of the model of industry dynamics is lucidly described. It was carried out not as an academic exercise but by the author working with a team of Shell managers, and made a serious contribution to Shell's strategic thinking about their industry context and its possible futures.

This illustrates an outstanding feature of John Morecroft's approach. All the work described was carried out in active engagement with managers facing problems.

Not for this author the too-familiar picture in which academics sit at their desks and write papers about other papers!

So this book is not 'academic' in the usual derogatory sense of that word. Nor is it a book to be read casually in an armchair, for it comes with website materials enabling readers to get a feel for situation dynamics by running simulators – including one containing the oil industry model.

Finally, although presented as a textbook, this volume is relevant on a broader canvas. When I was a manager in industry I found the then textbook management science irrelevant to my day-to-day concerns. However, since then a major shift in perspective has occurred. Originally the core concept ('hard') was to make models of assumed real-world systems, and then experiment on the models to find optimum ways of doing things. The richer current concept ('soft') illustrated here, is complementary to this. It uses models as transitional objects to aid learning. In his last chapter John Morecroft writes:

> The idea that there is a singular and objective world out there to be modelled is replaced with the softer notion that a formal model can help improve mental models ... through which we interpret and make sense of the world ...

For its lucidity, its practicality and its illustrations of the idea of consciously learning your way to 'action to improve', this book is a very welcome addition to the literature. It brings a fresh wind off the heath to the groves of academe.

Peter Checkland
Emeritus Professor of Systems
and Honorary Fellow
of Lancaster University

Preface to the Second Edition

In the second edition of *Strategic Modelling and Business Dynamics* I have refreshed the book while building on its strengths. The original 2007 book was well received. So I retained the pre-existing ten-chapter architecture and within this architecture I made numerous chapter-by-chapter revisions. For example chapters 1 and 9, on the fishing industry and *World Dynamics* refer to new research and web-based simulators about sustainability and climate change. The background to the oil industry in Chapter 8 reports changes to industry structure and the advent of shale oil. The references at the end of each chapter have been carefully reviewed and updated to include selected journal articles and books that point the way to important ongoing developments in the field such as group model building and computationally intensive analytical methods.

But there is more too. I want the book to be an enduring bridge from traditional to contemporary system dynamics, and so I have created two accompanying websites – the Learners' website and the Instructors' website.[1] Traditional system dynamics involves a distinctive 'style' of modelling and analysis. It lays strong emphasis on clear visualisation and documentation of real-world feedback structure backed-up by rigorous yet easy-to-read equation formulations. Understanding of dynamics comes from careful narrative interpretation of simulations. I use these style guidelines for modelling and analysis throughout the book and I believe it is important for all students of system dynamics to master them. To reinforce the message I have provided, on the Learners' website, selected articles from the working paper archives of the MIT System Dynamics Group.[2] I hope readers will enjoy these historical glimpses of the field. On the Instructors' website I have provided annotated and graded solutions to course assignments showing exemplary work by students who have followed the style guidelines. My thanks to Chris Baker, Zahir Balaporia, Bill Grace and John Kapson (graduates of WPI's online programme in system dynamics) for agreeing to display their anonymised assignments for the benefit of other learners. It is worth noting that, when

---

[1] Please see the About the Website Resources section at the back of the book.

[2] The articles are reproduced with permission of MIT's Technology Licensing Office. They come from a special DVD archive collection of all the working papers and PhD theses in the D-memo series of MIT's System Dynamics Group, covering a period of almost 50 years, starting in the early 1960s. In total the collection contains around five thousand articles, originally printed on paper, which have each been scanned to create electronic pdf files. Copyright of the entire collection resides with MIT and the DVD is available from the System Dynamics Society www.system dynamics.org.

enrolled in the course, they each held responsible full-time posts in business or government.

From this foundation of rigour-with-accessibility it is then possible for learners to reach out securely to complementary methods and ideas, whatever form they might take. For example, the book already connects with contemporary behavioural and resource-based views of the firm, as described in the Preface from the 1st Edition of the book (see the next section). These ideas, from modern economics and strategy, fit neatly with asset stock accumulation and the *information feedback view of the firm* found in traditional system dynamics. In addition, and scattered throughout the book, there are references to contemporary analytical methods for dynamic models. And finally, for model conceptualisation, there is mention of tried-and-tested protocols for group model building.

I have added two new electronic topics that can be found in learning support folders on the Learners' website (see the About the Website Resources section). The topics are the 'dynamics of diversification' and 'managing metamorphosis'. Diversification is an important part of corporate (multi-business) strategy and complements material in Chapters 6, 7, 8 and 10 on the dynamics of single-business firms and of entire industries. Metamorphosis is a process of managed adaptation to change in the business environment; change that is often ushered in by firms, industries and societies as they co-exist and innovate while competing for resources and markets. When the environment changes organisations must reliably sense the change. Then they must take timely action to re-configure their assets and operating policies in order to survive and contribute to the formation of a new and beneficial future environment. The material on metamorphosis is novel and somewhat experimental. It can be seen as a way to extend the range of strategic modelling to include surprise disruption to firms' core business arising from technical and social innovations – and covert side-effects. The new electronic content includes video lectures from my online course at Worcester Polytechnic Institute (WPI). I am grateful to Khalid Saeed and Jim Doyle at WPI for enabling and supporting the use of this video content.

All the simulators used in the book are now stored on the Learners' website in chapter-by-chapter learning support folders. They are accompanied by an evergreen link to the latest iThink modelling software. My thanks to Karim Chichakly at isee systems for providing this link and for implementing, within the evolving software, special functionality on which my book relies – in particular sketchable time charts and the capability for users to conduct instructive 'tours' of initial simulator conditions (by hovering-over model icons to view the numerical values they hold).

My thanks also to the editorial and book production team at Wiley for their friendly and professional support throughout the 2nd edition project. Jenny Ng worked diligently with me on design and content changes. She also expertly managed permissions and ensured everything was completed on time. Tessa Allen skilfully guided the book through it's multi-stage production process while Caroline Quinnell sharpened numerous phrases during copy editing. My secretary Suzanne Shapiro has steadfastly and cheerfully supported my work at London Business School for more than 25 years. During this period Suzanne and I have been based in two different subject areas: Strategy & Entrepreneurship (1986–1996); and Management Science & Operations (1997–present). Thank you Suzanne! Finally, I thank my wife Linda who provides the motivation, love, stability and perspective of family life that lies behind all my work.

Preface from the First Edition[3]

I first became interested in models and modelling when I studied physics as an undergraduate at Bristol University. Or perhaps my interest was really awakened much earlier when, as a boy of nine or 10, my friend Alan Green introduced me to the board game of Monopoly. I soon became fascinated with board games of all sorts and accumulated a collection that included Cluedo (a detective murder mystery game, also known as Clue), Railroader (a game to build and operate your own wild-west railroad in competition with rival railway companies), and Buccaneer (a game of pirate ships and treasure collecting). I was intrigued by the colourful tokens, the chance cards, the rules and the evocative boards that showed city sights, a murder mansion, a treasure island or whatever was needed to fire the imagination. In Buccaneer, the game's clever distinction between the 'sailing power' and 'fighting power' of a treasure-seeking frigate is something I still appreciate today. And as a modeller I admire the game designer's artful representation of a pirate's world, set out on a blue-and-white chequered board that serves as an ocean.

Later, after graduating from Bristol, I joined Ford of Europe's operational research department, where computational decision models replaced the abstract and elegant models of physics. There I worked on investment appraisal (justifying the decision to build a new Fiesta car factory in Spain) and dealer location (whereabouts within Bromsgrove, Bury St Edmunds, or other English towns and cities, to site new car dealerships). During the second of my three years with Ford, the company sponsored me on an MSc degree in operational research at London University's Imperial College. It was at Imperial that I first encountered system dynamics, albeit briefly in an elective course on quantitative methods, and this chance encounter eventually led me to apply to the doctoral programme at MIT's Sloan School of Management for a PhD in system dynamics. Hence began the journey that I have pursued ever since.

When I look back over my 40-plus years in the field I see five different phases of work, all of which have contributed to the content of this book and led me to the friends and colleagues who have shaped my thinking. My names for these phases are: (1) manufacturing dynamics and information networks; (2) bounded rationality and behavioural decision making; (3) modelling for

---

[3]Full details of articles and books referred to in the Preface can be found in later chapters by cross-referencing with author names in the index.

learning; (4) the dynamics of strategy; and (5) soft systems and complementary modelling methods.

Manufacturing Dynamics and Information Networks

The first phase coincided with my doctoral dissertation at MIT when I worked on manufacturing and supply chain dynamics in Cummins Engine Company and Harley-Davidson. I was fortunate, back then, to have Jay Forrester as my PhD thesis supervisor, Jim Lyneis as a collaborator/faculty adviser on the Cummins project, and Nathaniel Mass as a faculty instructor. I learned many valuable modelling skills from them and from MIT's intensive academic apprenticeship with its special educational blend of theory and real-world practice. I still remember the sense of excitement as a first-year doctoral student, arriving by plane in Columbus Indiana, headquarters of Cummins Engine Company. There, I worked on the Cummins manufacturing dynamics project and found myself applying the inventory control, forecasting and production planning formulations I had learned at MIT. The simple factory model in Chapter 5 contains echoes of these same formulations. Further archive material on manufacturing dynamics can be found in the learning support folder for Chapter 5 on the Learners' website (see the About the Website Resources section).

My doctoral thesis topic arose from an on-the-job discovery that circumstance presented. I was working simultaneously on manufacturing models of Cummins and Harley-Davidson. When I set out the 10–15 page diagrams of these two models side-by-side on my apartment floor in Cambridge (Massachusetts), I noticed that the information flows which coordinated multi-stage production in the two factories were arranged in different patterns. Every stage of production in Harley, from final assembly of motorcycles to sub-assemblies and raw materials, was coordinated from a master schedule – a kind of top-down control. There was no such master schedule in Cummins's factory at the time. Stages of production followed local order-point rules. It turned out that Harley-Davidson was operating a computer-driven top-down material requirements planning (MRP) system, which was entirely new to manufacturing firms at the time (and, back then, had scarcely featured in the academic literature on operations management). My thesis compared the long-term dynamic performance of these alternative approaches to production planning and control. A striking result was that traditional order-point rules outperformed MRP (in terms of operating cost, production stability, inventory availability and lead-time predictability). Only under special and hard-to-achieve factory conditions was MRP superior, despite the cost-savings touted by advocates of MRP. And so my curiosity about information networks began.

As an aside, I should mention that the basis for the manufacturing models in my thesis was the production sector of the MIT group's National Economic Model. The production sector was essentially a generic model of the firm, residing within a system dynamics model of the US economy. The premise of the group's research at the time was that the US economy could be conceived as a micro-economic collection of interacting firms, households and banks. Macro-economic behaviour arises from micro-structure. Jay Forrester was leading the National Model project, so he knew the production sector intimately. As my thesis supervisor he was able to swiftly critique and guide my efforts to adapt this generic model of the firm to fit what I had discovered from the company-specific models of Cummins and Harley. I learned a great deal about model formulation and behaviour analysis from those encounters. I also learned from other doctoral students in system dynamics who, at the time, included David Andersen, Alan Graham, Mats Lindquist, Ali Mashayeki, George Richardson, Barry Richmond, Khalid Saeed and Peter Senge; and then later Nathan Forrester, John Sterman, Jack Homer, Jim Hines and Bob Eberlein.

It was while working with the production sector, which was a visually complex model, that I took to drawing boundaries around sets of model symbols that belonged with a given policy function, such as capacity utilisation or scheduling and ordering. This visual simplification procedure later led to policy structure diagrams as a high-level way of representing the coordinating network in system dynamics models. I use both policy boundaries and policy structure diagrams throughout the book.

Bounded Rationality and Behavioural Decision Making

My thesis showed that sparse and 'simple' information networks in firms can often deliver business performance that is superior to more complex and sophisticated information networks. This observation led me, as a newly-appointed junior faculty member at MIT Sloan, into the literature of the Carnegie School and Herbert Simon's work on bounded rationality. The idea that the 'structure' of a firm's information feedback network determines the firm's performance and dynamic behaviour is central to system dynamics.[4] The Carnegie literature helps to bring the information network into clear focus and to explain why human decision makers, faced with complexity and

---

[4]See also a guest lecture I delivered at WPI in 2009 entitled 'Reflections on System Dynamics and Strategy'. It can be found on the Learners' website in a folder entitled 'A Glimpse of Learning Phases in the Preface'. The same lecture can also be viewed on YouTube by searching under 'System Dynamics and Strategy'.

information overload, prefer sparse information networks. People and organisations are boundedly rational. They cannot gather or process all the information needed to make 'best' (objectively rational) decisions. Whenever people take decisions that lead to action, they selectively filter information sources, disregarding or overlooking many signals while paying attention to only a few. Well-designed policies recognise this human trait, while functional 'stovepipes' are an unfortunate corollary that stem from poor design (or no design at all). In practice, bounded rationality leads to departmentalised organisations in which the left hand quite literally doesn't know (and shouldn't need to know) what the right hand is doing. Loose coordination among functions, departments or sectors is normal.

Bounded rationality helped me to identify, interpret and better understand information feedback loops in business and social systems. Puzzling dynamics nearly always arise from 'hidden' coordination problems and this idea is woven throughout the book, beginning with the simple fisheries model in Chapter 1, continuing in Chapter 4's world of showers and in Chapter 5's factory model, and culminating in Chapter 7's market growth model. The information/coordination theme continues in Chapter 8 (the oil industry), in part of Chapter 9 (a return to fisheries) and in Chapter 10 (product growth dynamics in fast-moving consumer goods).

I was not alone at MIT in working on bounded rationality and system dynamics. John Sterman too was studying the topic, and using it to make sense of long-term economic cycles generated by the National Economic Model. Through conversations, seminars and papers I gained a better appreciation of the information processing assumptions of system dynamics that distinguish the subject from traditional micro-economics on the one hand and optimisation methods in management science on the other.

Modelling for Learning

After more than 10 years at MIT, I returned to England in 1986 to join London Business School. John Stopford made possible this return and I joined him in the School's Strategy department. From this new academic base I entered a productive and enjoyable phase of 'modelling for learning'. I was invited by Arie de Geus to collaborate with his Group Planning department in Royal Dutch/Shell, based at the headquarters of Shell International in London. There, over a period of six years, a series of modelling projects (some conducted by me, and others conducted by David Kreutzer and David Lane) unfolded within the framework of Arie's 'planning as learning' initiative. The idea was to take a fresh view of planning and decision making in organisations and see them as collective learning processes. A vital empirical finding, from educational psychologists' studies of child learning, was that learning and doing often go hand-in-hand; children learn as they play. Arie de Geus made the logical step from child's play to decision making by play. It was a big step. But it was insightful if you took the idea seriously, as he and others in Group Planning did. Modelling and simulation fit naturally with this new approach to planning since models are in essence representations of reality (toys) and simulators allow role-playing with a modelled (and much simplified) reality.

An important consequence of my collaboration with Arie and Shell was the launch, at London Business School, of a week-long residential executive education programme called Systems Thinking and Strategic Modelling (STSM). The programme used learning-by-doing to engage executives with the core principles of feedback systems thinking and system dynamics modelling. Chapter 2 (Introduction to Feedback Systems Thinking) and Chapter 3 (Modelling Dynamic Systems) are derived from STSM. Moreover, the programme brought together, for a period of 10 years, a faculty team at London Business School that helped to develop system dynamics in many important ways and materially contributed to the content of this book. The team members were Arie de Geus, Erik Larsen, Ann van Ackere and Kim Warren and then later Shayne Gary. I enjoyed working with this special group of people and know that together we accomplished a great deal. Thanks to you all.

The shower models in Chapter 4 were sparked by Erik Larsen who felt, in the spirit of modelling for learning, that we shouldn't simply lecture STSM participants about the tricky balancing loop in a shower 'system'. Instead, we should build a simulator that would allow participants to see (or even experience) the resulting dynamics. So together we developed prototype simulators that became the basis for the World of Showers A and B models in Chapter 4. Alessandro Lomi and Ari Ginsberg later joined us to write a journal article based on these models, entitled 'The dynamics of resource sharing – a metaphorical model'. Two MBA students at London Business School, Thomas Furst and Derrick D'Souza, helped me to develop an early version of the gaming interface, and my wife Linda Morecroft worked on the user guide and interface enhancements for World of Showers.

There is an anecdote to accompany the shower project. After Erik Larsen and I had formulated the model's equations, we needed to supply parameters. Erik suggested that the 'desired temperature' of the shower should be set at 25°C. I asked him if that number was high enough. He said it didn't matter as the choice would make no difference to the resulting dynamics, which was what we wanted the model to demonstrate. He was right in principle, but in practice (as I discovered by taking a thermometer into my home shower) water at 25°C feels distinctly cool. Erik was not easily moved by this piece of empirical evidence and so, as an amusing compromise, we decided to locate the model's imaginary shower taker in a hot and humid climate where a cool shower would be both desirable and plausible.

Perhaps the most memorable project from the modelling for learning era was a study of the structure and long-term dynamics of global oil markets. This study, conducted with the help of Kees van der Heijden, led to the Oil Producers' model described in Chapter 8. At the time, Kees was head of Group Planning's renowned scenario development team. He brought together 10 Shell managers who contributed to the model's conceptualisation. The project was a good opportunity to engage these managers with the model building process and to build a model that captured a collective view of their oil world as the basis for subsequent scenario development. The original Oil Producers' model was developed in the iThink modelling language. But several years later, prompted by a suggestion from Erik Larsen, the model's equations were transported into Visual Basic and a dramatic new interface was overlaid as the basis for experimental work on decision making in dynamically complex environments (the global oil industry is certainly dynamically complex). This work was carried out by Paul Langley as part of his doctoral thesis at London Business School ('An experimental study of the impact of online cognitive feedback on performance and learning in an oil producer's microworld', November 1995).

Systems Thinking and Strategic Modelling ran twice a year for 15 years and brought system dynamics to hundreds of managers and senior staff from organisations around the world.

The Dynamics of Strategy

Around 1995, I began working with Kim Warren on the dynamics of strategy. This development was motivated by our shared interest in strategy (we were both in the Strategy department at the time) and also by our familiarity with a widely cited paper in the academic management literature entitled 'Asset stock accumulation and sustainability of competitive advantage'. The paper was written by INSEAD's Ingemar Dierickx and Karel Cool and appeared in *Management Science* in 1989. Their argument was that the sustainability of firms' competitive advantage could be better understood by thinking about the way firms accumulate the asset stocks or resources that underpin their business. A firm might achieve competitive advantage by building a distinctive set of asset stocks that rivals would find difficult to imitate. Sustainability of competitive advantage would stem in part from the time it takes to accumulate or reconfigure such assets or resources. We realised that here was a dynamic view of firm performance that could be further developed by formally linking system dynamics with the resource-based view of the firm (an important branch of contemporary strategy theory and practice).

Our way of carrying out this synthesis was to jointly design and launch an MBA elective course at London Business School, which we called the Dynamics of Strategy. Applied research projects followed, including PhD theses at London Business School by Edoardo Mollona, Shayne Gary, Abhijit Mandal and Martin Kunc.

Dynamic resource-based models of the firm were devised to study important strategy topics such as diversification and competitive advantage. The research partners for doctoral projects included François Delauzun from BBC World Service and Bill Howieson from Scottish Power. Another partnership was with the London Office of McKinsey & Co., during 1996–2000, when the Business Dynamics practice was in full swing. The company assembled a strong team of consultants with expertise in modelling, and they provided a sounding board for many fledgling ideas about system dynamics and strategy. My thanks to Andrew Doman who led the Business Dynamics initiative in London and to Maurice Glucksman, Paul Langley, Norman Marshall, Panos Ninios and Hendrick Sabert who collaborated with London Business School on a variety of projects and publications.

There are samples of this strategy dynamics work on the Learners' website and in the book. See in particular the materials on People Express Airlines in the learning support folder for Chapter 6 and the materials on diversification dynamics and metamorphosis in the v-Lecture folders. Also, Chapter 10 includes edited extracts from Martin Kunc's dissertation about product growth dynamics and industry competition in fast moving consumer goods. Kim Warren went on to further develop the SD-RBV theme in his Forrester Award-winning book, *Competitive Strategy Dynamics*.

Soft Systems and Complementary Modelling Methods

In November 2001, I was invited by Mike Pidd of Lancaster University Management School to join the INCISM network, and it was here, in a series of meetings that spanned two years, that I learned much more about soft systems than I had previously known. INCISM is an abbreviation for Interdisciplinary Network on Complementarity in Systems Modelling and its meetings were funded by the UK's Engineering and Physical Sciences Research Council

(EPSRC). The network brought together a mix of academics and practitioners to explore the combined use of what have become known as 'hard' and 'soft' approaches to systems modelling. One result was a book entitled *Systems Modelling – Theory and Practice.* Through the network, the book and subsequent conversations with both Peter Checkland and Mike Pidd, I have come to better understand where system dynamics fits on the hard–soft model spectrum. It seems to me that the juxtaposition of system dynamics and soft systems methodology (SSM) reveals, in tangible terms, quite a lot about the abstract philosophy of modelling – by which I mean the different ways in which modellers interpret situations in business and society. I touch on this topic in Chapter 2 (under 'event-oriented thinking'), in Chapter 5 (under 'modelling for learning and soft systems') and again in Chapter 10 (under 'mental models, transitional objects and formal models'). INCISM also inspired a plenary session on soft systems and modelling at the 2004 International Conference of the System Dynamics Society in Oxford. Presentations by Mike Pidd and Peter Checkland described the territory covered by hard and soft modelling approaches and opened up discussion about the role of both qualitative and quantitative system dynamics. In the UK there is a long tradition of qualitative system dynamics which was started by Eric Wolstenholme and Geoff Coyle. The Oxford conference built on this tradition with its theme of collegiality as a social and scientific process to mediate between competing or complementary world views.

My interest in complementary modelling methods was further reinforced through collaboration with the Operational Research and Management Sciences group at Warwick Business School. There I found colleagues working at the interface of operational research and strategy. We had much in common. The use of complementary models and frameworks for strategic development became the focus of activity for an informal research group that included Robert Dyson, Maureen Meadows, Frances O'Brien, Abhijit Mandal and Alberto Franco (all from Warwick at the time), Jim Bryant (from Sheffield Hallam) and me.

At Warwick, I also found experts in discrete-event simulation (DES). We soon discovered a shared interest in simulation methods that transcended our differences. With Stewart Robinson, I conducted a mini-project that compared system dynamics and discrete-event models of fishery dynamics. We each built a small model of a fishery following the normal modelling conventions of our respective fields. Then we compared notes. The project led to many interesting conversations about modelling and simulation. Some of our thoughts and conclusions are reported in the appendix of Chapter 9 on alternative simulation approaches. Although both system dynamics and discrete-event simulation are commonly viewed as hard system modelling approaches, their comparison illustrates an interplay and clash of world-views worthy of a soft systems study. In a sense, this comparison was our mini-project as we built separate fishery models and then reflected how our professional backgrounds led us to interpret and represent the problem situation in fisheries. The fishery models also opened the door to the discrete-event simulation community, making possible further collaborative research with Ruth Davies, Sally Brailsford and others at the boundary of system dynamics and DES.

How to Use This Book

To get the most out of *Strategic Modelling and Business Dynamics* it is important to develop a good intuitive feel for 'dynamics' – how and why things change through time. Personal experience of simulated dynamics is a good way to learn. So the book comes with chapter-by-chapter learning support folders, which are available on the Learners' website (see the About the Website Resources section). Each folder contains models and gaming simulators that allow readers to run simulations for themselves and to reproduce the time charts and dynamics described in the text. The models come to life in a way that is impossible to re-create with words alone. It is easy for readers to spot opportunities for learning support. A spinning gyroscope is printed in the page margin alongside text that explains how to run the simulator.[5] Examples include unintended drug-related crime, the collapse of fisheries, perverse hotel showers, persistent manufacturing cycles, boom and bust in new products and services, promising market growth, unfulfilled market growth, competitive dynamics, hospital performance and price volatility in global oil.

There are also PowerPoint slides with notes to accompany the book. They are available on the Instructors' website (see the About the Website Resources section). The slides include lectures and workshops which are organised chapter-by-chapter. They can be supplemented with assignments which are also to be found on the Instructors' website.

There are many ways to use the book, models and slides in university and management education, some of which are outlined below. No doubt instructors will adapt and tailor the materials to suit their own needs, but the following comments may trigger some useful thoughts.

MBA and Modular/Executive MBA

The book is derived from an MBA elective of the same name (Strategic Modelling and Business Dynamics SMBD) that I ran at London Business

---

[5]A spinning gyroscope is 'dynamically complex' and is therefore a good visual metaphor to signal the simulation of dynamics in business and society. A gyroscope behaves in surprising ways. For example, when prodded on its top-most point it moves at right angles to the direction of the push; a counter-intuitive response. A gyroscope is also self-balancing. It stands on a pointed-end, like an upright pencil. Yet instead of falling over, as might be expected, it appears to defy gravity by remaining upright with its axis horizontal; again a counter-intuitive response.

School for many years.[6] It therefore has a track record in graduate management education. To run a similar elective course at another business school I recommend starting with the well-known 'Beer Distribution Game' in the opening session and then working through a selection of book chapters complemented with workshops and assignments based on the learning support models. The Beer Game is a role-playing exercise for teams of students that examines supply-chain dynamics and coordination problems in a multi-stage production-distribution chain comprising retailers, wholesalers, distributors and a factory. The game can be purchased at modest cost from the System Dynamics Society *www.systemdynamics.org* and is a vivid way to introduce students to modelling, representation, simulation and puzzling dynamics. On this foundation can be built lectures and workshops that introduce feedback systems thinking and modelling (Chapters 2 and 3); examine the cyclical dynamics of balancing loops (Chapters 4 and 5); and overlay the growth dynamics of reinforcing loops to study limits to growth, stagnation and decline (Chapters 6 and 7). By the end of Chapter 7 students have covered the key concepts required to conceptualise, formulate, test and interpret system dynamics models. Then instructors can select among the applications presented in Chapters 8, 9, and 10 (complemented with system dynamics materials from other sources) to create a complete course with 30 or more contact hours offered in modular or weekly format. The material is best spread out across an academic term or semester to allow adequate time for reading, preparation and model-based assignments.

A full-semester twenty-eight session course suitable for graduate students can be found on the Instructors' website in the folder entitled Course Outlines. A fourteen session taster course specially designed for PhDs can also be found in the same website folder.

Non-Degree Executive Education

Materials from the book have also been successfully used in a popular one-week residential Executive Education programme called *Systems Thinking and Strategic Modelling* (STSM) which ran at London Business School throughout the 1990s. The purpose of this programme was rather different than a typical MBA course in strategic modelling and business dynamics. Participants were often senior managers and/or their experienced staff advisers. For these people it was important to communicate how they should *use* modelling and simulation for strategic development and organisational

---

[6]Over the years Strategic Modelling has also been taught by Ann van Ackere, Shayne Gary and Scott Rockart, who each brought their own interpretations to the core materials. My thanks to them for the innovations and refinements they introduced.

change. Mastering the skills to build models and simulators was secondary to their need for becoming informed model users, by which I mean people capable of initiating and leading strategic modelling projects in their own organisations – as many STSM participants subsequently did. So the programme was designed to emphasise the conceptual steps of model building including problem articulation and causal loop diagramming. The course also provided syndicate teams with a complete, compact and self-contained experience of the steps of a group modelling project from problem definition, to model formulation, testing and simulation. This compact experience was delivered through mini-projects, chosen by the teams themselves, and developed into small-scale models under faculty supervision.

The programme began in the same way as the MBA course, with the Beer Distribution game used as an icebreaker and an entertaining introduction to feedback systems thinking, dynamics and simulation. Participants then learned, through lectures and syndicate exercises, the core mapping and modelling concepts in Chapters 2 and 3. It may seem surprising that executives would take an interest in hotel showers and drug-related crime (the examples in Chapters 2 and 3 that illustrate causal loop diagrams, feedback structure, equation formulation and simulation), but they always did. Real-world applications were then demonstrated with lectures about serious and successful modelling projects such as the Oil Producers' model in Chapter 8 or the Soap Industry simulator in Chapter 10. In addition guest speakers from business or the public sector, sometimes past-participants of STSM, were invited to talk about their experiences with modelling. Participants also spent half a day or more using a strategy simulator such as the People Express Management Flight simulator (referred to in Chapter 6) or the Beefeater Restaurants Microworld, available from *www.strategydynamics.com*. Working in small teams of three or four, participants discuss and agree a collective strategy for their assigned company and then implement the strategy in the corresponding simulator. Invariably, when dealing with dynamically complex situations, the best laid plans go astray and teams' experiences provide much valuable material for a debriefing on the pitfalls of strategy making. The final two days of the programme are spent on the team mini-projects mentioned above.

Ten and twelve session taster courses suitable for MBAs and Executives can be found on the Instructors' website in the folder entitled Course Outlines.

Undergraduate and Specialist

Masters Courses

I am confident that the content of this book works for MBA and Executive Education. It has also proven to be suitable for undergraduate and specialist masters courses in modelling and simulation. Obviously undergraduates lack the business experience of typical MBAs. They will therefore find it harder to make sense of the coordination problems that routinely crop up in organisations and contribute to puzzling dynamics, chronic underperformance and failures of strategy. Here the book's website models perform a vital function. They bridge the experience gap by enabling younger readers to simulate puzzling dynamics and to experience coordination problems for themselves.

Otherwise the sequencing of materials can be much the same as for an MBA course, with perhaps more emphasis given to non-business examples and cases. For example, it is possible to devote an opening session to the fisheries gaming simulator in Chapter 1 as a replacement for the Beer Distribution Game. Alternatively in order to retain, at the start of the course, a vivid role-playing exercise and social 'icebreaker' then simply replace the Beer Game with the Fish Banks simulator. Like the Beer Game, Fish Banks is also available at modest cost from the System Dynamics Society *www.systemdynamics.org*. The game debrief can be supplemented with the model and materials in Chapter 1. Then after the game, instructors can cover the core modelling Chapters 2 through 5 and selectively add content from Chapters 6 through 10 to suit the audience. For example students who are not especially interested in firm-level business dynamics and strategy may prefer to spend more time on public sector applications in Chapter 9 and on the industry-level simulator of the global oil producers in Chapter 8.

A ten session taster course for Masters in Management students and for undergraduates can be found on the Instructors' website in the folder entitled Course Outlines.

Chapter 1
The Appeal and Power of Strategic Modelling

- Introduction
- A New Approach to Modelling
- The Puzzling Dynamics of International Fisheries
- Model of a Natural Fishery
- Operating a Simple Harvested Fishery
- Preview of the Book and Topics Covered
- Appendix – Archive Materials from *World Dynamics*

Introduction[1]

I have always been fascinated by models and games and particularly by model conceptualisation, the process by which people represent and simplify situations from the real world to make sense of them. Consider for example, the popular board game of Monopoly. Players find themselves as property developers in an imaginary city. It could be London or New York, except of course (and this is the curious thing) the board doesn't look remotely like a real city or even like a geographical map of either city. The game board is just a large square of card on which are printed neatly labelled and coloured boxes displaying familiar place names like cheap and cheerful Old Kent Road in brown, bustling Trafalgar Square in red and elegant Mayfair in dark blue. There are houses and hotels, but no streets. There are stations, but no railway lines. There is a community chest, but no community of people. There is a jail, but no police department. Players move around the city with a throw of the dice in a curious assortment of vehicles: a boot, a ship, a horse, an iron, a cannon and even a top hat. It is a fantasy world, a much simplified view of

---

[1]The introduction contains edited extracts from my 2000 paper, 'Creativity and Convergence in Scenario Modelling'.

real estate in a city, and yet it captures something real – the essence of commercial property ownership and development in a growing competitive market. The more property you own and control, the more you earn. Bigger is better, winner takes all.

The challenge of any kind of modelling lies precisely in deciding, among myriad factors, what to include and what to leave out. The same principle applies whether you are devising a board game like Monopoly or building a simulator for a management team in BMW, Dow Chemical, Goldman Sachs, Harley-Davidson, Mars Inc., Microsoft, Royal Dutch/Shell or Transport for London. The starting point is essentially, 'what's important here?' What do you and others have in mind when you think about the strategy and future success of a business, a city or an entire industry? What is the issue under investigation and which factors need most attention to address the issue? These practical questions in turn raise a more basic philosophical question about how we conceptualise the enterprises in which we live and work. How do people, whether they are leaders, advisers or commentators, make sense of firms, industries or societies, explain them to others, and anticipate outcomes well enough to shape and communicate intelligent strategy and policy?

I can recall this fascination with conceptualisation from a time when business dynamics, or more generally system dynamics (and its specialist visual language of stocks, flows and information feedback), was entirely new and unfamiliar to me. It was back in the early 1970s. The *Limits to Growth* study, a research project exploring how to create an economically and ecologically sustainable society, was attracting attention worldwide. The project was conducted at the Massachusetts Institute of Technology (MIT) and two influential books based on this work, *World Dynamics* (Forrester, 1971) and *Limits to Growth* (Meadows *et al.*, 1972), had already been published. Further work on the paradox of global growth and sustainability was in full flow. Thousands of miles away I was a graduate student at London University's Imperial College, completing a masters degree in operational research. I had only just encountered *Industrial Dynamics*, the seminal book that marked the beginning of system dynamics (Forrester, 1961).

Nevertheless, I experienced a sense of excitement about the possibility of using computer models to visualise and simulate issues that were foremost in the minds of business and political leaders and important for our everyday lives. Certainly I was no novice to computer modelling, but up until then I had used computational power for optimisation and decision support. What I found appealing in this new area of system dynamics was the promise of a subject aimed at broad policy making backed up by the discipline of model building and the power of simulation.

Imagine you are contemplating the dilemma of fast-growing global population in a world of finite resources. Today, there are 7 billion of us on the planet. Back in 1850 there were just over one billion. By 2050 there could be as many as nine billion people. Is it really possible that mankind could outgrow the planet and overexploit its abundant natural resources to usher in a dark age of pollution, poverty and suffering? Why might this happen and when? How do you begin to answer such questions and how do you conceive a 'global system' in your mind? I was captivated by a representation in *World Dynamics* that limited itself to only two pages of symbols whose clearly defined purpose was to explore alternative future time paths for global industrial society. It was a bold sketch on a compact canvas.

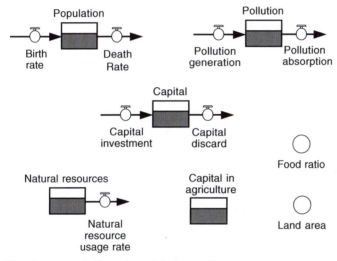

Figure 1.1   Stock accumulations for global growth
Source: Adapted from Forrester (1971, pp. 20–21).

For those who have read *World Dynamics*, Figure 1.1 will evoke memories of the model. However, for most readers who are new to system dynamics you will glimpse what I saw as a graduate student: strange symbols and familiar phrases which claim to set some sort of boundary on the set of factors that will shape the environmental and economic destiny of mankind. I have deliberately chosen to show a much-simplified diagram that leaves out many intermediate variables and the complex network of connections, because that is how I first perceived the model. There are only four stock accumulations (shown as rectangles with inflows and outflows), representing aspects of our world, that have grown steadily and relentlessly over many centuries: population, capital, pollution and natural resources (which have declined). This fact alone I found remarkable for its brevity yet common-sense appeal. To understand global limits to growth one surely has to think hard about the drivers of population (birth rate and death rate, shown as small circles with tiny taps superimposed on arrows); the engines of human economic activity (capital investment, capital discard and the usage rate of natural resources); and the consequences of human activity on the global environment (the processes of pollution generation and absorption).

These factors must co-evolve over time. But what forces or influences make sure they evolve in a balanced way that can satisfy the aspirations and sustain the living standards of a healthy global population? My picture does not show the full web of coordinating forces. That is something you will learn to model and interpret later in the book. For now you just have to imagine there is such a web operating behind the scenes that determines how, for example, the birth rate depends on population, capital and pollution, or how capital investment depends on population and natural resources. But can a sustainable balance be achieved? Is there a coordinating web that will steer global growth within the constraints of finite natural resources, limited land area, and biological/physical laws (that govern the world's ecology), while at the same time meeting the needs of billions of global stakeholders (parents and families, investors in productive capital, exploiters of natural resources)?

It came as a shock all those years ago to realise there is no nation, no government and no responsible business community that has the power or the information to mastermind a global growth engine.[2] A coordinating web is certainly there (reproduced in the Appendix as Figure 1.13), but it is a weak and imperfect invisible hand. In the long run, this invisible hand will achieve a ruthless balance of population, resources and human activity. But the time path to this ultimate balance may involve a catastrophic decline of living standards and population or spiralling pollution.

Figure 1.2 compares two (among many) alternative time paths that summarise the message as I recall it from my early encounter with system dynamics (Randers, 1980). Bear in mind these are rough hand-drawn sketches, not formal simulations. Nevertheless, the century-long timescale on these charts is representative of the time horizon in the original study and left a deep impression about the ambition of the field to understand the long term by simulating the interaction of human decisions-and-actions with enduring natural forces. On the left is a likely scenario. Global carrying capacity (defined as how much human activity the globe can sustain) starts high in the uncrowded world of the 1950s. Human activity starts low. As population and capital grow, human activity rises steadily and exponentially, approaching the

---

[2]The same idea of limited ability to control situations applies to firms in competitive industries and, to some extent, to business units and functional areas inside corporations and firms. Management teams can devise strategy (the intended strategy), but a whole organisation stands between their ideas and resulting action, so the implemented strategy is often different than intended. The levers of power are only loosely connected to operations.

finite (but unknown) global capacity around the turn of the millennium. There is no particularly strong signal to announce that this hidden capacity limit has been reached, nor any coalition of stakeholders with the power to restrict human activity once the limit is exceeded. So 'the band plays on' for another 20 years. Collectively, we live beyond the generous but limited means of our planet. This overexploitation of resources and the environment leads to a steady erosion of global carrying capacity and a consequent rapid decline in human activity. In human terms, this multi-decade period of decline is a dark age of low living standards, high pollution, food shortage, premature death and economic depression. It is a dramatic story arising from simple yet plausible assumptions about human behaviour and planetary limits.

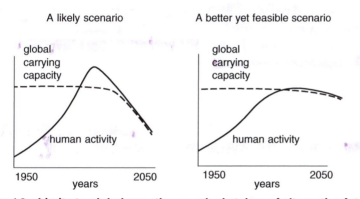

Figure 1.2   Limits to global growth – rough sketches of alternative futures

The story has not really changed in the four decades since it was first simulated. But there was always another, much more optimistic story. This alternative and sustainable future is sketched on the right of Figure 1.2. I won't say here what differences in the coordinating web can lead to this new outcome. Instead, I invite you to think about the task of balancing the stock accumulations in Figure 1.1 in light of what you learn from the book. I also refer you to the comprehensive simulations of the *Limits to Growth* team (Meadows *et al.*, 1972; 2002 and Cerasuolo, 2013) and to two of the original simulations from *World Dynamics* reproduced in the Appendix as Figure 1.14.

A New Approach to Modelling

World Dynamics and *Limits to Growth* anticipated a new and participative approach to modelling and simulation. People's ability to manage their complex world can be improved by visualising and simulating it. Plans and alternative futures become clearer by rehearsing them (O'Brien and Dyson,

2007). Only now is this approach coming to be widely appreciated in business, political and academic circles. During the 1970s, models were still viewed as instruments for accurate prediction whose validity rested primarily on short-term predictive power, conformance with established economic theory and goodness-of-fit to historical data. Modelling for learning, of the kind presented in this book and intended to complement people's mental models, was in its infancy.

The idea of rehearsing alternative futures is fundamental to contemporary strategic modelling and scenario development. The purpose of models and simulations is to prepare organisations and individuals for alternative futures by bringing these futures to life so they are imagined more vividly than would otherwise be possible. Moreover, as you will see throughout the book, strategic models not only help people to generate alternative futures for their firms and industries, but also to challenge, shape, change and enrich their interpretation of a complex world.

An important objective for modellers (and arguably for anyone in a leadership position who has to make sense of complex business or social situations, devise strategies and communicate them) is to find a compact 'shareable' description of how a firm, industry or social system operates. Sooner or later, the creative and divergent thoughts that are present at a very early stage of enquiry (captured in the phrase 'there's a lot going on out there') must be turned to convergent thoughts that focus group attention on the essence of the situation at hand (by agreeing, through ruthless pruning, what's really important and what can be safely ignored). In business dynamics, this creative process of simplification (known as 'conceptualisation') takes shape as a picture of a firm or industry that the modeller agrees with the project team. There are of course guidelines to follow. You begin by identifying so called stock accumulations and feedback loops, the visual building blocks of system dynamics models and simulators. Striking the right balance of creativity and convergence is an essential art of modelling. The parsimonious structure of the *World Dynamics* model is evidence of creativity and disciplined convergence in model conceptualisation. The model's enduring appeal and power to communicate lies partly in its concise yet compelling representation of a massively complex reality.[3]

---

[3]Modelling can be controversial. *World Dynamics* was and still is a thought-provoking model, a potent catalyst for political debate and an instrument for serious policy making. It was also a focus of learned criticism about the nature and use of modelling and simulation in the social sciences. Quotations from the press and academic literature at the time convey the impact, both positive and negative, of the model on opinion leaders: 'This is likely to be one of the most important documents of our age ...', *New York Times*; 'There are too many assumptions that are not founded, and there is too high a level of aggregation in the model', *Science*; 'This year will not see the publication of a more important book than Forrester's *World Dynamics*, or a book more certain to arouse dislike', *Fortune*; 'This is a piece of irresponsible nonsense, a publicity stunt ... extremely simplistic, given the

The Puzzling Dynamics of International Fisheries

By now I hope your curiosity about modelling is stirred, but before probing the basic concepts and tools used by system dynamics modellers, I want to show you a model, a small model, designed to address an important contemporary issue facing society. I will explain its main assumptions, demonstrate some simulations and then give you the opportunity to run the simulator for yourself.

The topic is fisheries. The problems of overexploitation facing international fisheries are well known, widely reported in the press and a subject of government policy in many nations. The performance of international fisheries is indeed puzzling. Fish naturally regenerate. They are a renewable resource, in apparently endless supply, providing valuable and healthy food for billions of consumers and a livelihood for hundreds of thousands of fishing communities worldwide. The fishing industry has been in existence since the dawn of civilisation and should last forever. Yet fish stocks around the world are volatile and some are even collapsing. Once rich fishing grounds such as Canada's Grand Banks now yield no catch at all. Stocks in other areas, such as the English Channel, the North Sea and the Baltic, are in terminal decline.

The issue is powerfully expressed by environmental journalist Charles Clover (2004) in his acclaimed book *The End of the Line*. Here is an excerpt from Chapter 1:

> Fish were once seen as renewable resources, creatures that would replenish their stocks forever for our benefit. But around the world there is evidence that numerous types of fish, such as the northern cod, North Sea mackerel, the marbled rock cod of Antarctica and, to a great extent, the west Atlantic bluefin tuna, have been fished out, like the great whales before them, and are not recovering ... The perception-changing moment for the oceans has arrived. It comes from the realisation that in a single human lifetime we have inflicted a crisis on the oceans greater than any yet caused by pollution. That crisis compares with the destruction of the mammoths, bison and whales, the rape of rainforests and the pursuit of bushmeat. It is caused by overfishing.
>
> (from *The End of the Line* by Charles Clover, published by Ebury. Reprinted by permission of The Random House Group Ltd and Charles Clover.)

---

current state of knowledge in the social sciences', economists from Yale. Notice the sharp division of opinion on the scope, size, adequacy and usefulness of the model. The serious press thinks the work is important for its readers and worthy of policymakers' attention. Academics question the model's apparent simplicity. Not surprisingly judgements vary about the complexity and accuracy required of models (or even ideas and theories) for them to offer useful guidance to business and society. Modellers need to strike a careful balance.

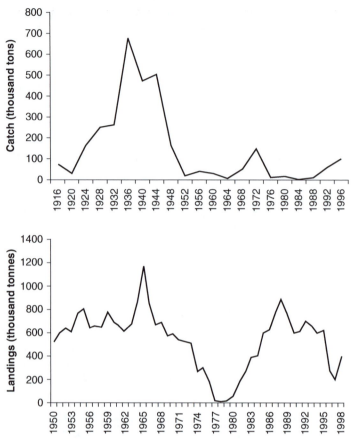

Figure 1.3 Pacific sardine catch (top) and North Sea herring catch (bottom) from Fish Banks debriefing materials (Meadows *et al.*, 2001)
Source: Nichols (1999).

Figure 1.3 shows evidence of overfishing from two real fisheries. This kind of time series data is a useful focus for model building because it contains the dynamics of interest. The top chart shows the Pacific sardine catch in thousands of tonnes per year over the period 1916–1996. The annual catch grew remarkably between 1920 and 1940, starting at around 50 thousand tonnes per year and peaking at 700 thousand tonnes per year – a 14-fold increase. Over the next four years to 1944, the catch fell to 500 thousand tonnes per year, stabilised for a few years and then collapsed dramatically to almost zero in 1952. Since then it has never properly recovered. The bottom chart shows a similar story for the North Sea herring catch in the period 1950 to 1998. However, in this case, following a collapse between 1974 and 1979, the fishery did recover in the 1980s and early 1990s with an average annual catch around 600 thousand tonnes per year – similar to the catch in the 1950s and 1960s.

Why does overfishing happen? We can be sure that no fishermen set out with the deliberate intention of depleting fisheries and wrecking their own livelihoods. Yet this outcome has been repeated in fishing communities around the world.[4] A good explanation is to be found in a fisheries gaming simulator called Fish Banks, Ltd (Meadows *et al.*, 2001; Meadows and Sterman, 2011). Since I am not an expert on fisheries, I will base my model on this popular simulator. Fish Banks has been used to teach principles of sustainable development to audiences that include politicians, business leaders and government policy advisers as well as fishing communities and high school students. Incidentally, it is no coincidence that the lead designer and author of Fish Banks, Dennis Meadows, was also a principal investigator in the *Limits to Growth* study. Fish Banks has proven to be a potent metaphor for sustainable development in many industries and enterprises, including the world itself viewed as a huge socio-economic enterprise.

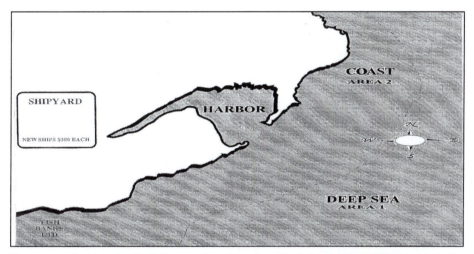

Figure 1.4   An imaginary fishery – the game board of the original FishBanks, Ltd
Source: Meadows, *et al.*, 2001

Figure 1.4 shows the Fish Banks game board and its imaginary fishery. There is a region of ocean, close to land, containing a single species of fish. Fish regenerate as a function of the existing population. The local fishing community buys ships from the shipyard and takes them to sea to harvest fish. The total catch depends on the number of ships, the fish population and other factors, such as the weather. In the game, as in real life, the fish population is not known accurately, although it can be estimated. Also, in the game, as in

---

[4]Clover describes the poignant scene at Lowestoft in recent years: the unrepaired doorways and shabby 1930s office buildings on the seafront, symbols of economic collapse. This town was once among England's greatest fishing ports, famous the world over, with a history spanning 600 years.

real life, the process of fish regeneration is not fully understood by those in the system (players or fishermen). Regeneration is related to the (unknown) fish population, but the relationship is complex and may involve other external factors.

Model of a Natural Fishery

I have taken the situation and factors outlined above and used them to create a simple fisheries model (though the scaling I use is different from Fish Banks and there are no competing fishing companies). Figure 1.5 shows the fish population and regeneration. For now there are no ships or fishermen – they appear later. So what you see is a natural fishery, free from human intervention.[5] The fish population or fish stock, shown as a rectangle, accumulates the inflow of new fish per year (here the inflow is defined as births minus deaths). Initially, there are 200 fish in the sea and the maximum fishery size is assumed to be 4000 fish. Incidentally, the initial value and maximum size can be re-scaled to be more realistic without changing the resulting dynamics. For example, a fishery starting with a biomass of 20 thousand tonnes of a given species and an assumed maximum fishery size of 400 thousand tonnes would generate equivalent results.

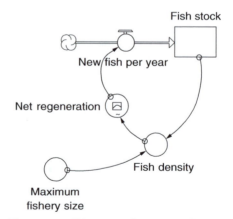

Figure 1.5   Diagram of a natural fishery

[5]The diagram was created in the popular iThink language (isee systems, 2014). The symbols are pretty much standard for all system dynamics models, though there are differences of detail between the main alternative modelling software packages. Here, in Chapter 1, I briefly explain each symbol when I first refer to it in the text. Later, in Chapter 3, there is a more formal introduction to modelling symbols and equations, with a fully documented example.

The flow of new fish per year is shown by an arrow. The size of the inflow varies according to conditions within the fishery, as explained below. This idea of a modulated flow is depicted by a tap or 'flow regulator' placed in the middle of the arrow. At the left end of the arrow is another special symbol, a pool or cloud, depicting the source from which the flow arises – in this case fish eggs.

A very important relationship is the effect of fish density on net regeneration, a causal link shown by a curved arrow. Since fish density itself depends on the number of fish in the fishery region, the result is a circular feedback process in which the size of the fish stock determines, through various intermediate steps, its own rate of inflow.[6] The relationship is non-linear as shown in Figure 1.6.

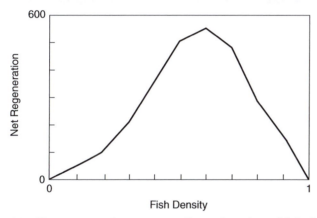

Figure 1.6   Net regeneration as a non-linear function of fish density

When the fish density is low there are few fish in the sea relative to the maximum fishery size and net regeneration is low, at a value of less than 50 fish per year. In the extreme case where there are no fish in the sea, the net regeneration is zero. As fish density rises the net regeneration rises too, on the grounds that a bigger fish population will reproduce more successfully, provided the population is far below the presumed theoretical carrying capacity of the ocean region.

As the fish density continues to rise, there comes a point at which net regeneration reaches a peak (in this case almost 600 fish per year) and then begins to fall because food becomes scarcer. Ecologists say there is increasing

---

[6]Interestingly, some people dispute the existence of this circularity. They argue that the number of juveniles reaching fishable size each year has nothing to do with the number of parents in the sea because fish such as cod can produce upwards of seven million eggs in a season – most of which perish due to predation and environmental factors. However, the number of fish eggs is certainly related to the population of fish.

intraspecific competition among the burgeoning number of fish for the limited available nutrient. So when, in this example, the fish population reaches 4000 the fish density is equal to one and net regeneration falls to zero. The population is then at its maximum natural sustainable value.

Simulated Dynamics of a Natural Fishery

If you accept the relationships described above then the destiny of a natural fishery is largely pre-determined once you populate it with a few fish. To some people this inevitability comes as a surprise, but in system dynamics it is an illustration of an important general principle: the structure of a system (how the parts connect) determines its dynamic behaviour (performance through time). A simulator shows how. The simulation in Figure 1.7 shows the dynamics of a 'natural' fishery over a period of 40 years, starting with a small initial population of 200 fish. Remember there are no ships and no investment. Fishermen are not yet part of the system.

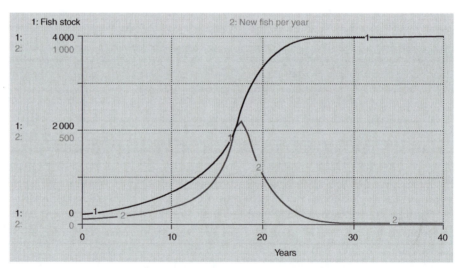

Figure 1.7   Simulation of a natural fishery with an initial population of 200 fish and maximum fishery size of 4000

The result is smooth S-shaped growth. For 18 years, the fish stock (line 1) grows exponentially. The population grows from 200 to 2500 fish and regeneration (new fish per year, line 2) also increases until year 18 as rising fish density enables fish to reproduce more successfully. Thereafter, crowding becomes a significant factor according to the non-linear net regeneration curve shown in Figure 1.6. The number of new fish per year falls as the population density rises, eventually bringing population growth to a halt as the fish stock approaches its maximum sustainable value of 4000 fish.

Operating a Simple Harvested Fishery

Imagine you are living in a small fishing community where everyone's livelihood depends on the local fishery. It could be a town like Bonavista in Newfoundland, remote and self-sufficient, located on a windswept cape 200 miles from the tiny provincial capital of St Johns, along deserted roads where moose are as common as cars. 'In the early 1990s there were 705 jobs in Bonavista directly provided by the fishery, in catching and processing' (Clover, 2004). Let's suppose there is a committee of the town council responsible for growth and development that regulates the purchase of new ships by local fishermen. This committee may not exist in the real Bonavista but for now it's a convenient assumption. You are a member of the committee and proud of your thriving community. The town is growing, the fishing fleet is expanding and the fishery is teeming with cod.

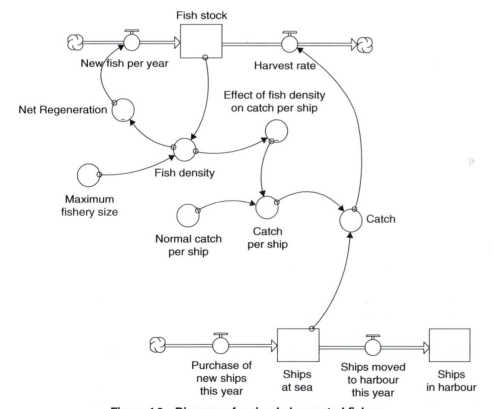

Figure 1.8   Diagram of a simple harvested fishery

Figure 1.8 shows the situation. The fish stock in the top left of the diagram regenerates just the same as before, but now there is an outflow, the harvest rate, that represents fishermen casting their nets and removing fish from the sea. The harvest rate is equal to the catch, which itself depends on the number of ships at sea and the catch per ship. Typically the more ships at sea the bigger the catch, unless the fish density falls very low, thereby reducing the catch per ship because it is difficult for the crew to reliably locate fish. Ships at sea are increased by the purchase of new ships and reduced by ships moved to harbour, as shown in the bottom half of the diagram.

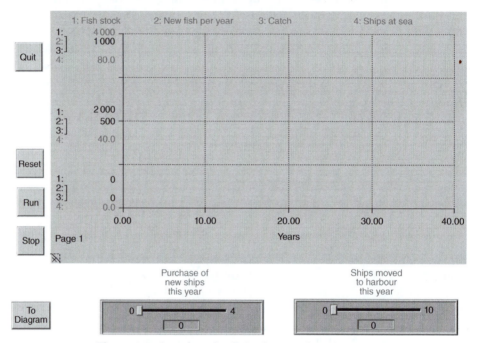

Figure 1.9　Interface for fisheries gaming simulator

The interface to the gaming simulator is shown in Figure 1.9. There is a time chart that reports the fish stock, new fish per year, catch and ships at sea over a time horizon of 40 simulated years. Until you make a simulation, the chart is blank. The interface also contains various buttons and sliders to operate the simulator and to make decisions year by year. There are two decisions. Use the slider on the left for the purchase of new ships and the slider on the right for ships moved to harbour. You are ready to simulate! Open the file called 'Fisheries Gaming Simulator' in the learning support folder for Chapter 1. The interface in Figure 1.9 will appear in colour. First of all, simulate natural regeneration over a period of 40 years, a scenario similar, but not identical, to the simulation in Figure 1.7. The only difference is that the initial fish population is 500 fish rather than 200. What do you think will be the trajectories of the fish stock and new fish per year? How will they differ from the trajectories in Figure 1.7? Would you expect any similarities? To find out, press the button on the left labelled 'Run' (but don't alter either of the two sliders, which are deliberately set at zero to replicate a natural fishery). You will see a five-year simulation. The fish stock (line 1) and new fish per year (line 2) both grow steadily. You can observe the exact numerical values of the variables by placing the cursor on the time chart, then selecting and holding. Numbers will appear under the variable names at the top of the chart. At time zero, the fish stock is 500 and new fish are regenerating at a rate of 63 per year. If you look carefully you will see that the catch (line 3) and ships at sea (line 4) are, as expected, running along at a value of zero, alongside the horizontal axis of the time chart. Press the 'Run' button again. Another five simulated years unfold showing further growth in the fish stock and in new fish per year. Continue until the simulation reaches 40 years and then investigate the trajectories carefully and compare them with the time chart in Figure 1.7. Why does the peak value of new fish per year occur so much earlier (year 10 instead of year 16)? Why is the final size of the fish stock identical in both cases?

Harvesting in Bonavista, Newfoundland – A Thought Experiment

Back to Bonavista, or at least a similar imaginary fishery, scaled to the numbers in the simulator. The fishing fleet has been growing and along with it the catch and the entire community supported by the fishery. As a member of the town's growth and development committee you want to explore alternative futures for the fishery and the simulator is one way to do so. You conjure up a thought experiment. Starting as before with an initial stock of 500 fish, you first simulate growth, through natural regeneration of fish, for a period of 10 years. The result is a well-stocked fishery similar to the one existing some 20 years ago when the hamlet of Bonavista, as it was then, began to expand commercial fishing. You know from the previous experiment that this scenario will lead to plenty of fish in the sea, but in reality you and the fishermen themselves don't know how many.

To replicate this fundamental uncertainty of fisheries you should 'hide' the trajectories for fish stock and new fish per year by colouring them grey so they blend into the background of the time chart. Some playing around with the software is necessary to bring about this change, but the result is important and worthwhile. First, press the 'Reset' button on the left of the time chart. The trajectories will disappear to leave a blank chart. Next move the cursor to the tiny paintbrush icon at the right of the tools bar at the top of the interface. Select and hold. A palette of colours will appear. Move the cursor to the bottom line containing greys and blacks. Select the light grey colour on the extreme left. Release the mouse button and move the cursor back onto the time chart where it will now appear as a paint brush. Select and the background of the chart will turn grey. Return to the colour palette and select the light grey colour *second from the left*. Now move the paintbrush cursor so that it lies exactly on top of the phrase 'Fish stock' at the top left of the time chart. Select and the phrase will turn from blue to grey and will, as intended, be virtually indistinguishable from the background grey. Repeat the same painting procedure for the phrase 'New fish per year'. Your time chart is now ready.

Press the 'Run' button twice to recreate 10 years of natural fishery growth. At first glance the simulated chart will appear quite blank and uninteresting. That's how it should be! Now move the slider for 'Purchase of new ships this year' to a value of 2 by selecting, holding and dragging the slider icon until the number 2 appears in the centre box. This setting means that each simulated year two new ships will be purchased and used by Bonavista fishermen. Press the 'Run' button three times in succession to simulate fleet expansion for years 10–25, a period of historical growth for the imagined Bonavista fishery. Ships at sea (line 4) increase linearly from zero to 30 as you would expect from an investment policy that adds two new ships a year over 15 years. The catch (line 3) increases proportionally in a similar linear pattern. Press the 'Run' button once more to simulate continued fleet expansion for years 25–30. Ships at sea continue the same relentless linear expansion, but notice a dramatic change in the trajectory of the catch (line 3). In year 26, after 16 years of steady growth, the catch levels out and peaks at 786 fish per year even though new ships are being added to the fleet. (To check the numerical values move the cursor onto the time chart, then select, hold and drag.) In year 27 the catch declines for the very first time in the fishery's simulated history. At the start of year 29, the catch is down to 690 fish per year, a decline of 12 per cent from the peak. Imagine the situation in Bonavista. The town's main business is in a downturn. A community, which has become used to growth and success, begins to worry and to ask why. Perhaps the past two years have been unlucky – poor weather or adverse breeding conditions. However, year 29 sees continued decline. The catch falls below 450 fish per year while the fleet grows to 40 ships. A downturn has become a slump.

At this point you can imagine pressure building in the community to do something about the problem. But what? The fishery is in decline. Perhaps the answer is to halt the purchase of new ships and to require some ships to remain in harbour. Such measures may seem logical if you believe that overfishing is to blame. But others will argue the decline is due to a run of exceptionally bad luck and that, sooner or later, the catch will return to normal. And remember nobody knows for certain the size of the remaining fish stock or the regeneration rate. That's all happening underwater. So, as in all practical strategy development, there is scope for argument and conflict about the true state of affairs and how best to react. Moreover, it is politically and economically painful for any community or business to cause itself to shrink deliberately. There are bound to be more losers than winners.

Nevertheless, imagine Bonavista agrees a conservation policy involving a total ban on the purchase of new ships for the next five years and an effective reduction in the fleet size to be achieved by moving five ships per year into the harbour. A little mental arithmetic reveals that in its first year of operation this policy idles 12.5% of the active fleet (5 ships out of 40), then 14.3% in the second year (5 ships out of 35), then 16.7% in the third year (5 ships out of 30). After five years, a total of 25 ships have been idled, which is fully 62.5% of the original fleet – a huge reduction in a short time. Adjust the sliders to represent the implementation of this stringent conservation policy. First set the slider for the 'Purchase of new ships this year' to zero, either by dragging the slider icon to the extreme left or by selecting the slider's 'Reset' button (denoted by 'U') in the bottom left of the slide bar. Then, set the slider for 'Ships moved to harbour this year' by dragging the slider icon to the right until the number 5 appears in the centre box. Press the 'Run' button to see the results of the policy. You will notice that ships at sea (line 4) decline steeply as enforced idling takes place. By year 35 of the simulation, the active fleet size is 15 ships at sea, back to where it had been in the early growth heyday of the fishery almost 20 years ago in year 17. Despite the cuts and huge economic sacrifices, however, the catch has declined to less than 10 fish per year, scarcely more than 1 per cent of the peak catch in year 26. In a single decade our imagined Bonavista fishery has gone from productive prosperity to extreme hardship. Each day the community awakes to see the majority of the fishing fleet idle in its once busy harbour, and the remaining active ships returning with a dismally tiny catch. You can imagine that by now many will have lost heart and lost faith in the conservation policy.

To finish the simulation reset to zero the slider for 'Ships moved to harbour this year' and then press 'Run'. In these final years it is no longer possible to enforce further reductions in the active fleet. The number of ships at sea remains constant and the catch falls practically to zero. It's a depressing story, but entirely consistent with the facts of real fisheries. Harvested fisheries are prone to catastrophic decline that nobody involved – fishermen, community leader or consumer – would wish on themselves. Yet this situation in particular, and others like it, arise from nothing more than a desire to purchase ships, catch fish and grow a prosperous community. Why? Fisheries provide but one example of puzzling dynamics that are the focus of this book. As we will see, modelling and simulation can shed useful light on why such puzzling dynamics occur and how to bring about improvement.

A Start on Analysing Dynamics and Performance Through Time

Much of the problem with managing fisheries lies in properly coordinating the number of ships at sea in relation to the number of fish. A sustainable fishery, one that provides a reliable and abundant harvest year after year, regenerates fish at about the same rate as they are being caught. Successful replenishment requires an appropriate balance of ships and fish. Balancing is easier said than done when in practice it is impossible to observe and count the number of fish in the sea, when fishing technology is advancing and when there is a natural human propensity to prefer growth and the prosperity it brings. Imagine we could reliably count the fish stock and observe the regeneration of fish through time. What new light would this new data shed on the rise and fall of Bonavista and the policy options to avoid catastrophic decline in the fish population? In our simulator we can choose to observe and report variables that, in real life, would be unobservable. Use the colour palette and paintbrush to reinstate the original coloured trajectories for the Fish stock (blue) and New fish per year (red). You will find the appropriate colours on the top row of the palette. (If you accidentally set the background colour of the chart to blue or red, which can happen if you don't align the paintbrush with the variable name, don't panic. Simply return to the colour palette, select light grey, and repaint the background. Then try again to re-colour the trajectories.) The resulting chart will look like Figure 1.10, with all the trajectories clearly visible, except that yours will be in colour.

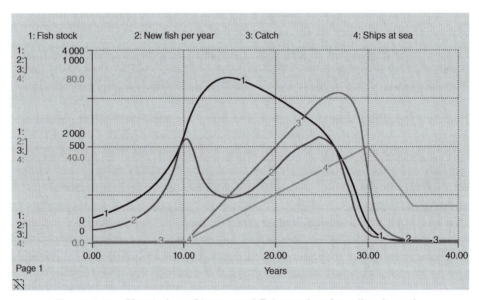

Figure 1.10 Simulation of harvested fishery showing all trajectories

Consider the behaviour over time of the fish stock (line 1). For the first 10 years of the simulation the number of fish grows swiftly because effectively there is a natural fishery (no ships) that is underpopulated relative to its carrying capacity. In years 10–15 commercial fishing begins and each year more ships are sent to sea (line 4). Nevertheless, the fish population continues to increase. These are the early growth years of the Bonavista community. During this entire period the catch is rising (line 3), but is always below the rate of regeneration (new fish per year, line 2). The fishery is sustainable with growing population. In years 15–20 the catch continues to rise steadily in line with fleet expansion, but the fish stock begins to decline gently as the catch exceeds the number of new fish per year (line 3 rises above line 2). This excess of catch over regeneration is not necessarily a problem for long-term sustainability because harvesting is actually stimulating the regeneration of fish, as shown by the steady increase in new fish per year. A harvested fishery, even a well-run one, will always have a fish population considerably lower than the maximum fishery size.

Herein lies a fundamental dilemma for fisheries management. Who is to say whether a decline in fish population is a problem or not? It could just be a sign of effective harvesting in a period of growth. Moreover, and this is vitally important to remember, nobody knows for certain how many fish of a given species are in the fishery. At best there are estimates subject to measurement error, bias and even manipulation. So it is very difficult in practice to make fish stock itself (how many fish are believed to be in the sea) the basis for investment policy (how many ships to purchase). Much more persuasive evidence comes from the catch. The simulation shows catch rising all the way through to year 25 and beyond. The temptation, even in years 20–25, is to believe that further fleet expansion is both desirable and justified. The conflicting signals from fish stock (a weak signal at best) and the catch (a strong and tangible signal of immediate economic and personal importance to fishermen and fleet operators) form the basis of the coordination problem in fisheries. Throughout year 25 and even into year 26 it is not unreasonable to continue fleet expansion even though the invisible fish population is in steady decline.

However, in year 25 something of vital significance happens under water, hidden from all but the fish themselves. The number of new fish per year (line 2) peaks and then starts to decline. This is the first evidence, a kind of early warning signal, that the fishery is being overfished. Fish density is now so low that regeneration is suppressed. The fishery teeters on the brink of catastrophe. The rate of population decline (the steepness of line 1) increases. But the catch keeps on rising throughout year 26 so no action is taken to curtail fleet expansion. In year 27 the catch itself peaks and then declines, gradually at first. This is the first tangible evidence of stock depletion underwater, but even so the signal is likely to be ignored until the trend proves conclusive and until the fishing community persuades itself to limit fishing. In the simulator, we assume that new ship purchasing continues apace until year 30. By then the fish stock has fallen to around 400, only 10% of the maximum fishery size. The regeneration rate (new fish per year) is still in decline and far below the much reduced catch. Measures to halt investment and to idle ships in years 30 to 40, drastic though they are, are too little too late. Bonavista's fish have all but gone and with them the industry on which the community depends. By year 35 there are so few fish left (only 16!) that, even with a total ban on fishing, it would take two decades to rebuild the stock to its value in year 10 when our imagined Bonavista first began commercial fishing.

Saving Bonavista – Using Simulation to Devise a Sustainable Fishery

Now you are familiar with the gaming simulator, you can use it to test alternative approaches to growing and developing the Bonavista fishery. First press the 'Reset' button to obtain a new blank time chart and to re-initialise the simulator. Next, without altering either slider, press the 'Run' button twice in order to simulate 10 years of natural growth in the fish population so that Bonavista inherits a well-stocked fishery. Then re-simulate the same fleet expansion as before – two ships per year for years 10–25. You will find yourself back in Bonavista's heyday with a fleet of 30 ships and a history of 15 years of steady growth in the catch. Now it is your responsibility to steer the community toward a sustainable future that avoids the errors of the past. For realism you may, as before, want to 'grey-out' the trajectories for fish stock and new fish per year. What is happening to the fish stock underwater is difficult to know, vague and often subject to controversial interpretation. Also bear in mind the practical political difficulties of curtailing growth and of idling ships in a community that depends on fishing. Think about *plausible* adjustments to the two sliders at your disposal. It is a good discipline to note your intentions, and the reasoning behind them, *before simulating*. Imagine you first have to convince the Bonavista community and fishermen to adopt your plan. Then, when you are ready, simulate, analyse the trajectories and try to make sense of the outcome. Was the result what you expected? If not then why? If you don't like the result then try again.

Dynamic Complexity and Performance Through Time

Although in principle it is possible to create a sustainable Bonavista it is very difficult to do so in practice or even in a simulator, particularly when you inherit a fleet of 30 ships following 15 years of successful economic growth. The fisheries simulator is one example of a dynamically complex system, of which there are others in this book and many more in life. Often such systems give rise to puzzling performance through time – performance far below the achievable and, *despite the best of intentions*, not what people (stakeholders in the system) want. In this case, the fishery is prone to catastrophic decline when perhaps all that fishermen desire, and the fishing community wants, is growth, more and better ships, and a higher standard of living. Dynamic complexity stems from the connections and interdependencies that bind together social and business systems. When a change happens in one part of the system (e.g. more ships are purchased) sooner or later it has implications elsewhere, and vice versa. Moreover, these implications are not always obvious and are often counterintuitive (e.g. more ships can lead to a *greater* rate of fish regeneration, but not always).

Dynamic complexity does not necessarily mean big, detailed and complex, involving hundreds or thousands of interacting components. Indeed, as the fisheries simulator shows, dynamic complexity and puzzling performance can arise from only a few interacting components. What matters is not so much the raw number of components but the intricacy with which they are bound together.

Such intricacy involves time delays, processes of stock accumulation (such as the accumulations of ships and of fish), non-linearities (such as the hump-shaped relationship between fish density and fish regeneration), and closed feedback loops (such as the reinforcing relationship between fish stock, fish density, fish regeneration and fish stock). These special terms, the language of feedback systems thinking, will become clearer later. For now it is sufficient to appreciate that dynamic complexity stems from intricate interdependencies of which there are many, many examples in our increasingly interconnected world. Sometimes it is possible to reduce dynamic complexity by making interdependencies less entwined and more understandable. Indeed, this goal of simplification is really the ultimate aim of policy design in system dynamics – redesigning social and business systems so that, despite their complexity, normally-competent people can run them successfully.

Why are fisheries so dynamically complex? What changes would make them less prone to sudden and catastrophic decline? Herein lies the whole area of fisheries policy involving fishermen, fishing communities, governments, marine scientists, consumers and fish themselves. There is a lot that could be modelled about the interactions among these stakeholders and arguably a serious fisheries policy simulator would be much bigger and would involve many more variables and relationships than those in our small Bonavista model. Nevertheless, at the heart of any such model will be a representation of the factors – biological, economic, political and social – that determine the balance of ships at sea and fish in a commercial fishery.

A vital part of dynamic complexity in fisheries lies in the relationship between the catch and fish density. Not surprisingly, if the fish density is very low then it is difficult for fishermen to locate fish and the catch is lower than normal. But the relationship is non-linear as shown in Figure 1.11. Here, fish density is measured on a scale from zero to one, where one is the highest possible density (the number of fish is equal to the carrying capacity) and zero is the lowest (there are no fish). The vertical axis shows the effect of fish density on catch per ship, also on a scale from zero to one. In our imagined Bonavista, the normal catch per ship is 25 fish per ship per year – remember this is a scale model. The actual catch per ship is obtained from the product of normal catch (25) and the effect of fish density.

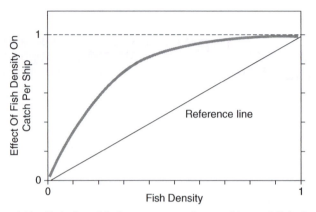

Figure 1.11   Relationship between catch per ship and fish density

When the fish density is high, in the range between 0.7 and one, the catch per ship is stable at 25 because there is little or no depressing effect from fish density. The sea is full of fish and they are easy to find and catch. When the fish density is lower, in the range 0.4 to 0.7, the catch is still very close to normal (25). The assumption, borne out empirically in real fisheries, is that fish are still quite easy to find even when there are fewer, because they tend to cluster. Only when the fish density falls very low, in the range between zero and 0.4, does scarcity make fishing more difficult. In this narrow range the effect of density falls swiftly from 0.9 (almost normal) to zero.

The non-linearity, the sudden depressing effect of density on the catch, makes fisheries management difficult. You can appreciate why if you imagine the argument between a marine biologist and a fisherman about the need to conserve stocks. When the fish population falls to half the maximum (fish density equal to 0.5) the marine biologist argues that stocks are too low. But the fisherman reports (accurately) there is no difficulty catching fish, so what's the problem? In all likelihood, the fisherman thinks the fish stock is actually higher than the marine biologist's estimate. The biologist is exaggerating the problem, or so it seems to someone whose livelihood depends directly on the catch. When the fish population falls to one-quarter of the maximum (fish density equal to 0.25) the marine biologist is frantic and even the fisherman is beginning to notice a reduction in the catch, down by about one-third relative to normal. That outcome, though worrying, is not obviously fatal. Perhaps with a bit more effort and luck the poor catch can be rectified, and why believe the marine biologist now, when he/she was seemingly so wrong and alarmist before? The non-linearity creates confusion in the attribution of causality – what causes what in the system – and such confusion is a typical symptom of dynamic complexity.

Cunning Fish – A Scenario with Reduced Dynamic Complexity

If we lived in a world where fish were cunning and took steps to avoid capture when they noticed a decline in their numbers (as though responding to a census) then the dynamic complexity of fisheries would be reduced and, ironically, fish stocks would be easier to manage for sustainability. To represent this thought experiment the effect of fish density on catch per ship is modified. Instead of being non-linear it becomes linear, as shown by the reference line in Figure 1.11. As fish density falls the fish take action to protect themselves. Suppose they disperse instead of clustering. So now, even with a slight decline in density, it is more difficult for fishermen to fill their nets. The effect of density falls below one and the catch per ship is reduced. The lower the density, the lower the catch per ship – a simple linear relationship. Now let's simulate the same Bonavista growth 'strategy' as before: purchase two new ships per year from years 10–30; and then, in years 30–40, stop new purchases and idle some ships by keeping them in harbour.

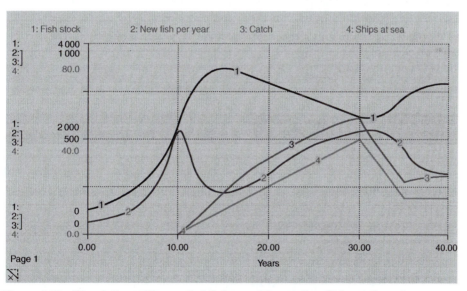

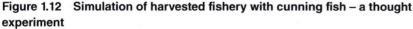

Figure 1.12   Simulation of harvested fishery with cunning fish – a thought experiment

The result is shown in Figure 1.12. This is a scenario of reduced dynamic complexity and is created by running the model called 'Fisheries Gaming Simulator – Cunning Fish' in the learning support folder for Chapter 1. Admittedly it is imaginary and fanciful but nevertheless interesting. The most obvious difference by comparison with Figure 1.10 is that the fish stock (line 1) no longer collapses in the period between years 25 and 30.

Instead, there is a steady and gradual decline in the number of fish from about 2800 in year 25 to 2400 in year 30. Crucially, the trajectory of the catch (line 3) is also different even though Bonavista's fleet profile (line 4) is identical to the profile in Figure 1.10. Here we see the practical effect of cunning fish. Trace the precise shape of the catch in the period between years 10 and 25 and compare it year-by-year with the catch in Bonavista's original years of growth and prosperity in Figure 1.10. Between years 10 and 15, the two trajectories are almost visually identical, a result that is not too surprising because fish are plentiful and growing in number and the fleets are of equal size. However, between years 15 and 20, quite early in Bonavista's growth surge, there is a noticeable difference in the two catches. The rate of increase in Figure 1.12 begins to slow as fish, whose numbers are just beginning to decline, evade capture – at least some of them do. By year 20, the catch is 400 fish per year whereas in Figure 1.10 it is 500 fish per year, 25% higher. The divergence continues through to year 25, with a catch of 530 cunning fish per year in Figure 1.12 versus 750 normal fish per year in Figure 1.10, which is 40% higher. Moreover, it is already becoming apparent to fishermen that cunning fish are fewer in number because the catch per ship is less than it used to be (roughly 18 fish per ship per year in year 25 – obtained by dividing a catch of 532 fish per year by a fleet of 30 ships versus 22 fish per ship per year in year 15 – obtained by dividing a catch of 220 fish per year by 10 ships). By year 30, the fortunes of the two Bonavistas are dramatically reversed. In Figure 1.12, the catch is 615 cunning fish per year and rising by comparison with 380 normal fish per year in Figure 1.10 and plummeting.

In the cunning fish scenario it is much easier to take effective corrective action to save the fishery. By year 30 there is still a reasonably large fish population of almost 2500 fish. However, marine biologists can argue that the stock is significantly depleted (to just over 60 per cent of the fishery's maximum size of 4000 fish) and fishermen will be inclined to agree because the catch per ship they are experiencing is now only about 15 fish per ship per year (615 fish per year by 40 ships) – a productivity decline of 17% in five years and 25% in 10 years. The exact same fleet reduction measures as before now work successfully to revitalise the fishery. Starting in year 30, a combination of enforced idling of five ships per year plus a ban on new purchases causes the active fleet to fall (line 4). Note that by the end of year 30 the catch (line 3) has fallen to equal the regeneration rate of new fish per year (line 2), so the fish population stabilises. By the third quarter of year 32, less than two years after the first cuts in fleet size, the fish stock is growing and fishermen are noticing an increase in catch per ship, up by 7% to 16 fish per ship per year from 15 in year 30. The enforced idling of 10 ships over two years is still very painful for the community, but at least there are positive results to show for the sacrifice. By year 35, the end of enforced idling, the active fleet or ships at sea (line 4) is down to 15, the catch (line 3) is down to 270 fish per year and the catch per ship is up to 18 fish per ship per year – an improvement of 20% over five years. In the final interval to year 40, the active fleet size remains constant at 15 ships. New fish per year (line 2) gradually converge to equal the catch (line 3) so that by year 40 the fishery is in long-term equilibrium with almost 3200 fish. The Bonavista community with its fishermen and its nearby colony of cunning fish has achieved a sustainable future.

Preview of the Book and Topics Covered

The fisheries simulator demonstrates a general point that dynamic complexity within business and social systems makes management and strategy development difficult. The performance of firms and industries over time rarely unfolds in the way we expect or intend. The purpose of strategic modelling and business dynamics is to investigate dynamic complexity by better understanding how the parts of an enterprise operate, fit together and interact. By modelling and simulating the relationships among the parts we can anticipate potential problems, avoid strategic pitfalls and take steps to improve performance.

The rest of the book demonstrates the art and science of system dynamics modelling. Chapter 2 introduces causal loop diagrams as a powerful conceptual tool to visualise interdependencies and take a strategic overview of operations. Chapter 3 introduces the additional concepts and tools required to translate causal loops into algebraic models and simulators. Chapter 4 provides an opportunity to experiment with a simulator and gain insight into cyclical dynamics by 'managing' the water temperature in an imaginary hot water shower. At first glance, World of Showers is far removed from the worlds of business or public policy, but the gaming simulator vividly illustrates the coordination problem at the heart of balancing loop dynamics found in many practical management situations. Players can also redesign the shower model to improve personal comfort, just as business simulators are used to redesign operating policies to improve corporate performance.

Chapters 5, 6 and 7 present a variety of business applications, covering topics such as cyclicality in manufacturing, market growth and capital investment. The models in these chapters are deliberately small and concise so their structure and formulations can be presented in full and used to illustrate principles of model conceptualisation, equation formulation and simulation analysis. Chapters 8 and 9 present larger models that arose from real-world applications. Chapter 8 investigates the upstream oil industry and the dynamics of global oil producers that affect us all through the volatile price of oil and gasoline. The chapter includes a description of the model's conceptualisation, a thorough review of the resulting feedback structure of global oil markets, a sample of equation formulations and a comprehensive set of simulations. Chapter 9 presents public sector applications of strategic modelling. We briefly review a classic model about the growth and economic stagnation of cities. Next there is a model that investigates the dynamics of hospital doctors' workload and patient care. Then we return to fisheries and further develop the gaming simulator from this chapter into a fully endogenous model of fisheries that includes investment and regulatory policy. Finally, Chapter 10 addresses the important topic of model validity and confidence building, using a model of product innovation in fast-moving consumer goods to illustrate a variety of tests of model integrity and quality. The chapter ends with a review of all the models covered in the book and some philosophical yet practical comments on realism, model fidelity and learning.

Throughout the book there are exercises with simulators that illustrate the dynamics of interest and allow readers to conduct their own tests and policy experiments. The simulators can be downloaded from the book support website (www.wiley.com/go/strategicmodelling2e). Each is designed with an interface that makes it easy to run simulations, interpret the time charts, change selected parameters and explore the underlying model structure and equation formulations. They offer a useful way to experience dynamic complexity and to develop an intuition for the causes and cures of puzzling dynamics in businesses and society.[7,8]

---

[7]Here, at the end of Chapter 1, is a good place to issue a challenge for readers who, on completing the book, wish to further develop their modelling skills on a really important dynamic problem. The task is to rebuild the *World Dynamics* model to address the effects of global warming, with the intention of creating a small-scale simulator that can be used to raise public awareness of the need for us all to cut carbon emissions. By public awareness I mean awareness in your community, company, department, university or school. Background material for this personal project can be found in *2052: A Global Forecast for the Next Forty Years* (Randers 2012), *The Vanishing Face of Gaia* (Lovelock, 2009) and in *Last Call*, a documentary film about the *Limits to Growth* project (Cerasuolo, 2013)). More ideas can be found in the 30-year update of *Limits to Growth* (Meadows, *et al.*, 2002), in Thomas Fiddaman's prize-winning work on a climate–economy model (Fiddaman, 2002) and in *A Rough Ride to the Future* (Lovelock, 2014). But remember, the main objective in this challenge is to create a compact and vivid model to raise local public awareness of the effects of climate change rather than to develop a calibrated climate–economy model for climate scientists and policy advisers. Incidentally I decided to set myself the task of rebuilding the *World Dynamics* model. An overview of my approach can be found in 'Metaphorical Models for Limits to Growth and Industrialization' (Morecroft, 2012). Sample models and supporting materials are available online from the System Dynamics Society www.systemdynamics.org. See Morecroft ISDC Workshops 2011–2013 for more details.

[8]See also John Sterman's online interactive simulator on climate change. The simulator, available at http://web.mit.edu/jsterman/www/GHG.html (accessed 20 February 2015), is based on the 'bathtub dynamics' experiments carried out at the MIT System Dynamics Group (Sterman & Booth Sweeney, 2007). The results show that even highly educated people with strong backgrounds in mathematics and the sciences have great difficulty relating the flow of greenhouse gas (GHG) emissions to the stock of greenhouse gases in the atmosphere. Further material on the 'bathtub dynamics' of greenhouse gases can be found in *World Climate*, a vivid interactive role play negotiation of a global climate agreement using a simulator called C-ROADS (Sterman, *et al.*, 2011).

There are also two electronic topics that can be found in the folders for 'v-Lectures 1 and 2' on the Learners' website. The topics are 'dynamics of diversification' and 'managing metamorphosis'. Diversification is an important part of corporate (multi-business) strategy and complements material in Chapters 6, 7, 8 and 10 on the dynamics of single-business firms and of entire industries. Metamorphosis is a process of managed adaptation to change in the business environment.

Appendix – Archive Materials from *World Dynamics*

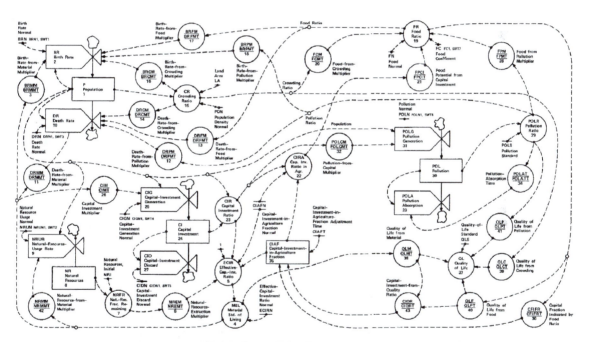

Figure 1.13   Diagram of the original *World Dynamics* model

This world model is a beginning basis for analysing the effect of changing population and economic growth over the next 50 years. The model includes interrelationships of population, capital investment, natural resources, pollution and agriculture. *Source:* Forrester, Jay W., *World Dynamics*. 1973, pp. 20–21, Reproduced by permission of Jay W. Forrester.

Basic world model behaviour showing the mode in which industrialisation and population are suppressed by falling natural resources

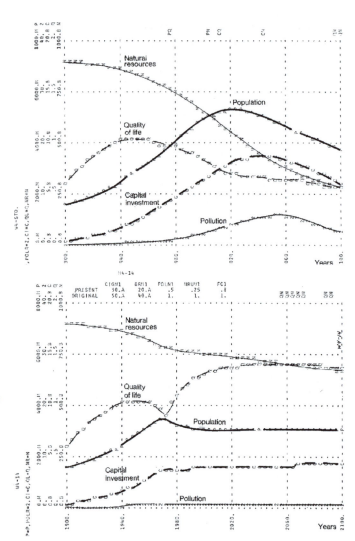

One set of conditions that establishes a world equilibrium at a high quality of life. In 1970 normal capital investment rate is reduced by 40 per cent, normal birth rate is reduced by 50 per cent, normal pollution generation is reduced by 50 per cent, normal natural resource usage rate is reduced by 75 per cent, and normal food production is reduced by 20 per cent

Figure 1.14   Simulations of the original world dynamics model

Source: pages 225 and 232 of 'Counterintuitive Behavior of Social Systems', Chapter 14 in the *Collected Papers of Jay W. Forrester*, originally published by Wright-Allen Press, 1975, available from the System Dynamics Society www.systemdynamics.org, Reproduced by permission of Jay W. Forrester.

References

Cerasuolo, E. (2013) *Last Call*. A documentary by Italian film director Enrico Cerasuolo about the history, impact and main protagonists of the Limits to Growth project www.lastcallthefilm.org/ (accessed 17 January 2014).

Clover, C. (2004) *The End of the Line*. London: Ebury Press.

Fiddaman, T. (2002) Exploring policy options with a behavioral climate-economy model. *System Dynamics Review*, 18(2): 243–267.

Forrester, J.W. (1961) *Industrial Dynamics*. available from the System Dynamics Society www.systemdynamics.org; originally published by MIT Press 1961.

Forrester, J.W. (1971) *World Dynamics*. available from the System Dynamics Society www.systemdynamics.org; originally published by Wright-Allen Press, Cambridge, MA.

Forrester, J.W. (1971 and 1975) Counterintuitive Behavior of Social Systems. *Technology Review*, 73, 52–68. Also re-published in 1975 as Chapter 14 in the *Collected Papers of Jay W. Forrester*, available from the System Dynamics Society www.systemdynamics.org; originally published by Wright-Allen Press, Cambridge MA.

isee systems (2014) iThink modelling software, visit www.iseesystems.com.

Lovelock, J. (2009) *The Vanishing Face of Gaia – A Final Warning*. London: Allen Lane, an imprint of Penguin Books.

Lovelock, J. (2014) *A Rough Ride to the Future*. London: Allen Lane, an imprint of Penguin Books.

Meadows, D.H., Meadows, D.L., Behrens, W.W. III, *et al*. (1972) *Limits to Growth*. New York: Universe Books.

Meadows, D.L., Fiddaman, T. and Shannon, D. (2001) *Fish Banks, Ltd. A Micro-computer Assisted Group Simulation That Teaches Principles of Sustainable Management of Renewable Natural Resources* (5th edn). The FishBanks Ltd game was developed by Professor Dennis Meadows, co-author of *Limits to Growth*. The board game kits which include the game software, PowerPoint slide sets for introducing and debriefing the game, instructions for playing the game, the role description, game board and pieces are sold through the System Dynamics Society www.systemdynamics.org/. Email: office@systemdynamics.org.

Meadows, D.H., Randers, J. and Meadows, D.L. (2002) *Limits to Growth: The 30 Year Update*. White River Junction, VT: Chelsea Green Publishing Company.

Meadows, D.L. and Sterman, J.D. (2011) *Fishbanks: A Renewable Resource Management Simulation*. MIT Sloan Learning Edge (an online learning resource for management education). https://mitsloan.mit.edu/LearningEdge/simulations/fishbanks/Pages/fish-banks.aspx (accessed 17 January 2014).

Morecroft, J.D.W. (2000) Creativity and convergence in scenario modelling. In Foschani, S., Habenicht, W. and Waschser, G. (eds), *Strategisches Management im Zeichen von Umbruch und Wandel* (Festschrift honouring Erich Zahn). Stuttgart: Schaeffer-Poeschel-Verlag, pp. 97–115.

Morecroft, J.D.W. (2012) Metaphorical Models for Limits to Growth and Industrialization, *Systems Research and Behavioral Science*, 29(6): 645–666.

Morecroft, J.D.W. Online ISDC Workshops. (2011–2014). In the Online Proceedings of the International System Dynamics Conferences for 2011–2013, http://conference.systemdynamics.org/past_conferences/.

Nichols, J. (1999) Saving North Sea Herring. *Fishing News*, February.

O'Brien, F.A. and Dyson, R.G. (eds) (2007) *Supporting Strategy*. Chichester: John Wiley & Sons.

Randers, J. (1980) Guidelines for model conceptualisation. In Randers, J. (ed.), *Elements of the System Dynamics Method*. available from the System Dynamics Society www.systemdynamics.org, originally published by MIT Press, Cambridge MA, 1980.

Randers, J. (2012) *2052: A Global Forecast for the Next Forty Years*. Vermont: Chelsea Green Publishing.

Sterman, J.D. and Booth Sweeney, L. (2007) Understanding public complacency about climate change: Adults' mental models of climate change violate conservation of matter. *Climate Change*, 80(3–4): 213–238. Available at http://web.mit.edu/jsterman/www/Understanding_public.html (accessed 20 February 2015).

Sterman, J.D., Fiddaman, T., Franck, T., *et al.* (2012) *World Climate: Negotiating a Global Climate Change Agreement*, https://mitsloan.mit.edu/LearningEdge/simulations/worldclimate/Pages/default.aspx (accessed 20 February 2015).

Chapter 2
Introduction to Feedback Systems Thinking

- Ways of Interpreting Situations in Business and Society
- A Start on Causal Loop Diagrams
- Structure and Behaviour Through Time – Feedback Loops and the Dynamics of a Slow-to-Respond Shower
- From Events to Dynamics and Feedback – Drug-related Crime
- Purpose of Causal Loop Diagrams – A Summary
- Feedback Structure and Dynamics of a Technology-based Growth Business
- Causal Loop Diagrams – Basic Tips
- Causal Loop Diagram of Psychological Pressures and Unintended Haste in a Troubled Internet Start-Up

In this chapter, the basic concepts of feedback systems thinking are introduced. The approach helps you to develop an overview of organisations and to see the big picture. It enables you to step back from operating detail, and to visualise how the parts of a business, industry or society fit together and interact. Pictures are important in this kind of work. You will learn how to draw causal loop diagrams (word and arrow charts that show interdependencies), and how to pick out the important feedback loops of circular cause and effect. You will also begin to appreciate that the structure of a given system, its particular combination of feedback loops, determines performance through time. From there it's just a short step to the most fundamental tenet of the field that 'structure gives rise to dynamical behaviour'.

Ways of Interpreting Situations in Business and Society

The idea that there is an enduring structure to business and social systems, which somehow predetermines achievable futures, is not necessarily obvious.

Some people argue that personalities, ambition, chance, circumstance, fate and unforeseen events hold the keys to the future in an uncertain world. But an interpretation of what is happening around you depends on your perspective. What appears to be chance may, from a different perspective, have a systemic cause. For example, when driving on a busy highway you may experience sporadic stops and starts. Does that mean you are at the mercy of random events like breakdowns or accidents? Not necessarily. Trapped in a car at ground level you don't see the waves of traffic that arise from the collective actions of individual drivers as they try to maintain a steady speed while keeping a safe distance from the car in front. There is an invisible structure to the 'system' of driving on a crowded motorway that causes sporadic stops and starts, without the need for accidents (though, of course, they do happen too). You can sense such structure, or at least something systemic, in the pattern of traffic density (alternating bands of congestion and free flow) observable from a nearby hillside overlooking the motorway, where you have the benefit of an overview. The same benefit of perspective applies to all kinds of business and social problems. So, in a way, this chapter is quite philosophical. It is about challenging you to think differently, more broadly and systemically, about the social world, including the organisations people find themselves in, and the multiple intentions, goals and actions of those organisations. Perspectives matter. In particular there are two contrasting perspectives that people bring to bear on policy and strategy development: an event-oriented approach and a feedback (or joined-up) approach. In many ways, they are polar extremes.

Event-oriented Thinking

An event-oriented perspective is pragmatic, action oriented, alluringly simple and often myopic. Figure 2.1 depicts this mindset in the abstract. It reflects a belief that problems are sporadic, stemming from uncontrollable events in the outside world. Life is capricious. Events come out of the blue or at least there is no time to worry about their causes. What's important is to fix the problem as soon as possible.

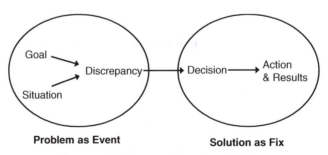

Problem as Event   **Solution as Fix**

Figure 2.1   Event-oriented world view

The typical thinking style here is linear – from problem-as-event to solution-as-fix. The problem presents itself as a discrepancy between an important shared goal and a capricious current situation. Through decision and action those responsible for the shared goal arrive at a solution and then move on to the next problem. Event-oriented thinking is widespread and often compelling. It can lead to swift and decisive action, but there are limitations to this open-loop, fire-fighting mode of intervention.

Consider a few practical examples depicted in Figure 2.2. Binge drinking is often in the news. Among other things, it leads to unruly behaviour in towns and cities late at night. A local solution is to deploy more police to arrest the main troublemakers.

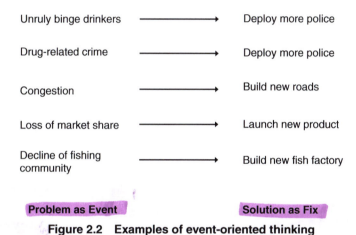

Figure 2.2   **Examples of event-oriented thinking**

Such an approach may reduce violence and accidents on a given night, but it does not get to grips with why people are binge drinking in the first place. Similarly, a quick-fix solution to drug-related crime is to deploy more police in order to seize drugs and arrest drug dealers, but that does not deter addicts. In a totally different area of public policy, traffic congestion is a chronic problem for motorists and transportation planners alike. One practical solution is to build new roads, an approach that does work, at least in the short run. However, experience suggests that in the long run congestion returns. This can be seen with the case of the M25 orbital motorway around Greater London, originally a six-lane highway with a circumference of 160 miles, completed in the mid-1980s. Thirty years later there are sections with 12 lanes and still it is overcrowded. An example from business is the strategic decision to launch a new product to prevent loss of market share. Even if the product is a success with consumers, the business ramifications can be far-reaching if the new product cannibalises a staple traditional product or invokes greater rivalry.

Event-oriented thinking is also common in fisheries management, as mentioned in Chapter 1, and further illustrated in the following example. In the late 1990s, the 370-year-old fishing community of Gloucester, Massachusetts found itself in economic decline due to the collapse of the white fishery from overfishing of groundfish stocks such as cod and haddock. Local unemployment was rising. An innovative solution proposed by community leaders was to build a new fish factory in empty wharf space to process abundant surface-water (pelagic) fish, such as herring and mackerel, and turn them into profitable 'Surimi' minced-fish products. In fact, this was a creative strategy that helped the Gloucester community in a difficult time. But the solution was a temporary fix in that the exploitation of herring and mackerel could easily undermine the revival of cod and haddock as these fish feed on pelagics. Moreover, competition for pelagics would intensify if the opening of the factory inspired other fishing communities to tap into the lucrative Surimi business. A more sustainable solution, devised by two modellers (Otto and Struben, 2004) in consultation with town leaders, addressed the fish factory's growth in the wider context of the traditional white fishery, regulation, trawler use and community well-being.

Feedback Systems Thinking – An Illustration

The Gloucester case brings us to feedback systems thinking. Otto and Struben adopted a feedback view of the problem facing Gloucester's community leaders and supporters of the new fish factory. A feedback approach is different from event-oriented thinking because it strives for solutions that are 'sympathetic' with their organisational and social environment. Problems do not stem from events, and solutions are not implemented in a vacuum. Instead, problems and solutions coexist and are interdependent.

Consider, for example, Figure 2.3, which is a causal loop diagram of factors contributing to road use and traffic congestion (Sterman, 2000). The rules for constructing and interpreting such a diagram are introduced later, but for now just focus on the cause and effect links that depict far-reaching interdependencies between highway capacity and traffic volume. Four feedback loops are shown. The top loop depicts road construction by the government agency responsible for transportation. As motorists experience an increase in travel time relative to desired travel time (the amount of time they are willing to spend on travel) there is growing pressure on planners to reduce congestion. This pressure leads to road construction which, after a time delay of several years, results in more highway capacity. More highway capacity reduces travel time as motorists are able to reach their destinations more quickly on less crowded roads. The four links described so far make a closed feedback loop labelled capacity expansion. Interestingly, this loop includes an event-oriented link from 'pressure to reduce congestion' to road construction, which is similar to the connection in Figure 2.2 from congestion to 'build new roads'. But this isolated connection is now placed in the context of many other factors, side effects if you like, deemed relevant to the big picture.

Based on a figure from *Business Dynamics*, Sterman 2000. Traffic volume depends on congestion, closing several feedback loops that cause traffic to increase whenever new roads are built.

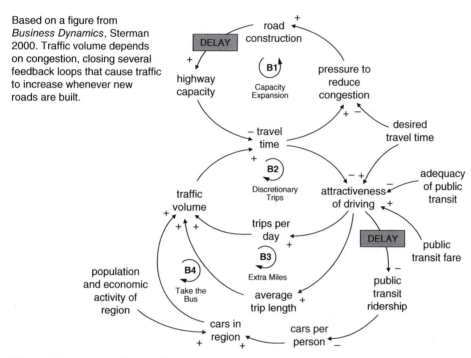

Figure 2.3 A causal loop diagram about road congestion
Source: Adapted from Sterman, J.D., *Business Dynamics: Systems Thinking and Modeling for a Complex World*, 2000, Irwin McGraw-Hill, Boston, MA. Reproduced with permission of the McGraw-Hill Companies.

One important side effect is shown in the middle loop labelled 'discretionary trips'. Here a reduction in travel time leads to an increase in the attractiveness of driving. Attractiveness itself depends on a variety of factors including desired travel time, adequacy of public transit and public transit fare. The greater the attractiveness of driving then (eventually) the more trips per day taken by motorists, the more traffic volume and the higher the travel time, thereby closing the loop. Here already is a vital side effect that can, in the medium to long term, defeat the objective of new road building programmes aimed at reducing congestion. Bigger and better roads make it more attractive to drive. So people make extra journeys. This particular side effect is largely responsible for the failure of London's M25 orbital motorway to relieve traffic congestion in and around the Greater London area, as drivers took to commuting regularly between places they would otherwise seldom visit.

The lower middle loop shows a related side effect labelled 'extra miles'. For the same attractiveness reasons drivers not only make extra journeys, they also take much longer journeys. The aggregate traffic effect is similar. Traffic volume increases, leading to longer journey times. I can report this phenomenon from personal experience. Some years ago I was on sabbatical and spent part of my time at Warwick Business School, which is located in the English Midlands, on the edge of the city of Coventry, close to the medieval town of Warwick and near William Shakespeare's home town of Stratford-upon-Avon. Warwick University is 80 miles from my home. I would never have considered driving were there not a relatively new highway, sweeping west through the rolling Chiltern Hills, across the Oxford plain and then north toward Coventry. The journey takes only 90 minutes. It's a swift yet pleasant drive. The attractiveness of driving is high even though there is an excellent train-then-bus service from my home town to the university. However, the combination of train and bus takes two hours on a good day. So sometimes the car is better, despite my green intentions.

The bottom loop labelled 'take the bus' shows another side effect, a potential long-term impact from public transit. Here, as the attractiveness of driving increases, public transit ridership decreases, causing cars per person to increase. (The direction of these causal effects can be read accurately from the diagram, but first you have to be familiar with the meaning of the '+' and '−' signs near the arrow heads, which is explained later in the chapter.) With more cars per person there are more cars in the region and traffic volume increases, thereby closing the bottom loop.

If you reflect for a moment on the picture as a whole, you realise it is a sophisticated view of the congestion problem. There are 15 concepts connected by 19 links. A lot of complexity is condensed into a small space. Compare the picture with the single stark arrow in Figure 2.2 from an event-oriented perspective. Obviously there is much more to think about and discuss in the causal loop diagram. Such richness is typical of good feedback systems thinking. The approach gives pause for thought by showing that often there is more going on (in public policy or in business strategy) than people first recognise. In fact, it is not difficult to extend the road congestion diagram. Sterman (2000) presents a bigger diagram containing in total 11 feedback loops, 20 concepts and 33 connections. In this more elaborate representation, all the effects, except desired travel time, are endogenous. In other words, the status of the road transportation system depends almost entirely on conditions *within* the system itself, which is broadly defined to include loops for road capacity expansion, discretionary trips, extra miles, take the bus (all as before) and in addition new loops for public transit capacity expansion, fare increase, public transit cost cutting, route expansion, as well as long-term side effects from opening the hinterlands and migration to the suburbs. Ultimately, road congestion depends on the interplay of all these factors.

Where exactly to draw the boundary on the factors to include is a matter of judgement and experience. Usually there is no one right answer and therefore the process of constructing diagrams, and tying them to a dynamic phenomenon, is important too. People responsible for strategy development and facing problematic situations often have in mind partial and conflicting views of these situations. It is therefore well worth spending time to capture their individual perspectives, develop an overview, share the big picture and thereby try to anticipate the ramifications, knock-on consequences, and side effects of strategic change. These are the advantages of feedback systems thinking.

A Shift of Mind

In his influential book *The Fifth Discipline*, Senge (1990) makes the point that feedback systems thinking is a 'shift of mind', a new way of interpreting the business and social world, and a kind of antidote to silo mentalities and narrow functional perspectives often fostered (inadvertently) by organisations and by our tendency to carve up problems for analysis. Figure 2.4 summarises this shift of mind. Essentially problems and solutions are viewed as intertwined.

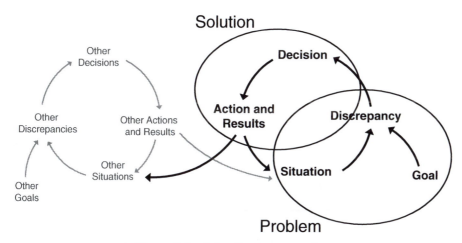

Figure 2.4   A feedback perspective

The typical thinking style here is circular – starting from a problem, moving to a solution and then back to the problem. The important point, as shown on the right of the figure, is that problems do not just spring from nowhere, demanding a fix. They are a consequence of the cumulative effect of previous decisions and actions, sometimes intentional, but often with hidden side effects. As before, a problem presents itself as a discrepancy between an important goal and the current situation. Those responsible for achieving the goal arrive at a solution in the form of a decision leading to action and results that change the current situation. If all goes to plan then the current situation moves closer to the goal, the size of discrepancy is reduced and the problem is alleviated. But this feedback response is not viewed as a once-and-for-all fix. It is part of a continual process of 'managing' the situation in order to achieve an agreed goal (or goals). Moreover, there is a recognition that other influences come to bear on the current situation. There are other stakeholders, with other goals, facing other situations and taking their own corrective action as shown on the left of Figure 2.4. The performance of the enterprise as a whole arises from the interplay of these interlocking feedback processes, just as we saw in the transport example where the stakeholders included motorists, transportation planners, bus companies and bus passengers.

The Invisibility of Feedback

There is more to feedback systems thinking than feedback loops alone. It is equally important to appreciate that many feedback processes are almost invisible in practice. They make themselves felt through unanticipated side effects, unexpected resistance to change and surprising outcomes. One way to grasp this abstract idea is to think about the unfortunate fate of the man in the stone circle shown in Figure 2.5.

Figure 2.5　The trouble with 'hidden' feedback
Source: The New Yorker Collection 1976 Arnie Levin from cartoonbank.com. All Rights Reserved. The two smaller panels are edited extracts from the original cartoon.

There are two entirely different ways to interpret this situation depending on the perspective you adopt. The picture on the right shows the perspective of the systems thinker. Here the seated man in the stone circle is evidently setting in motion a catastrophic sequence of events that will surely lead to his own destruction. He pushes over the stone to his left (the reader's right). It is clear, with the advantage of an overview, that this standing stone is in fact part of a stone circle. Inevitably the other stones will fall like giant dominoes, one after the other. Eventually the last stone will fall, with a crushing blow, landing on top of the seated man. Yet he is evidently oblivious to this fate. Why? Because where he is seated he doesn't see the stone circle. Instead, he sees just two standing stones, one on either side, as shown in the two small panels on the left of Figure 2.5. From this limited perspective he (in his last conscious moments) interprets the catastrophe differently. The sudden toppling of the last standing stone is a complete surprise. It comes out of the blue, unconnected with his pushing over the first stone. Ironically he seals his own fate but he doesn't even know it. And that's the trouble with hidden feedback.

The message from the stone circle is widely applicable. We live and work in systems of circular causality – but like the stone circle (viewed from within), feedback paths and consequences are not obvious. Often they are hidden. And so, in everyday situations, we experience a variety of perplexing phenomena that only begin to make sense as the network of cause and effect that lies behind them is revealed. Examples from common experience include the bull-whip effect in supply chains (where factories face huge changes in demand even though customers order at a steady rate), boom and bust in new product sales, volatile oil and gas prices, disappearing cod in fisheries (even though fish regenerate), mystery hold-ups on motorways, and the elusive comfort of hotel showers (too hot or too cold). These phenomena are often attributed to uncontrollable events or are blamed on others, but there is usually an alternative and better feedback explanation.

A Start on Causal Loop Diagrams

A causal loop diagram is a visual tool for the feedback systems thinker. As in the transportation example, such diagrams show cause and effect relationships and feedback processes. All causal loop diagrams are constructed from the same basic elements: words, phrases, links and loops – with special conventions for naming variables and for depicting the polarity of links and loops. Figure 2.6 is a very simple causal loop diagram, just a single loop, connecting hunger and amount eaten in a tiny model of appetite. Deliberately there is very little detail. Imagine the situation for yourself. You are hungry, so you eat. How would you describe the process that regulates food intake? Common sense and experience says there is a relationship between hunger and amount eaten and this connection is shown by two causal links. In the top link hunger influences amount eaten, while in the bottom link amount eaten has a reverse influence on hunger. Each link is assigned a polarity, either positive or negative. A positive '+' link means that if the cause increases then the effect increases too. So an increase in hunger causes an increase in the amount eaten. A negative '−' link means that if the cause increases then the effect decreases. So an increase in the amount eaten causes a decrease in hunger. In fact, the assignment of link polarity is just a bit more sophisticated. In general it is better to imagine the effect (whether an increase or decrease) relative to what it would otherwise have been, in the absence of an increase in the cause. This turns out to be a more robust test.[1] In any case, the two concepts, hunger and amount eaten, are mutually dependent, and this two-way dependence is shown as a closed feedback loop. The feedback loop represents, in outline, the control of food intake.

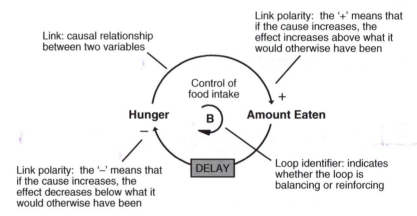

Figure 2.6   Simple causal loop diagram of food intake

There are a few more details to explain in the diagram. The bottom link contains a box labelled 'DELAY'. This symbol shows a time delay in a causal link where a given cause leads to an effect, but not immediately. There is a lag. So here the more you eat the less hungry you feel, but it takes a while for hunger pangs to diminish. Such time delays add dynamic complexity because cause and effect is less obvious. Where eating is concerned, a time delay of 20 minutes or so can make it much more difficult to regulate food intake. Overeating is a common result. In the centre of the diagram there is another special symbol, a 'B' inside a small curved arrow, a loop identifier to indicate a balancing feedback loop. Generally speaking a feedback loop can be either balancing or reinforcing. The names give a clue about the way the feedback

---

[1]This more sophisticated assignment of link polarity works not only for normal causal links but also for links that correspond to stock accumulation processes. The distinction will become clear in Chapter 3 where stock accumulation is introduced as a vital concept for modelling and simulating dynamical systems.

process operates. In a balancing loop a change in the condition of a given variable leads to a counteracting or balancing change when the effects are traced around the loop. A simple thought experiment illustrates the idea. Imagine you take a long walk and return home feeling hungry. Hunger rises and the feedback loop swings into action. Amount eaten rises and eventually hunger declines. The feedback effect of the loop is to counteract the original rise in hunger, which is a balancing process. By comparison a reinforcing loop amplifies or reinforces change. In a realistic multi-loop system, such as the transport example mentioned earlier, behaviour through time arises from the interplay of balancing and reinforcing loops. It is useful, when interpreting a web of causal connections, to identify the main loops as a way of telling a story of what might unfold. At the same time, it is a good discipline to name each loop with a mnemonic for the underlying feedback process. Hence, in Figure 2.6, the balancing loop is called 'control of food intake'. Similarly, in Figure 2.3, a feedback view of road congestion is depicted vividly as the interplay of balancing loops for 'capacity expansion', 'discretionary trips', 'extra miles' and 'take the bus'.

Structure and Behaviour Through Time – Feedback Loops and the Dynamics of a Slow-to-Respond Shower

Causal loop diagrams are a stepping-stone to interpreting and communicating dynamics or performance through time. The best way to appreciate this point is to see a worked example. Here I present a hot water shower like the one at home or in a hotel room. In this example, we start from dynamics of interest and then construct a causal loop diagram that is capable of explaining the dynamics. Our analysis begins with a time chart as shown in Figure 2.7.

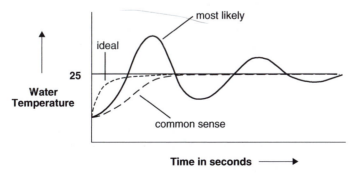

Figure 2.7   Puzzling dynamics of a slow-to-respond shower

On the vertical axis is the water temperature at the shower head and on the horizontal axis is time in seconds. Imagine it is a hot summer's day and you want to take a nice cool shower at 25°C. When you step into the cubicle the shower is already running but the water temperature is much too cold. The time chart shows three alternative time paths or trajectories for the water temperature labelled 'ideal', 'common sense', and 'most likely'. The ideal outcome is that you quickly adjust the tap setting by just the right amount and the water temperature immediately rises to the desired 25°C after which it remains rock steady. You are comfortably cool. Common sense says this ideal can't happen because, like most showers, this one is slow to respond. There is a time delay of a few seconds between adjusting the tap and a change in the water temperature. To begin with, the common-sense trajectory is flat and the water temperature remains too cold. Then, after a while the temperature begins to rise and quite soon settles at the desired 25°C. Unfortunately, bitter experience contradicts common sense. The most likely trajectory is quite different. Again the temperature starts too cold. You adjust the tap and gradually the temperature rises. After a few seconds the temperature is just right. But annoyingly it continues to rise. Before long you are much too hot, so you reverse the tap. It makes no immediate difference. So you reverse the tap even more. At last the temperature begins to fall and after a few more seconds you are again comfortably cool at 25°C. However, your comfort is short-lived as the water temperature continues to fall and you are right back where you started – too cold. The cycle continues from cold to hot and back again.

The most likely trajectory is a classic example of puzzling dynamics, performance over time that is both unintended and surprising. Who would deliberately set out to repeatedly freeze and scald themselves? The feedback systems thinker looks for the structure, the web of relationships and constraints involved in operating a shower that causes normal people to self-inflict such discomfort. It is clear from Figure 2.7 that the dynamic behaviour is essentially goal seeking. The shower taker *wants* the water temperature to be 25°C, but the actual water temperature varies around this target. The feedback structure that belongs with such fluctuating behaviour is a balancing loop with delay, and that's exactly what we are looking for in modelling or representing the shower 'system'. This notion of having in mind a structure that fits (or might fit) observed dynamics is common in system dynamics modelling. It is known formally as a 'dynamic hypothesis', a kind of preliminary guess at the sort of relationships likely to explain a given pattern of behaviour through time.

Figure 2.8 shows a causal loop diagram for a slow-to-respond shower. First consider just the words. Five phrases are enough to capture the essence of the troublesome shower: desired temperature, actual water temperature, temperature gap, the flow of hot water and the flow of cold water. Next consider the causal links. The temperature gap depends on the difference between desired and actual water temperature. The existence of a temperature gap influences the flow of hot water. This link represents the decision making and subsequent action of the shower taker. You can imagine a person turning a tap in order to change the flow of hot water and to get comfortable. The flow of hot water then influences the actual water temperature, but with a time delay because the shower is slow to respond. Also shown is a separate inflow of cold water, represented as a link on the left. The water temperature obviously depends on both water flows, hot and cold.

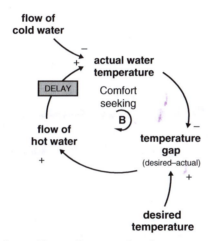

Figure 2.8   Causal loop diagram of a slow-to-respond shower

The end result is a balancing feedback loop, labelled 'comfort seeking', which is just what we are looking for to explain cyclical behaviour. The loop type can be confirmed by adding signs (positive or negative) to each link and telling a 'story' about the process of temperature adjustment around the loop. For convenience, imagine the desired water temperature is greater than actual at time zero – in other words the shower taker feels too cold and the temperature gap is greater than zero. Now consider the polarity of the first link. If the temperature gap increases then the flow of hot water becomes greater than it would otherwise have been. This is a positive link according to the polarity conventions. In the second link, if the flow of hot water increases, then the actual water temperature increases, albeit with a delay. This too is a positive link. (Note that in making the polarity assignment the flow of cold water, which also affects water temperature, is assumed to be held constant.) In the third and final link, if the water temperature increases then the temperature gap becomes smaller than it would otherwise have been. This is a negative link according to the polarity conventions. The overall effect around the loop is for an increase in the temperature gap to result in a counteracting decrease in the temperature gap, which signifies a balancing loop.

Incidentally, there is another way to work out loop polarity besides telling a story around the loop. It is also possible to simply count the number of negative links around the loop. An odd number of negative links (1, 3, 5 …) signifies a balancing loop while an even number of negative links (0, 2, 4 …) signifies a reinforcing loop. The reason this rule-of-thumb works is that any story about propagation of change around a loop will result in a counteracting effect for an odd number of negative links and a reinforcing effect for an even number. In this case, there is one negative link around the loop (between actual water temperature and the temperature gap) and so it is a balancing loop. The other negative link in the diagram (between flow of cold water and actual water temperature) does not count since it is not part of the closed loop.

Processes in a Shower 'System'

A typical causal loop diagram shows a lot about connectivity in a small space. It is a purely qualitative model, a sketch of cause and effect, particularly good for highlighting feedback loops that contribute to dynamics and to dynamic complexity. Usually there are many practical operating details about causality that lie behind the scenes. Although not shown in the diagram, it is important to be aware of this detail, particularly when building an algebraic simulator of the same feedback structure. Then it is vital to be clear and precise about how such links actually work in terms of underlying behavioural responses, economic and social conventions and physical laws. It is also important to know the numerical strength of the effects. This skill of seeing the big picture while not losing sight of operating detail is a hallmark of good system dynamics practice, known as 'seeing the forest and the trees' (Senge, 1990; Sherwood, 2002). It is a skill well worth cultivating.

One way to forge the connection from feedback loops to operations is to ask yourself about the real-world processes that lie behind the links. In the case of the shower there is an interesting mixture of physical, behavioural and psychological processes. Take, for example, the link from the flow of hot water to actual water temperature. What is really going on here? The diagram says the obvious minimum: if the flow of hot water increases then sooner or later, and all else remaining the same, the actual water temperature at the shower head increases too. The sooner-or-later depends on the time delay in the hot water pipe that supplies the shower, which is a factor that can be estimated or measured. But how much does the temperature rise for a given increase in water flow? The answer to that question depends on physics and thermodynamics – the process of blending hot and cold water. In a simulation model you have to specify the relationship with reasonable accuracy. You do not necessarily need to be an expert yourself, but if not then you should talk with someone who knows (from practice or theory) how to estimate the water temperature that results from given flows of hot and cold water – a plumber, an engineer or maybe even a physicist. Consider next the link from actual water temperature to the temperature gap. Algebraically the gap is defined as the difference between the desired and actual water temperature (temperature gap = desired water temperature − actual water temperature). But a meaningful temperature gap in a shower also requires a process for sensing the gap. The existence of a temperature gap alone does not guarantee goal-seeking behaviour. For example, if someone entered a shower in a winter wetsuit, complete with rubber hood and boots, they would not notice a temperature gap, and the entire feedback loop would be rendered inactive. Although this case is extreme and fanciful, it illustrates the importance of credibly grounding causal links.

The final link in the balancing loop is from temperature gap to the flow of hot water. Arguably this is the single most important link in the loop because it embodies the decision-making process for adjusting the flow of hot water. There is a huge leap of causality in this part of the diagram. The common-sense interpretation of the link is that when any normal person feels too hot or too cold in a shower, he or she will take corrective action by adjusting the flow of hot water. But how do they judge the right amount of corrective action? How quickly do they react to a temperature gap and how fast do they turn the tap? All these factors require consideration. Moreover, the key to over-reaction in showers arguably lies in this single step of causality. Why do people get trapped into a repetitive hot–cold cycle when all they normally want to achieve is a steady comfortable temperature? The answer must lie in how they choose to adjust the tap setting, in other words in their own decision-making process. Later on, in Chapter 4, we will investigate a full-blown algebraic model of a shower and review the main formulations in the balancing loop. For now it's enough to know that behind the three links of this alluringly simple loop lie practical processes for blending hot and cold water, for sensing a temperature gap and for adjusting the flow of hot water.

Simulation of a Shower and the Dynamics of Balancing Loops

Figure 2.9 shows the simulated dynamics of a slow-to-respond shower over a period of 120 seconds generated by a simulation model containing all the processes mentioned above. As before, the desired water temperature is a cool 25°C. However, in this scenario the water temperature starts too high at 40°C. Corrective action lowers the temperature at the shower-head to the desired 25°C in about 10 seconds, but the temperature continues to fall, reaching a minimum just below 24°C after 12 seconds. Further corrective action then increases the temperature, leading to an overshoot that peaks at 27°C after 21 seconds. The cycle repeats itself twice in the interval up to 60 seconds, but each time the size of the temperature overshoot and undershoot is reduced as the shower taker gradually finds exactly the right tap setting for comfort. In the remainder of the simulation, from 60 to 120 seconds, the temperature at the shower-head remains steady at 25°C. The overall trajectory is a typical example of goal-seeking dynamics arising from a balancing loop with delay.

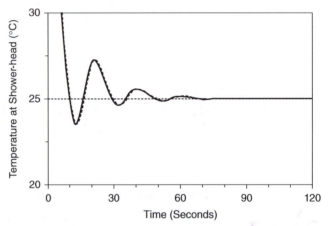

Figure 2.9　Simulated dynamics of a slow-to-respond shower

It is worthwhile to remember this particular combination of feedback structure and dynamic behaviour because balancing loops crop up all over the place in business, social, environmental and biological systems. Wherever people, organisations or even organisms direct their efforts and energy to achieving and maintaining specific goals in the face of an uncertain and changing environment there are balancing loops at work. Companies set themselves sales objectives, quality standards, financial targets and goals for on-time delivery. Governments set targets for economic growth, inflation, hospital waiting times, literacy, exam pass rates, road congestion, and public transport usage. The human body maintains weight, balance, temperature and blood sugar. The ecosystem sustains an atmosphere suitable for the animals and plants within it. The vast global oil industry maintains a supply of oil sufficient to reliably fill our petrol tanks. The electricity industry supplies just enough electricity to keep the lights on. Economies generate enough jobs to keep most people employed. The list goes on and on.

In some cases, like people's body temperature or domestic electricity supply, the balancing process works so well that it is rare to find deviations from the 'goal' – a degree or two from normal body temperature is a sign of illness and, in the electricity industry, it is unusual (at least in the developed world) for the lights to dim. In many cases, like sales objectives or hospital waiting times, the goals are known, but performance falls chronically short or else gently overshoots and undershoots. In other cases, however, like employment in the economy or inventory levels in supply chains, the balancing process is far from perfect. Performance deviates a long way from the goal, too much or too little. Corrective action leads to over- and under-compensation and the goal is never really achieved, at least not for long.

From Events to Dynamics and Feedback – Drug-related Crime

A shift of mind (from event-oriented thinking to feedback systems thinking) is not easy to achieve. The best way to make progress is through examples of feedback systems thinking applied to real-world situations. Instead of hot water showers we now consider something entirely different – drug-related crime. A typical description of the problem, by the victims of crime, might be as follows.

> Drugs are a big worry for me, not least because of the crimes that addicts commit to fund their dependency. We want the police to bust these rings and destroy the drugs. They say they're doing it and they keep showing us sacks of cocaine that they've seized, but the crime problem seems to be getting worse.

Expressed this way drug-related crime appears as a series of disturbing events. There is a concern about crime among the members of the community affected by it. They want action backed up with evidence of police attempts to fix the problem by busting rings and seizing drugs. But, despite these efforts, more crimes are happening. The feedback systems thinker re-interprets the description and draws out those aspects concerned with performance through time (dynamics) that suggest an underlying feedback structure, one or more interacting feedback loops, capable of generating the dynamics of interest. Of particular significance are puzzling dynamics, performance through time that people experience but do not want or intend. Some of the most interesting and intractable problems in society and business appear this way.

Figure 2.10 shows the unintended dynamics of drug-related crime that might be inferred from the brief verbal description above. This is just a rough sketch to provide a focus for structuring the problem. On the horizontal axis is time in years. On the vertical axis is drug-related crime defined in terms of 'incidents per month'. There are two trajectories. The upper line is a sketch of crime reported by the community. We assume a growth trajectory because 'the crime problem seems to be getting worse'. The lower line is a sketch of tolerable crime, a kind of benchmark against which to compare the actual level of crime. We assume a downward sloping trajectory because the community wants less crime and fewer drugs, and the police are taking action to achieve this end by seizing drugs and arresting dealers.[2]

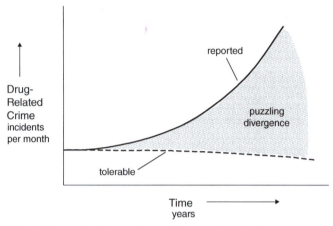

Figure 2.10   Unintended dynamics of drug-related crime – a rough sketch

The divergence between reported and tolerable crime is of particular interest to the feedback systems thinker. What feedback structure could explain this phenomenon? Reported crime is growing and we know that growth arises from reinforcing feedback. So where could such a malignant feedback process come from and why would it exist at all if those involved want less crime, not more? The persistence of unwanted growth in crime suggests a feedback loop that weaves its way around society (crossing the boundaries between police, the community and drug users) and by doing so it goes unnoticed.

A Feedback View

Figure 2.11 is a causal loop diagram for drug-related crime. First, consider the words and phrases alone. They provide the basic vocabulary of the causal model, the factors that drive up crime, or at least are hypothesised to do so. They also give clues to the boundary of the model, which parts of society are included. Of course there is drug-related crime itself, the variable of central

---

[2]You may be thinking this method of creating time charts is rather loose and in a sense you are right because we have very little data about the problem. But even in practice, with real clients, the information sources for modelling are always a pragmatic blend of informed opinion, anecdote, objective facts and clear reasoning. For a good example of this balanced approach in the area of drug policy see Homer (1993) and Levin, *et al.* (1975).

interest and concern to the community. There is a 'call for police action' and drug seizures that take us inside the police department. Then there is supply, demand and price that belong in the world of drug users who commit crime.[3]

Figure 2.11   Causal loop diagram for drug-related crime

These factors join up to make a closed loop of cause and effect. The loop brings together disparate parts of society to reveal a surprise. Hidden in the connections is a reinforcing feedback process responsible for (or at least contributing to) escalating crime. To confirm, let's trace the effect, around the loop, of an imagined increase in drug-related crime. In this kind of analysis the reason for the initial increase does not matter, it is the feedback effect that is of central interest. The story begins at the top of the diagram. An increase of drug-related crime leads to a call for more police action. More police action (raids and arrests) leads to more drug seizures. So far so good. But the paradox lies in what happens next as available drugs are traded on the streets. An increase in drug seizures causes the supply of drugs to decrease. This supply cut then causes the price of drugs to increase, just like any traded goods subject to market forces, assuming of course that higher price does not depress demand. And crucially for illegal drugs, price has little effect on demand because most users are addicts, dependent on their daily fix. So an

---

[3]Notice that all the terms in the diagram are nouns or so-called 'noun-phrases'. This is an important diagramming convention because you want concepts to denote things, attributes or qualities that can, in imagination, be unambiguously increased or decreased. Then, and only then, is it possible to assign polarity cleanly to causal links and thereby deduce the loop types – balancing or reinforcing. Take, for example, price and drug-related crime. It is easy to imagine the price of drugs going up or down and separately to imagine drug-related crime increasing or decreasing. Therefore, when a causal link is drawn between these two concepts, it is meaningful to ask whether an increase in one leads to an increase or decrease in the other. This thought experiment would make no sense if one or other concept were labelled as an activity, say pricing instead of price.

increase in price merely boosts crime as desperate drug users steal even more to fund their addiction. The reinforcing loop is plain to see. There is a 'crime spiral' in which any increase of drug-related crime tends to amplify itself through the inadvertent actions of police, drug dealers and addicts.

Scope and Boundary of Factors in Drug-related Crime

There could be more, much more, to the problem situation than the six concepts shown. I am not saying these six factors and this single reinforcing loop is a perfect representation of escalating crime in a community plagued with drug addicts. Rather it is a useful way of thinking about the problem that raises the perspective above the narrow confines of a single stakeholder. In fact, three stakeholders are united in this particular view and, just as we noted in the shower case, there is a lot going on behind the scenes of the stark causal links; detail that would need to be fleshed out in thinking more carefully about the problem and in building a simulation model to test alternative intervention policies. There is the community suffering from crime and calling for police action. There is the police department, concerned with all sorts of law enforcement, allocating police officers to priority tasks, among which is drug busting. Then there is the shady world of drug dealers sourcing drugs and covertly selling them to addicts who *must* consume, no matter what the cost. In the next chapter, we see how this qualitative feedback diagram is transformed into a full-blown simulator, but for now I want to end the discussion of drug-related crime by inviting you to think about what else *might* be included in a conceptual model of the problem.

One area of the diagram to expand is demand and supply. (Another good idea in practice is to gather more time series data to help refine the dynamic hypothesis, but we will bypass that step in this small illustrative example.) What if there is growth in demand because addicts and dealers themselves recruit new users? This possibility adds a whole new dimension to escalating crime not dealt with in our current picture, a new theory if you like. What if, as is surely the case, the available supply of drugs increases as the price rises? Does that mean drug seizures perversely expand the whole illegal drug industry (in the long run) by artificially boosting prices? Such industry growth could exacerbate the crime problem, particularly if the relevant time frame is a decade or more rather than just a few years. These questions, and others like them, are worth probing and may usefully expand the scope and boundary of our thinking. The point, however, in any such conceptualisation task, is to avoid unnecessary complexity and focus on finding plausible loops, often unnoticed in the pressure of day-to-day operations, that not only challenge conventional event-oriented thinking but also produce dynamics consistent with the observed problem.

An Aside – More Practice with Link Polarity and Loop Types

I have explained the origin of the reinforcing loop in Figure 2.11 by tracing an imagined change in crime all the way around the loop and showing that it leads to even more crime. As mentioned earlier, another way to find the loop type is to use the counting rule. Count the negative links around the loop. If the number of links is odd then the loop is balancing and if the number is even the loop is reinforcing. Let's do this exercise now. First we need to assign link polarities using the standard test. Any individual link connects two concepts A and B where A is the cause and B is the effect. For each link imagine an increase in the cause A and then work out the effect on B. In this thought experiment all other influences on B are assumed to remain unchanged, the *ceteris paribus* assumption. The link is positive if, when A increases, B increases above what it would otherwise have been. The link is negative if, when A increases, B decreases below what it would have been. Note that the mirror image test works too. So when A decreases and B also decreases the link is positive, but when A decreases and B increases the link is negative. What matters for polarity is whether or not there is a reversal.

We start at the top. All else equal, if drug-related crime increases then the call for police action (complaints from the community) increases above what it would otherwise have been, a positive link. When the call for police action increases then drug seizures increase, another positive link. Note there is a large leap of causality here that relies on all else remaining equal, *ceteris paribus*. We implicitly assume that a call for action really leads to action (in this case more police allocated to drug busting), rather than being ignored. Moreover, we assume that more police leads to more seizures. In the next link, an increase in seizures leads to a decrease in supply, below what it would otherwise have been, a negative link. Then a decrease in supply leads to an increase in price, another negative link coming this time from a mirror image test. Here there is a particularly clear instance of *ceteris paribus* reasoning because price depends both on supply and demand. The assumption behind the polarity test is that demand remains constant. An equivalent test on the demand-to-price link shows it is positive: an increase in demand leads to an increase in price, assuming supply is held constant. Finally, an increase in price leads to an increase in drug-related crime, a positive link that completes the loop. Counting up there are two negative links around the loop, an even number, so the loop type is reinforcing.

Purpose of Causal Loop Diagrams – A Summary

As we have seen, causal loop diagrams offer a special overview of business and society, showing what is connected to what and how changes in one part of the system might propagate to others and return. People often say we live in an interconnected world but have no way, other than words, to express this complexity. Causal loop diagrams, concise and visual, reveal the interconnections, both obvious and hidden. Moreover, they can be used to elicit and capture the mental models of individuals or teams and to expand the boundary of people's thinking beyond the parochial.

There is more than just connections, however. Causal loop diagrams also capture hypotheses about dynamic behaviour. Here is the beginning of the shift of mind so vital to feedback systems thinking. The future time path of any organisation is partly and significantly pre-determined by its structure, the network of balancing and reinforcing feedback loops that drive performance through time. Causal loop diagrams embody this important philosophical view by making plain the important feedback loops believed to be responsible for observed performance (Perlow *et al.*, 2002).

Feedback Structure and Dynamics of a Technology-based Growth Business

The first project I undertook after completing my PhD was to model a technology-based growth company operating in Salt Lake City, Utah. With an MIT colleague, Jack Homer, I made the 2000-mile plane journey from Boston to Utah on several occasions to interview the management team and capture their understanding of the business. The company made automated materials handling systems. These systems are expensive and technically complex, but the principle is simple enough. You have probably seen forklift trucks used in factories to move goods from place to place. They are an example of materials handling, with human operators as drivers. Nowadays, the process is largely automated. Visit a manufacturing firm and you will find specialised robotic machines moving materials. They pick stock items from huge multi-storey racks and deposit them on conveyor belts for production and assembly. At the end of the production line they receive finished goods, count them and store them in a warehouse ready for shipping. The technology is a sophisticated blend of mechanical engineering, electrical engineering and computer science. Product designers are often recruited from the aerospace industry. The equipment is very expensive and is built to order with a long lead time. An automated storage and retrieval system for use say in Harley-Davidson's motorcycle factory in Pennsylvania or BMW's MINI factory in Oxford might cost several million pounds sterling and take more than a year to build and install. Each system is a self-contained engineering project that includes design, proposal writing, competitive bidding, construction and installation.

At the time of the modelling project, automated materials handling systems were new. There was a belief among the management team, and others in the industry, that the market for these complex products was potentially very large. But the fledgling industry had teething problems. Growth was not as fast as expected. Automated handling was still perceived by customers (factory owners and operators) to be inflexible. It was difficult to trade off promised labour savings against the large capital cost. Customers needed persuasion and reassurance to invest. Nevertheless, there had been a few years of promising growth, but now the product was meeting resistance in the market and there were signs of a downturn in sales. Was growth sustainable? What factors might halt growth? These were the questions the management team wanted to investigate. A series of meetings took place to map out the operation of the business. The scope of the analysis was deliberately broad, extending across functional areas, into the market and including competitors.

The causal loop diagram in Figure 2.12 emerged from the meetings (Morecroft, 1986). It shows four interacting loops. At the top is a 'real growth loop', a structure capable of powering business expansion. Of central importance is the salesforce. The Utah company viewed itself as a leader in automated materials handling and its salesforce was responsible for wooing customers and persuading them of the merits of automation. The bigger the salesforce ~Delay the larger the pool of customers interested in the technology. However, customers do not immediately buy. They first request a feasibility study with a formal costed proposal for a competitive bid. The more customers, the more study requests, the more study completions and, *ceteris paribus*, the greater the number of contracts won. More contracts boost the budget for the salesforce enabling a bigger salesforce. The result is a reinforcing loop in which an increase in the salesforce eventually leads to enough extra business to justify a further increase in salesforce, and so on. This single loop in isolation is how the business might look to an established monopoly producer, or to a myopic and optimistic producer unaware of competitors. Admittedly, it is just a brief sketch concentrating on technology diffusion, but it shows a growth engine. Providing the basic economic proposition to customers is good (i.e. automation is reliable and cost effective) then the business will grow steadily, limited only by the time it takes to educate customers about the technology, design systems and agree contracts.

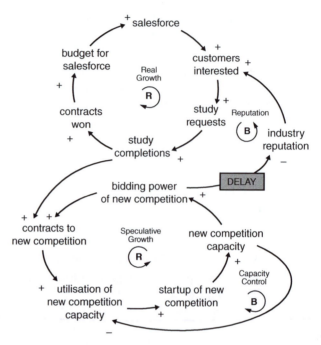

Figure 2.12 Feedback loops in the growth of the automated materials handling business

Source: Adapted from The Dynamics of a Fledgling High-Technology Growth Market, *System Dynamics Review*, 2(1), 36–61, Morecroft, J.D.W, 1986 © John Wiley & Sons Limited. Reproduced with permission.

If such a growth engine is really at work, why might it falter? Meetings revealed commercial pressure from new entrants which, it turned out, was able to explain the temporary stagnation already observed. This pressure is captured in three feedback loops that extend the boundary of the model to rivals, their combined capacity and, crucially, their collective impact on industry reputation. The hypothesis here is that rapid entry of new firms, attracted by the growth potential of the industry, eventually undermines industry reputation thereby making it much more difficult for any producer (new or established) to woo customers. The industry reputation loop is a good place to start. Here we imagine that study completions (proposals from the established producer in Salt Lake City) are open to competitive bids by new rivals. As no single producer has a monopoly, an increase in study completions leads to more contracts awarded to new competition. The loss of contracts is not, however, the only problem here. It is the knock-on consequences that matter most. An increase in contracts to new competition leads to higher utilisation of new competition capacity. So existing new firms are busy and this success signal leads to an increased start-up of new competition and an expansion of new competition capacity. With more capacity the collective bidding power of new competition rises, but this can hurt the industry. The product is complex and some new entrants are still learning the technology. So as their bidding power rises industry reputation is depressed leading eventually to a reduction in customers interested, fewer study requests and fewer study completions. The result is a balancing loop, the reputation loop, which undermines real growth by attracting naïve and opportunist producers to an industry whose growth depends on the confidence of customers in the merits of a complex product.

The reputation problem is exacerbated by speculative growth of new entrants, shown by the loop at the bottom of Figure 2.12. Here an increase of contracts awarded to new competition leads, as before, to an increase in the bidding power of new competition. New firms compete more vigorously for the available contracts and they win more, thereby attracting even more new firms. The growth process is speculative because new entrants do little to woo customers. Instead, they hijack customers already nurtured by established producers. New firms bid aggressively, win contracts and reinforce the impression that the market is growing.

The final loop is labelled 'capacity control', but in the context of speculative entry it is weak and myopic. If new competition capacity rises then, all else remaining equal, the utilisation of capacity falls thereby deterring entry and stabilising capacity. But all else does not remain equal and speculative growth creates the illusion of capacity shortage. The illusion quickly fades if real growth (in the top loop) becomes negative due to low industry reputation. Then contracts to new competition diminish, utilisation falls and the reality of stagnant or falling demand becomes apparent to new producers and potential new entrants alike.

Causal Loop Diagrams – Basic Tips

In this chapter, several causal loop diagrams have been presented. Despite their variety they all follow the basic tips of good practice.

Picking and Naming Variables

The choice of words is vital. Each variable must be a noun. Avoid the use of verbs or directional adjectives. For example, a causal diagram can use the word 'sales', but not 'sales planning' or 'increased sales'. Simple nouns like 'accounts' or 'staff' can be augmented with adjectives to give phrases like 'large accounts' or 'experienced staff'. Sticking to these basic naming rules helps when assigning polarity to causal links and explaining how changes propagate around loops.

Words are versatile, but they should also be grounded in facts. The range of concepts that can be included in causal loop diagrams extends from the hard and easily measureable, such as 'new products' and 'recruits', to the soft and intangible such as 'morale' or 'customer perceived quality'. A powerful feature of feedback systems thinking and system dynamics is its ability to incorporate both tangible and intangible factors. However, for any variable no matter how soft, you should always have in mind a specific unit of measure, a way in which the variable might be quantified, even if formal recorded data do not exist. Hence, you might imagine morale on a scale from 0 (low) to 1 (high) or product quality on a scale from 1 (low) to 5 (high). Be sure to pick words that *imply* measureability, such as 'delivery lead time' thought of in weeks or months, rather than a vague concept like 'delivery performance'.

Meaning of Arrows and Link Polarity

Arrows show the influence of one variable on another – a change in the cause leads to a change in the effect. The assignment of link polarity (+) or (−) makes the direction of change clear. In Figure 2.13, an increase in marketing budget leads to an increase in sales, which is a positive link.

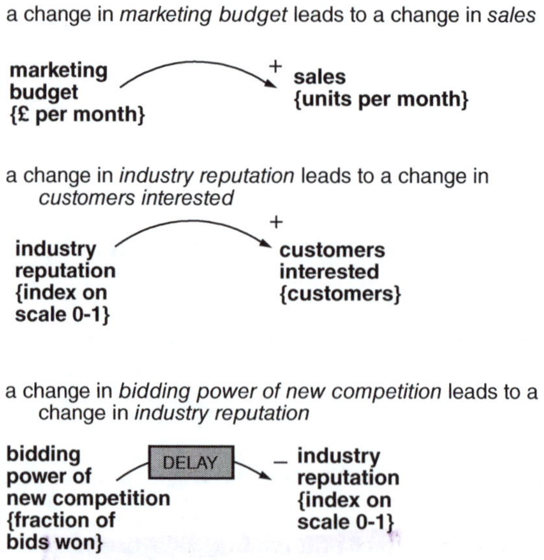

a change in *marketing budget* leads to a change in *sales*

marketing budget
{£ per month}
+ sales
{units per month}

a change in *industry reputation* leads to a change in *customers interested*

industry reputation
{index on scale 0-1}
+ customers interested
{customers}

a change in *bidding power of new competition* leads to a change in *industry reputation*

bidding power of new competition
{fraction of bids won}
DELAY
− industry reputation
{index on scale 0-1}

Figure 2.13 Arrows and link polarity

A useful refinement in polarity assignment is to note whether the effect of a given change is an increase (or decrease) *greater than it would otherwise have been.* The use of this extra phrase avoids ambiguity in situations where the effect is cumulative. Hence, an increase in industry reputation leads to an increase in customers interested; but since customers were accumulating anyway, we really mean more customers than there would otherwise have been. Polarity assignment works equally well for intangible variables. Industry reputation here is viewed as an intangible concept measured on a scale from 0 to 1. In the particular case of the materials handling business described earlier, industry reputation depends on the bidding power of new competitors. An increase in bidding power (measured as the fraction of bids won by new firms in the industry) leads to a decrease in industry reputation, below what it would otherwise have been, a negative link. As reputation takes a long time to change, a delay is shown on the link.

Drawing, Identifying and Naming Feedback Loops

For the systems thinker, feedback loops are the equivalent of the sketches created by political cartoonists. They capture something important about the situation or object of interest. Just as a few bold pen lines on a canvas can characterise Barack Obama, Nelson Mandela, Vladimir Putin, Osama bin Laden or Angela Merkel, so a few feedback loops on a whiteboard can characterise an organisation. Like celebrity sketches feedback loops should be drawn clearly to identify the dominant features, in this case important loops. Sterman (2000) identifies five tips for visual layout:

1 Use curved lines to help the reader visualise the feedback loops
2 Make important loops follow circular or oval paths
3 Organise diagrams to minimise crossed lines
4 Don't put circles, hexagons, or other symbols around the variables in causal diagrams. Symbols without meaning are 'chart junk' and serve only to clutter and distract.
5 Iterate. Since you often won't know what all the variables and loops will be when you start, you will have to redraw your diagrams, often many times, to find the best layout.

(Sterman, J.D., *Business Dynamics: Systems Thinking and Modeling for a Complex World,* © 2000, Irwin McGraw-Hill, Boston, MA. Reproduced with permission of the McGraw-Hill Companies.)

As we have already seen, for the hot water shower and drug-related crime, there are two main loop types, balancing and reinforcing. A loop type is identified by imagining the effect of a change as it propagates link-by-link around the loop. A reinforcing loop is one where an increase in a variable, when traced around the loop, leads to a further increase in itself. Such an outcome requires an even number (or zero) of negative links. A balancing loop is one where an increase in a variable, when traced around the loop, leads to a counterbalancing decrease in itself. Such an outcome requires an odd number of negative links. Once you have identified loop types it is good practice to label them R for reinforcing and B for balancing, the letter encircled by a small curved arrow shown clockwise for clockwise loops (and vice versa). By following these tips and by studying the examples in the chapter you should be able to create, label and interpret your own causal loop diagrams.

Causal Loop Diagram of Psychological Pressures and Unintended Haste in a Troubled Internet Start-Up

Although causal loop diagrams are nothing more than specialised word-and-arrow charts they can nevertheless provoke a 'shift of mind' about puzzling phenomena in organisations. A good example is to be found in a study by Perlow *et al.* (2002) of a troubled internet start-up company (Notes.com) whose founders inadvertently became trapped into making important decisions too quickly. Eventually and covertly this self-induced collective impatience, dubbed 'the speed trap', undermined the performance and competitive advantage of the very enterprise the founders had worked so hard to create. The Perlow paper presents, step-by-step, four carefully crafted causal loops to distill an endogenous (feedback) view of the speed trap, based on ethnographic data (minutes of meetings, observations, interviews) about the firm's style of decision making. This exceptionally detailed material was gathered over 19 months of close collaboration between the founders and researchers. Figure 2.14 shows the completed causal loop diagram, which is the culmination of some eight pages of loop-by-loop presentation. The text that accompanied the figures is reproduced below and the complete article can be found in the learning support folder for Chapter 2.

> The speed trap is composed of the four feedback processes shown in Figure 2.14. Notes.com's rapid entry into the Internet market, supported by fast decision making, led to cues from which participants formed beliefs about the potential market and the time horizon over which that market could be realized. If these early cues had been negative, the investment might have been abandoned. But instead, these early cues suggested the potential market was substantial. The assessed potential of the investment grew and fed back to increase both urgency and the perceived value of fast decision making, thereby creating the reinforcing accelerating aspirations loop. As more people visited its web site, Notes.com significantly raised its expectations for site usage and its final valuation. Rising expectations further reinforced the need to act quickly.

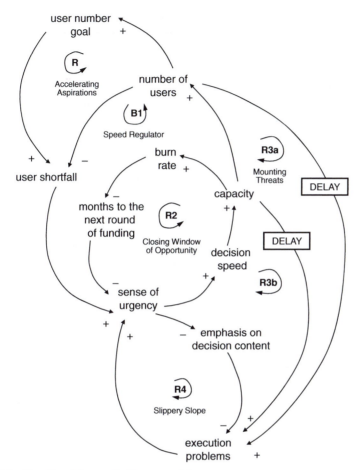

Figure 2.14   Feedback loops in the speed trap
Source: The Speed Trap, Perlow *et al.* 2002.

Rapid decisions coupled with high expectations led to commitments that fixed or reduced the time period over which objectives had to be achieved. By 'growing' the organization and hiring more people, the management shortened the time until they needed additional funding. At the same time, fast decisions led to an increasing number of commitments (borrowed money, career opportunities foreclosed, equipment purchased) that decreased the likelihood that people would revisit core decisions. These links create the second feedback process, the *closing window of opportunity* loop (R2), which further increased the sense of urgency.

These two loops were instrumental in creating Notes.com's early success, but, because leaders did not perceive fundamental threats to the enterprise, the loops also led to substantial commitments being made in advance of complete knowledge concerning the company's viability. Unfortunately, given the shrinking time horizon, once significant threats did appear, there was little the organization could do about them. The perceived urgency they created only reinforced the belief that major changes of course would sabotage any chance of success. Therefore, despite serious threats to the firm, the combination of escalating commitments and a shrinking time horizon created a situation in which the only plausible course of action was to move even more quickly. The consequence of the mounting threats was thus to increase urgency further, leading to even hastier decisions and the firm's being trapped in the *mounting threats* loops (R3a and R3b).

Finally, the combination of high expectations, a shrinking time horizon and mounting threats caused participants to increasingly value decision speed over decision content. Not only was their increasingly abbreviated decision process justified as 'necessary given the dynamics of the market', but also, those who dared challenge this view were seen as immature and lacking an understanding of the Internet market. A focus on decision speed at the expense of more careful consideration pushed the organization onto the *slippery slope* created by a vicious cycle of declining attention to decision content and an increasing number of issues that required decisive action. For Notes.com, getting caught in the speed trap meant that a focus on making fast decisions, while initially a source of competitive advantage, eventually became an internally generated and self-destructive need for speed.

I included the speed trap excerpt to show another example of high quality causal loop diagramming. The more examples you see, the better. The speed trap is, in many ways, an exceptional and unusual feedback system study. As already mentioned, it arose from long and intense collaboration between organisational researchers and the client company; a process described by the authors as 'full ethnographic immersion'. The study was qualitative yet rigorous. As far as I know, there was not an intention to develop a simulator. Nevertheless the work shows there is value in good causal loop diagramming. The resulting journal article, with its careful loop-by-loop analysis of feedback structure, serves as a quality benchmark for would-be qualitative modellers.

It pays to invest serious time and effort in 'loop discovery' and 'loop construction': understanding the organisational setting, using familiar and well-grounded vocabulary, choosing words and phrases to ensure reliable attribution of causality and link polarity; sketching clear loops; and labelling loops according to the process each depicts. It also pays to write a lucid narrative interpretation of the loops and their likely effects on performance of the organisation or business.

In subsequent chapters we turn our attention to formal models and simulators of feedback processes. Such models also call for close scrutiny of operations, to discover realistic interlocking factors that lie behind dynamics. But as we will see, simulation modelling brings additional rigour and fun to feedback systems thinking.

References

Homer, J. (1993) A system dynamics model of national cocaine prevalence. *System Dynamics Review*, 9(1): 49–78.

Levin, G., Roberts, E.B. and Hirsch, G. (1975) *The Persistent Poppy: A Computer-Aided Search for Heroin Policy*. Cambridge, MA: Ballinger.

Morecroft, J.D.W. (1986) The dynamics of a fledgling high technology growth market. *System Dynamics Review*, 2(1): 36–61.

Otto, P. and Struben, J. (2004) Gloucester Fishery: insights from a group modelling intervention. *System Dynamics Review*, 20(4): 287–312.

Perlow, L.A., Okhuysen, G.A. and Repenning, N.P. (2002) The Speed Trap: Exploring the Relationship Between Decisionmaking and Temporal Context. *Academy of Management Review*, 45(5): 931–955.

Senge, P.M. (1990) *The Fifth Discipline: The Art and Practice of the Learning Organization*. New York: Doubleday.

Sherwood, D. (2002) *Seeing the Forest for the Trees: A Manager's Guide to Applying Systems Thinking*. London: Nicholas Brealey.

Sterman, J.D. (2000) *Business Dynamics: Systems Thinking and Modeling for a Complex World*. Boston, MA: Irwin McGraw-Hill (see in particular Chapter 5 on Causal Loop Diagrams).

Chapter 3
Modelling Dynamic Systems

- Asset Stock Accumulation
- The Coordinating Network
- Modelling Symbols in Use: A Closer Look at Drug-related Crime
- Equation Formulations
- Experiments with the Model of Drug-related Crime
- Benefits of Model Building and Simulation

Causal loops diagrams are very effective for expanding the boundary of your thinking and for communicating important feedbacks. However, they are not especially good as the basis for a full-blown model and simulator that computes dynamics and performance through time. For a working model, we need better resolution of the causal network. It turns out, not surprisingly, that there is more to causality and dynamics than words and arrows alone. The main new concepts required to make simulators are introduced in this chapter. They transform a simple sketch of causality into a portrait (or better still an animation) that brings feedback loops to life, by specifying the realistic processes that lie behind causal links as the basis for an algebraic model and simulator.

Asset Stock Accumulation

Asset stock accumulation is a very important idea in system dynamics, every bit as fundamental as feedback and in fact complementary to it. You can't have one without the other. Asset stocks accumulate change. They are a kind of memory, storing the results of past actions. When, in a feedback process, past decisions and actions come back to influence present decisions and actions they do so through asset stocks. Past investment accumulates in capital stock – the number of planes owned by an airline, the number of stores in a supermarket chain, the number of ships in a fishing fleet. Past hiring accumulates as employees – nurses in a hospital, operators in a call centre, players in a football squad, faculty in a university. Past production accumulates in inventory and past sales accumulate in an installed base.

All business and social systems contain a host of different asset stocks or resources that, when harnessed in an organisation, deliver its products and services. Crucially, the performance over time of an enterprise depends on the balance of these assets and resources (Warren, 2002; 2008). An airline with lots of planes and few passengers is out of balance and unprofitable. Empty seats bring no revenue. A factory bulging with inventory while machines lie idle is out of balance and underperforming. Inventory is expensive.

To appreciate how such imbalances occur we first need to understand the nature of asset stock accumulation – how assets build and decay through time. A process of accumulation is not the same as a causal link. Accumulations change according to their inflows and outflows in just the same way that water accumulates in a bathtub. If the inflow is greater than the outflow then the level gradually rises. If the outflow is greater than the inflow then the level gradually falls. If the inflow and outflow are identical then the level remains constant. This bathtub feature of assets in organisations is depicted using the symbols in Figure 3.1. Here an asset stock or resource is shown as a rectangle, partially filled. On the left there is an inflow comprising a valve or tap superimposed on an arrow. The arrow enters the stock and originates from a source, shown as a cloud or pool. A similar combination of symbols on the right represents an outflow. In this case, the flow originates in the stock and ends up in a sink (another cloud or pool). The complete picture is called a stock and flow network.

Figure 3.1   Asset stock accumulation in a stock and flow network

Consider, for example, a simple network for university faculty as shown in Figure 3.2. Let's forget about the distinction between professors, senior lecturers and junior lecturers and call them all instructors.

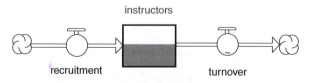

Figure 3.2   A simple stock and flow network for university faculty

Instructors teach, write and do research. The stock in this case is the total number of instructors. The inflow is the rate of recruitment of new faculty – measured say in instructors per month, and the outflow is turnover – also measured in instructors per month. The source and sink represent the university labour market, the national or international pool of academics from which faculty are hired and to which they return when they leave. The total number of instructors in a university ultimately depends on all sorts of factors such as location, reputation, funding, demand for higher education and so on. But the way these factors exert their influence is through flow rates. Asset stocks cannot be adjusted instantaneously no matter how great the organisational pressures. Change takes place only gradually through flow rates. This vital inertial characteristic of stock and flow networks distinguishes them from simple causal links.

Accumulating a 'Stock' of Faculty at Greenfield University

The best way to appreciate the functioning of stocks and flows is through simulation. Luckily it is only a small step from a diagram like Figure 3.2 to a simulator. In the learning support folder for Chapter 3, find the model called 'Stock Accumulation – Faculty' and open it. A stock and flow network just like Figure 3.2 will appear on the screen. To make this little network run each variable must be plausibly quantified. Imagine a new university called Greenfield. There is a small campus with some pleasant buildings and grounds, but as yet no faculty. The model is parameterised to fit this situation. Move the cursor over the stock of instructors. The number zero appears meaning there are no instructors at the start of the simulation. They will come from the academic labour market. Next move the cursor over the valve symbol for recruitment. The number five appears. This is the number of new instructors the Vice Chancellor and Governors plan to hire each month. Finally move the cursor over the symbol for turnover. The number is zero. Faculty are expected to like the university and to stay once they join. So now there is all the numerical data to make a simulation: the starting size of the faculty (zero), intended recruitment (five per month) and expected turnover (zero per month).

Press the 'Run' button. What you see is stock accumulation as the 'bathtub' of instructors gradually fills up. This steady increase is exactly what you expect if, each month, new instructors are hired and nobody leaves. Now double select the graph icon. A chart appears – a colour version of Figure 3.3 – that plots the numerical values through time of instructors (line 1), recruitment (line 2) and turnover (line 3). The horizontal time axis spans 12 months. The number of instructors begins at zero and builds steadily to 60 after 12 simulated months. Meanwhile recruitment remains steady at five instructors per month and turnover is zero throughout. Numerically the simulation is correct and internally consistent. Recruitment at a rate of five instructors per month for 12 months will, if no one leaves, result in a faculty of 60 people. That's all very obvious, and in a sense, stock accumulation is no mystery. It is simply the result of taking the numerical difference, period by period, between the inflow and the outflow and adding it to the stock size. An equation shows the simple arithmetic involved:

$$\text{instructors}(t) = \text{instructors}(t - dt) + (\text{recruitment} - \text{turnover}) * dt$$
$$\text{INIT instructors} = 0$$

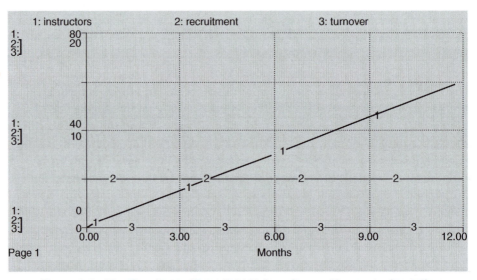

Figure 3.3   **Faculty size at Greenfield University – a 12-month simulation**

Here, the number of instructors at time t (this month) is equal to the number of instructors at time t−dt (last month) plus the difference between recruitment and turnover for an interval of time dt. The interval is a slice of time convenient for the calculation, the so-called delta-time dt. So if dt is equal to one month then the calculation is a monthly tally of faculty. The initial value of instructors is set at zero.

All stock accumulations have the same mathematical form, no matter whether they represent tangible assets (machines, people, planes) or intangible assets (reputation, morale, perceived quality). The relationship between a stock and its flows is cumulative and naturally involves time. It is *not* the same as a simple causal link.[1] The stock of instructors accumulates the net amount of recruitment and turnover *through time*. Mathematically speaking, the stock *integrates* its inflow and outflow. The process is simple to express, but the consequences are often surprising.

To illustrate, let's investigate a 36-month scenario for Greenfield University. Recruitment holds steady at five instructors per month throughout, but after 12 months some faculty are disillusioned and begin to leave. To see just how many leave double select the 'turnover icon'. A chart appears that shows the pattern of turnover across 36 months. Now select the 'Points' tab to display a table of the corresponding numerical values at intervals of three months. For a period of 12 months, turnover is zero and faculty are content. Then people start to leave, at an increasing rate. By month 15 turnover is two instructors per month, by month 18 it is four instructors per month and by month 21 it is six instructors per month. The upward trend continues to month 27 by which time faculty are leaving at a rate of ten per month. Thereafter turnover settles and remains steady at ten instructors per month until month 36. (As an aside it is worth noting this chart is just an assumption about future turnover regardless of the underlying cause. In reality instructors may leave Greenfield University due to low pay, excess workload, lazy students, etc. Such endogenous factors would be included in a complete feedback model.)

To investigate this new situation, it is first necessary to extend the simulation to 36 months. Close the turnover chart by selecting the small grey arrow in the left margin of the Graph display window. Then find 'Run Specs' in the pull-down menu called 'Run' at the top of the screen. A window appears containing all kinds of technical information about the simulation. In the top left, there are two boxes to specify the length of simulation. Currently the simulator is set to run from 0 to 12 months. Change the final month from 12 to 36 and select 'OK'. You are ready to simulate. However, before proceeding, first sketch on a blank sheet of paper the faculty trajectory you expect to see. A rough sketch is fine – it is simply a benchmark against which to compare model simulations. Now select the 'Run' button. You will see the 'bathtub' of faculty fill right to the top and then begin to empty, ending about one-quarter full. If you watch the animation very carefully you will also see movement in the dial for turnover. The dial is like a speedometer – it signifies the speed or rate of outflow. Now move the cursor over the 'turnover icon'. A miniature time chart appears showing the assumed pattern of turnover. Move the cursor over 'recruitment' and another miniature time chart appears showing the

---

[1]For more ideas on stock accumulation see Sterman (2000), Chapter 6, 'Stocks and Flows', Warren (2002), Chapter 2, 'Strategic Resources – the Fuel of Firm Performance' and Chapter 7, 'The Hard Face of Soft Factors – the Power of Intangible Resources'.

assumed steady inflow of new faculty from hiring. Finally, move the cursor over the 'stock of instructors'. The time chart shows the calculated trajectory of faculty resulting from the accumulation of recruitment (the inflow) net of turnover (the outflow).

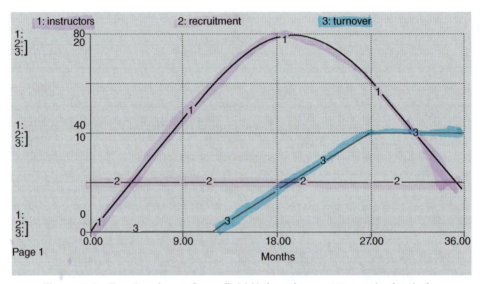

Figure 3.4   Faculty size at Greenfield University – a 36-month simulation

All three trajectories can be seen in more detail by double selecting the 'graph icon'. The chart in Figure 3.4 appears. Study the time path of instructors (line 1). How does the shape compare with your sketch? For 12 months, the number of instructors grows in a straight line, a simple summation of steady recruitment (line 2). Then turnover begins to rise (line 3). The faculty therefore grows less quickly. By month 20 turnover reaches five instructors per month, exactly equal to recruitment, and line 3 crosses line 2. The process of accumulation is perfectly balanced. New faculty are arriving at the same rate that existing faculty are leaving. The number of instructors therefore reaches a peak. Beyond month 20 turnover exceeds recruitment and continues to rise until month 27 when it reaches a rate of ten instructors per month, twice the recruitment rate. The faculty shrinks even though turnover itself stabilises.

Notice that although the number of instructors gently rises and falls, neither the inflow nor the outflow follows a similar pattern. The lack of obvious visual correlation between a stock and its flows is characteristic of stock accumulation and a clear sign that the process is conceptually different from a simple causal link. You can experience more such mysteries of accumulation by redrawing the turnover graph and re-simulating. Double select the turnover icon and then hold down the mouse button as you drag the pointer across the surface of the graph. A new line appears and accordingly the numbers change in the associated table. With some fine-tuning you can create a whole array of smooth and plausible turnover trajectories to help develop your understanding of the dynamics of accumulation. One interesting example is a pattern similar to the original but scaled down, so the maximum turnover is no more than five instructors per month.

Asset Stocks in a Real Organisation – BBC World Service

Figure 3.5 shows the asset stocks from a model of BBC World Service, created in a series of meetings with an experienced management team.

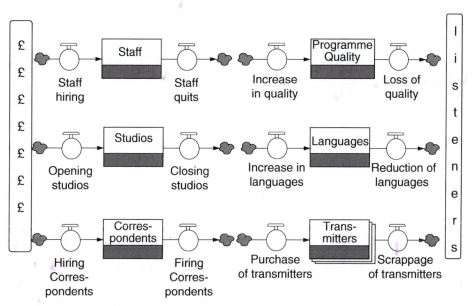

Figure 3.5   Asset stocks at BBC World Service
Source: Morecroft, J.D.W., 1999, Visualising and Rehearing Strategy, *Business Strategy Review*, 10(3) 17–32. Blackwell Publishing.

World Service is a renowned international radio broadcaster specialising in news and current affairs. At the time of the study in the mid-1990s, the organisation was broadcasting over 1200 hours of programming per week in 44 languages from 50 transmitters that reached 80% of the globe. It had 143 million listeners, an audience double its nearest rival. Although World Service is a part of the BBC, it was (at the time) separately funded by the British Foreign and Commonwealth Office (FCO), with a budget in the mid-1990s of £180 million per year.

The model was developed and used to explore 10-year strategy scenarios and to support the organisation's bid to government for future funding (Delauzun and Mollona, 1999). For this purpose, World Service was conceived as a dynamical system in which public funds from Government on the left are deployed in various ways to build assets that collectively attract listeners on the right. There is a rich mix of tangible and intangible assets. The tangibles include staff and studios located at Bush House, the former headquarters of World Service on the Strand in London. There are also foreign correspondents stationed in the numerous countries that receive World Service broadcasts, and an international network of transmitters (short-wave, medium-wave and FM) that beam programmes to listeners across the globe. (There was no internet radio back then, though if one were to update the model it would be possible to add a new asset stock to represent online capacity.) The intangibles include the portfolio of languages as well as soft yet vital factors such as programme quality, programme mix and editorial reputation. A successful broadcaster like World Service builds and maintains a 'balanced' portfolio of tangible and intangible assets that attract enough of the right kind of listeners at reasonable cost. Behind the scenes there is a complex coordinating network of feedback loops that mimic the broadcaster's operating policies and strive to maintain an effective asset balance. Parts of the structure are presented later in this chapter, but, for now, the purpose is simply to show a practical example of stocks and flows in a real business.

The Coordinating Network

Feedback loops are formed when stock and flow networks interact through causal links, in other words when the inflows and outflows of one asset stock depend, directly or indirectly, on the state or size of other asset stocks. In principle, all the stocks and flows in an organisation are mutually dependent because conditions in one area or function may cause or require changes elsewhere. For example, in BBC World Service the more staff employed, the more hours are available for programme making. This extra staff effort results in a gradual increase in programme quality. Better programmes eventually attract more listeners. In this case, the stock of staff affects the inflow to programme quality (an intangible asset) that in turn affects the inflow to the stock of listeners. Coordination is achieved through a network that relays the effect, direct or indirect, of particular stocks on a given flow.

The symbols used for the coordinating network are shown on the left of Figure 3.6. A causal link is drawn as an arrow with a solid line, exactly the same as in a causal loop diagram. An information flow is drawn as an arrow with a dotted line. It too depicts an influence of one variable on another, though in a subtly different way than the effect transmitted by a causal link.

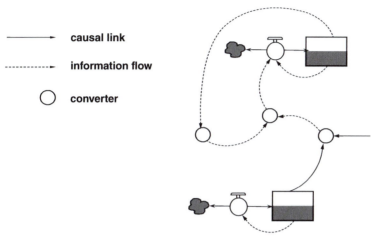

Figure 3.6   Symbols in the coordinating network that connects stocks and flows

A converter represents a process that converts inputs into an output and is depicted as a circle. Converters receive causal links or information flows and transform them according to whatever rules, physical laws or operating policies apply. In a simulator there is an equation behind each converter that specifies the rules. For example, a converter to represent water temperature in a shower model receives, as inputs, flows of hot and cold water. The converter combines these inputs to yield the water temperature. The process can be expressed quantitatively in an equation, derived from physical laws, that computes water temperature as a function of the flows of hot and cold water. Another example is a converter to represent the relative price of two competing products, say well-known brands of beer. In this case the converter receives information about the shelf price of each beer and then computes the ratio.

The diagram on the right of Figure 3.6 shows how all the symbols fit together. In this illustration there are two stock and flow networks joined by a coordinating network containing three converters. This assembly is a feedback representation because the two flow rates not only accumulate into the two stocks but are themselves regulated by the magnitude of the stocks. The picture can readily be extended from two to 20 stocks or more depending on the complexity of the situation at hand. No matter how large the picture, it captures an elaborate process of bootstrapping that arises from nothing more than cause, effect, influence and accumulation found in all organisations.

Modelling Symbols in Use: A Closer Look at Drug-related Crime

To see all the modelling symbols in use we revisit the problem of drug-related crime from Chapter 2.[2] Recall the original intention was to identify systemic factors that explain growth in drug-related crime despite the drug busting efforts of police. Figure 3.7 shows the sectors of society involved and one important feedback loop, a reinforcing crime spiral.

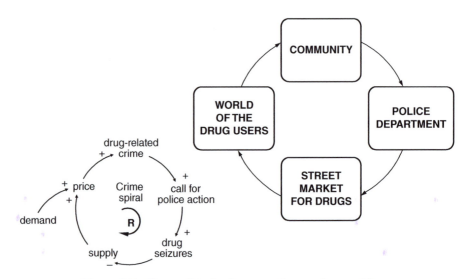

Figure 3.7   Drug-related crime – sectors and causal loop

There are four sectors: the community itself (suffering from crime), the police department (trying to control crime), the street market for drugs and the world of the drug user. A simulatable model of this situation represents the stock accumulations, causal links, information flows and operating policies that lie behind the reinforcing crime spiral. The model is presented sector by sector.

Figure 3.8 shows the causal links in the community. The community is concerned about drug-related crime and raises its collective concern through a call for police action. Notice that each concept is accompanied by units of measure that help ground the model and subsequently aid quantification. The

---

[2]Another way to gain familiarity with the modelling symbols is to work through the iThink tutorial in the learning support folder for Chapter 3. You will build a tiny model of population dynamics, develop equations and simulate it. Please bear in mind that you are unable to save the model because the licence for the software that accompanies the book does not allow newly-built models to be saved. But that doesn't matter in this exercise – the point is to gain familiarity with symbols and conventions of visual modelling in system dynamics.

search for practical and consistent units of measure is an important modelling and thinking discipline. Drug-related crime is expressed as incidents per month. A practical measure of the community's 'call for police action' is complaints per month. The link here is the same as in the causal loop diagram, but the difference in units between the cause and the effect shows the need for another concept, community sensitivity to crime, to operationalise the original link. Community sensitivity can be thought of in terms of complaints per incident. A community that is very sensitive to crime will generate more complaints per incident than a community resigned or indifferent to crime, thereby bringing to bear more pressure for police action.

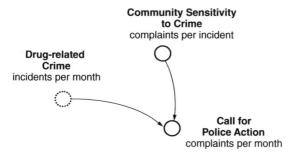

Figure 3.8   Community reaction to crime

Figure 3.9 takes us inside the police department. Notice that the police department converts the call for police action (in complaints per month) into drug seizures (in kg per month).

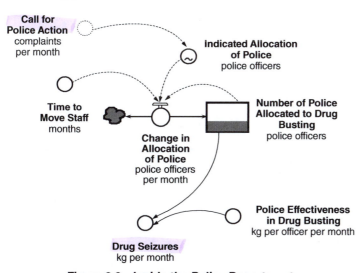

Figure 3.9   Inside the Police Department

In the causal loop diagram, this conversion of complaints into seizures is achieved in a single causal link. The stock-and-flow diagram reveals the operating detail behind the link. In the middle of the diagram there is a stock accumulation representing the number of police allocated to drug busting. The policy controlling the allocation of police is in the top half of the diagram and is a typical goal-seeking adjustment process. Call for police action leads to an indicated allocation of police – the number of police officers deemed necessary to deal with the drug problem. This goal is implemented by reallocating police between duties. The change in allocation of police (measured in police officers per month) depends on the difference between the indicated allocation, the current number of police allocated to drug busting and the time it takes to move staff. In reality the process of reallocating police takes time and organisational effort, all of which is captured by the stock and flow network for number of police. Incidentally, the 'cloud' on the left of this network represents the total pool of police in the department, currently working on other duties, who might be called into drug busting.[3] The amount of drug seizures is proportional to the number of police allocated. To operationalise this link it is necessary to introduce a new concept, 'police effectiveness in drug busting', measured in kilograms per officer per month – a kind of drug busting productivity.

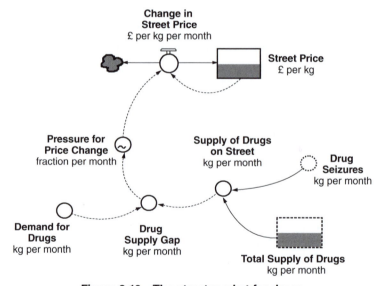

Figure 3.10   The street market for drugs

The street market for drugs adjusts the street price of drugs according to the supply and demand of drugs, as shown in Figure 3.10. The supply of drugs on

---

[3]By using a cloud symbol we assume that the pool of police officers assigned to duties other than drug busting is outside the boundary of the model. If for some reason we wanted to track the number of officers in this pool, then the cloud symbol would be replaced by a stock accumulation with its own initial number of officers. It would then be apparent from the diagram that shifting more officers to drug busting reduces the number available to work on other duties.

the street is equal to the total supply of drugs less drug seizures. The drug supply gap is the difference between demand for drugs and supply on the street (all measured in kilograms per month). The existence of a supply gap generates pressure for price change, which in turn drives the change in street price that accumulates in the street price (measured in £ per kilogram). The pricing 'policy' here is informal – an invisible hand. Note there is no target price. The price level continues to change as long as there is a difference between supply and demand.

In Figure 3.11 we enter the world of drug-dependent users with an addiction and craving that must be satisfied at all costs, even if it involves crime. Addicts need funds (in £ per month) to satisfy their addiction. In a given geographical region the funds required by addicts are proportional to their collective demand for drugs (in kilograms per month) and the prevailing street price (in £ per kilogram).

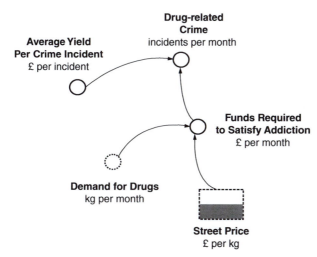

Figure 3.11   World of the drug users

Drug-related crime is the amount of crime (in incidents per month) necessary to raise the funds required. This conversion of funds into crime depends also on the average yield per crime incident (measured in £ per incident), which is a measure of criminal productivity and reflects the wealth of the burgled community.

Equation Formulations

The final step in developing a simulator is to write algebraic equations. Diagrams are a good starting point because they show all the variables that must appear in the equations. Nevertheless, there is skill in writing good algebra in a way that properly captures the meaning of the relationships depicted.

Drug-related Crime

Consider the formulation of drug-related crime. We know from the diagram that drug-related crime depends on the funds required (by addicts) to satisfy their addiction and on the average yield per crime incident. These two influences are reproduced in Figure 3.12, but how are they combined in an equation? Should they be added, subtracted, multiplied or divided? The top half of Figure 3.12 is a plausible formulation where drug-related crime is equal to funds required divided by average yield. This ratio makes sense. We would expect that if addicts require more funds they will either commit more crimes or else operate in a neighbourhood where the yield from each crime is greater. Hence, funds required appears in the numerator and average yield in the denominator. The ratio expresses precisely and mathematically what we have in mind.

Drug-Related Crime [incidents/month]	=	Funds Required to Satisfy Addiction [£/month]	/	Average Yield Per Crime Incident [£/incident]

Dimensional Analysis

Left hand side: [incidents/month]

Right hand side: [£/month]/[£/incident] = [£/month]*[incident/£] = [incidents/month]

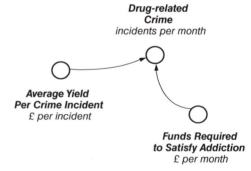

Figure 3.12   Equation formulation for drug-related crime

An alternative formulation, such as the product of 'funds required' and 'average yield', contradicts common sense and logic. A simple numerical example shows just how ludicrous such a multiplicative formulation would be. Let's suppose there are 10 addicts in a neighbourhood and collectively they require £1000 per month to satisfy their addiction. On average, each crime incident yields £100. A multiplicative formulation would imply that drug-related crime in the neighbourhood is (1000 * 100), in other words one hundred thousand – which is numerically implausible and wrong. The correct formulation results in (1000/100), or 10 incidents per month.

There are numerous guidelines for equation formulation to help modellers write good algebra that means what they intend. One of the most useful is to ensure dimensional consistency among the units of measure in an equation. This guideline is always useful in situations like the one above where the main formulation challenge is to pick the right arithmetical operation. Dimensional consistency requires that the units of measure on left and right of an equation match. In this case, 'drug-related crime' on the left is measured in incidents per month. So the operation on the right must combine 'funds required' and 'average yield' in such a way as to create incidents per month. Taking the ratio of funds required [£/month] to average yield [£/incident] achieves this outcome, as shown in the inset of Figure 3.12. No other simple arithmetic operator such as +, −, or * leads to this result. For example, the units of measure for a multiplicative formulation would be £2 per month per incident, a bizarre and meaningless metric that reveals a fatal formulation error.

Funds Required to Satisfy Addiction

The formulation for funds required is shown in Figure 3.13. We know from the diagram that 'funds required' depends on demand for drugs and the street price.

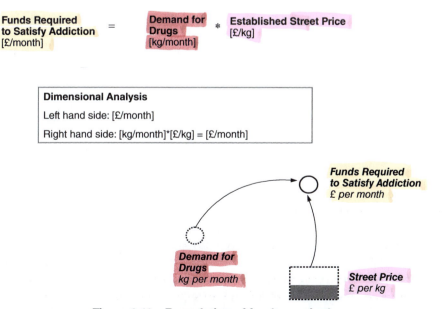

Figure 3.13 Formulation of funds required

The greater the demand, or the higher the street price, the more funds required. Moreover, a combination of greater demand and higher street price calls for even more funds and therefore suggests a multiplicative formulation. Thus, the equation for 'funds required' is expressed as the product of demand for drugs and the street price. A dimensional analysis shows the units of measure are consistent in this formulation.

Street Price and Price Change

The street price of drugs is a stock that accumulates price changes. The change in street price is a function of street price itself and 'pressure for price change'. This pressure depends on the drug supply gap, in other words whether there is an adequate supply of drugs on the street. The diagram and corresponding equations are shown in Figure 3.14.

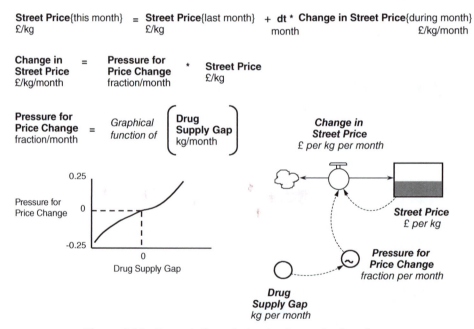

Figure 3.14 Formulation of street price and price change

The first equation is a standard formulation for a stock accumulation. The street price this month is equal to the price last month plus the change in price during the month. The change in street price arises from informal, covert trading of illegal drugs on street corners. It is an important formulation that depends both on street price itself and the pressure for price change. This pressure is itself a function of the drug supply gap, a graphical function whose shape is sketched in the lower left of Figure 3.14. To understand the price change formulation, first imagine the drug supply gap is zero – there is just enough volume of drugs being supplied by dealers to satisfy demand. Under this special condition the pressure for price change is logically zero and so too is the change in street price itself. The multiplicative formulation ensures no price change when the pressure for price change is zero. Now suppose there is a shortage of drugs on the street. The drug supply gap is positive and, through the graph, the pressure for price change is also positive. Moreover, as the gap grows the pressure rises more quickly than a simple linear proportion. The relationship is non-linear, with increasing gradient. A mirror image applies when there is a surplus of drugs and the drug supply gap is negative. Pressure for price change is expressed as a fraction per month, so the resulting change in price is the street price itself multiplied by this fraction per month. The units of price change are £/kilogram/month and an inspection of the price change equation shows the required dimensional balance.

Notice that the price itself feeds back to influence price change. This is quite a subtle dynamic formulation and has the curious, though realistic, implication that there is no pre-determined market price or cost-plus anchor toward which price adjusts. The only meaningful anchor is the current price. Hence, if there is a chronic undersupply the price will relentlessly escalate, and conversely if there is a chronic oversupply the price will steadily fall. Price settles at whatever level it attains when supply and demand are balanced, no matter how high or low.

Allocation of Police

The formulation for the allocation of police is shown in Figure 3.15. It is a classic example of an asset stock adjustment process. At the heart of the formulation is a stock accumulation of police officers guided by an operating policy for adjusting the allocation of police. The first equation is a standard stock accumulation in which the number of police allocated to drug busting this month is equal to the number allocated last month plus the change in allocation during the month. The second equation represents the policy for redeploying police to drug busting. The change in allocation of police depends on the gap between the indicated allocation of police and the current number of police allocated to drug busting. If there is pressure on the police department from the community to deal with crime then this gap will be positive and measures how many more police officers are really needed. However, officers are redeployed gradually with a sense of urgency captured in the concept 'time to move staff'. The greater this time constant, the slower the rate of redeployment for any given shortfall of police officers.

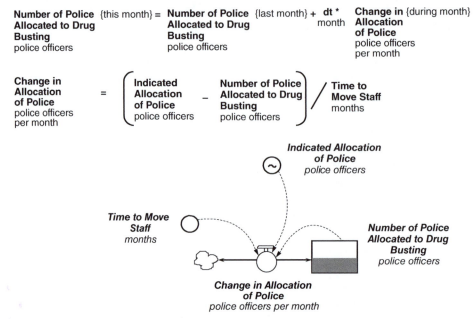

Figure 3.15   Formulation for the allocation of police

The formulation divides the shortfall by the time to move staff, resulting in a dimensionally balanced equation with appropriate units of police officers per month.

Experiments with the Model of Drug-related Crime

A Tour of the Model

Open the file called 'Crime and Drugs' in the learning support folder for Chapter 3. An overview diagram like Figure 3.16 appears showing the main sectors, stock accumulations and links.[4]

---

[4]The reinforcing feedback loop that drives growth in drug-related crime is not visible in the sectorised diagram in Figure 3.16. The reason is that concepts which are the link pins between sectors are duplicated in each of the joined sectors. So, for example, drug seizures appear in the police department and again in the street market. Similarly, the street price appears in the street market and again in the drug users sector. Drug-related crime appears in the drug users sector and again in the community. Finally, the call for police action appears in the community and again in the police department. This duplication is achieved in the software by 'ghosting' a variable name. A special ghost icon is placed on top of a variable and, when selected, a copy of the variable's icon appears which can be moved and placed at any point on the model page. When deposited, a

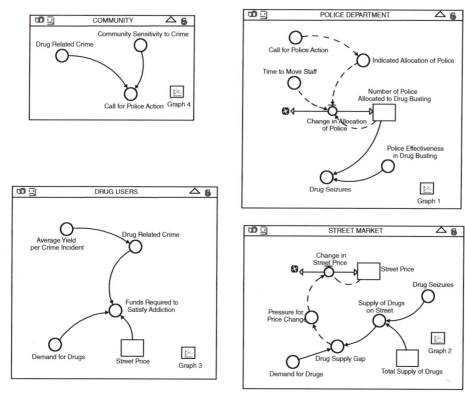

Figure 3.16   Overview of the drug-related crime model showing sectors, stocks and links

First let's tour the model and note the starting conditions in this imaginary world. To generate the correct starting conditions press the 'Run' button in the lower centre of the screen. When the simulation is complete, press the other button labelled 'Reset to Time Zero'. Now move the cursor into the world of the drug users, to the phrase 'drug-related crime'. This is a good place to begin. A little box pops up containing the number 200, meaning that, when the simulation begins, drug addicts are already committing 200 crimes per month. Move backwards in the causal chain. You will find that addicts collectively need £200 000 per month to fund their addiction (from demand of

---

ghost-like manifestation of the variable appears with a dotted outline. This replica carries with it the variable's underlying algebraic formulation for use in the new location. Other system dynamics software packages offer similar functionality under different names, such as clone. It is not essential to use ghosting or cloning in a sectorised model. Active links can instead be drawn between variables in different sectors. However, in large models the use of ghosting or cloning is to be recommended as it greatly reduces visual complexity and the daunting sight of a spaghetti-like tangle of connections. Even in small models like drugs and crime there is merit in such clarity. Moreover (and this is important) the absence of overt visual links between sectors is a reminder of the invisibility of feedback loops that weave their way across organisational boundaries.

500 kilograms per month at a street price of £400 per kilogram) and that each crime yields £1000 on average. Now visit the community and check the 'sensitivity to crime' and 'call for police action'. Typically a crime leads to five complaints, so the call for police action takes a value of 1000 complaints per month (200 * 5) received from the community.[5]

Next, move to the police department to probe what's happening there. Initially there are 10 police officers allocated to drug busting but, due to the volume of complaints, the indicated allocation (the number of officers really needed) is 13.[6] Police effectiveness in drug busting, a productivity measure, is 10 kilograms per police officer per month. Hence, drug seizures start at 100 kilograms per month (10 officers each seizing 10 kilograms monthly on average).

Now step out of the police department and into the street market. The total supply of drugs brought to the neighbourhood is assumed to be 500 kilograms per month, but the supply that actually reaches the street is 400 kilograms per month due to the effect of seizures. Demand for drugs is 500 kilograms per month, so the drug supply gap is 100 kilograms per month. This initial shortage leads to pressure for price increase of one per cent per month. Our tour of initial conditions is complete.

Escalating Crime – The Base Case

Now we are ready to simulate. Press the 'Run' button and watch the stock accumulations for street price and the number of police allocated to drug busting. They start small and, as time goes by, they quickly escalate. Press the 'Run' button again and now watch the little dials. What you see, over 48

---

[5]Note of warning: the parameter values in this small pedagogical model have not been carefully calibrated and would likely benefit from more field research and logical thought. For example, the street price of drugs is crudely initialised at £400 per kilogram (kg) and the total supply of drugs on the street is set at 500 kg per month. In a real-world modelling project both these numbers should be set as accurately as possible based on experts' judgements and/or published data in government reports or the press; and should then be double-checked with a dose of logical reasoning. Some numbers are easier to pin down than others and once set can help clarify the values of other related parameters in a kind of logical bootstrapping. For example, in the drug–crime model the average yield per crime incident can be estimated on common-sense grounds. Knowledge of that number may then, through a process of logical reasoning, shed more light on the street price of drugs in £ per kg.

[6]The numerical value of the change in allocation of police officers is displayed as 0.833333. Obviously some judgement is needed in interpreting this numbingly precise value. It means that, on average, at the start of the simulation, the re-allocation of police officers to drug busting increases by the equivalent of about 80% of a single full-time equivalent police officer per month. Modellers should beware of misleading precision in a simulator's calculations and round the numbers to a precision consistent with the problem situation.

simulated months, are the changes and knock-on consequences that unfold when drug addicts commit crimes, disturb a community, and invoke a response from police. There is a lot going on so it is a good idea to make several runs and study the dials sector by sector. After 48 months (4 years) of drug busting and escalating crime, conditions are much worse.

To investigate how much conditions have changed by the end of the simulation, repeat the same tour of variables you began with. In the world of the drug user, crime has risen to 446 incidents per month and is still growing fast. In the police department, 30 police officers are allocated to drug busting and seizures have reached 296 kilograms per month. Meanwhile, the supply of drugs on the street has dwindled to 204 kilograms per month and the street price has reached £893 per kilogram.

To explore the dynamics in more detail, open the graphs located in the lower right of each sector. The time charts shown in Figure 3.17 will appear showing how conditions unfold from the perspective of each stakeholder.

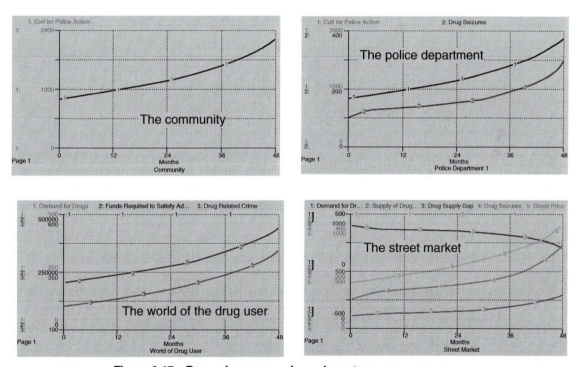

Figure 3.17   Dynamics as seen in each sector

Begin with the police department (Graph 1). The call for police action (line 1) starts at 1000 complaints per month and grows steadily to more than 2000 after 48 months. More complaints lead to growth in drug seizures (line 2) from

100 to almost 300 kilograms per month. The underlying re-allocation of police officers to drug busting is shown on a separate page of the graph, which can be viewed by selecting the 'page' tab in the bottom left of the chart. A new page appears (not included in Figure 3.17) that shows the indicated allocation of police (line 1) growing in response to complaints. Following the indicated allocation with a slight time lag, there is a corresponding increase in the number of police allocated to drug busting (line 2).

Meanwhile, in the street market (Graph 2), demand for drugs (line 1) remains steady at 500 kilograms per month while drug seizures (line 4) grow. Therefore, the supply of drugs on the street falls (line 2) and the drug supply gap (line 3) rises. This shortage forces up the street price of drugs (line 5) from £400 to almost £900 per kilogram over four years. The result, in the world of the drug user (Graph 3), is a steady escalation of funds required (line 2) that induces a corresponding increase in drug-related crime on a parallel trajectory (line 3). Meanwhile, demand for drugs (line 1) remains steady, at the same value already seen in the street market. Finally, from the community's viewpoint (Graph 4), drug-related crime is rising (line 1), provoking more complaints and an ever greater call for police action (line 2).

Drilling Down to the Equations

Feedback structure gives rise to dynamic behaviour, and the most detailed expression of feedback structure is to be found at the level of algebraic equations. The equations of the drug-related crime model can be found by 'drilling down' below the diagram. Select the 'equation' tab on the left of the screen and a whole page of equations is revealed, which are reproduced in Figures 3.18 and 3.19. The formulations are identical to the ones presented earlier in the chapter and you are invited to browse them. Notice they are conveniently organised by sector, starting with stock accumulations, then algebraic converters and finally graphical converters. Moreover, there is a one-to-one correspondence between the equations and the diagram, making it easy to move back and forth between the visual representation and its algebraic equivalent. The equations are readable like sentences and replicate the full variable names used in the diagram. The intention is to create 'friendly algebra', easy to communicate and interpret. For example, in the police department, the change in the allocation of police is equal to the difference between the 'indicated allocation of police' and the 'number of police allocated to drug busting', divided by the 'time to move staff'. This expression, though algebraic, is pretty much plain English, and normally modellers strive to achieve such transparency, both to clarify their own thinking and to communicate the algebra to others.

COMMUNITY

Call for Police Action = Drug Related Crime * Community Sensitivity to Crime {complaints per month}

Community Sensitivity to Crime = 5 {complaints per incident}

POLICE DEPARTMENT

Number of Police Allocated to Drug Busting(t) = Number of Police Allocated to Drug Busting(t-dt) +

(Change in Allocation of Police) * dt

INIT Number of Police Allocated to Drug Busting = 10 {police officers}

Change in Allocation of Police = (Indicated Allocation of Police - Number of Police Allocated to Drug Busting) /

Time to Move Staff {police officers per month}

Drug Seizures = Number of Police Allocated to Drug Busting *

Police Effectiveness in Drug Busting {kg per month}

Police Effectiveness in Drug Busting = 10+STEP(0,12) {kilograms per officer per month}

Time to Move Staff = 3 {months}

Indicated Allocation of Police = GRAPH(Call for Police Action)

(0.00, 10.0), (500, 10.0), (1000, 12.5), (1 500, 16.5), (2000, 26.5), (2 500, 47.5), (3000, 69.5), (3 500, 81.0), (4000, 88.0), (4500, 93.0), (5 000, 95.0)

Figure 3.18   Equations for the Community and Police Department

STREET MARKET

Street Price (t) = Street Price (t-dt) + (Change in Street Price) * dt

INIT Street Price = 400 {£ per kg}

Change in Street Price = Street Price * Pressure for Price Change {£ per kg per month}

Total Supply of Drugs (t) = Total Supply of Drugs (t-dt)

INIT Total Supply of Drugs = 500 {kg per month}

Drug Supply Gap = Demand for Drugs – Supply of Drugs on Street {kg per month}

Supply of Drugs on Street = Total Supply of Drugs – Drug Seizures {kg per month}

Pressure for Price Change = GRAPH (Drug Supply Gap)

(–1 000, –0.203), (–800, –0.142), (–600, –0.0925), (–400, –0.0475), (–200, –0.02), (0.00, 0.00), (200, 0.02), (400, 0.0525), (600, 0.105), (800, 0.153), (1000, 0.223)

WORLD OF THE DRUG USERS

Average Yield per Crime Incident = 1000 {£ per incident}

Demand for Drugs = 500 {kg per month}

Drug-related Crime = Funds Required to Satisfy Addiction / Average Yield per Crime Incident {incidents per month}

Funds Required to Satisfy Addiction = Demand for Drugs * Street Price {£ per month}

Figure 3.19   Equations for the street market and world of the drug users

The same transparency applies to stock accumulations and even to non-linear relations in graphical converters. For example, in the street market, the street price of drugs at time t is equal to the street price at the previous time (t–dt) plus the change in street price over the period dt (the interval of time between t–dt and t). The change in street price is then expressed as the product of 'street price' and 'pressure for price change'. In turn, the pressure for price change is formulated as a non-linear graph function of the drug supply gap.

The shape of this graph is specified by the paired numbers shown at the end of the equation, where the first number is the size of the drug supply gap (in kilograms per month) and the second number is the corresponding value of the pressure for price change (the fractional change per month). The actual shape can be seen by double selecting the model icon representing pressure for price change. A window appears containing a graph constructed from these numbers. The drug supply gap is on the horizontal axis and the pressure for price change is on the vertical axis.

Anomalous Behaviour Over Time and Model Boundary

A simulator is a relentless and unforgiving inference engine – it shows the logical implications of all the assumptions it contains; the behaviour over time that *will* unfold given the structure. This enforced consistency between assumptions and outcomes has the power to surprise people and is a major benefit of simulators for strategy development. Surprise behaviour often reveals flaws and blind spots in people's thinking. Modellers themselves are the first beneficiaries of such ruthless consistency during the early diagnostic testing of a new model. The drug-related crime model provides a simple example.

Recall the dynamic hypothesis behind the model. Escalating crime is attributable to police drug busting that removes drugs (and drug dealers) from the streets. A side effect is to push up the street price of drugs and this price inflation inadvertently forces addicts to commit more crime, leading to more drug busting and so on. The structure is a reinforcing loop and the simulator shows that crime escalation is possible given reasonable operating assumptions about the police department, street market, the community and addicts themselves.

An extension of the simulation from 48 to 60 months pushes this logic beyond the limits of common sense and reveals a world in which the price of drugs is sky high, crime has increased six-fold and the supply of drugs on the street is negative! Figure 3.20 shows this anomalous scenario in more detail. To create these charts open the model called 'Crime and Drugs – 60 months'[7] and press the 'Run' button. Open Graph 1 in the police department. The call for police action (line 1) begins at 1000 complaints per month and escalates to more than 6000 after 60 months (five years). Notice the steep upward trajectory typical of exponential growth from a reinforcing feedback loop.

---

[7]This model is identical to the previous one but the length of the simulation has been increased to 60 months by changing 'run specs' in the pull-down menu headed 'Run'. In addition, the vertical scale of chart variables has been adjusted so the simulated trajectories do not go out of bounds.

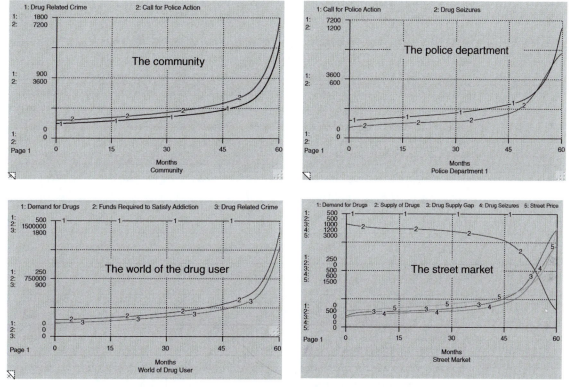

Figure 3.20   Anomalous dynamics in a 60-month simulation

Meanwhile, drug seizures rise in a similar exponential pattern until month 55 when the rate of increase begins to moderate. The reason for this slowdown is that police are being overstretched and it is increasingly difficult for department leaders to re-allocate officers to drug busting, despite the rising call for police action. Turn to page 2 of the police department chart to see the overstretch effect in more detail. The indicated allocation of police (line 1) rises exponentially to 70 police officers in month 54, as the police department recognises the escalating call from the community for police action. However, in the final six months of the simulation the department encounters its own manpower limit to drug busting, since (by assumption) no more than 95 officers can be allocated to the task, no matter how great the call from the community. The indicated allocation gradually levels out at 95 officers and the growth in the actual number of police allocated to drug busting (line 2) begins to slow down.

So far so good, in the sense that the trajectories are plausible from an operational viewpoint. But the full consequences are quite surprising. The cap on police effort does not stop crime escalation. To understand why step into the 'street market' and open Graph 2. The demand for drugs (line 1) is steady at 500 kilograms per month throughout the entire 60 months, reflecting the assumption that addicts will seek their daily fix regardless of supply. Meanwhile drug seizures (line 4) are rising. Between months 30 and 45 they increase from 160 to 244 kilograms per month. By month 54 seizures are 500 kilograms per month – equal to the entire supply. So according to this scenario by month 54 there are no more drugs available on the street – they have all been seized. Moreover, by month 60, police officers are seizing more drugs than the dealers themselves can obtain and the supply of drugs on the street (line 2) is negative. Clearly this extreme situation is illogical – a fallacy in the model revealed by simulation. Common sense says police cannot seize more drugs than are supplied. There is one more subtle twist in this diagnostic simulation. The drug supply gap (line 3) fuels an exponential rise in street price (line 5), which shows no sign of slackening, despite the levelling-off of police effort at the end of the simulation.

A modeller faced with these contradictions returns to the model's assumptions to find the fallacy. A few possibilities come to mind. The simplest, and least disruptive to the integrity of the model, is that police effectiveness in drug busting is not constant (as assumed) but depends on the supply of drugs on the street. As supply is reduced through drug seizures it becomes more and more difficult for police to trace the few drugs that remain – an example of the 'law of diminishing returns'. This formulation requires a new causal link and a graphical converter that shows police effectiveness as a non-linear function of the supply of drugs on the street.[8] Such a re-formulation would solve the

---

[8]If you try to add this connection to the diagram an error message is generated saying 'sorry, but that would create a circular connection'. The software is pointing out a new fallacy. In a dynamical system every feedback loop must contain at least one stock accumulation that stores the changes generated around the loop. In this case, the supply of drugs on the street could be reformulated as a stock accumulation:

$$\text{Supply of drugs on the street } (t) = \text{supply of drugs on the street } (t - dt)$$
$$+ (\text{change in street supply}) * dt$$
$$\text{INIT supply of drugs on the street} = 400 \text{ \{kilograms per month\}}$$

INFLOWS:

$$\text{Change in street supply} = (\text{indicated supply of drugs on the street}$$
$$- \text{supply of drugs on the street}) \text{ / time to affect street supply}$$
$$\text{Indicated supply of drugs on the street} = \text{total supply of drugs} - \text{drug seizures}$$
$$\text{Time to affect street supply} = 1 \text{ (month)}$$

To complete the new formulation simply add diminishing returns to police effectiveness:

$$\text{Drug seizures} = \text{number of police allocated to drug busting} * \text{police effectiveness in drug busting}$$
$$\text{Police effectiveness in drug busting} = 10 * \text{GRAPH (supply of drugs on the street)}$$
$$\{\text{kilograms per officer per month}\}$$

Sketch your own graph, which should be non-linear on a scale between zero and one. When the supply of drugs on the street is high then police effectiveness should be at a maximum value of one. When the supply of drugs on the street is significantly reduced (say less than half its initial value) then police effectiveness begins to decline, and should reach zero when the supply on the street is zero.

absurdity of negative supply, but would not necessarily deal with price escalation (line 5). The problem here is that any sustained supply shortage, even a 20% shortfall or less, will invoke an upward drift in price, because there is no cost anchor for the price of drugs. Recall that the rate of change of price is proportional to the current street price and the drug supply gap. Such price behaviour is plausible in a market where demand is totally inelastic; yet endless price escalation is clearly unrealistic. This inconsistency suggests the need for a more radical change to the model – a rethink not only of individual formulations but also an expansion of the model boundary. One idea is to include the dynamics of supply. The current model assumes the total supply of drugs is fixed, so drug seizures create a permanent shortage on the street. However, if the street price is high then, sooner or later, the supply of drugs will increase to compensate for drug busting, thereby re-establishing an equilibrium of supply and demand.

Not surprisingly, the small pedagogical model of drugs and crime in this chapter has its limitations. It illustrates principles of model building but would not be an adequate model to address drugs policy. However, the same modelling principles can and do lead to useful policy models in the context of serious applications projects, exemplified in Homer's (1993) study of national cocaine prevalence in the USA.

Benefits of Model Building and Simulation

In this chapter we have seen what it takes to convert qualitative feedback loops into a dynamical model and simulator complete with stock accumulations, causal links, information flows and dimensionally balanced algebraic equations. There is a lot of work involved and considerable skill needed to develop robust formulations that mean the same algebraically as you intend. But the pay-off from this extra effort is well worthwhile because the result is far, far more than a diagram. It is a simulator: an inference engine to diagnose performance problems; a virtual world to experience dynamic complexity and stimulate imagination; and a laboratory to design and test new policies and strategies.

There are other benefits, too, that come from the modelling process. There is the discipline of combining operational detail with feedback systems thinking, thereby 'seeing the forest' without losing sight of the trees. There is greater clarity and precision about causality and interdependence in business and society that stems from modelling explicit stock accumulation and representing the information network that drives decision making and coordinates action. There is the opportunity (particularly for models built with management teams) to develop shared vocabulary and concepts relevant to strategy. The focus on units of measure in equation formulation sharpens people's thinking about the quantification of strategy and draws on their powerful collective mental database. A diagram of stocks, flows and feedback loops is an intermediate step to an algebraic model that helps communicate model assumptions and provides a framework for data collection. The diagram guides equation formulation and helps to ensure that the algebraic model remains consistent with people's descriptions of how the parts of a complex organisation fit together.

References

Delauzun, F. and Mollona, E. (1999) Introducing system dynamics to BBC World Service: An insider perspective. *Journal of the Operational Research Society*, 50(4): 364–371.

Homer, J. (1993) A system dynamics model of national cocaine prevalence. *System Dynamics Review*, 9(1): 49–78.

Sterman, J.D. (2000) *Business Dynamics: Systems Thinking and Modelling for a Complex World*. Boston, MA: Irwin McGraw Hill.

Warren, K. (2002) *Competitive Strategy Dynamics*. Chichester: John Wiley & Sons.

Warren, K. (2008) *Strategic Management Dynamics*. Chichester: John Wiley & Sons.

Chapter 4
World of Showers

- Getting Started
- Redesigning Your World of Showers
- Inside World of Showers
- Simulations of World of Showers B

In Chapter 2, a hot water shower was introduced as an example of a dynamically complex system involving balancing loop feedback. The shower-taker tries to align water temperature with a goal or 'desired temperature' by regulating the flow of hot water. This seemingly straightforward goal-seeking task is not always easy to achieve and often results in repeated overshoot and undershoot of water temperature and self-inflicted discomfort. World of Showers is a gaming simulator that enables players to take the role of a shower-taker – without getting wet. You enter an imaginary shower and adjust the water temperature to the desired level by adjusting the hot water supply. The mix of hot and cold water is controlled by a tap setting – just like a normal shower. The simulator traces the movement of temperature over time and displays the results of your efforts to control the system. The simulator illustrates the coordination problem at the heart of balancing loop dynamics and even enables players to redesign the shower system to improve performance and personal comfort. A shower, with its local goal and adjustment process, is a metaphor for goal-seeking behaviour in organisations and it illustrates dynamic complexity. It provides insight into the challenges of managing performance in self-regulating systems where obvious interventions often produce surprise consequences and when an action has one set of consequences locally and a very different set of consequences in another part of the system.

Getting Started

Open the file called 'World of Showers A' in the learning support folder for Chapter 4. The opening screen looks like Figure 4.1.

World of Showers A
This is a shower simulator. You are the one taking a shower. Your goal is to shower at 25°C. There is only
one thing you can conrol: The water tap in your shower. The water tap can be set on a continuous scale between zero
and one. It mixes the cold and hot water. If it is set to zero, only the cold water (10 °C) will come out, if it
is set to one, only the hot water (70 °C) will come out.

Your task is to adjust the tap setting so that you reach a stable desired temperature of 25 °C as quickly as
possible. To enter your shower, press the button labelled 'To Charts and Controls'. There you will find a time chart
that displays water temperature and a slide bar to control the tap setting. To start the simulator press 'Run'. The red line
shows the temperature in your shower, while the blue line shows the desired temperature you are trying to achieve. After
the simulation, scroll down for more information. Have fun!

Figure 4.1   Opening screen of World of Showers A

Taking a Shower in World of Showers A

Situation: A cool shower in a five-star hotel

You are on a consulting assignment in the South of France. You arrive at your
five-star hotel after a long flight and a harassing taxi journey along a crowded
motorway near Marseilles in mid-summer. Unfortunately, your cab has no
air-conditioning. You are desperate for a cool shower. So you rush to your
room. Immediately you set the shower running, without looking particularly
closely at the controls. You start to get undressed. Your shoelace becomes
knotted and you spend a frustrating two minutes unpicking the tiny knot. By
the time you are finished the shower has settled to a steady temperature,
though you don't yet know how high or low. You enter the shower cubicle. As
you expect, the water temperature is controlled by a tap setting that mixes the
hot and cold water supply. You reach for the tap. Press the button labelled 'To
Charts and Controls' on the opening screen to see a graph for displaying
simulated temperature as shown in Figure 4.2. Below the graph you will see a
slide bar to control the tap setting.

You are now in the shower! Press the 'Run' button to start your simulated
shower. The temperature trajectories will begin to appear. It happens that the
initial tap setting you chose (when you first rushed into the room) supplies
water at a steady temperature of 35°C. That's much too hot.

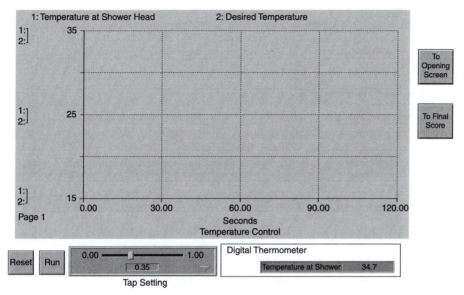

Figure 4.2   The tap setting control and temperature graph

You want a cool shower at a steady 25°C, so you need to adjust the tap setting by moving the pointer on the slide bar. The digital thermometer displays an accurate reading of the current water temperature. The graph displays a plot over 120 simulated seconds of the water temperature you experience (temperature at shower head, line 1) and also the temperature you are seeking (desired temperature, line 2). By comparing these two temperatures you can easily tell whether your shower is too hot or too cold. To increase the water temperature move the slider to the right while keeping the mouse button pressed. To decrease the water temperature move the slider to the left, still keeping the mouse button pressed. The slide bar is set on a continuous scale from 0 to 1.

Scroll down to the next graph showing a record of your tap setting, as illustrated in Figure 4.3.

Scroll down further on the screen to see a graph of your final score as shown in Figure 4.4. The score cumulates the absolute deviation between temperature at the shower head and desired temperature and is a measure of your performance while 'managing' the shower. Lower is better.

To take another simulated shower press on the button 'To Charts and Controls' and then select 'Reset'. The temperature graph will be cleared and the tap setting restored to its initial value of 0.35. It is important always to reset before running a new simulation in order to ensure that the starting conditions are the same in each experiment. Play as many times as you like to see how quickly you can reach and maintain the desired temperature.

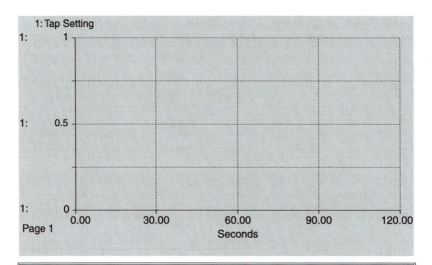

Now take a look at how you adjusted the tap over the 120 seconds (Tap Setting) and compare it with how the temperature varied over that same time period (in the previous graph). Then go on and replay as many times as you want to see what yields the best results. Have fun!

Figure 4.3   The tap setting graph

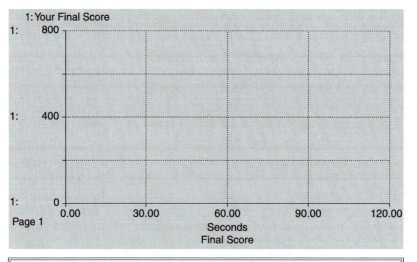

Now here is your final score, calculated as the accumulated difference between the desired shower temperature and the actual shower temperature. In other words, the lower your final score, the better. So go ahead, and give it another shot. Unlike in *Donkey Kong*, the question here is: 'How low can you go?'

Your Final Score   10

Figure 4.4   Your final score

Your role in the simulator is analogous to that of a functional business manager. You have a specific target to achieve (a comfortable temperature) and a resource (hot water) to help you meet the target. You apply rational thought in the deployment of this resource. However, like the functional manager, you don't always get the resource you need the moment you request it. There is a time lag in the system whose impact you may not fully appreciate and which creates the dynamic complexity of the world you seek to manage.

Taking a Shower in World of Showers B

Situation: Cool shower in a two-star hotel

Later that summer you are on holiday in the Costa del Sol. You are still paying off the debt on your recent MBA, so you've gone for a low budget package deal. It is late summer and the weather is very hot and humid. You arrive at your two-star hotel, anxious for a cool shower after a long and frustrating journey on an overbooked plane through overcrowded airports. You are with a friend. You go to your separate rooms. You are pleasantly surprised to find there is a working shower, so you set it running. You start to get undressed. Once again your shoelace becomes knotted (you make a mental note to find a new shoe shop). You console yourself that at least the shower should have settled to a steady temperature by the time you are ready. You enter the shower cubicle. Amazingly the controls look identical to the ones you remember from your five-star hotel in the South of France (maybe this isn't such a bad place after all). You reach for the tap and adjust the temperature toward a cool and steady 25°C.

Open the file called 'World of Showers B' in the learning support folder for Chapter 4. The opening screen is similar to World of Showers A. Select the button 'To Charts and Controls' to find identical simulator controls, the same slide bar and the same graph for temperature. Select the button 'To Final Score' to review your performance. Notice the additional score for a hidden shower-taker (your friend) whose role is played by the computer. Select the button 'To Temperature Comparison' to reveal an extra graph that compares the temperature movements in your shower with the temperature in the hidden shower.

Press the 'Run' button to start the simulation. As before, play as many times as you like to see how quickly you can reach and maintain the desired temperature. After each simulation, press 'Reset' to restore all the charts and simulator controls to their initial values for easy comparison of results.

World of Showers B exposes you to unseen forces and increased dynamic complexity that can defeat well-intentioned objectives to keep cool. Back in the organisational world you often face analogous dynamic complexity where seemingly rational means to achieve agreed objectives are defeated by the system. Functional managers strive to achieve local departmental goals only to find their efforts frustrated by hidden dependence on other functions with different or conflicting goals. Executives strive to achieve ambitious strategic targets for their business unit only to find their efforts frustrated by subtle pressures from corporate goals that (often unintentionally) deny key resources or create damaging internal competition for resources.

Redesigning Your World of Showers

In World of Showers A, the plumbing in your five-star hotel is of the highest quality. It is well-designed so that adjustments to the tap setting correlate closely with movements of temperature, albeit with a time delay. In other words, your decisions lead to the outcome you intend (once you have mastered the impact of the delay). It is a manageable world of low dynamic complexity in which you have the freedom to act independently of others who may also be taking showers in the hotel at the same time.

In World of Showers B, the quality of plumbing in your two-star hotel is distinctly inferior. Comments in the guest register suggest you are not the only one who has had problems with the hotel's showers. Your friend has confirmed this view, recalling in particular her experiences on the day you both arrived: 'It was impossible to get the temperature right. The tap was totally useless. I almost ripped it off the wall.' As you peruse a litany of similar criticism from long-departed guests, you realise that the hotel's shower problems probably arise because different rooms unwittingly share the supply of hot water. Showers interfere with each other. Hence, if you need more hot water, someone else (invisible to you) receives less and vice versa. It is a less manageable world of high dynamic complexity and interdependence. Cause and effect are not closely correlated and your actions inadvertently have an impact on others, which can worsen their performance relative to goal.

You have time on your hands, so you start wondering how this down-and-out hotel might improve its showers. Unfortunately, the faults of the hot water system can't be eliminated without upgrading all the pipes and tearing down walls and ceilings, but that's life. Competition for scarce resources is endemic and you can't rebuild society overnight. Why should a two-star hotel be different? So, what else could be done? You muse idly over this puzzle. It is another warm and sultry Spanish summer afternoon. Your thoughts drift . . .

All of a sudden you find yourself back in your shower cubicle. You notice some new controls in the shower that were not there before. To locate these new controls, press on the button 'To Policy Levers' to reveal the screen shown in Figure 4.5. There are two slide bars that allow you to modify your shower world.

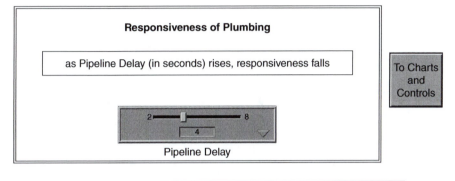

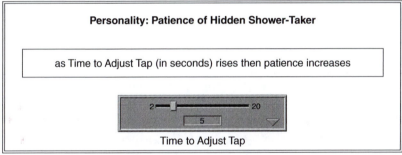

Figure 4.5   Policy levers for responsiveness and patience

The top slider alters the responsiveness of the plumbing by changing the pipeline delay (in seconds) between a turn of the tap and a change in water temperature. The shorter the delay, the more responsive is your shower and all other showers in the hotel.

The bottom slider gives you unimaginable power to influence personality – you can change the patience of any hidden shower-takers who may share your shower world! A patient shower-taker is someone who reacts only gradually to a temperature gap. Such a person is willing to tolerate some discomfort and therefore moves the tap only gradually when the water is too hot or too cold. The longer the time to adjust the tap (in seconds), the more patient the person. (You reflect momentarily on where you yourself lie on this scale of patience.)

Responsiveness and personality are set before you take your simulated shower and are then fixed for the duration of each run. They cannot be altered during a simulation. To reset the two policy levers to their default values, select the

'U' button in each slider box. If you cannot see the button, the default value is already set. Choose new slider values for your first policy design experiment. (Hint: To begin with, alter only one slide bar per experiment. That way you will have a clearer idea of the impact of each policy lever.)

To take another shower in your modified shower world, select the button 'To Charts and Controls'. Note that if you press the 'Reset' button, in order to clear the graphs, then you will also restore the policy levers to their default values. If so, just revisit the policy levers and set them back to the values you intended. Then return to the charts and controls. To start the simulation, press the 'Run' button and experience 120 simulated seconds. Is your new shower world better? Has your final score improved? Do you feel more in control of your own destiny or more at the mercy of unseen system forces? In the light of your experience, redesign the system once again by selecting new values on the slide bars for responsiveness and personality. Play as many times as you like. Can you equal the best score you achieved in World A? Which design changes are most effective and best recreate the feel of World A? Why?

You hear a voice calling. You awake. You are in the hotel lobby with the guest book on your knee. The warmth of a Mediterranean summer still surrounds you. Gradually your mind clears. Those new controls were just a dream after all … You don't have the power to change personalities or even plumbing, but your imaginary shower world left you a message. Hotel showers are a microcosm of typical organisations – lots of people, striving for a variety of different goals, fulfilling their needs and coping with dynamic complexity. You now appreciate that dynamic complexity can be managed. It is possible to shape an organisation (responsiveness, mix of personalities, incentives, goals) to empower people, so that they have the freedom to succeed as individuals while contributing to collective ambitions and strategy. Already you see your name on the General Manager's door.

Reflections on the World of Showers

Economists recognise the problem of 'invisible' dependency as an externality. Externalities occur whenever a person's decisions and actions alter the frame of reference for others (Schelling, 1980). Externalities pose two basic problems for effective management. The first problem is that inefficiencies systematically arise because decision makers cannot possibly take into full account all the costs and benefits of their interdependent actions (the assumption of bounded rationality explained later in Chapter 7). The second problem is that specific individuals and groups are often put in a position of defending suboptimal allocations that satisfy local interests, but are collectively worse than the target efficient allocation.

[Handwritten margin note: Externalities: A persons decisions & actions alter the frame of Ref. for others.]

Feedback systems thinking deals with externalities by explicitly representing the hidden dependencies from which externalities arise. In a sense, they are no longer 'external'. Nevertheless, due to blind spots in their understanding of dynamic complexity, decision makers will behave as though they are facing externalities (Sterman, 1989).

The World of Showers shows that you don't need much dynamic complexity for inefficiencies to crop up in the management of shared resources. Even in World of Showers A, most players have difficulty producing a smooth yet fast convergence to the desired temperature. Yet a fluctuating temperature is clearly inefficient – it causes more discomfort than is strictly necessary.

The dynamic structure that baffles players in World of Showers A is the so-called 'balancing loop with delay', introduced in Chapter 2 and reproduced in Figure 4.6. Typical players acting toward the goal of desired temperature adjust the flow of hot water in response to delayed feedback. If they are not conscious of the delay, or don't know how to take proper account of it (as is usually the case), they end up taking more corrective action than needed, causing the temperature to overshoot. Further corrective action may cause overshoot in the other direction leading to a cyclical pattern of temperature adjustment.

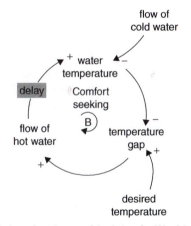

Figure 4.6   Balancing loop with delay in World of Showers A

World of Showers B couples two balancing loops to produce a structure with considerably more dynamic complexity, as shown in Figure 4.7. Here the flow of hot water in either shower depends not only on the temperature gap experienced by the shower-taker but also on the flow of hot water in the other hidden shower. Besides the baffling effect of the time delay, there is the added effect of mutual dependence and invisible sharing of a common resource.

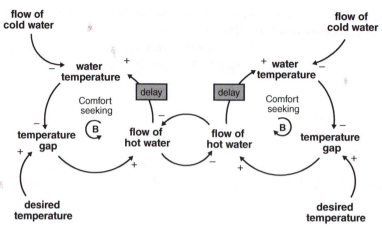

Figure 4.7   Interacting balancing loops in World of Showers B

Metaphorical Shower Worlds in GlaxoSmithKline, IBM and Harley-Davidson

Interdependent structures of this kind repeatedly crop up in functional and divisional organisations. Imagine, for example, that two divisions of a firm arrange to market their products through a shared salesforce. This pooled arrangement is common in organisations like GlaxoSmithKline (GSK) or IBM that employ professional sales people to explain complex products and services to customers and persuade them to buy. Suppose that two drug-producing divisions of GSK (A and B) are pursuing ambitious sales targets. To achieve its target, division A must capture a larger proportion of salesforce time, thereby denying division B. As a result, division B's sales fall well below target prompting efforts to win back the salesforce. Salesforce time switches back and forth between divisions, leading to self-induced cyclical instability in sales and, in addition, costly manufacturing.

A second example of interdependence occurs when product lines of a manufacturing firm share capacity, as shown in Figure 4.8.

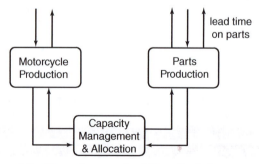

Figure 4.8   Managing product lines that share capacity

The diagram is based on a strategic modelling project with the Harley-Davidson motorcycle company (Morecroft, 1983). Motorcycle production and parts production both use the same machine tools to make components. The project team identified a performance puzzle surrounding the parts business. The company was losing market share in its highly profitable parts business even though competitors were just small job shops making look-alike Harley parts. A model to address this issue included the supply chain for both parts and motorcycles, extending from the factory to dealers and customers. The diagram shows the upstream factory end of these two supply chains. The explanation for loss of parts market share lies in the dynamic complexity of the interlocking supply chains.[1] Bikes and parts share capacity (just as shower-takers share hot water) and the operating policies that control capacity expansion and capacity allocation are inadvertently biased in favour of motorcycles (the big, glamorous and politically powerful part of the company – even though return on sales of parts is higher than bikes). Moreover, demand in the two supply chains is amplified and correlated (demand for bikes and parts rises quickly in the springtime).[2] The result is that the parts business suffers periodic capacity shortages and is unable to compete with job shops who can offer short and reliable lead times – a key competitive variable in any parts business.

A useful management principle accompanies the troublesome feedback structure behind the business examples above, and echoes the lessons of the shower simulator. In a slow-to-respond system with shared resources, aggressive corrective action to achieve local divisional or departmental goals leads to instability and underperformance in the organisation as a whole. For better results, either be patient or reduce interdependence and make the system more responsive. In the case of Harley-Davidson, the solution was to reduce interdependence between the motorcycle and parts businesses by investing in a large finished inventory of motorcycles. With plenty of motorcycles in the supply chain at the start of the spring selling season there

---

[1]There are many supply chain models to be found in the system dynamics literature, starting with the original production distribution system model in Chapters 2 and 15 of *Industrial Dynamics* (Forrester, 1961) and continuing in a special issue of the *System Dynamics Review* devoted to the dynamics of supply chains and networks (Akkermans and Dellaert, 2005). The Harley-Davidson model represents the bikes and service parts businesses as two supply chains that share capacity.

[2]Incidentally, any individual supply chain contains vertically integrated balancing loops, each with a delay. This stacked structure leads to demand amplification and the bull-whip effect as characteristic dynamics of supply chains. In principle, the same effect should be produced by 'stacking' two or more shower systems one on top of the other so that turning the tap in shower 1 (to control temperature) depletes a tank of hot water observable in shower 2 and under shower 2's control. Turning the tap in shower 2 (to control temperature) then depletes a tank of hot water in shower 3 and under shower 3's control, and so on. This 'cascaded' World of Showers C would likely be even more difficult to manage than World B. A variation on this structure is for the outflow of water from shower A to be the inflow of water to shower B and so on – a kind of thrifty World of Showers C. The reader is invited to develop and test these novel Shower Worlds.

was less internal competition for scarce capacity. As a result, the parts business was much more responsive to dealer demand and able to offer lead times equal to or better than specialist job shops.

Inside World of Showers

To examine the model behind the gaming simulator open World of Showers B and press the 'Model' tab on the left of the screen. There are two sectors – 'your shower' on the left and 'shower 2 – hidden' on the right. It is best to study shower 2 because this sector contains the complete balancing feedback loop for comfort seeking. (In 'your shower' the equivalent feedback loop is completed by you, the game player, and so the loop is not visible in the diagram.)

A Tour of Formulations in the Comfort-seeking Loop of the Hidden Shower

Let's get into shower 2 and talk through the operating structure as shown in Figure 4.9 and the corresponding equations in Figure 4.10. The temperature gap is the difference sensed by the shower-taker between desired temperature and the actual temperature at the shower head. In the equations, desired temperature is set at 25°C. The symbols on the left-hand side of the map show how the recognition of a temperature gap leads to a change in tap setting. This part of the map represents the decision making of a rational shower-taker who wants to stay comfortable.

The temperature gap leads to a fractional adjustment of the tap setting. Imagine what goes through the mind of the shower-taker. The water temperature is too cold. She decides to turn the tap part way round the scale in a direction that she believes will warm her up. In the equations this judgemental fractional adjustment is proportional to the temperature gap – the more degrees away from comfort, the greater the fractional adjustment envisaged, according to the judgemental calibration of the scale for the tap setting.

The shower-taker's thinking moves one step closer to action as she gauges the required adjustment to the tap setting. She glances at the tap and notes its current setting and the maximum and minimum settings to which it can be turned. If she feels too cold (temperature gap greater than zero) then she turns the tap toward the hot end of the scale. How far should she turn the tap between the current and maximum settings?

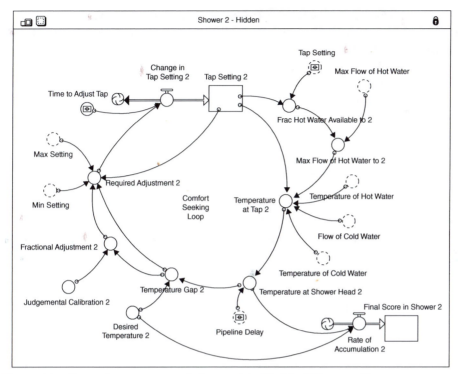

Figure 4.9   Operating structure of shower 2 in World of Showers B

Source: The Dynamics of Resource Sharing: A Metaphorical Model, *System Dynamics Review*, 11(4) page 293. Morecroft, J.D.W., Larsen, E.R., Lomi, A. and Ginsberg. A., 1995 © John Wiley & Sons Limited. Reproduced with permission.

Final Score in Shower 2 (t) = Final Score in Shower 2 (t - dt) + (Rate of Accumulation 2) * dt
INIT Final Score in Shower 2 = Rate of Accumulation 2
INFLOWS:
Rate of Accumulation 2 = ABS(Desired Temperature 2 –Temperature at Shower Head 2)

Tap Setting 2 (t) = Tap Setting 2 (t - dt) + (Change in Tap Setting 2) * dt
INIT Tap Setting_2 = 21/60 {dimensionless fraction of scale range}
INFLOWS:
Change in Tap Setting 2 = Required Adjustment 2 / Time to Adjust Tap
{fraction range of scale remaining/second}

Desired Temperature 2 = 25 {°C, the temperature at which the person in shower 2 feels comfortable}
Frac Hot Water Available to 2 = Tap Setting 2 / (Tap Setting +Tap Setting 2) {dimensionless}
Fractional Adjustment 2 = ABS (Temperature Gap 2*Judgemental Calibration 2) {fraction of scale range remaining}
Judgemental Calibration 2 = 1/10 {fraction of scale range remaining/°C, the judgemental calibration of the tap scale by the person in shower 2, represented as a fractional adjustment of tap setting within the visible scale remaining, per °C temperature gap}
Max Flow of Hot Water to 2 = Max Flow of Hot Water * Frac Hot Water Available to 2 {litres per second}
Max Flow of Hot Water = 1 {litre per second, which is equivalent to 60 litres per minute}

Required Adjustment 2 = If Temperature Gap 2 > 0 Then (Max Setting – Tap Setting 2) * Fractional Adjustment 2 Else
(Min_Setting-Tap_Setting_2)*Fractional_Adjustment_2 {fraction range of scale remaining}
Temperature at Tap 2 = (Flow of Cold Water * Temperature of Cold   Water + Tap Setting 2 *
Max Flow of Hot Water to 2 * Temperature of Hot Water) / (Flow of Cold Water + Tap Setting 2 *
Max Flow of Hot Water to 2) {°C}
Temperature at Shower Head_2 = SMTH3 (Temperature at Tap 2, Pipeline Delay) {°C}
Temperature Gap 2 = Desired Temperature 2 – Temperature at Shower Head 2
Time to Adjust Tap = 5 {seconds, the time taken to adjust the tap setting, combining both the judgemental delay and the physical delay in moving the tap}

Figure 4.10   Equations for shower 2 in World of Showers B

Here the shower-taker's judgement is key to her later comfort! In the model, the required adjustment is equal to the difference between the maximum and current tap settings (her room for manoeuvre, or angular distance remaining, on the scale) multiplied by the fractional adjustment (her estimate of the appropriate turn of the tap as a fraction of the remaining angular distance on the scale). The equation formulation can be seen in Figure 4.10. If she feels too hot then she follows a similar line of reasoning in gauging how far to turn the tap between the current and minimum setting.

All these thoughts, comprising her judgement on tap setting, flash through her mind in an instant. In fact, she is scarcely aware of the steps in the judgement. What she knows and feels is a sensation of being too cold or too hot, and so she turns the tap. In the model, the change in tap setting is set equal to the required adjustment divided by the time to adjust the tap setting. This portion of the map represents the part of the shower system where judgement and decision making convert into action. Her hand turns the tap and the tap setting changes. The angular movement of the tap accumulates in a level that represents the position of the tap on the hot–cold scale. Then the plumbing takes over, and she awaits the consequences!

On the right-hand side of Figure 4.9 the water temperature at the tap is shown to depend on the tap setting. The equivalent algebraic formulation is shown in Figure 4.10. The temperature at the tap depends on the flow of cold water, the temperature of the cold water, the tap setting, the maximum flow of hot water to shower 2 and the temperature of the hot water. The equation looks quite complex, but really it is just blending two flows of water, cold and hot, and calculating the resultant temperature. The flow of cold water is fixed at 15 litres per minute, at a temperature of 10°C. The maximum flow of hot water available to both showers is set at 60 litres per minute, at a temperature of 70°C. The flow of hot water in shower 2 is a fraction of this maximum flow, determined by the tap settings in shower 2 and in your shower (as explained below). As the tap setting changes from its minimum value of 0 (the cold end of the scale) to its maximum value of 1 (the hot end of the scale) then the water temperature moves from its minimum value of 10°C to its maximum blended value (a weighted average of 10°C and 70°C water).

The temperature at the shower head changes with the temperature at the tap, but only after a time delay, which is literally the pipeline delay in the pipe connecting the tap to the shower head. In the model, the pipeline delay is set at 4 seconds. As the water emerges from the shower head, we come full circle around the diagram, back to the temperature gap.

To summarise, shower 2 in World of Showers B is represented in three parts. On the left of Figure 4.9 is the behavioural decision-making process that translates a temperature gap into a required adjustment of the tap setting. At the top of the figure is the action of adjusting the tap that leads to a new tap setting. On the right of the map is the piping and water flow that convert the tap setting into hot water at the shower head.

Interdependence of Showers – Coupling Formulations

The crescent of links in the top right of Figure 4.9 shows the coupling connections between the two showers and Figure 4.10 shows the corresponding algebra (Morecroft, Larsen, Lomi and Ginsberg, 1995). The showers are supplied with a maximum flow of 60 litres of hot water per minute. The fraction of hot water available to shower 2 depends on the tap setting in both shower 2 and in your shower – hence the coupling. As the tap setting in shower 2 moves further toward the hot extreme of the scale, then (assuming no change in the tap setting in your shower) shower 2 gains access to a larger share of the available hot water supply. However, if the tap setting in your shower increases, then shower 2 loses a proportion of the hot water flow. Algebraically, the fraction of hot water available to shower 2 is represented as the ratio of tap setting 2 to the sum of tap setting 2 and the tap setting in your shower. The maximum flow of hot water available to shower 2 is the product of the fraction of hot water available to shower 2, and the maximum flow of hot water in the system as a whole (the shared resource constraint).

The coupling equations for your shower are similar to shower 2, but expressed in terms of the tap settings as they affect the flow of hot water in your shower. Hence, the fraction of hot water available to your shower is represented algebraically as the ratio of the tap setting in your shower to the sum of tap settings in your shower and in shower 2.

Simulations of World of Showers B

Figure 4.11 shows typical simulated behaviour of temperature at the two shower heads over a period of two minutes (120 seconds). Shower-takers both begin too hot and inadvertently end up in an endless cycle of conflict and discomfort. Neither shower-taker is able to achieve a condition of stable and comfortable 25°C water, despite the intention of both to do so. Instead of converging, the water temperature in both showers exhibits persistent fluctuations, sometimes reaching peaks of almost 35°C and troughs of less than 20°C. The strong coupling of the shower worlds is evident in the way temperature movements mirror each other – when the temperature is high in your shower (line 1), it is low in shower 2 (line 2), and vice versa.

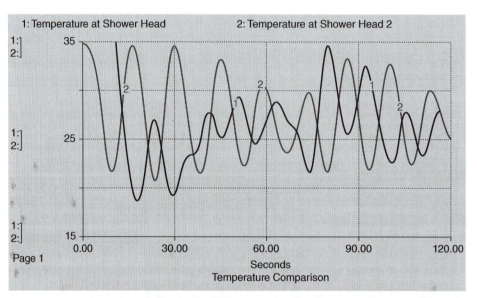

Figure 4.11   Typical simulation of two interacting showers in World of Showers B

Such a world is confusing and frustrating for decision makers. Well intentioned actions to stabilise temperature (and so increase comfort) have the perverse effect of inducing instability. Moreover, no amount of time spent changing the tap setting will improve the situation. Each shower-taker adopts an adjustment strategy and mindset appropriate to a single shower, reinforced by visual cues that confirm they are in a single shower world – separate cubicles, a single tap to adjust, no awareness of the other shower or its occupant (just like the functional or regional stovepipes that shape mindsets in organisations).

An effective way to improve performance is to reduce the pipeline delay and to increase the patience of the hidden shower-taker (by increasing the time to adjust the tap). Reducing the pipeline delay makes each shower more responsive to the comfort needs of the shower-takers. Increasing the time to adjust the tap mimics a hidden shower-taker who reacts more gradually to any temperature gap and so reduces internal competition for hot water. The combined effect of these two design changes is to reduce coupling between the two showers so each shower-taker feels more in control of their own destiny. The effective dynamic complexity of the shower system is reduced and World of Showers B behaves more like World of Showers A, with the water temperature in both showers converging quickly to the desired 25°C as shown in Figure 4.12.

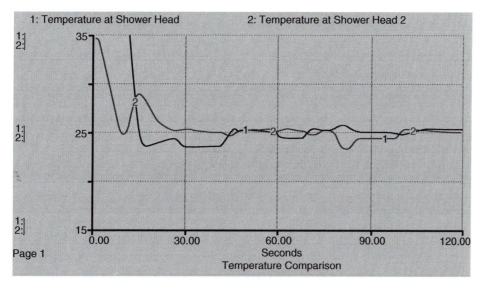

Figure 4.12   Simulation of two interacting showers in a redesigned World of Showers B with pipeline delay reduced from 4 to 2 seconds and time to adjust tap increased from 5 to 10 seconds

References

Akkermans, H. and Dellaert, N. (eds) (2005) The dynamics of supply chains and networks. *System Dynamics Review*, 21(3): 173–186.

Forrester, J.W. (1961) *Industrial Dynamics*. Available from the System Dynamics Society www.systemdynamics.org. (Originally published by MIT Press 1961.)

Morecroft, J.D.W., Larsen, E.R., Lomi, A. and Ginsberg, A. (1995) The dynamics of resource sharing: a metaphorical model. *System Dynamics Review*, 11(4): 289–309.

Morecroft, J.D.W. (1983) Managing product lines that share a common capacity base. *Journal of Operations Management*, 3(2): 57–66.

Schelling, T.C. (1980) *Strategy of Conflict*. Cambridge, MA: Harvard University Press.

Sterman, J.D. (1989) Misperceptions of feedback in dynamic decision making. *Organizational Behaviour and Human Decision Processes*, 43(3): 301–335.

Chapter 5

Cyclical Dynamics and the Process of Model Building

- An Overview of the Modelling Process
- Employment and Production Instability – Puzzling Performance Over Time
- Equation Formulations and Computations in Production Control
- Modelling Workforce Management and Factory Production Dynamics
- Equation Formulations in Workforce Management
- Chronic Cyclicality in Employment and Production and How to Cure It
- Modelling for Learning and Soft Systems
- Appendix 1: Model Communication and Policy Structure Diagrams
- Appendix 2: The Dynamics of Information Smoothing

Modelling is iterative. It begins with a concern about dynamics (performance over time) and preliminary ideas about feedback structure. Then gradually, in stages, a model takes shape that clarifies the concern and sharpens ideas about structure. The purpose is not to create a perfect model that replicates the real world situation in every detail. Rather it is to engage in a learning process using the model as an instrument for investigation, clarification and discovery.

An Overview of the Modelling Process

In system dynamics, five steps of modelling can be identified as shown in Figure 5.1. Usually there is lots of to-and-fro between the steps as understanding of the situation improves by sketching diagrams, quantifying concepts, writing friendly algebra and making simulations.

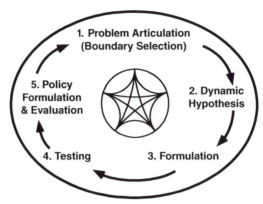

Figure 5.1 Modelling is an iterative learning process
Source: Sterman, J.D., *Business Dynamics: Systems Thinking and Modeling for a Complex World*,
© 2000, Irwin McGraw-Hill, Boston, MA. Reproduced with permission of the McGraw-Hill Companies.

Step 1 is problem articulation. It is the most important step of all because it shapes the entire study. Here the modeller or modelling team identifies the issue of concern, the time frame, the level of analysis (business unit, firm, industry, etc.), the boundary of the study and the likely scope of factors involved. Step 2 is a dynamic hypothesis, a preliminary sketch by the modeller of the main interactions and feedback loops that could explain observed or anticipated performance. Step 3 is formulation, the transformation of a dynamic hypothesis into a reasonably detailed diagram of feedback processes and corresponding algebraic equations. Step 4 is testing. The model is simulated to see whether or not its behaviour over time is plausible and consistent with available evidence from the real world. Step 4 fixes errors and begins to build confidence in the model's integrity. Step 5 is policy formulation and evaluation. By now there is confidence that the model's structure is sound and that it is capable of reproducing the dynamic symptoms of the original problem. Hence, attention shifts to policy changes intended to improve performance and to alleviate the perceived problem. The new policies are then simulated to see how well they work.

Notice these steps are shown as a cycle and not as a linear sequence. The web-like symbol in the middle of the diagram and the circle of arrows around the edge mean that iteration is a natural and important part of the process. For example, it is common for modellers to revise the problem and model boundary as they develop a dynamic hypothesis and causal loops. Thus, step 2 influences step 1. Similarly, formulation and testing can reveal the need for new equations or new structure, because initial simulations contradict common sense (as in the 60-month run of the drug model in Chapter 3) or else reveal that the original dynamic hypothesis is incapable of generating observed or expected behaviour over time. So steps 3 and 4 can influence steps 1 and 2 or each other.

Dynamic Hypothesis and Fundamental Modes of Dynamic Behaviour

From a modeller's perspective, a dynamic hypothesis is a particularly important step of 'complexity reduction' – making sense of a messy situation in the real world. A feedback systems thinker has in mind a number of structure–behaviour pairs that give valuable clues or patterns to look for when explaining puzzling dynamics. Figure 5.2 shows six fundamental modes of dynamic behaviour and the feedback structures that generate them.

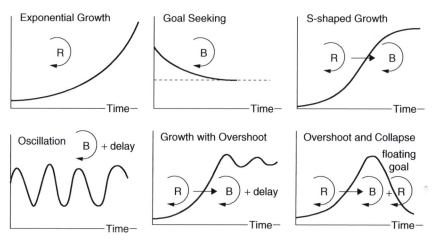

Figure 5.2   Dynamic hypothesis and fundamental modes of dynamic behaviour
Source: Sterman, J.D., *Business Dynamics: Systems Thinking and Modeling for a Complex World*, © 2000, Irwin McGraw-Hill, Boston, MA. Reproduced with permission of the McGraw-Hill Companies.

The trajectories in the top half of the diagram arise from simple feedback processes. On the left is pure exponential growth caused by a single reinforcing feedback loop in isolation. In the centre is pure goal-seeking behaviour caused by a balancing loop. On the right is s-shaped growth that occurs when exponential growth hits a limit. In this case, a reinforcing loop dominates behaviour to begin with, and then later (due to changing conditions) a balancing loop becomes more and more influential.

The trajectories in the bottom half of the diagram arise from more complex feedback processes. On the left is classic oscillatory, goal-seeking behaviour with repeated overshoot and undershoot of a target, caused by a balancing loop with a time delay. In the centre is growth with overshoot, a pattern of behaviour where growth from a reinforcing loop hits a limit that is not immediately recognised. This lagged limiting effect is represented as a balancing loop with delay. On the right is overshoot and collapse, which is a variation on growth with overshoot, but here the limit itself is a floating goal that adds an extra reinforcing loop. This set of six structure–behaviour pairs is not exhaustive, but illustrates the principle that any pattern of behaviour over time can be reduced to the interaction of balancing and reinforcing loops.

Some of the most intriguing and complex dynamics arise in situations where multiple feedback loops interact and each loop contains time delays and non-linearities. We meet two such models later in the book, the market growth model in Chapter 7 and the oil producers' model in Chapter 8. Even quite simple linear models with two or three interacting loops and time delays, however, can prove to be very interesting as we will see in the factory model in this chapter. The main point for now is to realise that all such models take shape in a structured yet creative process of discovering feedback processes in everyday affairs.

Team Model Building

Often models are built by teams that include a group facilitator, an expert modeller and of course the client group (the policymakers/stakeholders who are grappling with a problem situation). There are also a variety of 'modelling support roles' that have come to be recognised as distinctive and important for the success of team modelling projects. There is a process coach to observe and manage the group process, a recorder to take notes and a gatekeeper to liaise between the modellers and the client group. Sometimes one person can handle more than one of these roles, but it is nevertheless important for the team to bear in mind the role distinctions.

Although definitions of group model building differ, there is broad agreement that the essence is to meaningfully involve stakeholders in the process of developing a model, in the expectation that a more relevant model will result, with implementable insights (Richardson and Anderson, 1995; Vennix, 1996). Principles for the design and delivery of successful group model building workshops have become an important area of research and practice in system dynamics. For example, specific protocols and scripts for group model building are described in Andersen and Richardson (1997). Since these beginnings in the late 1990s a rich literature in 'participatory modelling' has taken shape as reported in Hovmand (2014) and creatively adapted for use in 'community based system dynamics'.

My purpose here is narrow relative to this literature. I do not intend to describe in detail the methods and processes used by group model builders, though I will refer to them. Rather I wish to make a specific point that in team model building, there are distinct phases of work that cut across the five iterative modelling steps shown in Figure 5.1 and described above. These phases, illustrated in Figures 5.3 and 5.4, show, in broad terms, when and where different team members are involved. The diagrams and accompanying text arise from my own experience of team model building in applied research projects such as the oil industry project in Chapter 8 and the soap industry project in Chapter 10.

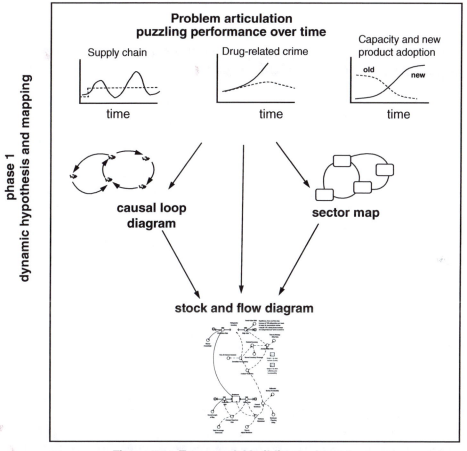

Problem articulation
puzzling performance over time

Supply chain

Drug-related crime

Capacity and new
product adoption

old

new

time

time

time

causal loop
diagram

sector map

stock and flow diagram

phase 1
dynamic hypothesis and mapping

Figure 5.3   Team model building – phase 1

Phase 1 is all about identifying the problem situation and mapping the relevant feedback structure. Normally the facilitator and expert modeller work with the client group to capture the group's understanding of the situation and to reframe it dynamically. Phase 1 begins with problem articulation and ends with a stock and flow diagram. Nowadays this vital phase is often designed and scripted using group model building protocols and delivered with support from the (roles of) process coach, recorder and gatekeeper. The first modelling challenge is to express the problem situation in terms of performance through time. The top of Figure 5.3 shows three examples. The time chart on the left is a sketch of volatile dynamics in a supply chain, where variations in factory production (the solid line) far exceed changes in retail demand (the dotted line). Why does the factory overreact in this way? The contrasting shape of the trajectories for production and demand is a good way to frame the factory's problem dynamically. The time chart in the centre shows drug-related crime as discussed in Chapters 2 and 3. The dynamic problem lies in the growth of crime (the solid line), which far outstrips tolerable crime (the dotted line). Finally, the time chart on the right shows trajectories for factory capacity in new product adoption. The strategic problem, expressed dynamically, is to retire old capacity (the dotted line) while growing new capacity (the solid line). The success of product adoption depends in part on how well the balance of old and new capacity is managed. A model examining this issue in fast-moving consumer goods is presented in Chapter 10.

A pattern of performance over time is a clue in the search for feedback structure. It is important to realise that feedback loops and asset stocks do not just conveniently present themselves to modellers. There is a highly creative task to discover, among the views and information provided by the team, enduring feedback structure that is capable of generating the dynamics of interest. A dynamic hypothesis is a good starting point. Often a hypothesis is nothing more than a hunch that the sought-for structure resembles a particular combination of feedback loops, such as a balancing loop with delay or a reinforcing loop linked to a balancing loop. The hunch can be refined in different ways to arrive at a refined causal loop diagram and ultimately a tailored stock and flow diagram that adequately fits the situation.

The rest of Figure 5.3 shows three alternative paths the facilitator and modeller can take in going from performance over time to a stock and flow diagram. The appropriate path depends on the situation at hand, and also on preferred modelling style and choice of scripts. One approach, shown on the left, is to sketch a causal loop diagram and then overlay the extra operating detail required for a full stock and flow diagram. This is the approach taken with the drug-related crime model in Chapter 3. However, in practice feedback loops may not be evident at first glance. Instead it is often helpful to create a sector map showing the main parts of the enterprise to be modelled and then to probe their interaction more deeply. This approach is shown on the right of Figure 5.3. It involves mapping the operating policies and stock accumulations in each sector in an effort to discover feedback loops, all the time bearing in mind the dynamic hypothesis. The resulting policy map is then converted into a detailed stock and flow diagram. Yet another approach is to draw the main asset stock accumulations, and then map the network of connections between them. This direct approach is shown in the centre of Figure 5.3.

Phase 1 defines the problem as well as the broad scope and architecture of the model and can be carried out quite quickly. It is not unusual for a team of 5–10 people to contribute. One or two days of work can yield maps of sufficient quality and content to guide algebraic modelling in phase 2. Active participation by policymakers and stakeholders in phase 1 also enhances buy-in to the project and reduces the likelihood that the client group will mistrust the model and treat it as a suspicious black box. For these reasons, it is entirely appropriate to involve senior managers and other experienced people in phase 1. Typically, they adopt a broad strategic view of the organisation consistent with the perspective of a feedback systems thinker (even if they themselves have never seen a causal loop before). Moreover, they usually enjoy the mapping process and the resulting overview of their organisation in causal loops or sector maps.

The group model building literature provides tailored and tested protocols and tools for use in phase 1. For example, among the scripts described by Andersen and Richardson (1997) there are 'scripts' to elicit from stakeholders patterns of performance over time (dynamic stories) and causal structures. There are also scripts to gently introduce stakeholders to the basic concepts of system dynamics, sometimes by showing them small stock and flow models (so-called 'concept models') whose minimal feedback structure nevertheless generates simulated dynamics relevant to the problem situation. Concept models, as diagrams, need to be small and versatile enough that participants, guided by the group facilitator, are able not only to understand the diagrams quickly, but also to modify them. Concept models can also take the form of generalizable causal loop diagrams or of sector maps that show the operating policies and stock accumulations within each sector. The key thing is for modellers to devise simple yet compelling visual models to stimulate group discussion of the problem situation and, in doing so, engage participants with the specialist visualisation tools of system dynamics. Once stakeholders are engaged with a concept model, then larger and more ambitious visual models and simulators can also take shape (if necessary). Understanding the relationship between visual representations in system dynamics and the role they play in team work is at the heart of effective group model building and has come to be associated with the powerful notion of boundary objects (Black and Andersen, 2012; Black, 2013). As Hovmand aptly notes, 'the essence of group model building is the explicit design and management of a process to socially construct boundary objects involving system dynamics visual representations' that capture feedback loops and naturally pave the way to formal simulators.

Phase 2 is algebraic modelling and simulation, as shown in Figure 5.4. The stock and flow diagram from phase 1 is converted into friendly algebra and a variety of diagnostic simulations are conducted.

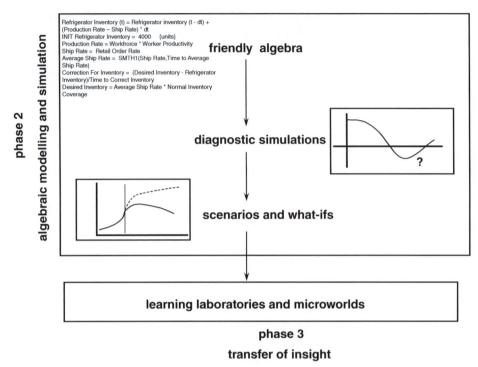

Figure 5.4   Team model building – phases 2 and 3

This work is demanding and time consuming and, in my experience, is best carried out by a dedicated modelling team, usually a subset of the project team, perhaps three or more people, including the facilitator, the expert modeller and at least one person who knows the organisation very well. It can take weeks or even months to create a robust and well-calibrated simulator. There are equations to be written, parameters to be obtained and graphical functions to be sketched. When the formulations are finished simulations can begin, but it is very rare indeed for a model to run plausibly first time. It is best to be highly sceptical of initial runs and treat them as diagnostic simulations that may reveal inadvertent modelling errors. Frequently equation formulations do not work as intended and cause totally implausible behaviour over time, such as price that climbs sky-high or market share that falls below zero. Fixing equations to remove such anomalies of behaviour gradually builds confidence that the model is ready to use with the project team for what-ifs and scenarios. Incidentally, when anomalies cannot be fixed they often reveal a flaw in the way people have been thinking about the dynamics of strategy. Persistent anomalies in simulated trajectories often arise because, upon close inspection, the model is showing counterintuitive behaviour from which people can learn something new.

Phase 3 is the transfer of insight organisation-wide. The model is transformed into a specially packaged simulator called a 'learning laboratory' or 'microworld', easy enough for anyone in the organisation to operate. It can be used in workshops to communicate the insights from a modelling project to hundreds or even thousands of people in an organisation. The shower simulator in Chapter 4 and the fisheries gaming simulator in Chapter 1 are small-scale examples of such technology, and there are other examples later in the book.[1]

Employment and Production Instability – Puzzling Performance Over Time

To illustrate the modelling process, consider the following dynamic puzzle facing a manufacturer of major household appliances. The company has been experiencing fluctuating employment and production in its refrigerator division. The employment level has varied over a ratio of about two to one (in other words the maximum workforce is roughly twice the minimum) with peak-to-peak intervals of two years. Conventional event-oriented thinking might suggest that macro-economic upturns and downturns are responsible for this costly and disruptive behaviour over time. However, the evidence in this case is that the economy has been stable. Something else is going on, but what? Feedback systems thinking will often (though not always) look to internal factors, the way the division is organised, coordinated and managed, to explain dynamic behaviour. Interactions among the firm's operating policies and the practical constraints of production may in themselves explain the puzzling behaviour and also hold the key to future improvements. Incidentally, the analysis of fluctuations in business goes right back to the earliest work in system dynamics. Readers are referred to Jay Forrester's original working papers in the learning support folder for Chapter 5, in a sub-folder called c05 Archive Materials. Here you will find D-0016 Formulating Quantitative Models of Dynamic Behavior of Industrial and Economic Systems and D-0046 Models of Dynamic Behavior of Industrial and Economic Systems. The manuscripts contain ideas that subsequently appeared in Forrester's seminal 1961 book *Industrial Dynamics*. There is also a description of the special 'J-K-L' time notation used in system dynamics models for many years. Familiarity with this

---

[1] A valuable set of case studies and interactive web-based simulators for strategy and sustainability can be found at the MIT Sloan *Learning Edge* website. The cases, simulators and other support materials are described in Sterman (2014a; 2014b). Additional interactive strategy simulators based on system dynamics can be found on the websites for Forio.com, isee systems and Strategy Dynamics.

notation will enable readers to understand the equation formulations of other models in the downloadable archive materials that accompany the book.

The situation is expressed dynamically in Figure 5.5. There are two time charts, both with a timescale of three years. The workforce is on a scale of 100–300 workers and production is on a scale from 0–2000 refrigerators per week. Both trajectories are strongly cyclical. How could these dynamics arise? A feedback systems thinker knows that a balancing loop with delay is capable of generating such oscillatory behaviour. This insight about dynamics is a useful structural clue, but where would such a loop be found among the factory's operations?

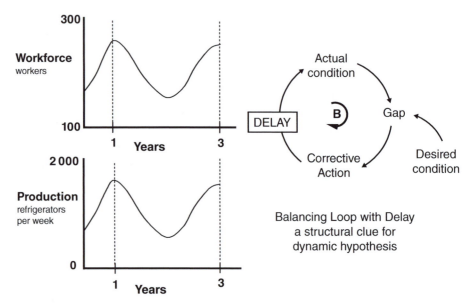

Figure 5.5   Employment and production cyclicality – puzzling performance and structural clue

The search for an appropriate balancing loop begins in this case with a sector map. Our dynamic hunch is that the factory's performance problems stem from the interaction between production control and workforce management. There is somehow a failure of coordination between these two important activities in the factory. Figure 5.6 shows the main connections. The production control sector receives incoming orders from retailers and makes shipments of refrigerators in return. A key question in our investigation is how the firm translates orders for refrigerators into the number of factory workers needed. Common sense suggests the volume of orders is related to the number of workers, but how? Managers responsible for production control decide the 'right' amount of production necessary to fulfil orders and to ensure reliable supply. The resulting production schedule is then used to adjust the workforce whose size determines the production rate. In the figure, you can already see a closed loop between the two sectors, formed by the production schedule and workforce, and it is this loop we want to examine in more detail.

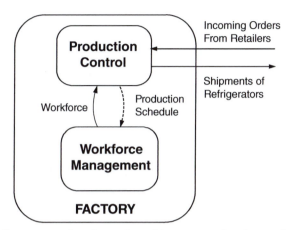

Figure 5.6   Sector map for dynamics of factory production and employment

A sector map shows the parts of the business, its recognisable functions, each with its own stock and flow network and its own operating policies. We can find the feedback processes within and between sectors by listing policies in use, sketching the stock and flow networks that belong in each sector and then identifying the influential connections. It is like building a jigsaw puzzle. The pieces are the policies and asset stocks, the connections are the clues for which pieces fit together and the resulting picture reveals the feedback processes. Figure 5.7 shows the pieces of the jigsaw for our factory model.

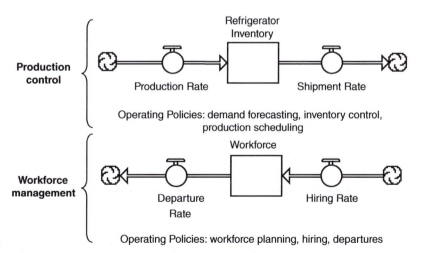

Figure 5.7   Asset stocks and list of operating policies in production control and workforce management

At the top is production control with policies for demand forecasting, inventory control and production scheduling, the kind of routine decision-making processes found in all factories. There is also a refrigerator inventory, an important asset stock that sits between the production rate and shipment rate and signals the current balance of supply and demand. At the bottom of the figure is workforce management. Here the policies are workforce planning, hiring and departures – all those routine processes that influence the size of the factory workforce. The workforce itself is the sector's asset stock that sits between the hiring rate and the departure rate.

Dialogue About Production Control

Figure 5.8 is a complete stock and flow diagram for production control. The three shaded regions represent the main operating policies and within these regions there is a more specific representation of information flows and converters.

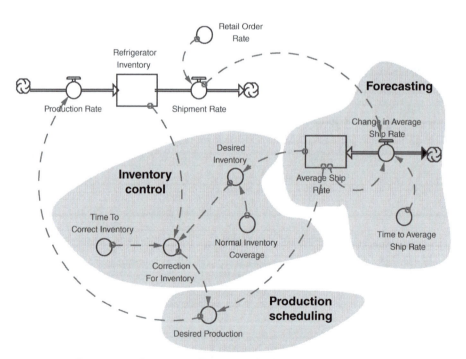

Figure 5.8 Stock and flow diagram for production control

Why use this particular picture? To understand, imagine the following dialogue between a modeller and factory expert:

Modeller: I imagine that forecasting is an important input to your production scheduling process. Tell me more about forecasting.

Factory expert:	Well forecasting is essentially how we estimate future demand from retailers.
Modeller:	What information do you use?
Factory expert:	There are many different information sources we could use. There is an annual forecast prepared by the marketing department. There is a factory database containing recent and historical records of retail orders and the shipment rate of refrigerators. General economic conditions are relevant too, whether we are in an economic boom or a recession.
Modeller:	OK, but would you say that some of these information sources are more reliable or better than others?
Factory expert:	Forecasts from the marketing department are usually viewed with scepticism in the factory. At least that is our experience in this particular factory (though I can imagine factories in other firms where marketing forecasts are taken more seriously). Realistically the only data we really trust is shipments. That's real demand without any marketing spin or bias, and much more tangible (and therefore believable) even than retail orders. We can actually see and count the number of refrigerators that leave the factory each day and, from the database, have a pretty good idea of how shipments vary from month to month. Hence, we have concluded that past shipments are actually a good guide to future demand.
Modeller's note to self:	In that case I can formulate forecasting as an average of the shipment rate itself, and downplay other influences.
Modeller:	So would it be fair to say that production scheduling is driven principally by a forecast of shipments?
Factory expert:	Yes, that's about right except that we also like to make sure we have enough finished refrigerators in stock to meet unexpected changes in demand. As a result we will sometimes schedule extra production to build finished inventory to a satisfactory level or else cut the schedule to reduce inventory if we think it's too high. It's a form of inventory control.
Modeller:	But how do you decide on a satisfactory inventory level?
Factory expert:	In our case that's just a rule of thumb, nothing too formal. Through experience we have come to the conclusion that it's sensible to carry about four weeks' worth of shipments.
Modeller:	So to summarise, production scheduling combines forecasting of shipments with inventory control?
Factory expert:	Yes, that's a reasonable description of what goes on.
Modeller's note to self:	So I can augment the forecast with an asset stock adjustment formulation to represent inventory control.
Modeller (on the next day, having created the stock and flow diagram in Figure 5.8):	Here is a picture of what you've told me so far about the factory. You will see the three main areas we talked about: forecasting, inventory control and production scheduling. There is a refrigerator inventory of finished units at the end of the production line. The inventory is increased by the production rate and reduced by the shipment rate. The rest of the diagram shows how production is coordinated.

Forecasting relies principally on information about the shipment rate and is essentially an average of past shipments (on the grounds mentioned that past shipments are a good guide to future demand). It matters how quickly this average responds to variations in the shipment rate. Forecasting should distinguish between routine day-to-day variations in shipments on the one hand and systematic trends on the other. This ability to discriminate is captured in the concept 'time to average ship rate', something that will need to be quantified in the algebraic model and has an important influence on the dynamics of production. The average shipment rate (or forecast) is used in two different ways to guide production planning. It feeds directly into production scheduling where it is one component of desired production. It also influences inventory control. The diagram shows four concepts used to capture the typical nature of inventory control. There is a 'desired inventory', which is an amount of inventory the factory aims to hold in order to avoid 'stockouts'. This desired inventory depends on the average ship rate and normal inventory coverage, consistent with the observation that it is good to carry about four weeks' worth of shipments. By comparing desired inventory with the current refrigerator inventory, factory managers decide whether to boost or cut production to ensure that the right number of refrigerators is in stock. The correction for inventory captures this managerial judgement and incorporates a concept called 'time to correct inventory' that represents the urgency with which factory managers correct an inventory shortage or surplus. Production scheduling then combines information on the average ship rate with the correction for inventory to arrive at desired production.

Thought Experiment: A Surprise Demand Increase in an Ideal Factory

To test this part of the model, suppose the retail order rate increases unexpectedly and permanently by 10% from 1000 to 1100 refrigerators per week. Will the factory be able to keep up with demand? Assume for now that the factory can always produce at a rate equal to desired production. In Figure 5.8, this temporary simplifying assumption is shown by connecting desired production directly to the production rate. The link portrays an ideal factory with no constraints on production. Although the situation is deliberately simplified, it is still worth investigating as a stepping-stone to understanding sources of variability in production.

Figure 5.9 is a simulation of this ideal factory generated by running the model called 'Production' in the learning support folder for Chapter 5. Press 'Run' and watch the screen icons. Then open Graph 1 which contains two tabbed pages corresponding to the two charts in Figure 5.9.

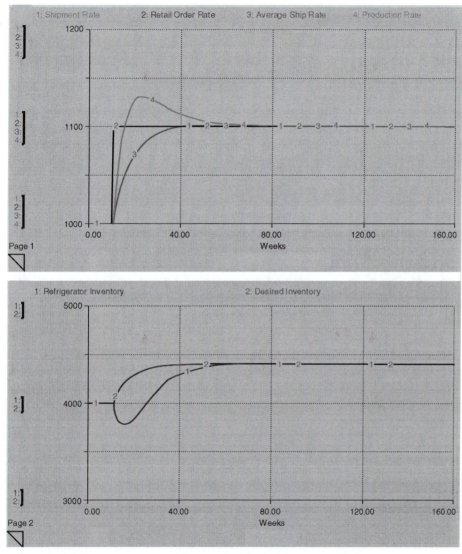

Figure 5.9   Simulation of a 10 per cent unexpected demand increase in an ideal factory

For the first 10 weeks, the factory is in perfect equilibrium, as though the retail order rate had been rock steady for a long time. In the top chart (page 1 of Graph 1), the shipment rate, retail order rate, average ship rate and production are all equal at 1000 refrigerators per week. In the bottom chart (page 2 of Graph 1), the refrigerator inventory is equal to desired inventory. Then in week 10, the retail order rate (line 2, top chart) increases permanently by 10%, consistent with our demand assumption. If you look very carefully at the time chart, you will see that the shipment rate (line 1) follows exactly the same trajectory as the retail order rate; in fact the two lines are superimposed. Thus, the factory is able to fully satisfy demand at all times, despite the unexpected increase in demand. The factory achieves this perfect supply by depleting inventory in the short run and then subsequently expanding production not only to meet demand but also to replenish inventory.

The story of factory adjustment begins in the bottom chart. In week 10, when demand increases, refrigerator inventory (line 1) starts to decline. Now look at the top chart. In the interval between weeks 10 and 15 the shipment rate/retail order rate (line 2) exceeds the production rate (line 4). In other words, the outflow of refrigerators exceeds the inflow, so the inventory must decline. Meanwhile, production is quickly catching up to shipments and by week 15 they are exactly equal. Inventory stabilises, but the factory is not yet in equilibrium. Inventory control calls for more production to replenish inventory. Notice that desired inventory (line 2 in the bottom chart) rises in proportion to the average ship rate (line 3 in the top chart) because of the factory's rule of thumb to hold four weeks' coverage of shipments. Hence, there is an interval between weeks 15 and 55 when production exceeds shipments. During those 40 weeks, the factory is producing for stock as well as for shipment. As inventory is gradually replenished the production rate falls until it equals the retail order rate and the factory is back in equilibrium. The important dynamical feature of the simulation is the factory's inevitable need for 'surplus' production, above and beyond the real increase in demand. This outcome is not intuitively obvious from the operating policies alone. It requires simulation to reliably trace the consequences.

Equation Formulations and Computations in Production Control

It is common for equation formulations to be organised in sectors and blocks that correspond as closely as possible to the visual model. We begin with inventory accumulation as shown in Figure 5.10. These are the standard equations for a stock and flow network. Refrigerator inventory at time t is equal to refrigerator inventory at the previous point in time t-dt, plus the net change resulting from production (the inflow) and shipments (the outflow) over the interval dt between t-dt and t. The initial inventory is set at 4000 refrigerators, deliberately chosen so that there are four weeks' coverage of initial shipments, exactly in line with the factory's rule of thumb. The production rate is identically equal to desired production, a temporary but convenient assumption that says the factory can always produce as many refrigerators as needed at just the right time.

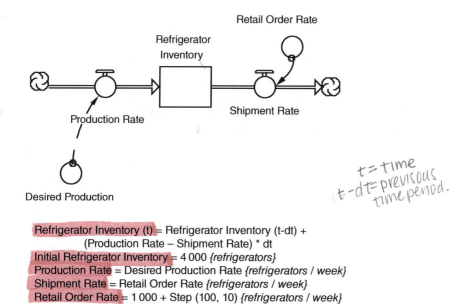

Retail Order Rate

Refrigerator Inventory

Production Rate

Shipment Rate

Desired Production

t = time
t − dt = previous time period.

Refrigerator Inventory (t) = Refrigerator Inventory (t-dt) +
(Production Rate − Shipment Rate) * dt
Initial Refrigerator Inventory = 4 000 {refrigerators}
Production Rate = Desired Production Rate {refrigerators / week}
Shipment Rate = Retail Order Rate {refrigerators / week}
Retail Order Rate = 1 000 + Step (100, 10) {refrigerators / week}

Figure 5.10   Equations for inventory accumulation

The shipment rate is equal to the retail order rate implying there is enough finished inventory available in the shipping bay to fill orders.[2] The retail order rate itself is formulated as a one-time step increase, a simple yet insightful exogenous change. The order rate begins at 1000 refrigerators per week and then, in week 10, rises by 10% (100 refrigerators per week).

---

[2]In practice some factories temporarily run out of inventory and/or deliberately choose to build to order. Such supply bottlenecks are usually modelled by introducing an order backlog in parallel with finished inventory. Retail orders then flow into the backlog. Both inventory and backlog are simultaneously reduced by the shipment rate, which is itself jointly a function of the size of the backlog and finished inventory. This is a classical dynamical representation of supply and demand. A typical formulation for the shipment rate is:

shipment rate = desired shipment rate * effect of inventory on shipments
desired shipment rate = backlog/normal delivery delay
effect of inventory on shipments = GRAPH (adequacy of finished inventory)
adequacy of finished inventory = finished inventory/desired finished inventory

Here the effect of inventory on shipments is a non-linear function that depends on the adequacy of finished inventory. The typical shape of the curve is convex – steep to begin with and then gradually flattening out. If there is no inventory at all then there are no shipments. With a small amount of well-chosen inventory, the factory can fill orders for its high volume products. With plenty of inventory the factory can ship everything it wants to. It is a useful exercise to extend the production and work-force model by adding a backlog and by modifying the shipments formulation along the lines outlined above. Complete formulations of inventory, backlog and constrained shipments are described in working paper D-3244-2 'Structures Causing Instability in Production and Distribution Systems'. The paper can be found in the learning support folder for Chapter 5, inside the subfolder c05 Archive Materials.

Forecasting Shipments – Standard Formulations for Information Smoothing

The formulations for forecasting shipments are shown in Figure 5.11. They are a specific example of standard formulations for 'information smoothing' that occur whenever people in organisations perceive, estimate or formally measure the conditions around them. In this case, factory managers are estimating future demand. We already know the factory regards past shipments as a reliable guide to future demand, but how is this idea expressed algebraically? At the heart of the formulations is a stock accumulation called the 'average ship rate' and a procedure for updating it. The average ship rate at time t (the current estimate of demand) depends on the average ship rate at time t-dt, modified or updated by the 'change in average ship rate' over the interval dt. The size of the update depends on the gap between the shipment rate and the average ship rate, divided by the 'time to average ship rate'. What does this really mean? The gap signifies change. The bigger the gap, the more demand has changed relative to its past average, and so the greater the scope for updating the forecast. But the speed of update is also important.

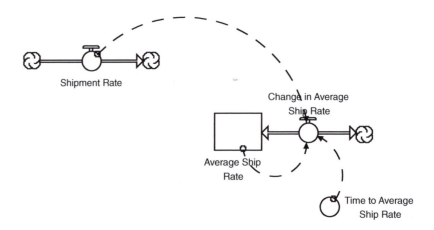

Average Ship Rate (t) = Average Ship Rate (t-dt) +
    Change in Average Ship Rate * dt
INIT Average Ship Rate = 1000 {refrigerators / week}
Change in Average Ship Rate = (Shipment Rate – Average Ship Rate) /
    Time to Average Ship Rate {refrigerators / week / week}
Time to Average Ship Rate = 8 {weeks}

Figure 5.11   Forecasting shipments through information smoothing

A large gap may just be a temporary blip and so factory managers may not want to fully adjust their estimate of demand. This wait-and-see idea is captured by the 'time to average ship rate'. If the averaging time is short then the update is swift, and if the averaging time is long the update is gradual. In this particular case, the averaging time is set at eight weeks. Computationally the average ship rate is updated by an amount per week equal to one-eighth of whatever gap exists between the shipment rate and the average ship rate.

Conceptually this means the factory forecast ignores short-term blips in demand but takes full account of systematic changes that persist over several months. The formulation is subtle and remarkably general. It can represent the natural smoothing that takes place in any process of monitoring or measurement (for example, in a thermometer used to measure air temperature where there is a noticeable delay in the reading if the thermometer is moved outside on a frosty day). Equally, the formulation can represent psychological smoothing that people apply to unfolding events (Makridakis, Chatfield, Hibon *et al.*, 1993). We tend to give most weight to recent events still vivid in memory and less to those in the distant past. Technically, the formulation corresponds exactly to so-called 'exponential averaging', where the average is computed from the sum of past observations, giving most weight to recent observations and progressively less to older ones, with a weighting pattern that decays exponentially (for a proof of this weighting pattern, see Forrester (1961), appendix E on smoothing of information and Sterman (2000), Chapter 11, section 11.3 on information delays).

Inventory Control – Standard Formulations for Asset Stock Adjustment

The equations for inventory control are shown in Figure 5.12. Here is another standard and classic collection of formulations. They can be used when modelling any kind of purposive, goal-directed behaviour in organisations. At the heart of these formulations is a vital distinction between the actual condition of an organisational asset and the desired condition. These two conditions can exist side-by-side and need not be the same. In practice, they differ most of the time and whenever they differ there is pressure for corrective action. In this case, the control or management of refrigerator inventory is of central interest. Factory managers know how much inventory they would like to be holding (the desired inventory) and can measure how much is currently in the factory (refrigerator inventory). A gap calls for corrective action, either cutting production to eliminate a surplus or increasing production to remedy a shortfall. The correction for inventory depends on the difference between desired inventory and refrigerator inventory. That much is intuitively obvious, but the inventory gap alone does not say how much production should change in response.

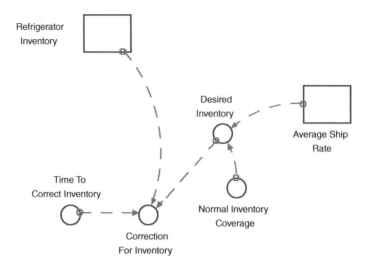

Correction for Inventory = (Desired Inventory − Refrigerator Inventory) /
Time to Correct Inventory {refrigerators / week}
Desired Inventory = Average Ship Rate *
Normal Inventory Coverage {refrigerators}
Time to Correct Inventory = 8 {weeks}
Normal Inventory Coverage = 4 {weeks}

Figure 5.12   Equations for inventory control

If the factory finds itself 2000 refrigerators short, it could (in principle) schedule all 2000 units for production in one week or it could build 200 per week for 10 weeks, or it could even ignore the gap entirely. This managerial sense of urgency is captured in the parameter 'time to correct inventory', which is set at a moderate value of eight weeks. The correction for inventory is equal to the inventory gap divided by the time to correct inventory. Desired inventory is formulated as the product of the average ship rate and normal inventory coverage. The coverage is set at four weeks consistent with the factory's rule of thumb to avoid 'stockouts'. Notice that the dimensions of all the equations balance properly.

Desired Production

Desired production is formulated as the sum of the average ship rate and correction for inventory. The two main pressures on production combine as shown in Figure 5.13. Not surprisingly, factory managers anchor their production plan to the average ship rate, which is their estimate or forecast of demand. They also adjust the plan to take account of any surplus or shortage of refrigerators signalled by inventory control.

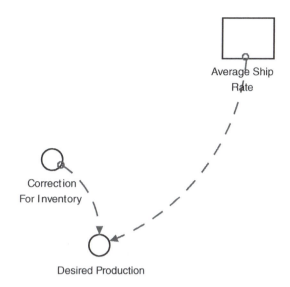

Desired Production = Average Ship Rate +
Correction for Inventory *{refrigerators / week}*

Figure 5.13   Desired production

The Computations Behind Simulation

So far, we have described the formulations for production control. Before moving on to consider the workforce, I will use the existing small algebraic model to demonstrate the computations that take place behind the scenes of any simulator. The model is the same one that generated simulations of the ideal flexible factory earlier in the chapter, which, as we saw, easily copes with an unexpected surge in orders. Nevertheless, there are some interesting dynamics associated with the depletion and rebuilding of inventory and the amplification of production. It is the computation of these dynamics I will now demonstrate.

At the start of any simulation, the initial values of all the stock variables are known. Collectively they determine the state of the system in much the same way that the levels of fuel, oil, coolant, screen wash and brake fluid tell you something about the state of your car. These stocks are connected to their inflows and outflows through the model's feedback loops. So, knowing the initial values, it is possible to work out the changes that will inevitably occur in the stocks during the coming interval of time. The stocks are updated according to their prescribed inflows and outflows to yield a new state of the system at the next point in time. By stepping through time (finely sliced) and repeating these calculations over and over again, the trajectories of the model's variables are made apparent.

Refrigerator Inventory (t) = Refrigerator Inventory (t-dt) +
(Production Rate − Shipment Rate) * dt

Initial Refrigerator Inventory = 4 000 *{Refrigerators}*

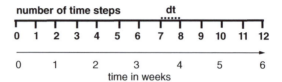

Stocks or levels are assigned initial values at time 0, and are then updated according to the inflow and outflow rates over the coming interval or time step dt

Rates of change for the coming time step (dt) depend on the value of stocks and converters (auxiliaries) at the end of the current period

Converters (auxiliaries) depend on stocks and other auxiliaries according to the relationships described in the information network

Figure 5.14   The computation process and time slicing

To illustrate the procedure, consider refrigerator inventory in the production control model as shown in Figure 5.14. The equation at the top of the diagram is the standard equation for stock accumulation that shows how refrigerator inventory is updated from one point in time (t-dt) to the next (t) according to the inflows and outflows over the interval dt between t-dt and t. Notice there are 4000 refrigerators at time zero to prime the calculation engine. In a larger model, it is necessary to provide initial values for every single stock. Time is sliced into tiny intervals of dt. This demarcation is a purely technical and computational artefact that overlays the time units in which the model is developed. In the production model, factory time is in weeks and dt is set to half a week, small enough to ensure numerical accuracy of the simulation.[3] The calculation proceeds in three stages. The stock is assigned its initial value of 4000 at the start of the simulation and then updated according to the inflow of production and the outflow of shipments over the coming interval or time step dt. Rates of change for the coming time step depend on the value of stocks and converters (also known as auxiliaries) at the end of the current period. In this case, the production rate is equal to the desired production rate and the shipment rate is equal to the retail order rate. Converters (auxiliaries) themselves depend on stocks and other auxiliaries according to the relationships described in the information feedback network. (Note that the meaning of the term 'auxiliary' is computational – it refers to variables that are auxiliary to the calculation of flow rates.) Such mutual dependence is a natural

---

[3]As a rule of thumb, dt should be no more than one-quarter of the shortest time constant in the model. In the production control model, dt is half a week and there are two time constants (time to average ship rate and time to correct inventory) both of eight weeks. So dt is one-sixteenth of the smallest time constant, comfortably within the rule.

consequence of feedback. The one exception is when a variable is assumed to be exogenous (not in a feedback loop) – such as the retail order rate.

Time (Week)	Refrigerator Inventory	Production Rate	Shipment Rate
0	4 000	1 000	1 000
1	4 000	1 000	1 000
2	4 000	1 000	1 000
3	4 000	1 000	1 000
⋮			
10	4 000	1 000	1 100
11	3 900	1 031.25	1 100
12	3 831	1 056	1 100
13	3 788	1 076	1 100
14	3 764	1 092	1 100
15	3 755	1 104	1 100

Handwritten annotations to the right of the table:
4000+1000 − 1100 = 3900
3900 + 1031 − 1100 = 3831
3831 + 1056 − 1100 = 3787
3787 + 1076 − 1100 = 3763
3763 + 1092 − 1100 = 3755
3755 + 1104 − 1100 = 3759

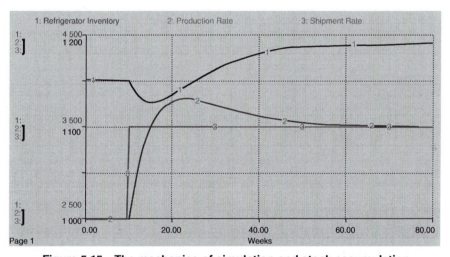

Figure 5.15   The mechanics of simulation and stock accumulation

Now we re-simulate the production control model to see the calculations step by step. Figure 5.15 contains a table of numerical values for refrigerator inventory, production rate and shipment rate over the period zero to 15 weeks. There is also a small time chart that shows the resulting trajectories all the way to week 80 (note this is only half the duration of the original simulation, so the trajectories appear stretched). Refrigerator inventory starts at 4000 and remains in equilibrium with the production rate exactly equal to the shipment rate of 1000 refrigerators per week. In week 10, shipment rate rises to 1100 mimicking the exogenous one-time increase in the retail order rate. The table shows the numerical consequences of this uplift in demand. The production rate builds slowly from a value of 1000, reaching 1104 by week 15. These particular week-by-week numbers are dictated by desired production whose computation is shown in the next figure. For five weeks, the refrigerator inventory falls because shipments exceed production.

$$\frac{4094 - 3831}{8} = 33$$

			*4	$(di_t - ri_t)/8$	$asr_t + ci_t$
Time (Week)	Shipment Rate	Average Ship Rate	Desired Inventory	Correction for Inventory	Desired Production
10	1 100	1 000 (4)=	4 000	0	1 000
11	1 100	1 012.5 (4)=	4 050	18.75	1 031.25
12	1 100	1 023.44 (4)=	4 093.75	32.8125	1 056.25
13	1 100	1 033.01 (4)=	4 132.03	43.0664	1 076.07
14	1 100	1 041.38 (4)=	4 165.53	50.2441	1 091.63
15	1 100	1 048.71 (4)	4 194.84	54.9545	1 103.66

Note sequence of computations

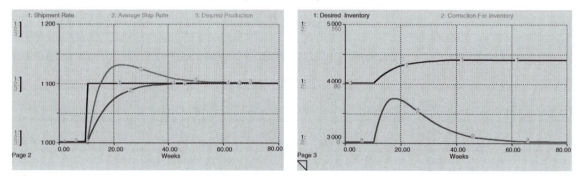

Figure 5.16   Computations in the information network

Meanwhile, the computations within the information network are proceeding as shown in Figure 5.16. Here the focus is on weeks 10–15. During this five-week interval, the shipment rate (2nd column) remains steady at 1100 refrigerators per week, in line with demand. The remaining columns show the numbers behind desired production. The average ship rate (3rd column) increases from 1000 to 1048.71 refrigerators per week, which is simply the numerical consequence of the assumed exponential smoothing. (Incidentally, simulators often display numbers with an unnecessary degree of precision and it is up to the modeller to interpret them appropriately. In this case, we are seeing the result of judgemental forecasting and it is best to round to the nearest whole number of refrigerators. The same common sense applies to the interpretation of numbers in the other columns and so I will report whole numbers.) Desired inventory (4th column) is defined as four times the average ship rate and the numbers reflect this rule of thumb, rising from 4000 to 4195 as factory managers re-appraise demand. The correction for inventory (5th column) is defined as one-eighth of the difference between the desired inventory and the refrigerator inventory. This fragment of algebra is repeated above the table using the abbreviation di_t for desired inventory at time t and ri_t for refrigerator inventory at time t. In week 10, desired inventory is 4000, exactly the same as the refrigerator inventory in week 10 from Figure 5.15. So the correction for inventory is zero. By week 11, desired inventory has risen to 4050 refrigerators while the actual number of refrigerators has fallen to 3900, a gap of 150. This gap calls for an additional 19 (150/8) refrigerators per week. Hence, at the start of week 11, desired production (6th column) is 1031 refrigerators per week: 1012 from the average ship rate (asr_t) and 19 from the correction for inventory (ci_t). It is this computed volume, still far below the shipment rate of 1100, that drives the production rate in week 11. As a result, refrigerator inventory (in Figure 5.15) falls to 3831 by the start of week 12.

The next round of calculations then takes place. In week 12, the shipment rate is 1100 and the average ship rate is 1023. Desired inventory is now 4094 (slightly more than 4*1023 due to rounding) and correction for inventory is 33 refrigerators per week (one-eighth of the difference between 4094 and 3831). Desired production is therefore 1056 refrigerators per week (1023 + 33) and this becomes the volume of production throughout week 13. Production is higher than the previous week, but still lower than the shipment rate of 1100, so inventory falls to 3788. The calculations continue into week 13 with an average ship rate of 1033, desired inventory of 4132, correction for inventory of 43, and desired production of 1076, and so on. By continuing the computations to week 80, the two time charts in Figure 5.16 are created.

So much for computation. Now we can proceed and develop the rest of the model.

Modelling Workforce Management and Factory Production Dynamics

Dialogue About Workforce Management

Figure 5.17 is a stock and flow diagram for workforce management. In this sector, the main policies are workforce planning, hiring and departures. Let's resume the imaginary dialogue between a modeller and factory expert that led to such a picture.

Modeller:	Tell me about workforce management.
Factory expert:	Usually a small committee comes together every week to discuss changes in the workforce. If there is a downturn in the business then normally we let workers go by attrition and don't replace them. If there is an upturn then we need more workers.

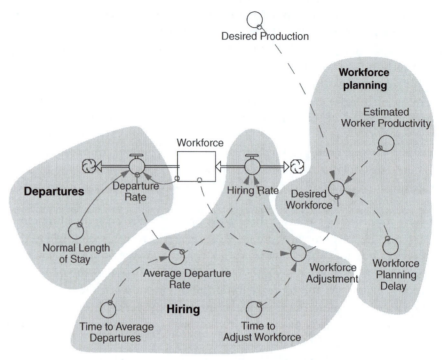

Figure 5.17   Stock and flow diagram for workforce management

Modeller:	How do you decide the number of workers you need in the factory?
Factory expert:	Well that's difficult to pinpoint. We know the weekly build schedule (desired production) and we monitor the productivity of our workers (based on a standard two-shift rota). From those two information sources we can estimate how many workers are needed.
Modeller:	So what happens if you have too many or too few workers?
Factory expert:	If we have too few workers we hire more. It takes time to fill vacancies because we like to honour employment commitments and that makes us fairly cautious about adding new people. If demand is growing we may be temporarily short of workers, which means we can't always produce exactly to plan. If we have too many workers, then we normally reduce the workforce through natural attrition, avoiding forced lay-offs, consistent with our employment commitments.
Modeller:	What causes workers to leave voluntarily?
Factory expert:	All factories experience regular turnover. Unfortunately turnover in this factory is high, partly a regional effect. Our human resource department estimates that workers typically stay for about a year and then move on. Of course, some people have been with us for much longer.

Modeller (on the next day, having created the stock and flow diagram in Figure 5.17):

Here is a picture based on our discussion. The workforce is increased by the hiring rate and reduced by the departure rate. Departures are proportional to the size of the workforce. The bigger the workforce the more departures, because the normal length of stay is roughly constant – about one year in this case. The hiring rate depends both on departures and a workforce adjustment. In the special case when demand on the factory is steady, then logically the workforce size is steady too, and the only pressure on hiring is from departures – the need to replace workers who leave. The average departure rate is the factory's estimate of the departure rate, measured over an interval called the 'time to average departures'. The workforce adjustment depends on the gap between the desired workforce and the workforce. Any such gap is corrected gradually over a number of weeks, reflecting the factory's traditional caution about adding new workers. This particular attitude to hiring is captured in the 'time to adjust workforce'. The desired workforce depends on desired production (the weekly build schedule) and estimated worker productivity. Here is an important link between production control and workforce management where the factory's production plans are transformed into a need for workers. This process of workforce planning does not happen instantaneously. There is a workforce planning delay to represent the administrative time it takes to reach agreement on the desired workforce.

Operating Constraint Linking Workforce to Production

To complete the visual model we need to reconsider how the production rate itself is determined. In our 'ideal' factory, we made the convenient simplifying assumption that production is always equal to desired production, but in reality production depends on workers, parts and machines. There needs to be enough of each. In principle, all these 'factors of production' can be modelled, but here we limit ourselves to just one realistic constraint, the effect of workers, and implicitly assume that the necessary parts and machines are always available. The relationship between workforce and production is shown in Figure 5.18. The production rate depends on the size of the workforce and on worker productivity. Notice that these two links are hardwired. They are practical operating constraints, not information flows. The bigger the workforce, the more production is possible, and vice versa. Worker productivity, in terms of output per worker per week, is important too. All else equal, high productivity boosts production and low productivity reduces it.

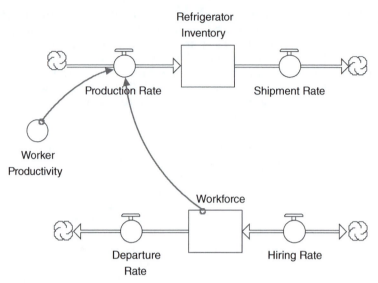

Figure 5.18   Operating constraint linking workforce to production

Simulation of the Complete Model: A Surprise Demand Increase in a Factory Where Production is Constrained by the Size of the Workforce

To investigate the dynamics of the complete model we again introduce a surprise increase in demand. Open the file called 'Production and Workforce' in the learning support folder for Chapter 5. You will see a diagram of the complete factory model. Press the 'Run' button on the left and watch the movement of the stocks and converter dials as the simulation progresses. Then open graph 1 on the right-hand side of the production control sector by double selecting the icon labelled 'Graph 1 for step, random and ramp'. The simulated trajectories are the same as shown in the top half of Figure 5.19. Press the 'page' tab in the lower left of the time chart to reveal page 2 of the graph pad, which shows simulated trajectories in the bottom half of Figure 5.19.

Once again the retail order rate (line 1, top chart) increases by 100 refrigerators per week in week 10. Now, however, factory production is constrained by the size of the workforce. As a result, the production rate (line 4) rises slowly. In fact, there is virtually no change in production in the four weeks immediately after the hike in orders. However, the factory still ships to order and, since production remains low, the only way to fill the extra orders in the short term is to deplete inventory. The refrigerator inventory (line 1, bottom chart) plunges to 3000 by week 24 and here is where the coordination problems for the factory begin. The steady decline of inventory

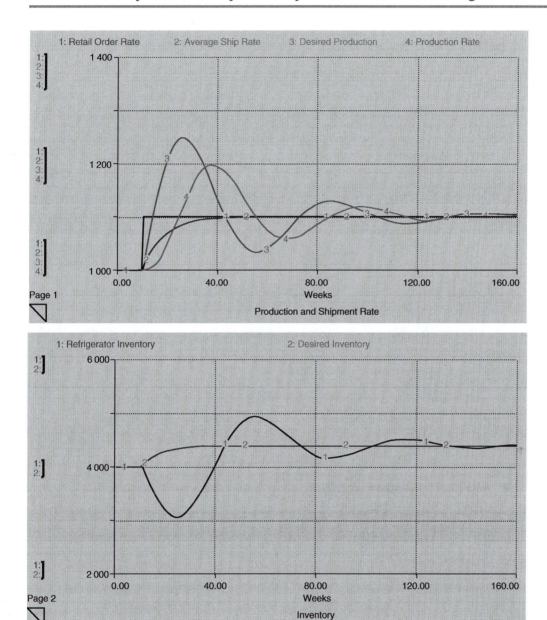

Figure 5.19   Simulation of an unexpected 10 per cent increase in demand.

over a period of 14 weeks creates enormous pressure from inventory control to boost production. This pressure is most clearly visible in desired production (line 3, upper chart) that soars to almost 1250 by week 26, a planned increase of 250 refrigerators per week against an increase in demand of only 100. The knock-on consequences are serious, because desired production is the signal that guides workforce planning.

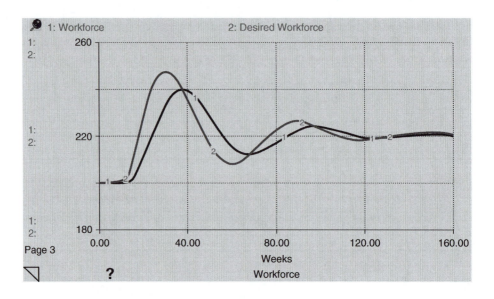

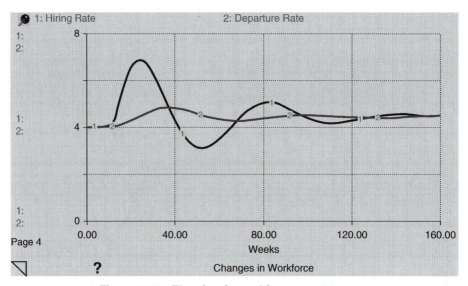

Figure 5.20   The view in workforce management

Figure 5.20 shows simulated trajectories in workforce management (which can be found on pages 3 and 4 of the graph pad). To begin with, workforce (line 1, top chart) is equal to desired workforce (line 2, top chart) and the factory has just the right number of workers (200) to produce the required 1000 refrigerators per week. After the hike in orders, the desired workforce rises in response to desired production, reaching a peak of almost 250 workers in week 30, an increase of 40%. The hiring rate (line 1, bottom chart) increases to fill the gap, but not all at once because factory managers are cautious in their approach to hiring. Hence, the workforce rises only gradually. As a result there is a sustained shortage of workers and it is this shortage that curtails production and then feeds back through inventory control to amplify desired production and desired workforce. Here we see in action a balancing loop with delay, creating havoc with factory planning and coordination.[4]

How does the confusion resolve itself? To investigate return to the production control variables in Figure 5.19 and review the situation in week 24. By this point in time the production rate (line 4) has finally caught up with the retail order rate (line 1). As a result, the refrigerator inventory stabilises and so too does desired production. However, there is still a need to rebuild inventory, a task that justifies the growing workforce. By week 42, refrigerator inventory is back on target and desired production is equal to demand, but now the consequences of past hiring come back to haunt the factory. The workforce is still near its peak and production is much higher than orders and shipments. Inventory therefore continues to grow, beyond desired inventory. The resulting excess inventory puts downward pressure on desired production and desired labour leading eventually to a reduction in the workforce and production. By week 72, inventory is back in line with desired inventory, but now the production rate is too low because the workforce has been allowed to shrink too much (through departures). However, the factory is gradually getting closer to matching production and shipments, while at the same time bringing inventory and the workforce in line with their targets. Another round of adjustments in the interval between weeks 70 and 130 brings the factory into long-term equilibrium. The simulation shows that equilibrium is hard to achieve, even in the seemingly easy case where demand increases permanently in a one-time step. In the face of a more variable demand pattern, the factory may never achieve the right balance and find itself locked in a syndrome of production and employment instability similar to the problem experienced by the real refrigerator manufacturer on which this example is based.[5]

[4]Throughout the book I demonstrate methods and principles for clear interpretation of time charts and careful design of simulation experiments to reveal sources of dysfunctional dynamics. This rigorous (yet non-technical) style of simulation analysis is a distinctive and important part of the core discipline of system dynamics. Readers who wish to see an early example of rigorous simulation analysis are referred to working paper D-2045-2 Understanding Oscillations in Simple Systems (Mass and Senge, 1975). The authors present a specially simplified version of the factory model that exhibits perfect undamped sinusoidal oscillations. The paper can be found in the learning support folder for Chapter 5, inside the subfolder c05 Archive Materials.

[5]The cycles in the factory model are slightly shorter than the two-year periodicity we set out to explain. It is a useful exercise to identify the parameters that determine periodicity and to adjust them for a better fit.

Pause for Reflection

This chapter has shown the typical steps in going from problem articulation to a feedback representation and simulation model. Most models start from a dynamic issue in terms of performance over time that is puzzling, dysfunctional, unintended or maybe just difficult to foresee. The modelling process is creative and iterative. The modeller begins with a hunch about which feedback loops are capable of generating the dynamics of interest. The hunch is underpinned by a philosophical view that dynamic behaviour arises endogenously from feedback structure rather than from external and uncontrollable events. The search for feedback loops then begins in earnest and can progress along a variety of different paths as outlined in Figure 5.3.

The factory dynamics model began as a sector map, which was then developed into a stock and flow diagram – a very common path in my experience. Sector maps show the main interlocking subsystems or functional areas in which feedback loops are to be found. They also convey a clear impression of the model boundary and assumed level of aggregation. Inside sectors are operating policies that guide asset stock accumulation. The operating policies depict decision-making processes and the information flows on which they depend. Feedback loops emerge by stitching together stock accumulations, operating policies, information flows and other practical operating constraints.

The factory model contained policies for forecasting, inventory control, production scheduling, workforce planning, hiring and departures, as well as a production function depicting the operating constraint of workforce on production. These six policies and single production function jointly guide the accumulation of workforce and finished inventory. At the heart of this coordinating network lies a powerful balancing loop with delay. Simulations of the factory model (in response to a one-time increase in demand) show cyclicality in production and workforce broadly consistent with the problem encountered by the real factory. By probing the way factories manage production we have found a credible feedback structure that offers an explanation of the instability phenomenon. We have transformed our vague dynamic hunch into a well-defined dynamic hypothesis and behavioural theory of factory performance.

Equation Formulations in Workforce Management

We begin with the workforce equation, which is formulated as an asset stock accumulation. In Figure 5.21, the workforce at time t is equal to the workforce at time t-dt plus the difference between the hiring rate and the departure rate over the interval dt. The initial workforce is 200 workers, deliberately chosen so that the factory starts in a perfect supply–demand equilibrium with production equal to shipments of 1000 refrigerators per month. This equilibrium number of workers is obtained by dividing demand of 1000 by worker productivity of five refrigerators per worker per week. The hiring rate is the sum of the average departure rate and workforce adjustment, a formulation we will return to later in the equations for hiring.

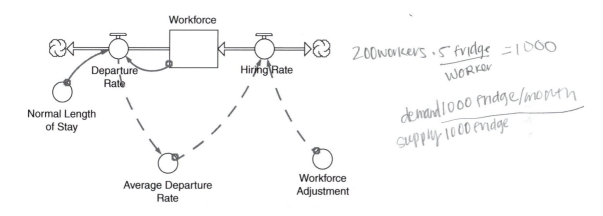

200 workers · 5 fridge = 1000
worker

demand 1000 fridge/month
supply 1000 fridge

Workforce(t) = Workforce(t-dt) + (Hiring Rate – Departure Rate) * dt
INIT Workforce = 200 *{workers}*
Hiring Rate = Average Departure Rate + Workforce Adjustment *{workers/week}*
Departure Rate = Workforce/Normal Length of Stay *{workers/week}* *=> 200/50 = 4 workers/week*
Normal Length of Stay = 50 *{weeks}*

Figure 5.21   Equations for workforce and departure rate

Departure Rate – Standard Formulation for Stock Depletion

The departure rate depends on the ratio of workforce to normal length of stay. Intuitively, the ratio makes sense. The more workers employed in a factory the more of them are likely to leave in a given period of time simply as a result of normal turnover. On the other hand, the longer the normal length of stay, the fewer workers will leave in a given period. Here we assume that the normal length of stay is 50 weeks, so with an initial workforce of 200 workers the departure rate is 200/50, four workers per week. Notice that the dimensions of the equation balance properly. By dividing the number of workers by the normal length of stay in weeks, the resulting departure rate is correctly expressed in workers per week.

The algebra of departures is a specific example of a standard formulation for stock depletion. In many (though not all) practical situations, the outflow from a stock accumulation is proportional to the size of the stock. A familiar example is the outflow of water from a bathtub, which is proportional to the depth of the remaining water. An industry example is the national or regional scrap rate of cars, which is proportional to the total number of cars on the road. The proportion is determined by the normal lifetime of a car, so the scrap rate is equal to the number of cars divided by the normal lifetime. Stock depletion can of course be more complex and depend on conditions other than the 'local' stock itself.[6] Nevertheless simple proportional loss is often a good first approximation.

Hiring – Standard Formulations for Asset Stock Replacement and Adjustment

Factory hiring (see Figure 5.22) includes the replacement of those workers who leave plus adjustments to the workforce size deemed necessary as a result of planned changes in production. These typical pressures on hiring are captured with standard formulations for asset stock replacement and adjustment. The hiring rate is equal to the average departure rate plus the workforce adjustment. First, we will investigate the effect of departures on hiring. A factory producing at a constant rate needs a stable number of workers, which can be achieved by hiring new workers at the same rate existing workers leave. Replacement is a kind of benchmark or anchor for hiring and the simplest equation would set the hiring rate equal to the departure rate. However, in practice, the departure rate takes some time to measure and factory managers may prefer to wait and see how many workers leave in a given period rather than activate hiring for each individual departure. This need for assessment suggests an information smoothing formulation. Hence, the hiring rate depends in part on the average departure rate, which is the actual departure rate smoothed over a period called 'the time to average departures' – four weeks in this case. The precise formulation is written as: Average Departure Rate = SMTH1 (Departure Rate, Time to Average Departures) {workers/week}. SMTH1 is just a convenient shorthand

---

[6]The quit rate of employees (or departures) might, for example, depend on relative pay. So then the standard depletion formulation could be modified as follows:

Departure Rate = Workforce/Length of Stay
Length of Stay = Normal Length of Stay ∗ Effect of Relative Pay

This new effect could be formulated as an increasing function of relative pay that takes a neutral value of one when relative pay itself is one (i.e. when there is pay parity).

for the standard information smoothing formulation first introduced in production control (Figure 5.11). This so-called 'built-in' function replicates the stock accumulation process at the heart of smoothing without the need for the modeller to create all the symbols. The function is called SMTH1 because there is just one stock accumulation in the underlying structure. (More complex smoothing and estimation procedures can involve two or three stock accumulations in series. See Appendix 2 for further details on smoothing, and in particular footnote 15 to which the Appendix refers.)

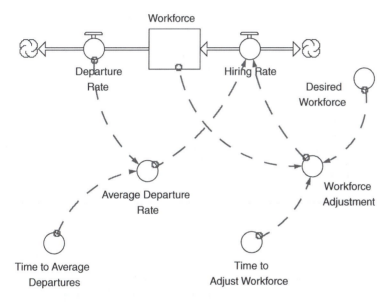

Hiring Rate = Average Departure Rate + Workforce Adjustment *{workers/week}*
Average Departure Rate = SMTH1(Departure Rate, Time to Average Departures)
        {workers/week}
Time to Average Departures = 4 *{weeks}*
Workforce Adjustment = (Desired Workforce – Workforce)/Time to Adjust
        Workforce *{workers/week}*
Time to Adjust Workforce = 8 *{weeks}*

Figure 5.22   Equations for hiring

The workforce adjustment is defined as the difference between desired workforce and workforce, divided by the 'time to adjust workforce'. This equation is a standard asset stock adjustment formulation (just like the correction for inventory in Figure 5.12) representing purposive goal-seeking behaviour – in this case factory managers' efforts to bring the workforce in line with desired workforce. The time to adjust workforce is set at 8 weeks to represent a cautious approach to hiring consistent with factory employment commitments.

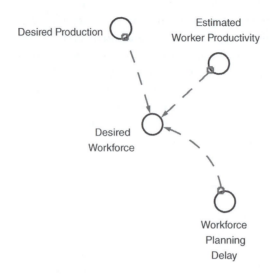

Desired Workforce = SMTH1(Desired Production/Estimated Worker Productivity,
   Workforce Planning Delay) *{workers}*
Desired Production = Average Ship Rate + Correction For Inventory   *{refrigerators/week}*
Estimated Worker Productivity = 5 + STEP(0,10) *{refrigerators/worker/week}*
Workforce Planning Delay = 4 *{weeks}*

Figure 5.23   Equations for workforce planning

Workforce Planning

The equations for workforce planning are shown in Figure 5.23. Desired
workforce is a key formulation, for it is here that factory managers decide how
many workers are needed. The main driver is desired production. The more
refrigerators the factory plans to produce per week, the more workers it
needs. The transformation from desired production into desired workforce,
however, is itself a decision-making process, requiring both time and
judgement. The formulation recognises the administrative nature of this
connection between production control and workforce. There is information
smoothing because it takes time for people to monitor the relevant
information and reach a decision on desired workforce. Judgement is involved
because worker productivity is not necessarily known objectively. Instead
there is estimated worker productivity. Currently, the estimate is set at five
refrigerators per worker per week, the same as actual productivity, but in
principle and in practice the estimated and actual productivity can differ, with
important implications for factory performance.[7] To summarise, the overall

---

[7]Consider the effect on factory output and production dynamics if the estimated worker productivity
is higher than the actual worker productivity. In other words factory managers think workers are
(or should be) capable of producing more refrigerators per week than they actually do. So, for

formulation says that desired workforce is the ratio of desired production to estimated worker productivity, smoothed over a period of time called the 'workforce planning delay'. Smoothing is achieved once again by using the SMTH1 function, with the planning delay set at four weeks.

Desired workforce brings us to the end of the workforce sector formulations. In the rest of the chapter, we continue our simulation analysis with scenarios and what-ifs typical of the kind of work conducted in phase 2 of a modelling project.

Chronic Cyclicality in Employment and Production and How to Cure It

The Curious Effect of Random Variations in Demand

Return to the model called 'Production and Workforce'. Open the icon for the retail order rate at the top of the production control sector. You will see the following equation:

$$\text{Retail Order Rate} = 1000 * \text{NORMAL}(1,0) + \text{STEP}(100,10)$$
$$+ \text{RAMP}(0,10) \ \{\text{refrigerators/week}\}$$

This is a versatile formulation for the exogenous retail order rate that allows a variety of different demand assumptions to be tested. We have already seen in Figures 5.19 and 5.20 the simulated effects of a one-time unexpected increase in demand from 1000 to 1100 refrigerators per month. This step change led to fluctuations in production and employment reminiscent of cyclicality experienced in the real factory, except that the fluctuations gradually subsided.

---

any given desired production, the desired workforce is too low. It is a good exercise to simulate the consequences of this bias using a scenario where the retail order rate is held constant at 1000 units per week, and workforce is initialised at 200 workers (the equilibrium workforce). You can run this thought experiment using the production and workforce model. Open the icon for the 'estimated worker productivity' and insert the value '1' in the step function to create a situation in which estimated productivity rises from 5 to 6 refrigerators per worker per week in week 10 (a 20% overestimate). Also, make sure to set the step change in retail order rate to zero in order to create a steady demand pattern. It turns out that when estimated productivity rises, the production rate falls at first as expected. Then it recovers and even overshoots the retail order rate. Eventually, in a diminishing cycle, the factory settles into a new equilibrium of supply and demand. This automatic re-alignment of production is a good example of error correcting by a balancing feedback loop. Factory managers do not need to know the exact real value of worker productivity in order to hire the right number of workers. If they overestimate productivity then finished inventory will be below desired and the resulting correction for inventory will create pressure to hire more workers, thereby compensating for the mis-estimation of productivity.

To inject more realism, we repeat the simulation with the addition of randomness in the retail order rate. In the equation for the retail order rate, rewrite NORMAL(1,0) as NORMAL(1,0.05), which means that demand is normally distributed around 1000 with a standard deviation of 0.05 or 5%. Meanwhile, the original step increase in demand still takes place in week 10.

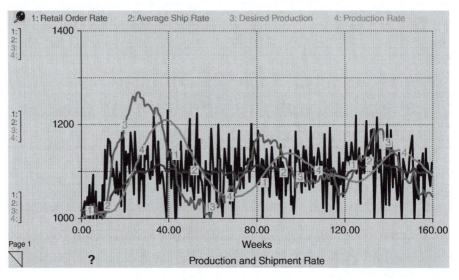

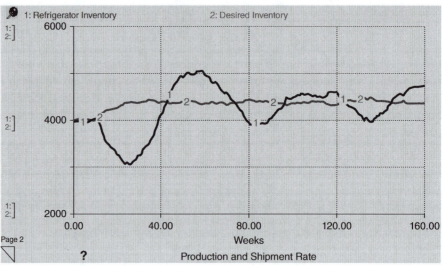

The view in production control

Figure 5.24   Simulation of a ten percent increase in demand and five percent random variation.

Press the 'Run' button to obtain, in Graph 1, time charts similar to those shown in Figure 5.24. Note there are detail differences between the time charts in the simulator and the book because each time the simulator runs it uses a different sample from the random process that characterises demand. The retail order rate (line 1, top chart) is highly variable from week to week, moving in a range between 1000 and 1200 refrigerators per week. The one-time increase in demand is masked by randomness. Nevertheless, and this is the interesting point, both the desired production rate (line 3) and the production rate (line 4) exhibit clear cyclicality, very similar to the deterministic pattern seen in Figure 5.19. Note, however, that the fluctuation persists throughout the entire 160-week simulation rather than gradually subsiding. Meanwhile, the average ship rate (line 2, top chart) clearly separates the uplift in demand from the random variations, just as one would expect from a process of information smoothing. Refrigerator inventory (line 1, bottom chart) also smoothes out randomness, so the remaining variation is cyclical. What we are seeing here is a vivid illustration of the principle that structure gives rise to dynamic behaviour. Even though retail orders vary randomly, the factory nevertheless finds itself locked into cyclical production and employment. Moreover, this instability will persist indefinitely if there is randomness to provoke it (for a more technical explanation of randomness and cyclicality in information feedback systems see Forrester (1961), appendix F on noise). The structure of asset stocks, flows, operating policies and information means that the factory is prone to chronic cyclicality – entirely consistent with the problem observed in practice. You could say the factory's mystery is solved.

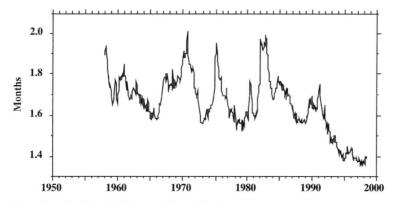

Figure 5.25   Cyclicality in US manufacturing industry
Source: Sterman, J.D., Business Dynamics: Systems Thinking and Modeling for a Complex World,
© 2000, Irwin McGraw-Hill, Boston, MA. Reproduced with permission of the McGraw-Hill Companies.

Industry Cyclicality and Business Cycles

The cyclical dynamics of the factory model are not confined to individual firms. There is evidence that similar processes of inventory control and workforce management are responsible for unwanted cyclicality in entire industries and in the economy as a whole (Mass, 1975). Figure 5.25 shows inventory coverage in US manufacturing industry over a period of 50 years from 1950 to 2000. (The data does not include finished inventories held by retailers and other distributors outside the manufacturing sector.) Coverage is on a scale from 1.3 to 2 months. The trajectory is strongly cyclical with a period of 5–8 years. This erratic pattern is typical of cyclicality in the real world where randomness interacts with feedback structure to cause fluctuations of varying periodicity. It is interesting to note the behaviour between 1990 and 2000 when inventory coverage falls far below its long-term average. Various explanations of this phenomenon are possible. It could be that widespread use of information technology and just-in-time systems enabled firms to operate with less inventory. Another explanation is that 1990–2000 was a period of sustained economic growth, accompanied by chronic inventory shortage.

Cyclicality also occurs in financial services. Figure 5.26 shows the insurance underwriting cycle between 1910 and 2000. Despite profound changes over these 90 years the cycle has been remarkably consistent. Underwriting profits, expressed as a percentage of earned premiums, fluctuate sharply although there are no physical inventories and materials in the supply chain. The detail business processes and procedures that create this cycle obviously differ from those in manufacturing, but somewhere among them are analogies to forecasting, inventory control and workforce planning that create a balancing loop with delay.

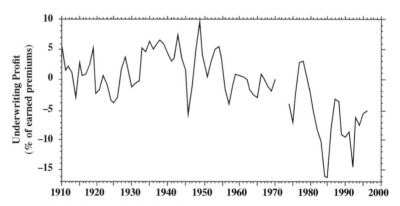

Figure 5.26   Cycles in service industries
Source: Sterman, J.D., *Business Dynamics: Systems Thinking and Modeling for a Complex World*, © 2000, Irwin McGraw-Hill, Boston, MA. Reproduced with permission of the McGraw-Hill Companies.

Policy Formulation and What-ifs to Improve Factory Performance

How might the factory's performance be improved? Such a question is natural at this stage of modelling, and brings us to the topic of policy formulation and what-ifs. What changes to operating policies might alleviate cyclicality? Various ideas come to mind and these ideas can all be tested with simulation. We know that cyclicality arises in the balancing loop that links inventory control, workforce management and production. What if we changed the policy for inventory control, say by halving the normal inventory coverage or doubling the time to correct inventory? What if we made the factory more responsive by slashing the workforce planning delay and trimming the time to adjust the workforce? All these are testable changes within the framework of the model. To illustrate, try doubling the time to correct inventory from eight to 16 weeks. Why this particular change? We know from earlier simulations that the process of rebuilding inventory tends to amplify demand changes, creating a misleading and exaggerated impression of desired production and desired workforce. Hence, if rebuilding were spread over a longer period of time, it may be easier for the factory to plan its workforce.

Figure 5.27 is a simulation of the new, more relaxed, inventory control policy in response to a 10% increase in demand, without randomness. There is a noticeable improvement in the stability of production and inventory by comparison with Figure 5.19. Desired production (line 3, top chart) peaks at 1187 refrigerators per week in week 30 compared with a peak of 1250 in Figure 5.19. Refrigerator inventory (line 1, bottom chart) falls to a minimum of 2838 in week 30, slightly lower than the minimum of 3000 in Figure 5.19. The factory is more willing to tolerate an inventory imbalance and because of this new attitude there is less short-term pressure to rebuild inventory. The knock-on consequence is a more gradual rise in desired production that translates, through the workforce, into more stable production. The production rate (line 4) rises to a peak of 1164 in week 45. There is much less amplification of production relative to retail orders and so the subsequent overbuilding of inventory in the period between weeks 60 and 75 is reduced, enabling the factory to achieve more easily a proper balance of supply, demand, inventory and workforce.

The essence of the policy change is for the factory not to overreact when inventory is too high or too low. Strong inventory control sounds good in principle but leads to unnecessary changes in the workforce that eventually feed back to destabilise production and inventory. Patience is a virtue in situations where corrective action depends on others. The same was true of the imaginary hotel showers in Chapter 4 where two shower-takers try to stay warm while unknowingly sharing hot water. It is better to be patient when there is interdependence. However, if local corrective action is genuinely possible, without delay, then it can pay to act swiftly, just as intuition would suggest. This phenomenon can be seen in the factory model by halving both the workforce planning delay and the time to adjust workforce. For easy comparison, the time to correct inventory is restored to eight weeks.

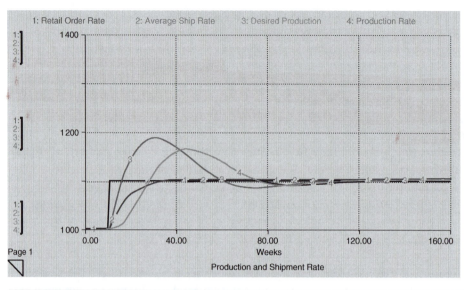

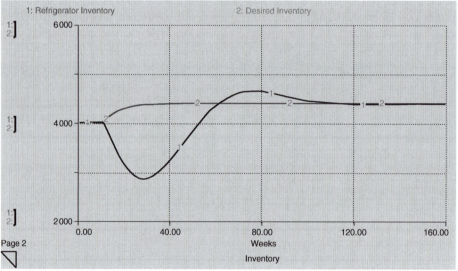

The view in production control

Figure 5.27   Simulation of a 10 per cent increase in demand when the time to correct inventory is doubled from 8 to 16 weeks.

So this is a factory with strong inventory control and a flexible workforce. The simulation is shown in Figure 5.28. The flexible factory avoids unnecessary fluctuations but is also faster to respond than the patient factory. By comparison with Figure 5.27, production (line 4, top chart) builds more quickly and inventory (line 1, bottom chart) falls less in the aftermath of the same uplift in demand. Moreover, the factory achieves equilibrium sooner.

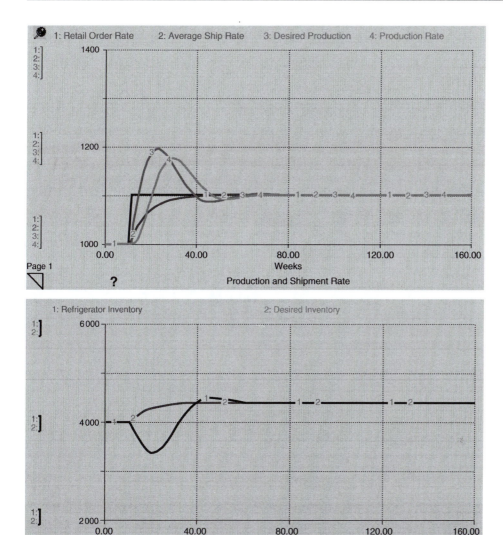

The view in production control

Figure 5.28   Simulation of a 10 per cent increase in demand when the workforce planning delay and time to correct workforce are both halved.

One conclusion is that a flexible factory can outperform another factory that is slow to adjust workforce (or capacity more generally). Perhaps even more important, however, is the observation that a patient factory can perform very well, much better than the base case, without the need for workforce flexibility. Success is achieved by ensuring that decisions in production control take into account the inevitable delays in planning and adjusting the workforce.

Modelling for Learning and Soft Systems

Modelling is not a cookbook procedure – it is fundamentally creative. At the same time, it is a disciplined, scientific and rigorous process that involves observing dynamic phenomena in the real world, surfacing and testing assumptions, gathering data and revising the model to improve understanding. In the absence of strategic modelling, people run business and society, with varied degrees of success, relying on judgement, experience and gut feel. The outer layer of Figure 5.29 shows this normal trial-and-error approach. Based on their mental models of organisations and industries, people devise strategy, structure and decision rules. They take strategic decisions (requiring organisational experiments) whose full implications are never clear at the outset. Then they observe what happens in the real world.

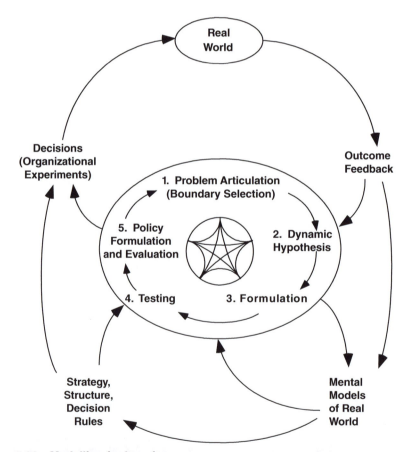

Figure 5.29   Modelling for learning

Source: Sterman, J.D., *Business Dynamics: Systems Thinking and Modeling for a Complex World,* © 2000, Irwin McGraw-Hill, Boston, MA. Reproduced with permission of the McGraw-Hill Companies.

The learning cycle is complete when people adjust their mental models on the basis of outcome feedback, in other words by comparing what was achieved with what was intended. The model building process described in this chapter complements the normal but fallible learning cycle. Modelling helps people to share, clarify and improve their mental models. It also enables them to test and refine strategic decisions and organisational experiments through simulation (before trying them out in the real world). The overall process we call 'Modelling for Learning' (Morecroft and Sterman, 1994).

A Second Pause for Reflection: System Dynamics and Soft Systems

Mention of the term 'learning' brings me to a philosophical point about models and modelling of social systems. To what extent should models represent something tangible 'out there' in the real world as opposed to perceptions in the minds of those who must take action in the real world? The distinction may seem of academic interest only, but it is of practical importance to all modellers – important enough that a group of academics and practitioners, funded by the UK Engineering and Physical Sciences Research Council (EPSRC), was convened to discuss the whole topic of hard and soft models (Pidd, 2004).[8] The group included representatives from Shell International, BT Exact Technologies, the UK Defence Science and Technology Laboratory (Dstl), the UK Inland Revenue and several academic institutions.[9] A useful picture to stimulate the group's discussion is shown in Figure 5.30 (Checkland, 2004). Here, a distinction is drawn between two approaches to business and social modelling. At the top is the approach of the 'hard' modeller, who observes systems in the real world that can be engineered and made to work better. Below is the approach of the 'soft' modeller, who observes complexity and confusion in the real world, but can organise exploration of it as a learning system. There is a big step from the hard outlook to the soft outlook.

Where does system dynamics fit in this scheme (Lane, 1994)? Many people automatically assume that because the approach involves equations and simulations it must therefore be a type of hard system modelling.

---

[8]The group called itself the 'Interdisciplinary Network on Complementarity in Systems Modelling' (INCISM) and its main interest was the combined use of hard and soft approaches in systems modelling.

[9]The academic institutions involved in the INCISM network were Lancaster University, Department of Management Science; the University of Strathclyde, Department of Management Science; Cranfield University/Royal Military College of Science; London Business School and the Open University.

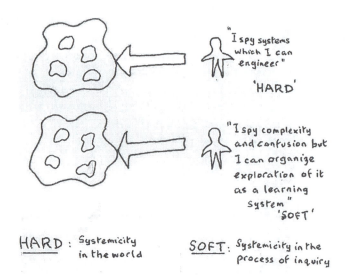

Figure 5.30 Two approaches to business and social modelling
Source: Checkland, P. (2004) Proceedings of the 2004 International System Dynamics Conference, Oxford, specially re-drawn by Peter Checkland in February 2015.

Equally, other people assume that soft or qualitative modelling, involving diagrams and words alone, is vague and woolly, lacking in discipline. These stereotypes are misleading. More important is whether problematical situations in business and society are thought to arise from a system in the real world or from multiple interacting perceptions of 'reality' in the minds of stakeholders. I will explore this abstract territory here as it relates to the practice of system dynamics, drawing on the factory model to illustrate my arguments. What could be more tangible in the business world than a factory?

Advice frequently given to beginning modellers in system dynamics is *not* to model the system. Setting out to replicate reality is considered to be a futile exercise that prevents people from exercising judgement about what to include and what to exclude from the model. So, to use the terminology of Figure 5.30, system dynamics modellers do not spy systems. Rather they spy dynamics in the real world and they organise modelling as a learning process, with the project team, to discover the feedback structure that lies behind the dynamics. Figure 5.31 is a reminder of this process from the factory model. We began with puzzling and undesirable cyclicality in factory production and employment. This phenomenon in the real world suggested to the modeller that, somewhere in the complexity and confusion of factory operations, there is a balancing loop with delay, which is capable of explaining the observed cyclicality. The search was then on for such a balancing loop – a search conducted in close consultation with factory managers to understand how they go about planning and coordinating production and workforce.

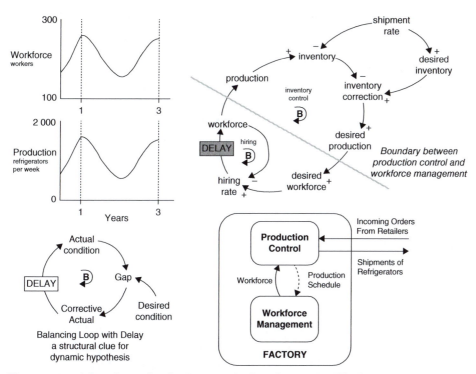

Figure 5.31   I Spy dynamics in the complexity of everyday life (factory operations in this case) and can discover underlying feedback structure

This investigation probed many aspects of manufacturing operations and policy from forecasting and inventory control to production scheduling and workforce hiring, and uncovered the feedback loops shown in the top right of Figure 5.31 (which summarise the main closed-loop connections in Figures 5.8, 5.17 and 5.18). There are two interacting balancing loops, one for hiring (that ensures there are enough workers) and the other for inventory control (that ensures there is enough finished inventory – neither too much nor too little). Crucially the inventory control loop is a balancing loop with delay, where the delay arises in adjusting the size of the workforce. This loop is mainly responsible for the observed cyclicality in production and employment.

The factory model is one particular case, but it is representative of broader practice. In system dynamics we take the view that, behind every dynamical problem, there is an enduring feedback structure waiting to be discovered. The structure may be well-hidden in the flux of everyday life, but nevertheless it is there and can be teased out in the ways illustrated with the factory model. The end result is a hard system model in the sense that the loops identified (in this case two balancing loops) are presumed to be there in the real world, stemming from much simplified, but nevertheless realistic, aspects of operations and policy. System dynamics delivers hard system models from a soft and interpretive modelling process (Lane, 2000).

Where in these models are the multiple interacting perceptions of reality that are the hallmark of soft systems? Such perceptions are to be found in the contrast between a whole system or global view (comprising several sectors and interlocking feedback loops) and a local view (comprising a single sector and just a few causal links).[10] Feedback loops that are responsible for puzzling dynamics nearly always weave their way across organisational boundaries (Wolstenholme, 1993). Consider the troublesome inventory control loop in the factory model that crosses the boundary between production control and workforce management. For that very reason, the loop is invisible at the functional level. A system dynamics project invariably expands the boundary of people's thinking, requiring them to see beyond the narrow confines of a single function or department to take proper account of organisational interdependencies. This broader view challenges narrow, departmental perspectives and helps to remedy the problems that arise from such myopia. For example, the factory model makes clear that the production department is not fully in control of its own destiny, no matter how much it would like to be. Production is not the same as desired production. If it were, then the two concepts would be directly connected in Figure 5.31 and the factory's feedback structure would reduce to a simple balancing loop without a delay and without cyclicality (as the simulations of an 'ideal' factory in Figure 5.9 showed).

The reality is that more production requires more workers and vice versa. If people in the production department (wishing to be responsive to demand) think the factory has the freedom to boost or cut production on the spur of the moment then the factory's cyclicality problems will persist. The volatile schedule resulting from this desire for responsiveness ripples into workforce planning and eventually feeds back to production. A feedback systems view makes the production and workforce planning departments aware of their mutual dependence and its knock-on consequences.

A Link to Soft Systems Methodology

A model that raises people's awareness of interdependence (by requiring them to 'think outside the box') is a particular example of a more general learning activity that takes place when using Soft Systems Methodology (SSM), as shown in Figure 5.32 (Checkland, 2004; Checkland and Poulter, 2006).

---

[10]For more examples of the contrast between global and local perspectives, see the causal loop diagram about road congestion in Chapter 2, and the many causal loop diagrams based on practical situations in Coyle (1996), Senge (1990), Sherwood (2002) and Wolstenholme (1990).

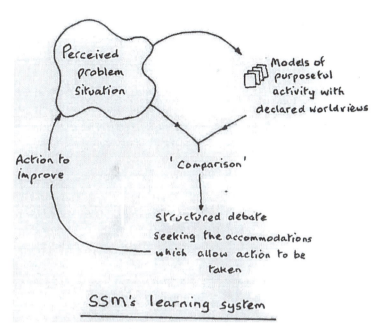

Figure 5.32   The learning system in soft systems methodology involves a comparison of alternative models of purposeful activity
Source: Checkland, P. (2004) Proceedings of the 2004 International System Dynamics Conference, Oxford, specially re-drawn by Peter Checkland in February 2015.

Underpinning this picture is the recognition that all problematical situations contain people who are trying to act purposefully or with intention. In any human organisation, many intentions are in play simultaneously and it is the interaction of these intentions that generates both progress and problems. Here, a perceived problem situation is deconstructed into alternative models of 'purposeful activity' within a declared worldview. These models are not necessarily descriptions of the world as it is, with its current real-world actions. The models are in people's minds and reflect an ideal or desired world consistent with a declared worldview, which may or may not correspond to hard reality. For example, as Checkland (2004) explains, a 'prison' can have a set of relevant models: it can be modelled as a punishment system, a rehabilitation system, a system to protect society or a system to train criminals. Any actual prison is a changing mix of all these perceptions and others. These alternative models of purposeful activity are sketched and then compared with each other and the problem situation in the real world. The comparison, facilitated by the modeller(s), leads to structured debate among the problem owners (often managers) that seeks the accommodations which allow action to be taken to improve the problem situation. And so a learning cycle is established.

Soft Systems Methodology then deals with models-in-the-mind and applies to a very broad class of problematic situations where action to improve is impeded because of conflicts in worldviews. By making clear the models of purposeful activity that belong with these worldviews, and seeking accommodations, the situation can be improved. The approach does not ignore the real world but sees reality as an ever-changing amalgam of idealised models that can co-exist either fruitfully (the goal of a soft system study) or destructively (as found in chronic problematic situations in which overt or hidden conflict is rife).

System dynamics tackles an important subset of these problematic situations where the 'problem' can be expressed dynamically and where dynamics arise from partial and idealised models that coincide with organisational, functional or political responsibilities.[11] When combined, such partial models reveal feedback loops in the real world.[12] While there is undoubtedly overlap between the two approaches, it is important to realise that the learning cycle in system dynamics seeks to discover enduring feedback structure as a hidden characteristic of the real world. This is hard system modelling dressed in soft clothing.

The overlaps between the approaches bear consideration. Among them is the central proposition that organisations contain people and groups who act purposefully. Purposeful action is at the heart of the goal-seeking behaviour generated by balancing loops. Moreover, problematic situations arise from interactions among purposeful actions motivated by conflicting worldviews. However, in system dynamics differences of purpose are distributed across organisations (to be found within functions or departments), whereas in SSM differences of purpose can exist within and between departments and even for the enterprise as a whole. These differences of purpose are deeply engrained in people's taken-as-given worldviews that SSM seeks to uncover.

The distinction I am drawing here is abstract and best illustrated with a practical example. The example uses system dynamics modelling symbols to sketch the kind of alternative models that characterise a soft systems approach. I should stress that this example does not adhere to the conventions and principles of SSM, and neither does it convey the rigour, discipline or richness of the approach. It does, however, illustrate the notion of soft models

---

[11]Strictly speaking this 'subset' of problematic situations handled by system dynamics is partly outside the boundary of situations handled by SSM, since it is difficult to reliably infer dynamics without the use of simulation.

[12]It is relevant to note that when system dynamics modellers conduct partial model tests they are effectively constructing imaginary models that are deliberately lacking real-world feedback loops, as in the 'ideal factory' simulations presented earlier in the chapter. These ideal worlds are conceptually similar to SSM's purposeful activity models though their stylised content and appearance is very different.

derived from a declared worldview. Readers who wish to learn the skills of soft system modelling are referred to Checkland and Poulter (2006) and to Checkland and Scholes (1990).

Alternative Views of a Radio Broadcaster

Imagine you are an executive from a successful commercial radio station in the USA and have been assigned to London to set up a rival to Classic FM, a very successful radio station that broadcasts classical music (with advertising and a sprinkling of news and weather) to a region greater than 200 miles around the capital. You want to find out more about broadcasting in the UK and have been invited to attend a budget and strategy meeting of another successful radio station in London (not Classic FM). You know nothing about this broadcaster (other than the fact that it too is successful), so you listen. Also, you recall your MBA strategic modelling class a decade ago and wonder if the concepts you learned back then will help you interpret the situation.

You soon realise that the organisation is keen to win listeners while remaining cost competitive with rivals. Those goals are no surprise. The available budget depends on the number of listeners, but how is this budget deployed? Members of the management team make clear that for them it is vitally important to have good staff and well-equipped studios. Also, to win and retain listeners requires the right mix of programmes as well as transmitters to reach the audience. So far, so good. Then you hear some views that surprise you. The team insists that a large fraction of the capital budget is spent on high-cost short-wave transmitters – the kind that can broadcast from a remote location in the UK to almost any part of the globe. Spare capital budget buys new FM transmitters to improve listening quality in selected cities. This transmission strategy is certainly not what you had in mind for your rival to Classic FM, but you continue to listen. The next two items in the discussion really surprise you. There is a strong and passionate case made for broadcasting in at least 40 different languages and maintaining a cadre of specialist correspondents in political hotspots such as Baghdad, Syria and the Ukraine. You know such specialists are really expensive and are puzzled how this organisation can be so financially successful. The final items make much more sense – the team agrees that high-quality programming and an excellent impartial editorial reputation is vital to continued success. Recalling your MBA modelling class you realise there is no mention at all of dynamics in this discussion, it has been all about management's priorities. Nevertheless, you muse on the list of asset stocks that would fit this description – if ever a dynamic model were to be created. The picture at the top of Figure 5.33 comes to mind. Here are 10 asset stocks that management believe are essential to attract the particular audience they have in mind.

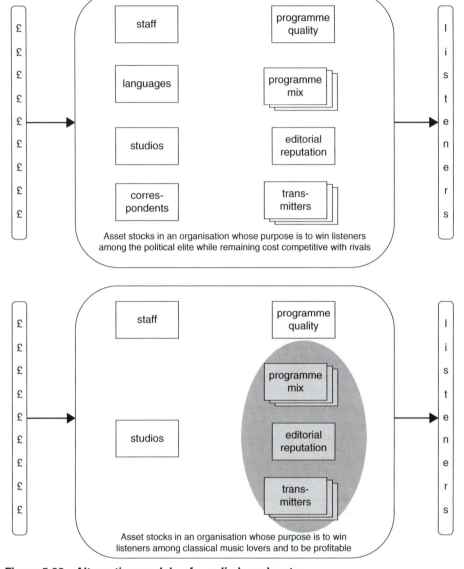

Figure 5.33   Alternative models of a radio broadcaster
Source: Morecroft, J.D.W. (2004) Proceedings of the 2004 International System Dynamics Conference, Oxford.

As you reflect on the conversation, you note that if you were running this organisation you would cut the language portfolio, redeploy the correspondents, change the programme mix, scrap the expensive short-wave transmitters and invest in a network of good local FM transmitters. The point here is that the model of the organisation you have in mind depends on the purpose you wish it to fulfil.

Your mission is to establish a new radio station that brings classical music to a large domestic audience, and does so profitably. A list of asset stocks that fits this purpose is shown in the bottom of Figure 5.33. There are fewer stocks than before and, of those remaining, the ones in the grey oval would be very different than at present. This second picture is a soft model in the sense that it shows the assets you believe are appropriate for a commercial broadcaster of classical music.

You subsequently discover the organisation you visited was BBC World Service, whose purpose is to be the world's best known and most respected voice in global radio broadcasting, and first choice among the international politically minded elite for authoritative and impartial news. In this example, the two different pictures of asset stocks are a bit like models of purposeful activity with different declared worldviews – one worldview coincides with the current reality and purpose of BBC World Service and the other worldview matches the purpose of a commercial radio station like Classic FM. If these two conflicting worldviews were to co-exist among the management team of a real radio station, then the team would be facing a problematical situation requiring significant accommodations on either side for action to be taken.

Note that neither of these pictures is a satisfactory basis for a conventional system dynamics model because there is no dynamical problem or issue guiding the selection of asset stocks or pointing to feedback loops that might explain dynamics.[13] More important, if a system dynamics modeller were working with a broadcaster like World Service, they would not normally build a model containing only the asset stocks in the lower picture (even if a member of the management team had in mind a new World Service like Classic FM) since these stocks contradict what is known about the current organisation.[14] However, if the modeller were helping a management team to investigate the start-up of a completely new commercial radio station then they might well develop a model with the slimmed-down assets shown. In that case, attention would focus on growth dynamics and the search would begin for the combination of reinforcing and balancing loops (containing the selected asset stocks) that determine growth. These growth structures are the focus of Chapters 6 and 7.

---

[13]A system dynamics model of BBC World Service was in fact built to investigate alternative government funding scenarios over a 10-year planning horizon. The problem situation was framed dynamically in terms of future trajectories for the number of listeners and the cost per listener. The project is described in Delauzun and Mollona (1999).

[14]In principle a dynamic hypothesis for World Service may exist that involves only the six asset stocks shown, but this is unlikely in practice since (for example) the language portfolio is so important in determining the number of listeners who tune in to an international news broadcaster.

Appendix 1: Model Communication and Policy Structure Diagrams

In this chapter I have used the factory model to illustrate the iterative steps in the model building process from problem articulation to simulation. It is a small model containing 22 concepts in total (two asset stocks, four flow rates, six converters, one built-in smoothing function, eight constants and one exogenous time series input) that just about fits on a single page. Nevertheless, as Figures 5.8, 5.17 and 5.18 show, there is considerable visual complexity in the model, which can inhibit communication. Communication is even more difficult with practical application models that contain hundreds or even thousands of concepts. There is a need for visual clarity, which can be achieved by grouping model concepts into meaningful clusters.

The factory model was divided into two main sectors, one for production control and the other for workforce management. Within the two sectors are the main operating policies that collectively guide and coordinate the accumulation of asset stocks. These policy functions can be indicated on a stock and flow diagram by using shading, as illustrated in Figures 5.8 and 5.17. Alternatively, much-simplified pictures can be drawn that focus on operating policies and strip away all the underlying formulation detail. The result is a 'policy structure diagram'. Figure 5.34 is an example.

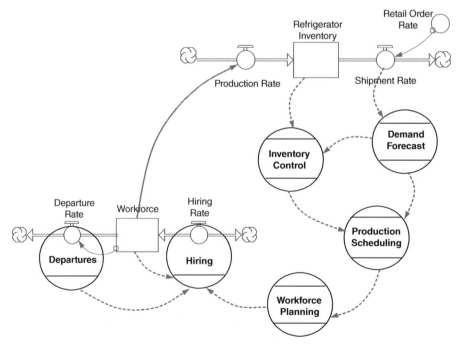

Figure 5.34   Policy structure of the factory model

It shows the factory model in terms of its main operating policies and stock accumulations. Here, an operating policy is represented as a large circle with information inputs and outputs. In some cases, the policy sits alone in a sea of information, a decision-making process – like the demand forecast or inventory control – that interprets information and hands it on to other parts of the organisation. In other cases, the policy subsumes a flow rate where a decision-making process, such as hiring, leads to action (the hiring rate).

Policy functions are similar to converters except that the transformations they bring about are more complex than can be expressed in a single conversion or a single algebraic equation. Policies involve several judgemental and computational steps. For example, inventory control involves goal formation (desired inventory), sensing a gap (the difference between desired inventory and actual) and corrective action (the amount of additional production to schedule in order to close the gap). Hence, the large circular symbol with horizontal lines represents a complex, multi-step conversion process.

The policy structure diagram provides a useful overview of factory coordination (or, more generally, firm coordination) without the full formulation detail. In fact, a wide variety of alternative formulations, with different steps of computation and different intermediate concepts and constants, might equally well fit within the framework of the diagram. This flexibility makes it easy to discuss the diagram with people who know factory and firm operations. In this case 22 concepts are reduced to only 11. Moreover, the vital information feedback network is formed from only six policy functions, each with a practical meaning to factory people.

I have found such diagrams very useful in my own professional work, both for model conceptualisation and communication. I will continue to use them throughout the book. As you will see in later chapters, where the selected models of firms and industries are larger, policy structure diagrams become increasingly effective as a concise way to visualise interlocking operations. Readers who wish to know more about the origins of the policy structure diagram, and see it deployed in classic factory and supply-chain models, are referred to my original working papers in the learning support folder for Chapter 5 downloads, inside the subfolder c05 Archive Materials. Here you will find D-3249-3 A Critical Review of Diagraming Tools for Conceptualizing Feedback System Models; D-3244-2 Structures Causing Instability in Production and Distribution Systems; and D-3293-3 Managing Product Lines that Share a Common Capacity Base. The manuscripts include full documentation of typical formulations for forecasting, inventory control, backlog control and supply-line control frequently used in system dynamics models of manufacturing firms and multi-echelon supply chains. These models and formulations can be seen as practical extensions of the simple factory model presented here in Chapter 5.

Appendix 2: The Dynamics of Information Smoothing

Information smoothing is so common in the day-to-day operation of business and society that it is worth examining more closely how it really works. Smoothing crops up in forecasts, expectations, perceptions, judgements and in any process of measurement or monitoring.[15] People do not instantly recognise the true conditions within an organisation. People do not change their minds immediately on the receipt of new information. Measurement, reflection and deliberation often take considerable time. Still more time is needed to adjust emotionally to a new situation before beliefs and behaviour change. Smoothing is a versatile way to capture this typical wait-and-see approach. A formulation for information smoothing is shown in Figure 5.35.

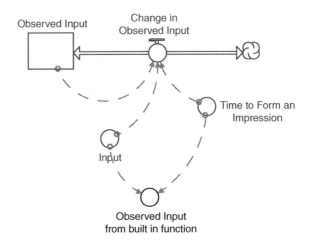

Observed Input(t) = Observed Input(t-dt) + (Change in Observed Input) * dt
INIT Observed Input = 1000 {units/week}
Change in Observed Input = (Input − Observed Input)/Time to Form an Impression {units/week/week}
Input = (1000 + STEP(100,10)) * NORMAL(1,0) {units/week}
Time to Form an Impression = 8 {weeks}
Observed Input from built in function = SMTH1(Input, Time to Form an Impression)

Figure 5.35   Information smoothing

---

[15]Forecasts and expectations can involve several interlinked smoothing processes in order not only to perceive the value of a given variable, but also to determine its trend. By knowing the trend, it is possible to project the value of the variable at a future point in time (according to the time horizon of the forecast). To find out more about forecasting formulations, examine the model called 'Trend Test' in the learning support folder for Chapter 5. Fully documented formulations for a trend function are available in Sterman (2000), Chapter 16. Interesting historical discussion about the trend function can be found in the accompanying subfolder c05 Archive Materials, Views on Trend Macro. The folder contains two memos: D-2544, A Review of the Trend Macro, by Barry Richmond, and D-2558, a response by Jay Forrester.

The smoothing process transforms an input into an observed input over an interval called the 'time to form an impression'. The formulation is similar to the average ship rate earlier in the chapter, but the terminology is generalised. In addition, an alternative SMTH1 function is included to demonstrate its precise equivalence to the standard single-stock formulation.

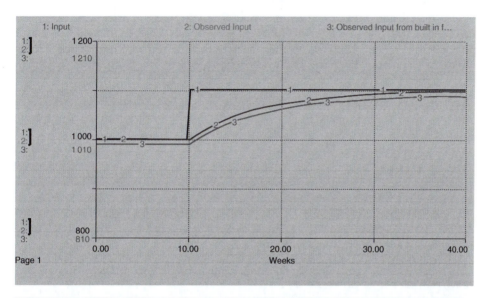

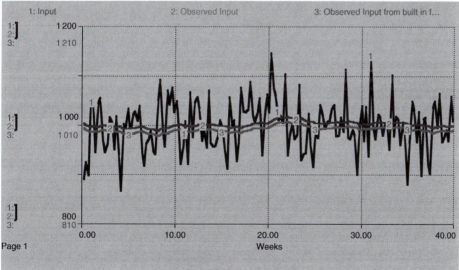

Figure 5.36   First-order (single stock) smoothing. Top: Smoothing of a step input that increases by 10 per cent. Bottom: Smoothing of a random input with standard deviation of five per cent

Two simulations are shown in Figure 5.36. They can be recreated by running the model called 'Information Smoothing' in the learning support folder for

Chapter 5. The top part of the figure shows smoothing of an input (line 1) that begins at 1000 units per week and increases to 1100 in week 10. The observed input (line 2) rises gradually from 1000 to 1100 as confidence builds that the one-time change in the input is permanent. Notice that the observed input from the SMTH1 built-in function (line 3) mimics line 2. In fact the numerical values of lines 2 and 3 are identical but the trajectories are deliberately placed on slightly displaced scales so they are both visible.

The bottom part of the figure shows smoothing of a random input (line 1). The observed input (line 2) captures the mean value of the input (1000 units per week) but filters out nearly all the variability. The time to form an impression is eight weeks and this interval is long enough to ensure that week-to-week variations of the input cancel each other out. The shorter the time to form an impression the more variability is observed.

References

Andersen, D.F. and Richardson, G.P. (1997) Scripts for model building, *System Dynamics Review*, 13(2): 107–129.

Black, L.J. (2013) When visual representations are boundary objects in system dynamics. *System Dynamics Review*, 29(2): 70–86.

Black, L.J. and Andersen, D.F. (2012) Using visual representations as boundary objects to resolve conflict in collaborative model-building applications. *Systems Research and Behavioral Science*, 29: 194–208.

Checkland, P. (2004) Working ideas, insights for systems modelling, item 092CHECK.pdf. Proceedings of the International System Dynamics Conference, Oxford. Available at http://www.systemdynamics.org/conferences/2004 (accessed 23 February 2015).

Checkland, P. and Poulter, J. (2006) *Learning for Action*. Chichester: John Wiley & Sons.

Checkland, P. and Scholes, J. (1990) *Soft Systems Methodology in Action*. Chichester: John Wiley & Sons.

Coyle, R.G. (1996) *System Dynamics Modelling*. London: Chapman and Hall.

Delauzun, F. and Mollona, E. (1999) Introducing system dynamics to BBC World Service. *Journal of the Operational Research Society*, 50(4): 364–371.

Forrester, J.W. (1961) *Industrial Dynamics*. Available from the System Dynamics Society www.systemdynamics.org; originally published by MIT Press, Cambridge MA 1961.

Hovmand, P.S. (2014) *Community Based System Dynamics*. New York: Springer.

Lane, D.C. (1994) With a little help from our friends: how system dynamics and 'soft' OR can learn from each other. *System Dynamics Review*, 10: 101–134.

Lane, D.C. (2000) Should system dynamics be described as a 'hard' or 'deterministic' systems approach. *Systems Research and Behavioral Science*, 17(1): 3–22.

Makridakis, S., Chatfield, C., Hibon, M. *et al.* (1993) The M2 competition: A real time judgementally based forecasting study. *International Journal of Forecasting*, 9(1): 5–22.

Mass, N.J. (1975) *Economic Cycles: An Analysis of Underlying Causes*. Cambridge, MA: MIT Press.

Morecroft, J.D.W. (2004) Working ideas, insights for systems modelling, Proceedings of the International System Dynamics Conference, Oxford. Available at http://www.systemdynamics.org/conferences/2004.

Morecroft, J.D.W. and Sterman, J.D. (1994) *Modeling for Learning Organizations*. Portland, OR: Productivity Press.

Pidd, M. (ed.) (2004) *Systems Modelling – Theory and Practice*. Chichester: John Wiley & Sons.

Richardson, G.P. and Andersen, D.F. (1995) Teamwork in group model building. *System Dynamics Review*, 11(2): 113–137.

Senge, P.M. (1990) *The Fifth Discipline: The Art and Practice of the Learning Organization*. New York: Doubleday.

Sherwood, D. (2002) *Seeing the Forest for the Trees: A Manager's Guide to Applying Systems Thinking*. London: Nicholas Brealey.

Sterman, J.D. (2000) *Business Dynamics: Systems Thinking and Modeling for a Complex World*. Boston, MA: Irwin McGraw-Hill. (See in particular Chapter 3, The Modeling Process, Chapter 11, Delays and Chapter 16, Forecasts and Fudge Factors: Modeling Expectation Formation.)

Sterman, J.D. (2014a) Interactive web-based simulations for strategy and sustainability; The MIT Sloan Learning Edge management flight simulators, Part 1. *System Dynamics Review*, 30(1–2), 89–121.

Sterman, J.D. (2014b) Interactive web-based simulations for strategy and sustainability; The MIT Sloan Learning Edge management flight simulators, Part 2. *System Dynamics Review*, 30(3): 206–231.

Vennix, J.A.M. (1996) *Group Model Building: Facilitating Team Learning Using System Dynamics*. Chichester: John Wiley & Sons.

Wolstenholme, E.F. (1990) *System Enquiry – A System Dynamics Approach*. Chichester: John Wiley & Sons.

Wolstenholme, E.F. (1993) A case study in community care using systems thinking. *Journal of the Operational Research Society*, 44(9): 925–934.

Chapter 6

The Dynamics of Growth from Diffusion

- Stocks and Flows in New Product Adoption – A Conceptual Diffusion Model
- The Bass Model – An Elegant Special Case of a Diffusion Model
- A Variation on the Diffusion Model: The Rise of Low-cost Air Travel in Europe
- Strategy and Simulation of Growth Scenarios
- Conclusion
- Appendix: More About the Fliers Model

Now we turn our attention from goal-seeking feedback and cyclicality to reinforcing feedback and the dynamics of growth. We begin with a product diffusion model responsible for S-shaped growth-and-stagnation in the sales lifecycle of new products and services. The model applies to a wide range of consumer goods from DVDs to web-sites, microwave ovens, low-cost air travel, mobile phones and solar panels. We examine the structure and dynamics of the well-known Bass diffusion model (Bass, 1969) and then propose a variation on this model to investigate growth strategy in the airline industry.

S-shaped growth appears in many guises. It is found in biological and ecological systems where for example exponential growth of a species runs up against a natural limit such as available land or food. A typical pattern of behaviour over time is shown at the top of Figure 6.1. Consider the qualitative features of the trajectory. In the early years, there is very little movement in the state of the system as exponential growth covertly gathers pace. In the middle years, the doubling power of exponential growth becomes dramatically apparent with a huge absolute change in the state of the system. In the final years, growth tails off and the state of the system settles into equilibrium. On the lower left is the corresponding feedback structure made up of two interacting feedback loops: a reinforcing loop, which is the growth engine, and a balancing loop as the limiting effect. The state of the system accumulates whatever is growing. It could be elephants in Uganda, nesting birds in Britain or visitors to a popular new ski resort. The more elephants, birds or visitors, the greater the net growth rate, though for elephants and birds growth is through births whereas for skiers growth is through word-of-mouth. The carrying capacity of habitat is important too: national parks for elephants, hedgerows for nesting birds and infrastructure for skiers. As the population grows, the state of the system approaches its carrying capacity and resource adequacy falls thereby reducing the fractional net increase. Eventually, a time comes when the state of the system is equal to the carrying capacity and the net growth rate falls to zero.

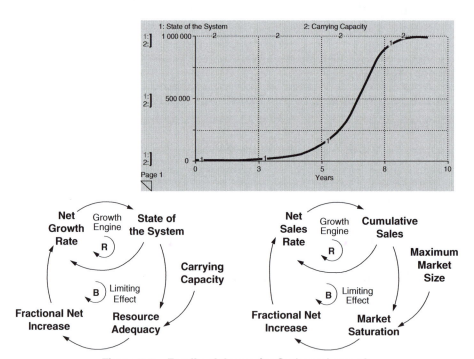

Figure 6.1   Feedback loops for S-shaped growth

On the lower right of Figure 6.1, the same feedback loops are re-labelled to represent sales growth and market saturation. The growth engine is powered by cumulative sales. The more units sold, the more visible the product and the greater the net sales rate. This kind of reinforcing effect applies to many fashion or lifestyle items such as Apple's iPhone or Sony's PlayStation. The limiting effect comes from market saturation (cumulative sales in relation to maximum market size). When the product is new then market saturation is low and the fractional net increase is high (perhaps as much as 0.5, or 50%, per month for the iPhone). As market saturation approaches 100% then the fractional net increase falls to zero because every consumer in the target market already owns the product.

Stocks and Flows in New Product Adoption – A Conceptual Diffusion Model

To transform this feedback view of diffusion into a simulation model we go straight to a stock and flow representation. The reason for this direct approach is that product adoption can be conceived very naturally in terms of a stock and flow network that moves consumers from one state (not owning the product) to another state (owning the product). However bear in mind that to achieve S-shaped growth two interacting feedback loops, a reinforcing growth engine and limiting effect, are also needed. Figure 6.2 shows a simple stock and flow network involving two stock accumulations linked by a single flow rate. Potential adopters on the left are converted to adopters on the right by the adoption rate.

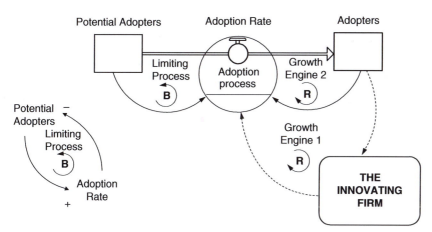

Figure 6.2   Stock and flow network and possible feedback loops in the adoption of a new product

To discover plausible feedback loops we need to think about the adoption process and the factors that influence it. Suppose we start with a dynamic hunch that a growth engine lies in the interaction between the innovating firm and the market. This is a reasonable assumption and leads to a feedback process of the kind depicted on the lower right of Figure 6.2. The innovating firm informs the market of its new product and persuades customers to adopt, so creating a link (an information link in this case) from the firm into the adoption process. What about the reverse link? One possibility is that as more and more adopters accumulate they enable the firm to become even more persuasive in winning over the remaining potential adopters. For now we don't need to know exactly how this link would work in practice. Rather, we simply note that if the link exists it creates the reinforcing loop we are looking for, shown as growth engine 1 in Figure 6.2.

Another entirely different growth engine could exist in parallel. Curiously, this loop need not pass through the firm at all. It represents an adoption process driven by social pressure and/or network effects. Here, the more adopters who already own the product the more attractive it is to the remaining potential adopters, independently of the actions of the firm. After a kick-start, the market converts itself with little need for persuasion from suppliers. Children's toys provide some good examples. The Tamagochi electronic pet and Rubik's cube puzzle were both popular toys that sold themselves through peer pressure and word-of-mouth. In this kind of selling there is a direct link from the number of adopters into the adoption process. The link is hardwired because it represents human social behaviour (the desire to mimic and be part of a social trend) rather than a cue for decision making. A powerful reinforcing loop, labelled growth engine 2, is formed as the adoption rate accumulates into adopters. In practice, product sales are likely to be driven by a combination of the two different growth engines with different weighting according to the relative importance of social pressures and firm persuasion.

The limiting process is often tangible and can be inferred on logical grounds. The basic idea is that, as the number of potential adopters falls and becomes very low (in relation to total market size), then the adoption rate must decline. In the extreme, when every single customer has adopted and the market is saturated, then the adoption rate is zero. This common-sense argument means there is a link from the number of potential adopters into the adoption process. It is a hardwired link that represents a physical/social constraint from the finite number of customers willing to purchase the product. As the market matures, only a few diehard potential customers remain and they are difficult to convert. The diehard link is woven into the stock and flow network to form a balancing loop of just the kind we are looking for. The loop runs from the stock of potential adopters into the adoption process and then backwards through the adoption rate into potential adopters. It is easier to see the loop in the causal loop diagram on the left. Here, potential adopters influence the adoption rate through a positive link exactly the same as before, but the adoption rate in turn influences potential adopters through a negative link to form the balancing loop. The negative link corresponds to the depletion flow in the stock and flow network (i.e. the adoption rate reduces potential adopters).

The Bass Model – An Elegant Special Case of a Diffusion Model

The Bass model offers a particular view of a socially-driven adoption process and elegant algebraic formulations with which to express a 'theory' or dynamic hypothesis for growth and saturation. Developed by marketing academic Frank Bass, the model was first published in *Management Science* in 1969. The article has since been voted among the top 10 most influential papers by INFORMS (Institute for Operations Research and the Management Sciences) members. Figure 6.3 shows how the principal influences on adoption are operationalised.[1]

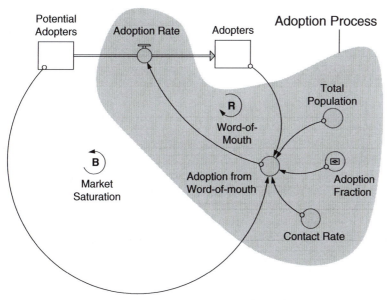

Figure 6.3   Stocks, flows and feedback loops in a contagion model of new product adoption

Essentially, it is a contagion model. Adopters 'infect' potential adopters through word-of-mouth thereby causing them to adopt. Note there is no influence whatever from the innovating firm on the adoption rate. In the full Bass model, this stark assumption is relaxed, but for now let's concentrate on the structure and formulation of contagion. There are two interacting feedback loops – a positive reinforcing loop representing word-of-mouth and a balancing loop representing market saturation. The more adopters, the greater the adoption from word-of-mouth. This contagion is limited as the number of potential adopters falls (since each new adopter comes from the pool of potential adopters and people are conserved!!). A contagion model is a good

---

[1]The model developed in Figures 6.3–6.8 of this chapter is the system dynamics equivalent of the original continuous time differential equations specified by Bass. However, Bass did not explicitly discuss the feedback loop structure of his model or identify the processes controlling adoption in terms of word-of-mouth and market saturation. The translation of the Bass model into the stocks, flows and feedback loops shown here was carried out by John Sterman and is described in Sterman (2000) *Business Dynamics* (Chapter 9).

way to capture the interplay of word-of-mouth and market saturation. Adoption from word-of-mouth is a function both of adopters and potential adopters. The contact rate and adoption fraction tell us something about the strength of the word-of-mouth effect. Next, we examine the algebraic formulation of these concepts.

Figure 6.4 shows the equations for adoption from word-of-mouth. Consumers interact socially. The total population is assumed to be one million people.

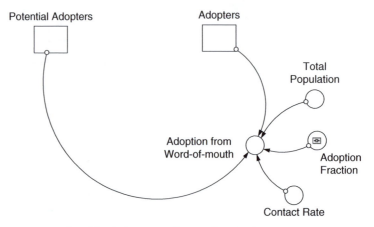

Adoption from Word-of-mouth = Contact Rate * Adopters
* (Potential Adopters / Total Population) * Adoption Fraction *{people / year}*
Contact Rate = 100 *{people per person / year}*
Total Population = 1 000 000 *{people}*
Adoption Fraction = 0.02 *{fraction}*

Figure 6.4   Equations for adoption through word-of-mouth – a social contagion formulation

They meet each other from time to time and may talk about their latest purchase. This propensity to socialise and chat is captured in the 'contact rate', set at a value of 100 and defined in terms of people contacted per person per year (which is dimensionally equivalent to 1/year). Hence, the number of encounters per year by adopters with the rest of the population is the product of the contact rate and adopters, which is the first term in the equation. Some of these encounters, the ones with potential adopters, lead to adoption (whereas an encounter between two adopters cannot, by definition, result in adoption). The probability that any randomly selected encounter is an encounter between an adopter and a potential adopter is equal to the proportion of potential adopters in the total population, which is the ratio in the second term of the equation. Note that this ratio naturally declines as adoption proceeds, reaching zero when the market is fully saturated. Not every encounter between an adopter and potential adopter results in adoption.

The fraction of successful encounters is called the adoption fraction and is set at a value of 0.02, meaning that 2% of encounters lead to adoption.

Figure 6.5 shows the equations for the stock and flow network of adopters and potential adopters. By now the formulation of these standard, yet vital, accumulation equations should be familiar. Incidentally, the model denotes time in years and the computation step or delta time dt is 1/16th of a year, small enough to ensure numerical accuracy. The number of adopters at a given point in time t is equal to the previous number of adopters at time (t-dt) plus the adoption rate over the interval dt. Conversely, the number of potential adopters at time t is the previous number minus the adoption rate over the interval. These symmetrical formulations ensure that the total population of customers remains constant. Initially, there are 10 adopters among a total population of one million. So the remaining 999990 people are potential adopters. The adoption rate is equal to adoption from word-of-mouth.

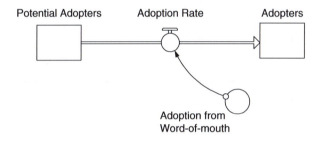

Adopters (t) = Adopters (t-dt) + (Adoption Rate)*dt
INIT Adopters = 10 {people}
Potential Adopters (t) = Potential Adopters (t-dt) − (Adoption Rate)*dt
INIT Potential Adopters = Total Population − Adopters {people}
Adoption Rate = Adoption from Word-of-mouth {people / year}

Figure 6.5   Stock accumulation equations for adopters and potential adopters

The Dynamics of Product Adoption by Word-of-mouth

Open the model called 'Bass Word-of-Mouth' in the learning support folder for Chapter 6 and browse the diagram and equations. Go to the graph where there is a time chart that displays adopters and potential adopters over a 10-year horizon. There is also a slider for the adoption fraction to test different assumptions about the strength of social contagion. The slider is initially set at 0.02 which is the value supplied in the equations above. Run the model to obtain the two charts shown in Figure 6.6.

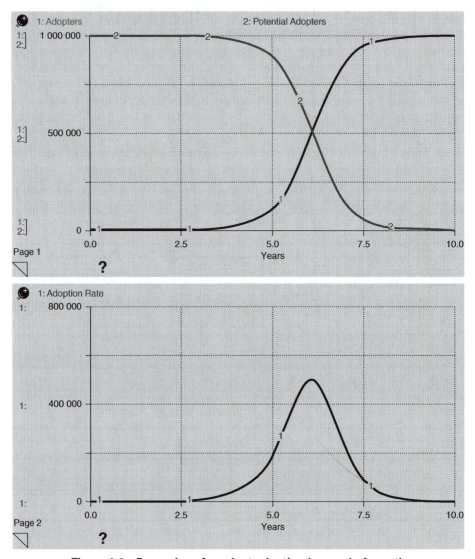

Figure 6.6   Dynamics of product adoption by word-of-mouth

The top chart shows adopters (line 1) and potential adopters (line 2) plotted on a scale from zero to one million. At the start there are only 10 adopters, a drop in the ocean. These few enthusiasts begin to spread the word. For four years, however, they and their growing band of followers appear to have almost no impact on the huge mass of potential adopters who have never heard of the product. Such slow early build-up is the nature of social contagion. For a long time, the enthusiasts are lone voices and the adoption rate in the bottom chart remains close to zero, though in fact steady exponential growth is taking place but on a scale dwarfed by the total population of one million people. During year 4, the number of adopters (top chart) swells from only 18 000 to more than 100 000 and they are beginning to be heard. Over the next year, the adoption rate (bottom chart) rises from 180 000 per year to a peak of almost 500 000 per year. The bulk of the million-person market is converted in the interval between years five and eight, by which time the adoption rate is much reduced as market saturation sets in.

The Need to Kick-start Adoption

Adoption peaks at 500 000 per year and yet four years after product launch the adoption rate is still less than one-tenth of its peak value. This barely perceptible build-up is typical of exponential growth that starts from a very small base. In the logical extreme where the initial number of adopters is zero then, even with one million potential adopters, there is no growth at all because the product is totally unknown and remains that way. Although such an extreme is unrealistic, it demonstrates the need to 'seed' the market with early adopters in order to kick-start word-of-mouth. That's where the firm has an important role to play through marketing of various kinds, such as advertising, promotions and trade shows. In practice, it would be necessary to investigate how marketing really works, starting from a rough picture like Figure 6.2 and adding the necessary operating detail inside the firm to discover new feedback loops that augment word-of-mouth. First, however, we consider the Bass model for a specific feedback representation of advertising and its effect on product adoption.

The Complete Bass Diffusion Model With Advertising

Advertising is represented as a separate influence on the adoption rate as shown in Figure 6.7. It is a subtle formulation (and once again elegant and compact) because advertising is cleverly woven into a feedback loop, a balancing loop in this case. The obvious part of the formulation is that advertising is capable of generating adoption separately from word-of-mouth. There are now two influences on the adoption rate: adoption from word-of-mouth and adoption from advertising. The clever part of the formulation is that adoption from advertising itself depends on potential adopters thereby providing the link that closes the new loop on the left. The basic idea is that well-targeted advertising converts a proportion of potential adopters in each period, where the proportion depends on advertising effectiveness. Hence, advertising has its biggest impact early in the adoption process when there are lots of potential adopters to reach and convert. At least that's what the Bass formulation assumes. If advertising really works this way then it dovetails neatly with word-of-mouth by providing exactly the early kick-start needed.

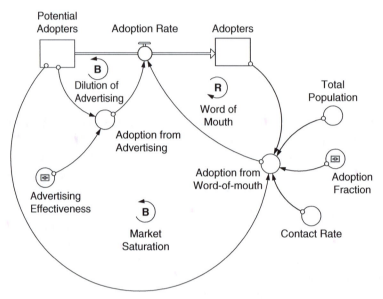

Figure 6.7   The complete bass diffusion model with advertising

The corresponding equations are shown in Figure 6.8. The adoption rate is the sum of adoption from advertising and adoption from word-of-mouth.

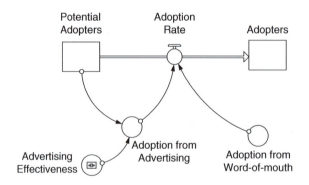

Adoption Rate = Adoption from Advertising +
               Adoption from Word-of-mouth {people/year}
Adoption from Advertising = Potential Adopters *
               Advertising Effectiveness {people/year}
Advertising Effectiveness = 0.011 {fraction/year
               meaning 1.1% per year of Potential Adopters}

Figure 6.8   Bass equations for adoption with advertising

Intuitively the equation makes sense because there are now two independent additive effects on the adoption rate. They are independent in the sense that advertising does not change the nature of social contagion (it just boosts the number of product advocates) and contagion does not influence advertising. Adoption from advertising is expressed as the product of potential adopters and advertising effectiveness and captures the ability of advertising to reach the masses early on, when word-of-mouth cannot. Advertising effectiveness is a constant fraction per year set at 0.011. The two equations together mean that advertising converts a fixed proportion of potential adopters in each period, at an annualised rate of just over 1% per year. It is useful to think about the numerical implications of the formulation at the start of the simulation when, as we have already seen, word-of-mouth is feeble. There are one million potential adopters (less 10 initial active adopters). Advertising reaches all of them and converts them at a rate of roughly 1% annually, or 10 000 people per year. This number is far, far more than the early word-of-mouth adoption but interestingly far, far less than the peak word-of-mouth adoption (which can number hundreds of thousands per year). Hence, advertising dwarfs word-of-mouth in the early years but is subsequently dwarfed by it. Such a shift of power between drivers of adoption is both dynamically and strategically important as simulations will clearly show.

The Dynamics of Product Adoption by Word-of-mouth and Advertising

The new trajectories of product adoption, boosted by advertising, are shown in Figure 6.9. There are striking differences by comparison with Figure 6.6. The adoption rate (bottom chart) rises sooner and peaks much earlier than adoption by word-of-mouth alone. The peak adoption rate in both cases is roughly 500 000 customers per year, increased only slightly to 505 000 with advertising. This similar scaling confirms the point that word-of-mouth ultimately dominates adoption. The trajectories for adopters and potential adopters (top chart) show that the whole adoption process is moved forward in time and is complete by year five, whereas before it was only just beginning in year five. The simulation shows just how strategically important advertising can be. It creates a huge timing advantage by unleashing the power of word-of-mouth much earlier.

To further investigate the dynamics of new product adoption let's conduct a simulation experiment. Open the model called 'Bass Diffusion with Advertising' in the learning support folder for Chapter 6. You will see the same time charts as in Figure 6.9. Also, there are two sliders to create what-ifs. Advertising effectiveness moves in the range between zero and 0.02 and the

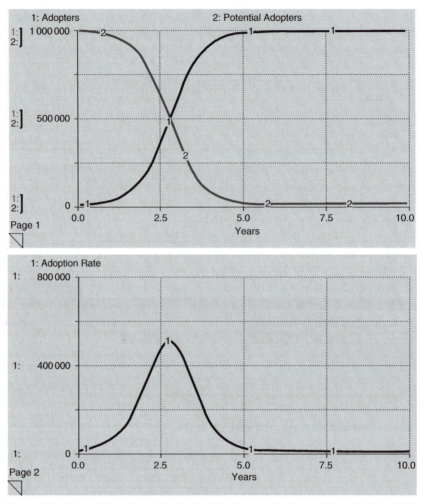

Figure 6.9 **Dynamics of product adoption by word-of-mouth and advertising**

adoption fraction moves between zero and 0.03. Now imagine launching a different product whose appeal is less obvious to consumers and so word-of-mouth is muted. The adoption fraction is halved from 0.02 to 0.01 meaning that only 1% of contacts between adopters and potential adopters result in adoption. Move the slider accordingly. Meanwhile advertising effectiveness is unchanged. Before simulating try to imagine the new trajectory of adopters. You can sketch your expectation by turning to page three of the graph pad (select the 'page' tab in the bottom left of the chart). There you will find the simulated trajectory of adopters (line 1) from the previous run. There is also another variable called 'sketch of adopters' (line 2) that runs along the time axis. To create your own sketch just select, hold and drag, starting anywhere along the line. A new trajectory appears that can be any shape you want. When you are finished, select 'Run' to simulate and check out your intuition.

The result of muted word-of-mouth is shown in Figure 6.10. The adoption rate (bottom chart) is noticeably flatter than before and reaches a peak of some 255 000 customers per year. Nevertheless, adopters (line 1, top chart) still show a clear pattern of S-shaped growth that rises more gradually. Interestingly, the muted adoption process is almost complete by the middle of year 7, the same timing as achieved in Figure 6.6 for an appealing product without advertising.

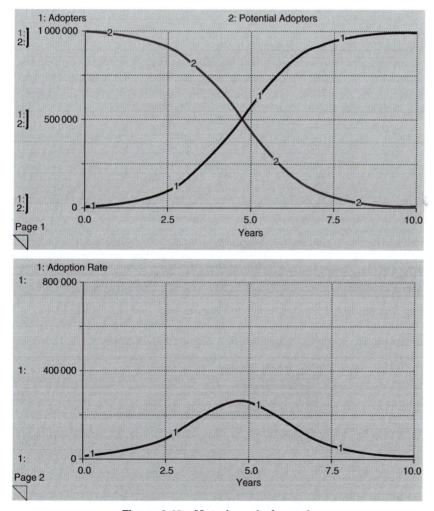

Figure 6.10   Muted word-of-mouth

A Variation on the Diffusion Model: The Rise of Low-cost Air Travel in Europe

The Bass model is a particular instance of the more general conceptual diffusion model introduced in Figure 6.2.[2] In this section, we examine another diffusion model with similar feedback loops but entirely different equation formulations written to fit the early growth strategy of easyJet, one of the UK's most successful no-frills airlines, at the dawn of low-cost flights in Europe. The model shows an alternative way to represent word-of-mouth and advertising that nevertheless retains the essential combination of balancing and reinforcing loops associated with adoption and S-shaped growth. It is recognisably a firm-level model where diffusion of low-cost air travel happens in competition with established airlines. It is a small model of some 27 equations in total.

To appreciate the model's boundary and scope, it is important to imagine the European airline industry not as it is today but as it was back in the mid-1990s when full-service air travel was the norm and low-cost flights were a new and unproven business concept.

easyJet – A Bright Idea, but Will it Work?

The historical situation is described in an article called 'easyJet's $500 Million Gamble' (Sull, 1999). The opening paragraph sets the scene:

> This case study details the rapid growth of easyJet which started operations in November 1995 from London's Luton airport. In two years, it was widely regarded as the model low-cost European airline and a strong competitor to flag carriers. The company has clearly identifiable operational and marketing characteristics, e.g. one type of aircraft, point-to-point short-haul travel, no in-flight meals, rapid turnaround time, very high aircraft utilisation, direct sales, cost-conscious customer segments and extensive sub-contracting. easyJet's managers identified three of its nearest low-cost competitors and the strategy of each

---

[2]A more detailed diffusion model, with explicit and detailed representation of firms' influence on adoption, is reported in *Strategy Support Models*, Morecroft 1984, also available in the learning support folder for Chapter 6 in the subfolder c06 Archive Materials. The modelling project investigated the migration strategy pursued by one of the Bell Operating Companies in the early 1980s, as it attempted to upgrade the private telephone switches used by business customers from traditional electromechanical technology to electronic. Thousands of customers generating several hundred million dollars per year of lease income needed to be persuaded to adopt electronic switches. The model included formulations for product pricing, sales targets, incentives, salesforce hiring, turnover and time allocation to represent the influences of the firm on market migration. For such a technically complex product, adoption was driven principally by sales force persuasion. Word-of-mouth sales were virtually non-existent.

of these airlines is detailed in the case study. But easyJet also experienced direct retaliation from large flag carriers like KLM and British Airways (Go). These challenges faced easyJet's owner, Stelios Haji-ioannou, as he signed a $500m contract with Boeing in July 1997 to purchase 12 brand new 737s.

Imagine yourself now in Mr Haji-ioannou's role. Is it really going to be feasible to fill those expensive new planes? In his mind is a bright new business idea, a creative new segmentation of the air travel market to be achieved through cost leadership and aimed at customers who are interested in 'jeans not business routines'. Feasibility checks of strategy are natural territory for business simulators, especially dynamic, time-dependent, strategy problems, such as rapid growth in a competitive industry. At the time, there were differences of opinion within the industry and even among easyJet's management team. Some industry experts had a dismal view of easyJet's prospects (in stark contrast to the founder's optimism), dismissing the fledgling airline with statements such as 'Europe is not ready for the peanut flight'.

To bring modelling and simulation into this debate, we have to visualise the dynamic tasks that face Mr Haji-ioannou and his team in creating customer awareness (how do you attract enough fliers to fill 12 planes?), and dealing with retaliation by rivals (what if British Airways or KLM engage in a price war, could they sustain such a war, what would provoke such a response?). The starting point is a map of the business, a picture created with the management team, to think with some precision about the task of attracting and retaining passengers and the factors that might drive competitor retaliation.

Visualising the Business: Winning Customers in a New Segment

Figure 6.11 shows how a start-up airline attracts new passengers and communicates its new low-cost, no-frills service to the flying public. The diffusion task is far from trivial, because when you think about it (and modelling really forces you to think hard about the practical details that underpin strategy), the company has to spread the word to millions of people if it is to fill 12 brand new 737s day after day.

Potential passengers represent the cumulative number of fliers who have formed a favourable impression of the start-up airline. Note that these passengers have not necessarily flown with easyJet, but would if they could.[3]

---

[3]We are drawing a distinction between wanting a product or service and actually buying it. The distinction is important in practice because customers often need time and further persuasion to buy (even though they are interested) and firms need to build capacity to supply. Interestingly, the Bass

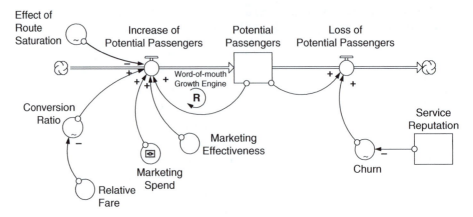

Increase of Potential Passengers = (Potential Passengers *Conversion Ratio + Marketing
Spend * 1 000 * Marketing Effectiveness) * Effect of Route Saturation
Conversion Ratio = GRAPH(Relative Fare)
Effect of Route Saturation = GRAPH(Route Saturation)
Marketing Spend = 2 500 {£ thousands per year}
Marketing Effectiveness = 0.05 {Passengers wooed per £ spent}

**Figure 6.11   Creating awareness of low-cost flights among potential passengers:
word-of-mouth and marketing**

Source: From *Supporting Strategy: Frameworks, Methods and Models,* Edited by Frances O'Brien
and Robert Dyson, 2007 © John Wiley & Sons Limited. Reproduced with permission.

This rather abstract way of thinking about passengers is a convenient
simplifying assumption that enables us to look at growth of interest in
low-cost flights independent of the firm's capacity to offer such a service. Such
simplification is justified for our limited purpose of exploring the feasibility of
filling 12 planes. Bear in mind, however, that the scope of a model always
depends on its purpose. For example, a model to study the growth of the
whole airline (rather than simply growth of potential passengers) would
include the company's internal operations such as hiring and training of staff
and investment in planes, as in Sterman's (1988) well-known People Express
management flight simulator.

The number of potential passengers starts very small (just 5000 in the model)
and grows over time. How does growth take place? The remaining parts of the
figure show the factors that determine both the increase and loss of

---

model makes no such distinction, an assumption that is not unreasonable for new product adoption
at the industry level when one might assume that the adoption fraction subsumes aggregate product
availability. So, for example, if there is chronic capacity shortage during the rapid growth phase then
the effective adoption fraction is lower than it would have been, had capacity been plentiful. For
explicit stock-and-flow modelling of the stages of consumer awareness in new product adoption,
see Finsgud (2004).

passengers. In practice, this information comes from the management team, coaxed out by a facilitator who is helping the team to visualise the business.

Passengers increase through a combination of marketing spend (posters, advertisements on the web, television, radio and newspapers) and word-of-mouth. The influences are similar to the Bass model, but the formulations are less abstract and not as elegant. Here, I provide a brief summary of the main concepts and equations. More information is provided in the Appendix of this chapter.

The increase of potential passengers depends on a host of influences. The first term in the equation represents word-of-mouth, formulated as the product of potential passengers and the conversion ratio. The strength of word-of-mouth is captured in the conversion ratio, which is itself a function of relative fare. The lower easyJet's fare relative to established rivals, the more potent is word-of-mouth. For example, at a dramatically low relative fare of 0.3 (i.e. 30% of rivals' fare) the conversion rate is assumed to be 2.5; meaning that each potential passenger on average converts two-and-a-half more potential passengers per year. When the fare is as low as this, it becomes a talking point among the travelling public, just as happened in real life.[4] At 50% of rivals' fare the conversion rate is reduced to 1.5 and at 70% it is only 0.3. Eventually, if easyJet's fare were to equal their rivals' then the conversion rate would be zero because a standard fare cannot sustain word-of-mouth.

The second term represents the separate effect of marketing on the increase of potential passengers, formulated as the product of marketing spend and marketing effectiveness. Marketing spend is set at a default value of £2.5 million per year. Marketing effectiveness represents the number of passengers wooed per marketing £ spent. It is set at 0.05 passengers per £, so marketing brings 125 000 potential passengers per year (2.5 million * 0.05).

Finally, the effect of route saturation represents the limits to growth arising from the routes operated by the 12 new planes. It is formulated as a graph function that multiplies the previous two effects. When very few potential passengers have heard of the new service (people who live in the catchment area of Luton airport, 30 miles north of London, who might use these routes and planes), then the effect of saturation takes a neutral value of one and has no detrimental impact on word-of-mouth or marketing. As more and more would-be fliers in the region form a favourable impression of the new service, the effect of route saturation falls below 1 and begins to curtail word-of-mouth

---

[4]In some cases, very low fares may deter passengers due to concerns about safety, but in this particular case easyJet was flying a fleet of brand new 737s, which instilled confidence.

and marketing effort. When all fliers in the region are aware of the new service, there is no one else left to win over and the effect of route saturation takes a value of 0. The formulations for route saturation are explained in more detail in the Appendix of this chapter and can be viewed by browsing the model that will be introduced shortly.

The loss of potential passengers depends on service reputation. The lower the reputation, the greater the loss. Industry specialists say that service reputation depends on ease-of-booking, punctuality, safety, on-board service and quality of meals. For short-haul flights, punctuality is often the dominant factor. The model does not represent all these factors explicitly but simply defines service reputation on a scale between 0.5 (very poor) and 1.5 (very good). If reputation is very good then fliers retain a favourable impression of the airline, so the annual loss of potential passengers is very small, just 2.5% per year. If reputation is poor then the loss of potential passengers per year is damagingly high, up to 100% per year.

Visualising Retaliation and Rivalry

Figure 6.12 shows one possible way to visualise the retaliatory response of powerful European flag carriers to low-cost airlines in the early years.

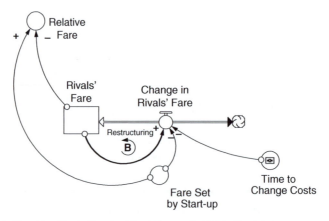

Rivals Fare(t) = Rivals Fare(t - dt) + (Change in Rivals Fare) * dt
INIT Rivals Fare = .25 {£/passenger mile}
Change in Rivals Fare = (Fare Set by Start-up – Rivals Fare)/Time to Change Costs
Fare Set by Start-up = .09 {£/passenger mile}
Time to Change Costs = 4 {years}
Relative Fare = Fare Set by Start-up / Rivals Fare {dimensionless}

Figure 6.12   Rivals and relative fare
Source: From *Supporting Strategy: Frameworks, Methods and Models*, Edited by Frances O'Brien and Robert Dyson, 2007 © John Wiley & Sons Limited. Reproduced with permission.

I must emphasise here the phrase 'one possible way', because there are many ways that a management team such as easyJet's might think about competitors. Part of the team's model-building task is to achieve the simplest possible shared image, drawing on the sophisticated (and sometimes conflicting) knowledge of the team members. A fundamental question is whether there is a need to model, in-depth, one or more competing firms. Do you need a detailed representation of British Airways or KLM to understand the threat such rivals might pose to the feasibility of easyJet's growth strategy?

The leader of a team modelling project should not impose a rigid answer on this question of how much detail to include. The modeller should be sensitive to the opinions of the management team while always striving for parsimony. After all, to achieve buy-in the model must capture their understanding of their world in their own vocabulary. In these situations, it is useful to bear in mind that experienced business leaders themselves simplify their complex world. If they didn't they couldn't communicate their plans. Good business modelling, like good business communication, is the art of leaving things out, and focusing only on those features of reality most pertinent to the problem at hand.

Figure 6.12 shows just enough about competitors to indicate how, collectively, they could stall easyJet's growth ambitions.[5] Recall that word-of-mouth feedback relies for its contagion on the start-up's fare being much lower than rivals. But what if competing firms try to match the start-up's low price? The figure shows how such price equalisation might take place. At the heart of the formulation is a balancing loop labelled 'Restructuring'. Rivals' fare is shown as a stock accumulation that takes time and effort to change. Competitors cannot reduce fares until they cut costs and a flag carrier like BA may take years to achieve cost parity with a low-cost start-up.[6]

To understand the formulation, suppose that rivals set themselves a target fare equal to the fare set by the start-up (in this case, £0.09 per passenger mile). The magnitude of the underlying cost equalisation task is now clear – it is the 64% difference between rivals' initial fare of 25 pence (£0.25) and easyJet's fare of nine pence. Such an enormous change can only be achieved through

---

[5]I have chosen a high level of aggregation for rivals. The purpose is to capture in broad, but dynamically accurate, terms how rival airlines respond to price competition.

[6]Large carriers will match low seat prices regardless of cost by providing some seats at a discount. Price cuts can be implemented very quickly through on-line yield management systems that allow dynamic pricing according to load factors. But it is a limited option. For example, out of 150 seats there may be 15 cheap ones. For very popular flights there are no cheap seats. Hence, the industry-wide effect of discounting is merely a partial adjustment to fully competitive prices. Only cost parity can deliver competitive prices that are profitable in the long term for a firm catering to a growing population of price-conscious fliers.

major restructuring of the business. The pace of restructuring depends on the time to change costs. Normally, one would expect this adjustment time to be several years, and in the model it is set at four years. The resulting equation formulation for the rivals' fare boils down to a standard asset stock adjustment equation where the change in the rivals' fare is equal to the difference between the fare set by the start-up and rivals' fare, divided by the time to adjust costs.[7]

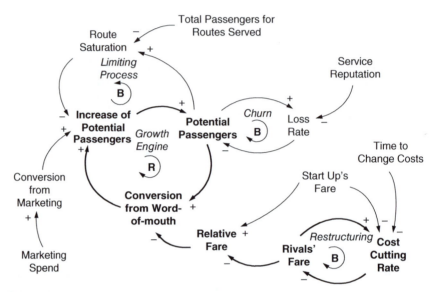

Figure 6.13   Feedback loops for the launch of a low-cost airline, a variation on the diffusion model

Source: From Supporting Strategy: Frameworks, Methods and Models, Edited by Frances O'Brien and Robert Dyson, 2007 © John Wiley & Sons Limited. Reproduced with permission.

Feedback Loops in the easyJet Model

Figure 6.13 shows the main feedback loops in the complete model. In the centre is the growth engine, involving potential passengers and conversion from word-of-mouth. Above is the limiting process in which route saturation eventually restricts the passenger conversion rate. These two loops are the equivalent of the reinforcing and balancing loops in the Bass model. In

---

[7]Sometimes, firms may seek ways to shortcut painful and slow cost-reduction programmes. For example in November 1997, only four months after Stelios signed the $500 million contract with Boeing, British Airways (BA) launched a new semi-autonomous airline called 'Go' to compete, free from the service traditions and cost constraints of the parent airline. Go offered reduced in-flight service and much lower fares than regular BA flights, to a variety of European destinations, from London's Stansted airport. Ultimately, this move proved to be a short-term fix. Go was subsequently sold and BA itself continued to implement cost-reduction programmes for many years.

addition, there are two new loops. In the bottom right of the figure is a balancing loop involving rivals' fare and cost cutting. The dynamic significance of this loop is that it tends to equalise rivals' fare with the start-up's fare. Relative fare rises gradually to parity, thereby reducing the strength of word-of-mouth. Finally, on the right is a balancing loop involving potential passengers and loss rate that captures churn in potential passengers arising from the start-up's service reputation.

Of course, this brief model of passengers and fares is a sketch of a more complex reality. Nevertheless, it contains enough detail to fuel team discussion about passenger growth and price retaliation. When simulated, it contains sufficient dynamic complexity to create thought-provoking growth scenarios.

Strategy and Simulation of Growth Scenarios

The main purpose of the model is to investigate easyJet's $500 million gamble to purchase 12 brand new Boeing 737s. Will it be possible to fill them? A rough calculation suggests the airline needs one million fliers if it is to operate 12 fully loaded aircraft – which is a lot of people.[8] What combination of word-of-mouth and marketing will attract this number of potential passengers? How long will it take? What are the risks of price retaliation by rivals? These are good questions to explore using the what-if capability of simulation.

Figure 6.14 shows simulations of the growth of potential passengers over the period 1996–2000 under two different approaches to marketing spend (bold and cautious) and under the assumption of slow retaliation by rivals. Bold marketing spend is assumed to be five times greater than cautious spend (at £2.5 million per year versus £0.5 million per year). In both cases, the horizontal straight line shows the 'required' number of passengers to fill

---

[8]Let's assume each aircraft carries 150 passengers and makes three round-trip flights a day. A fully loaded plane needs 900 passengers each day (150*3*2). A fully loaded fleet of 12 planes needs 10 800 passengers a day, or 3 888 000 passengers each year, which is very nearly 4 million. If we make the further assumption that each potential passenger is likely to fly the available routes twice a year on round-trip flights, then the start-up airline needs to attract a pool of almost one million fliers to ensure commercially viable load factors. This rough calculation is typical of the sort of judgemental numerical data required to populate an algebraic model. Perfect accuracy is not essential and often not possible. The best estimates of informed people, specified to order-of-magnitude accuracy (or better), are adequate, drawing on the informal but powerful knowledge base derived from experience.

12 planes. This line is a useful reference against which to compare the number of potential passengers. If and when potential passengers exceed required passengers, the strategy is deemed feasible.

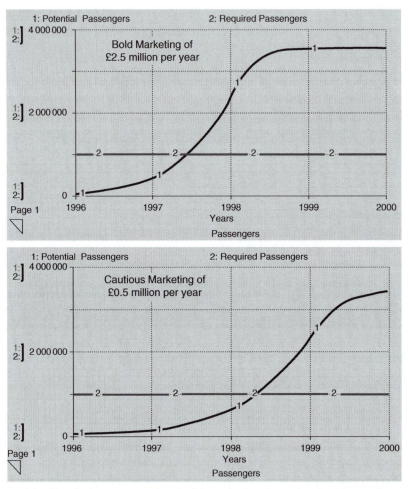

Figure 6.14 Simulations comparing bold marketing (top chart) with cautious marketing (bottom chart) assuming slow retaliation

Source: From *Supporting Strategy: Frameworks, Methods and Models*, Edited by Frances O'Brien and Robert Dyson, 2007 © John Wiley & Sons Limited. Reproduced with permission.

Consider first the timeline for bold marketing in the top half of the figure. The simulation begins in 1996 with a very small number of potential passengers, just 5000. The fledgling airline is virtually unknown to the flying public (despite its ambitions). In the first year of operation, bold marketing brings the airline to the attention of a growing number of fliers. By the end of 1996 there is a band of several hundred thousand enthusiastic supporters. Moreover, this band of supporters is beginning to recruit more followers through positive word-of-mouth. In the interval 1997–1998, the number of potential passengers rises sharply as word-of-mouth continues to stoke exponential growth. By mid-1997, the number of potential passengers has reached the target of one million required to fill the fleet. In the remainder of the year, reinforcing growth continues. There is a huge leap of more than one million potential passengers in the last six months of 1997 as the powerful engine of growth continues to gather momentum. Then, in the second quarter of 1998, growth ceases abruptly as the airline's message reaches all 3.5 million fliers in the imagined catchment region it serves.

The strategically important part of the timeline is the growth phase between the start of 1996 and early 1998. Bold marketing coupled with strong word-of-mouth unleashes a powerful engine of growth, which, in classic exponential fashion, begins small (and therefore invisible) and snowballs rapidly after 18 months.

Now consider the timeline in the bottom half of Figure 6.14, which traces the build-up of potential passengers from cautious marketing. Spend is cut by four-fifths from £2.5 million a year to only £0.5 million a year. As before, the simulation starts in 1996 with only 5000 potential passengers. In the first year, the airline wins few passengers – not surprising because marketing spend is much reduced. In the second year, there is healthy growth in passengers, despite the low marketing spend. Word-of-mouth is now beginning to draw in lots of new passengers. Once the growth engine is primed it gets rolling and in the second quarter of 1998 carries the airline's passenger base beyond the target required to fill the fleet. Growth continues into 1999 until nearly all 3.5 million fliers are aware of the new low-cost service. Cautious marketing simply defers growth (by comparison with bold marketing), but doesn't seem to radically alter the ultimate size of the passenger base. One can begin to appreciate a persuasive rationale for caution. By the year 2000, the simulated airline has saved £8 million in marketing spend (four years at an annual saving of £2 million), yet has still got its message out to 3.5 million fliers!

Figure 6.15 shows the same two marketing approaches (bold and cautious) under the assumption that rivals retaliate quickly. Price equalisation happens in half the time previously assumed and as a result both timelines are noticeably changed by comparison with the base case. From the viewpoint of strategic feasibility, however, the bold marketing timeline tells much the same story as before. At the start of 1996, the airline is almost unknown among the flying public, and by the third quarter of 1997 it has attracted enough potential passengers to fill 12 planes. Fast-acting rivals seem unable to prevent this rise of a new entrant from obscurity to commercial viability, though price equalisation measures do curtail the ultimate dissemination of the start-up airline's low-price message.

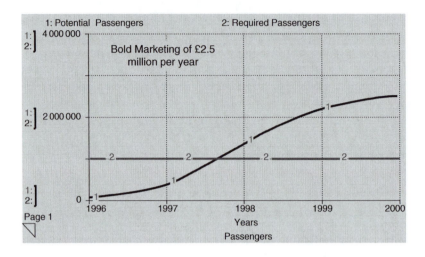

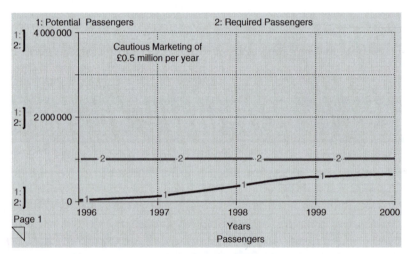

Figure 6.15 Simulations comparing bold marketing (top chart) with cautious marketing (bottom chart) assuming fast retaliation

Source: From *Supporting Strategy: Frameworks, Methods and Models*, Edited by Frances O'Brien and Robert Dyson, 2007 © John Wiley & Sons Limited. Reproduced with permission.

A strategically significant change is observable in the timeline for cautious marketing. The start-up airline is no longer able to fill its planes because it is unable to attract passengers. The rise from obscurity to prominence never happens. Cautious marketing attracts few converts and fails to ignite word-of-mouth. By the time the low-price message has reached a few hundred thousand fliers (at the end of 1997) it is no longer distinctive. Rivals are low price too. If this future were easyJet's, its planes would be flying half-empty and it would be losing money. Fast retaliation can prove fatal in a word-of-mouth market.

Using the Fliers Simulator to Create Your Own Scenarios

The Fliers simulator enables you to explore a variety of scenarios for a start-up low-cost airline. You can replay the simulations shown above, create new scenarios, and investigate the behaviour of many more variables. Open the model called 'Fliers Mini-Sim' in the learning support folder for Chapter 6 to see the opening screen as shown in Figure 6.16. There is a time chart for potential passengers and required passengers. Also there are numeric displays for potential passengers and relative fare, as well as sliders for marketing spend and time to change costs. Marketing spend is 2500 (in £ thousands per year) and the time to change costs is four years. These are the conditions for the base case scenario of bold marketing and slow retaliation already seen in Figure 6.14.

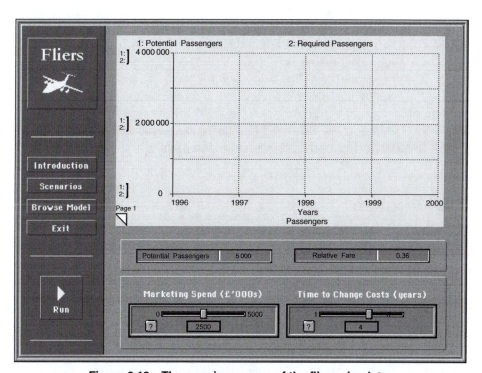

Figure 6.16   The opening screen of the fliers simulator

To get started, press the 'Run' button without altering either of the sliders. The first year of the simulation plays out. Scroll through the time charts to view the behaviour of the conversion ratio, the effect of route saturation, churn and the increase/loss of potential passengers. Press the 'Run' button again to see the next simulated year and so on to the end of the simulation in the year

2000. For a guided tour of the simulation, press the 'scenarios' button on the left. A new screen appears containing a menu of pre-prepared scenarios. Press the large green button for a year-by-year analysis of the base case. At the end of the analysis, press 'scenario explorer' to return to the opening screen. Then conduct your own experiments with other combinations of marketing spend and time to change costs. At any time you can learn more about the simulator by pressing the navigation buttons on the left of the screen. The introduction is a review of the easyJet case and the feedback structure of the model. The 'scenarios' button offers a guided tour of the four pre-prepared scenarios already covered in Figures 6.14 and 6.15. 'Browse model' allows you to see the detailed model structure and documented equation formulations.

Simulation, Predictions and Scenarios

It is important to remember that simulations are not predictions or forecasts of an inevitable future. Rather they are scenarios – alternative futures that may unfold if the assumptions behind the scenarios turn out to be true. In this case, the assumptions include: (1) all the structural relationships shown in the map; (2) all the numerical values and algebraic formulations in the simulator; and (3) the specific parameter changes that differentiate the scenarios (such as a five-fold increase in marketing spend going from cautious to bold). Simulations are a way of rehearsing the implications of our assumptions about strategy in order to reveal surprises and hidden pitfalls.

Conclusion

Dynamic processes of adoption and diffusion are widespread. As we have seen, the underlying feedback structure involves at least one reinforcing feedback loop that generates growth and at least one balancing feedback loop that exerts a limit to growth. Business and industry offer many variations on this basic feedback structure that apply not only to the adoption of new products and services but also to the adoption of new technologies such as alternative fuel engines for cars (Struben and Sterman, 2008; Keith, 2012), and solar panels (Sterman, 2010). In society-at-large the same (or very similar) structure applies to the spread of rumours and new ideas and to the spread of diseases such as HIV/AIDS (Dangerfield, Fang and Roberts, 2001) and avian flu.

The transition from growth to saturation is often of strategic importance to organisations but can be hard to detect in practice. Nothing grows forever, but exponential growth that gradually encounters a limit (through a non-linear saturation effect) can easily create an illusion of sustainable growth. A common result is that firms over-expand capacity and suffer a sharp decline in profitability as revenue levels off or falls while costs continue to rise. In these situations, awareness of the underlying feedback structure can be useful in recognising the early warning signs of stagnation and implementing changes that restore growth or pre-emptively cut costs. A particularly striking example of such pre-emptive strategic action is reported in a model-supported case study about the Refrigeration Sales Corporation of Ohio (Farr and Rockart, 2008; Farr, 2010). The CEO built his own Bass-like model of the US air conditioning business; a model which he shared with his management team. Simulations revealed impending saturation of the market for air conditioning units, leading to a probable sales downturn within five years (and the end of a growth era for the industry as a whole in the US). Armed with this strategic insight the CEO and his management team were emboldened to curtail capital investment and to reduce costs well ahead of rivals. As a result the company remained profitable, despite the predestined-yet-covert sales downturn. Meanwhile other firms in the industry were surprised by the downturn and lost money.

Organisations facing suspected limits to growth should beware of doing more of what worked in the past. For example, as we saw in the Fliers simulator, advertising provides a huge boost to awareness early in the diffusion cycle but has very little impact as the market saturates. Managers of growth businesses should try to anticipate upcoming limits and focus on freeing up the limiting forces or constraints. Low-cost airlines can open new routes. Software developers can provide new features. Consumer electronics manufacturers can release creative product variations aimed at new market segments, like Apple's highly successful iPad. Finally, firms should beware of self-induced limits that stem from failure to detect or address limiting conditions.

Appendix: More About the Fliers Model

A complete equation-by-equation description of the Fliers model is available within the Fliers Mini-Sim in the learning support folder for Chapter 6. Select 'browse model' from the list of buttons on the left of the opening page. A diagram similar to Figure 6.11 will appear. Then select any model icon to view the accompanying equation and documentation.

The formulations in the market sector of the Fliers model need more explanation than is available from the simulator. The equations for available passenger miles are shown in Figure 6.17. Essentially, the more planes owned by easyJet, the more passenger miles the airline can fly each year. Planes are represented as a stock accumulation with an initial value of 12. There is no inflow or outflow to this stock because, in the Fliers model, we are specifically interested in easyJet's $500 million start-up gamble to purchase and fill 12 new planes. Available passenger miles are defined as the product of planes, passenger miles per plane and service days per year. Passenger miles per plane is a measure of the daily travel capacity of a short-haul plane flying between European destinations. For example, a typical 737 aircraft carries 150 passengers and makes three flights of 1000 miles per day for a total travel capacity of 450 000 passenger miles per day. Service days per year is assumed to be 360, meaning that the typical new plane flies almost every day of the year. Hence, the total available passenger miles from easyJet's fleet of 12 planes is 12 * 450 000 * 360, which is roughly 1.9 billion passenger miles per year.

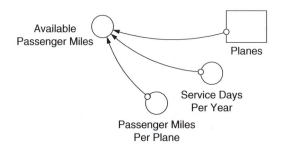

Available Passenger Miles = Planes *Passenger Miles Per Plane * Service Days Per Year
{passenger miles per year}

Planes(t) = Planes(t -dt)
INIT Planes = 12
Passenger Miles Per Plane = 450 000 {passenger miles/plane/day}
Service Days Per Year = 360 {days/year}

Figure 6.17   Equations for available passenger miles

The rest of the equations in the market sector convert this travel capacity to a potential market size expressed as the maximum passenger miles that could be flown by any one airline sharing the same routes operated by easyJet. The formulations are shown in Figure 6.18. Maximum passenger miles is the product of available passenger miles, average carriers per route, market share limit and maximum market size multiple. The reasoning is as follows. We assume that, on average, four carriers operate on the same routes as easyJet, including easyJet itself. So, as a rough approximation, the potential market size is four times easyJet's available passenger miles. Of this market it is reasonable to assume a market share limit of 50% (0.5) for any one airline. Moreover the existence of low fares could eventually double the market size. So the maximum market available to easyJet, with its fleet of 12 planes, is 1.9 * 4 * 0.5 * 2 = 7.6 billion passenger miles per year. This is the number that determines the limits to growth of potential passengers in the Fliers model.

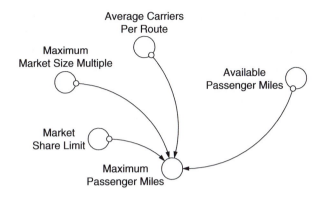

Maximum Passenger Miles = Available Passenger Miles * Average Carriers Per Route *
Market Share Limit * Maximum Market Size Multiple {passenger miles/year}
Average Carriers Per Route = 4
Market Share Limit = 0.5 {dimensionless}
Maximum Market Size Multiple = 2 {dimensionless}

Figure 6.18   Equations for maximum passenger miles

Back to the Future – From easyJet to People Express and Beyond

The formulations for easyJet's maximum market may look overly complex. Why not simply set up a stock of unaware customers who, through word-of-mouth and marketing, are converted to potential passengers for easyJet? The initial value of this stock would then be the maximum market size. Over time, these unaware customers are converted, through word-of-mouth and marketing, to potential passengers for easyJet. As the number of remaining unaware customers falls ever closer to zero, the conversion process slows. A single graphical converter linking unaware customers to the increase of potential passengers will do the job. As the number of unaware customers approaches zero, only the diehards remain and they cannot be easily moved. Thus, as unaware customers become fewer, their effect is to slow the rate of increase in potential passengers. Eventually, the flow is choked off entirely. I leave this formulation (involving a graph function) as an exercise for the reader. Note that the elegant Bass 'contagion formulations' would work too.

So why use eight concepts when two or three would do?[9] The reason is that the Fliers model was originally designed with two pedagogical purposes in mind. As we have seen in this chapter, it investigates the feasibility of easyJet

---

[9]Modellers normally try to adhere to 'Occam's Razor' – only add new concepts to the model if they are absolutely essential for the model's purpose – 'what can be done with fewer assumptions is done in vain with more' (William of Ockham 1285–1345 – Occam is the Latin spelling).

filling 12 planes – Stelios' $500 million gamble. The model was also designed, however, so that it could be extended to investigate the rise and fall of People Express airlines – a fascinating dynamic phenomenon in the same low-cost airline industry, but from an earlier era in the US market. For this additional purpose it is necessary to examine the growth of aircraft and staff and their joint effect on the service reputation of the airline. As the number of aircraft grows then the maximum market grows too (on the assumption that a growing low-cost airline establishes new routes as it acquires extra planes, thereby expanding the number of would-be fliers in the catchment area it serves). The formulations for the maximum market readily allow for this expansion of model purpose and boundary.

Readers are invited to build for themselves a People Express model using the airline model components in the learning support folder for Chapter 6. More information on how to proceed is provided there. However, it is a good idea, before plunging into this exercise, to read Chapter 7 about managing business growth. Here, we examine the managerial policies for building and coordinating strategic resources in a growth company in order to successfully and sustainably deliver new products and services to discerning customers. Coordination of growth was the key challenge facing Don Burr, the founder and CEO of People Express, in his company's bid to become a dominant player in the US domestic airline market and to change forever the competitive structure of the industry.[10,11]

The successful coordination of growth is a vital strategic task for many CEOs and top management teams. It is also a topic that has inspired some of the most creative and influential models in the system dynamics literature. Covert limits to growth can arise from a host of interlocking operational factors that

---

[10]There has been much debate about whether the rise and fall of People Express in the 1980s constituted a business failure. Those who disagree argue that in its brief lifetime the company changed the US airline industry beyond recognition. It also provided a memorable business experience for those involved – even those who suffered workplace burn-out toward the end of the company's brief and turbulent life. Judge for yourself the degree of failure or success and consider the following anecdote. A London Business School Executive MBA, who joined the programme in the early 1990s, had previously worked with People Express, through good times and bad. When asked if she would relive that part of her life again she replied yes, because of the atmosphere of excitement created by Don Burr and his top management team.

[11]The dramatic story of People Express is told in a popular Harvard Business School case study (Whitestone, 1983). The case is widely used in strategy courses alongside the People Express Management Flight Simulator (Sterman, 1988), which is itself based on the case. The model behind Sterman's vivid system dynamics gaming simulator is quite detailed and carefully calibrated to the case facts. Readers should be aware that Sterman's model is considerably more sophisticated than the airline model components in the learning support folder for Chapter 6. Nevertheless, both models can be viewed as variations on the 'growth and underinvestment' structure covered in Chapter 7. As far as I know, they share in common their formulations for rivals' fare (in terms of an asset stock adjustment process to represent restructuring of costs by traditional full-service airlines).

create surprise coordination problems. For example, extensions of the Bass model show the subtle constraining effects from capacity and infrastructure expansion on powerful word-of-mouth growth dynamics. The classic Market Growth model in Chapter 7 probes growth coordination inside the firm to reveal self-induced limits to growth. Variations, extensions and combinations of formulations in the Bass and market growth models (such as those used in the People Express model) indicate the broad applicability of system dynamics to growth management.

References

Bass, F. M. (1969) A new product growth model for consumer durables. *Management Science*, 15: 215–227.

Dangerfield, B.D., Fang, Y. and Roberts, C.A. (2001) Model-based scenarios for the epidemiology of HIV/AIDS: the consequences of highly active antiretroviral therapy. *System Dynamics Review*, 17(2): 119–150.

Farr, W. and Rockart, S. (2008) *Refrigeration Sales Corporation: The Evolution of a Closely Held Business*, Case Study, available from the first-named author Warren Farr III, President and CEO of Refrigeration Sales Corporation.

Farr, W. (2010) Using System Dynamics to Create Durable Business Strategy, Online Proceedings of the 2010 International System Dynamics Conference, Seoul, Korea. Available on the System Dynamics Society website www.systemdynamics.org. Also available through Google Scholar.

Finsgud, L. (2004) *Competing for Choice*. Monks Risborough, Bucks: Vola Publications.

Keith, D. (2012) Essays on the dynamics of alternative fuel vehicle adoption: insights from the market for hybrid-electric vehicles in the United States. The full text is available from the MIT DSpace database: http://dspace.mit.edu/handle/1721.1/79546 (accessed 24 February 2015).

Morecroft, J.D.W. (1984) Strategy support models. *Strategic Management Journal*, 5(3): 215–229.

Sterman, J.D. (1988) *People Express Management Flight Simulator: software and briefing materials*. Cambridge, MA: MIT Sloan School of Management.

Sterman, J.D. (2000) *Business Dynamics: Systems Thinking and Modeling for a Complex World*. Boston, MA: Irwin McGraw-Hill. (See Chapter 9 on S-Shaped Growth and in particular section 9.3.3 on the Bass Diffusion Model.)

Sterman, J.D. (2010) Eclipsing the Competition: The Solar PV Industry Simulation http://forio.com/simulation/mit-sloan-solar/index.htm (accessed 22 May 2014).

Struben, J. and Sterman, J.D. (2008) Transition challenges for alternative fuel vehicles and transportation systems. *Environment and Planning B: Planning and Design*, 35: 1070–1097.

Sull, D. (1999) easyJet's $500 million gamble. *European Management Journal*, 17(1): 20–38.

Whitestone, D. (1983) 'People Express (A)', Case No. 483-103, HBS Case Services Cambridge, MA.

Chapter 7
Managing Business Growth

The limiting conditions on growth in the previous chapter were largely external to the firm or at least somewhat beyond the firm's control. However, some of the most interesting constraints on business growth are internal to the firm. They are self-imposed or self-induced limits that arise from the way that an organisation expands its resources in marketing, distribution and manufacturing. Specifically, managerial policies in different functional areas, though intended to stimulate growth, may instead create hidden conflicts that undermine growth and lead to premature stagnation or even decline in a promising market. This kind of self-fulfilling prophecy stems from a coordination problem known as 'growth and underinvestment', common in many firms and industries (Senge, 1990: Chapter 7).

Figure 7.1 shows typical feedback structure that lies behind growth and underinvestment. There are four interacting feedback loops, making this the most dynamically complex situation we have investigated so far. The terminology is deliberately broad in order to emphasise the generic nature of the loops. At the top of the figure is a reinforcing growth engine formed by the links between demand and growing action.

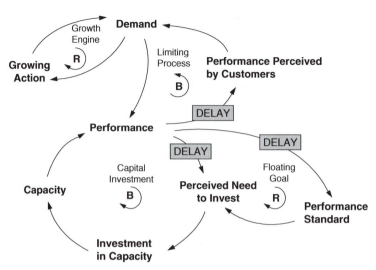

Figure 7.1   Growth and underinvestment feedback structure

The idea is that growing action by the firm (through expansion of marketing, sales force, distribution channels, etc.) leads to increased demand that in turn justifies further expansion. On the right is a limiting process that depends on performance (of the product or service) in the market. Performance could mean service quality, availability, reliability, value for money, or any one of a number of factors that attracts customers. The important point is that such customer-facing performance depends on the balance between demand and capacity. If, for some reason, the firm's capacity to deliver and support a product or service falls short of demand then performance will decline, and eventually performance perceived by customers will fall too and therefore curtail demand. On the other hand, if there is adequate capacity then demand will continue to grow under the influence of the growth engine. Note in this case the limit to demand growth is not external and fixed (as in the diffusion models of Chapter 6) but is itself a part of the feedback structure and can vary accordingly.

On the lower left of the figure is a balancing loop for capital investment. The loop connects performance, perceived need to invest, investment in capacity and capacity. This loop nurtures growth by striving for sufficient capacity to maintain satisfactory performance. However, appropriate investment is never easy to gauge. There is often ambiguity in investment plans and legitimate scope for differences of opinion in management teams about how much to invest and how soon. This ambiguity is captured in the concept 'perceived need to invest', which depends on performance relative to a performance standard. Performance below the standard is a signal to invest. If the performance standard were to be fixed and absolute then capacity adjustment would boil down to simple goal-seeking feedback. But there is an added sophistication, a subtle twist of dynamic complexity, in the form of a reinforcing loop called 'floating goal' that allows the goal itself to adapt. This loop, which is complementary to capital investment, connects performance to the performance standard, perceived need to invest, investment in capacity and capacity. If performance improves then, after a delay, the performance standard will improve too, leading eventually to more capacity, better performance and so on. The loop can operate as a virtuous or vicious cycle depending on the circumstances.

We will now discuss a model-supported, business case of growth that reveals a specific example of the growth and underinvestment archetype in action.

A Conceptual Model of Market Growth and Capital Investment

Most new companies fail. Some grow for a while and then stagnate. A few manage to grow but experience periodic downturns leading to crises of confidence and turnover of top management. Only a very small number of firms seem able to grow rapidly for extended periods of time. A classic model in the field of system dynamics, known as the 'market growth model' (Forrester, 1968), directly addresses this issue and arose from Jay Forrester's experience advising entrepreneurs and fledgling companies in technology-based firms around Boston, Massachusetts. Though compact, the model contains nearly everything of interest in dynamical business models such as multiple interacting loops, non-linearities, expectation formation, delays, bias and distortion in management information channels, and bounded rationality in operating policies.

Background to the Case

Imagine a division of a medium-sized electronics company producing specialist navigation equipment for use in luxury yachts and light aircraft. The division has recently launched a new state-of-the-art global positioning system and wants to explore the feasibility of various growth plans. The product is sold directly to firms that make luxury yachts and light aircraft rather than to the owners of boats and planes. Sales are generated by a direct sales force with the necessary technical knowledge to sell a sophisticated and expensive electronic product. The division is aiming for profitable growth while maintaining good service to customers. A sketch of future revenue time paths is shown in Figure 7.2. The plan is for steady revenue growth of about 50% per year, but no one really knows if the plan is achievable. Less desirable trajectories are growth with repeated downturns or growth followed by stagnation and decline.

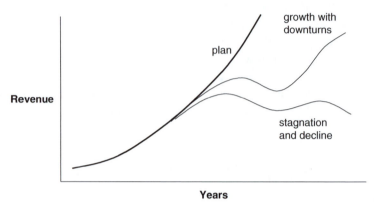

Figure 7.2   Future time paths for revenue

Adopting a Feedback View

Which circumstances might distinguish between these different outcomes? Downturns, stagnation and decline are often conveniently blamed on external factors such as a weak economy, aggressive rivals, limited market size or premature technology. However, we are looking for a different explanation involving factors within the control of management. Hence, we will assume there is a large potential market and that product quality is comparable to rivals, if not better. Our dynamic hunch is that the pattern of growth depends on the coordination of demand and supply. A sector map of suitable scope is shown in Figure 7.3. On the left is the firm represented in terms of sectors for sales force, production capacity and order fulfilment. Within these sectors are to be found operating policies such as hiring and investment. On the right is the market, represented in terms of customer ordering and the firm's influence on customers. Essentially, the task of the firm is to stimulate demand through sales effort and to adjust production capacity to satisfy the resulting customer orders.

The sectors are linked by four feedback loops as shown in Figure 7.4. At the top left is the sales growth loop involving the sales force and customer orders. At the top right is the customer response loop that depends on customers' perception of delivery delay. In the lower centre is the capital investment loop that expands capacity in response to the company's perception of delivery delay and on the lower right is a floating goal involving target delivery delay.

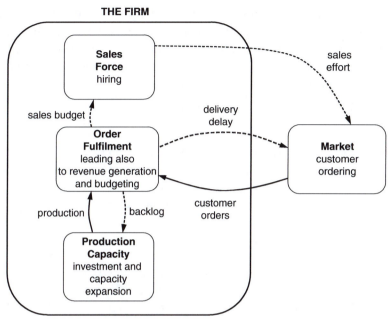

Figure 7.3   Sector map for dynamic hunch

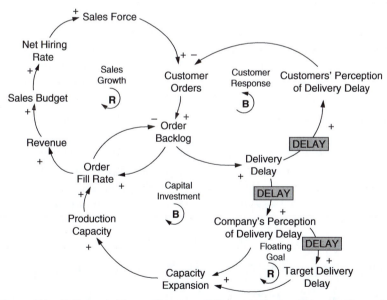

Figure 7.4   Full causal loop diagram of Forrester's market growth model

Although it is not possible to infer market growth dynamics from the diagram alone, an inspection of the individual loops provides some useful insight into the main dynamic processes at work. We start with the sales growth loop and imagine the effect around the loop of an increase in the sales force. A bigger sales force wins more customer orders (all else equal), resulting in a larger order backlog. Assuming adequate production capacity, then a larger backlog results in a greater order fill rate, more revenue and an increase in the sales budget. With a larger budget the firm can afford to hire more salesmen. So there exists a reinforcing loop in which any increase in the sales force stimulates extra orders and revenue that in turn justify a further increase in sales force.

Meanwhile, the capital investment loop expands capacity if there is evidence of unfilled demand. An increase in the order backlog leads to a rise in delivery delay because the factory takes longer to fill orders. The company's perception of delivery delay eventually rises too and this is the signal for capacity expansion. More production capacity leads to a higher order fill rate that reduces the order backlog and delivery delay. The result is a balancing loop in which any increase in delivery delay (above the company's target) leads to a compensating reduction in delivery delay through capacity expansion. The target delivery delay itself depends on the company's perception of delivery delay. This floating goal is part of a reinforcing loop that relieves chronic pressure for capital investment (due to rising delivery delay) by allowing the target delivery delay itself to rise.

While the company is attempting to match capacity with demand, the customer response loop limits demand if the product is not readily available. An increase in delivery delay leads to an increase in the customers' perception of delivery delay and a reduction of customer orders. Fewer orders lead to a smaller order backlog and a reduction in the delivery delay thereby completing a balancing loop. If the company cannot fill customer orders quickly enough, then demand falls to restore a conveniently short delivery delay.

The four loops provide a good multi-function overview of product–market growth; but why these particular loops? This is an important question to ask of any model, because the more plausible the feedback structure the more likely it will provide a convincing explanation of dynamics and performance through time.

Formulation Guidelines for Portraying Feedback Structure

It is sometimes said of our increasingly complex world that everything is connected to everything else, suggesting a huge tangle of interdependencies for people to manage and for the modeller to unravel. This is an overstatement. While it is true that more parts of business and society are connected now than in the past, through the internet, smartphones and laptops, many of the most important and useful connections are nevertheless sparse. Why? Anything that happens in organisations depends on the actions of ordinary people, who, no matter how talented, can handle only limited amounts of information as they communicate, collaborate and cajole to achieve their objectives. The complexity of society largely mirrors our own human capacity to process information and to coordinate action – and that capacity has not changed fundamentally since the industrial revolution or the Roman Empire. Therefore, the task for the feedback system modeller is to portray, as convincingly as possible, the relatively sparse network of connections through which people enact plans and strategies. The majority of the network is made up of information flows.

There are five formulation guidelines to help modellers identify the most influential and realistic connections among the myriad that could in principle exist (Sterman, 2000: Chapter 13 on modelling decision making). They are summarised in Figure 7.5. The first and most general is the 'Baker criterion', which requires that the inputs to all decision rules or policies must be restricted to the information actually available to real decision makers. Although this statement may seem obvious, it is vital for distinguishing, among the many potential influences on decision makers, those that really matter. Usually there are far fewer influences than one might at first suspect. In real life, managers use only a small fraction of the organisational information available to them to guide their decision making. Careful observation of managerial practice is therefore essential.

The Baker Criterion: the inputs to all decision rules (policies) must be restricted to information actually available to the real decision makers

The decision rules (policies) of a model should conform to managerial practice

Desired and actual conditions should be distinguished

Equilibrium and optimality should not be assumed

Decision rules should be robust under extreme conditions

Figure 7.5   Formulation guidelines
Source: Sterman, J.D., Business Dynamics: Systems Thinking and Modeling for a Complex World, © 2000, Irwin McGraw-Hill, Boston, MA. Reproduced with permission of the McGraw-Hill Companies.

The term 'Baker criterion' originates from Senator Howard Baker's famous question in the US Senate Hearings into the Watergate scandal in 1973: 'What did the President know and when did he know it?' The President (at that time Richard Nixon) could not be implicated in the scandal if he was unaware of the actions of his staff and subordinates. So figuring out just how much the President knew (and how much he should be expected to know) was of central importance. The same criterion can be usefully applied at any point of decision making in an organisation. What did the managers responsible for investment know and when did they know it? What did the people responsible for pricing know and when did they know it? What did customers know about the product or service and when did they know it. The point is that decision makers can't know everything and so, for the organisation as a whole, actions are only loosely coordinated and it can often appear that the left hand doesn't know what the right hand is doing. Such inconsistency is normal in management and is important for modellers to realistically portray.

The second guideline, a natural corollary of the Baker criterion, states that the decision rules or policies of a model should conform to managerial practice. All the influences on policies should be based on real-world counterparts and all variable names should be familiar to those working in the system. This advice leads to a descriptive model that represents the system as it currently operates, rather than an ideal model of how it should operate. Moreover, such a model is much more likely to engage managers and policymakers because it uses their own jargon and vocabulary.

The third guideline stresses the need for modellers to distinguish between actual and desired conditions in organisations. Actual conditions are what can be observed and measured such as capacity, workforce, price and so on. Desired conditions are in the minds of those with the power to act and reflect intentions, goals and aspirations. Nearly always, desired and actual conditions are different. Only by keeping the distinction clear is it possible to represent realistic disequilibrium pressures that drive corrective actions and contribute to dynamics.

The fourth guideline is a corollary of the third – equilibrium and optimality should not be assumed; they are convenient ideals but are not characteristic of the normal way organisations operate. Growth, fluctuation, stagnation, decline and overshoot are all disequilibrium phenomena and there is no guarantee that the various functions and sectors of an organisation that create such dynamics are optimally coordinated – far from it. A modeller who presumes optimal use of strategic resources or the existence of an efficient equilibrium between supply and demand is like a driving instructor who assumes that Sebastian Vettel or Lewis Hamilton are representative of typical motorists. Perfection in timing, action and reaction is an interesting benchmark, but is not a realistic way to think about normally competent drivers or normally competent organisations. The ideals of optimality and equilibrium require lots of coordinating information, much more than decision makers typically use, and fast reaction times too.

The fifth formulation guideline states that decision rules should be robust under extreme conditions. This guideline can expose flaws in equation formulations and give useful hints about when and where to expect non-linearities in feedback loops. Consider, for example, a linear pricing formulation where price reduction is proportional to the gap between target demand and current demand. A sudden halving of current demand would be an extreme condition. If this thought experiment were to result in a negative price (an unlikely outcome in reality) then it would suggest a need to modify the pricing formulation, by, for example, adding a new non-linear pressure from margin on price change.

Review of Operating Policies and Information Flows in the Market Growth Model

Now we will use the formulation guidelines to interpret the operating policies and information flows of the market growth model, thereby shedding light on the model's feedback structure and its portrayal of growth dynamics. The main policies within the model boundary are customer ordering, sales force hiring, budgeting and production capacity expansion. We examine these policies one by one and then show how they fit together to yield the four feedback loops already outlined.

Customer Ordering

Figure 7.6 shows the customer ordering policy. To identify the influential information flows we need to get inside the world of the customer.

Who are the customers? What are their incentives? Who and what influences them to place orders? To identify the *influential* information flows means getting inside the world of the customer – in this case experienced buyers in a purchasing department, who are knowledgeable about the product and concerned about quality, design and technology, component reliability, and availability.

Figure 7.6   Customer ordering policy

Remember our model represents the sale of a specialist technical product (advanced satellite navigation systems) to a manufacturer rather than to a consumer. So the 'customer' in this case is a knowledgeable, technical buyer who wants to know about the functionality of the product, is seeking quality and reliability and needs the product delivered on time. The buyer is not particularly price sensitive since the navigation system is only a small proportion of the cost of a light aircraft or small boat in which it is installed.

In principle, all six factors shown in the diagram (availability, quality, relative price, sales effort, advertising and word-of-mouth) could influence customer ordering, and others besides. Which should be included? Here the formulation guidelines can help to tease out, through questioning of managers and business experts, the dominant influences. For this type of technical product and commercial customer, the main influences on ordering are sales effort, quality/reliability and availability; priorities that would be apparent in managerial practice, just as Forrester found in his original study. The other potential influences (word-of-mouth, advertising and relative price) can be ignored here because they are not of central concern to this type of commercial customer.

A further simplification is possible. Quality and reliability can be eliminated entirely from the model if we assume they remain high and stable and therefore do not contribute to dynamics. This is a plausible assumption whose consistency with the facts can readily be checked. We are therefore left with only two influences on customer ordering: sales effort and availability – and ultimately a much simpler feedback representation. In conclusion, the essence of the ordering formulation lies in the technical nature of the product, sold by a professional sales force to commercial buyers who want absolutely reliable delivery.

Sales Force Expansion

Figure 7.7 shows the policy for sales force expansion. In formulating this policy, the modeller's central question is how the company justifies the hiring of sales people. Again many influences may come to bear and the diagram shows seven possibilities. The amount of information in all these influences is far more than any management team would normally use and the Baker criterion suggests a need to be selective in order to identify those influences that conform best to managerial practice. What does the management team know and really care about in hiring, and when do they know it? Among the influences shown, it is possible to distinguish two distinct managerial approaches to sales force expansion. The influences on the left correspond to a budget-driven policy, while those on the right correspond to a forecast-driven policy. A budget-driven policy is one in which hiring depends on the sales budget and sales force operating costs (which in turn depend on the current sales force size and salary). If the budget exceeds operating costs then additional hiring is permitted and vice versa for firing. A forecast-driven policy is one in which hiring is linked to a sales plan that might include a growth goal, sales objective or estimate of expected orders. Knowing the sales plan and sales force productivity yields a target sales force. Either approach to hiring is perfectly valid, but in reality one or the other is likely to dominate. There is a need to read between the lines of management practice to discern which is the most appropriate representation. In this case, we imagine the modeller has inferred from conversations that the sales department is budget driven. So the three factors on the left of the diagram are the active sources of information for the hiring policy. Once again a significant simplification is achieved in the information network and the resulting feedback structure.

How does the company justify expansion of the sales force? How does this policy depend on expectations about market growth and plans for capacity expansion? Imagine yourself inside a growing sales organisation as sales director or member of a sales management team

Figure 7.7   Sales force hiring policy

Budgeting

Figure 7.8 is a glimpse of the myopic and political world of budgeting as it affects the sales function. In principle, there is an optimal way for firms to budget by allocating funds to those activities that generate the greatest marginal returns. However, formulation guideline number four tells us to beware of optimal decision rules. A truly optimal allocation of funds requires far too much coordinating information to be a credible description of what goes on in practice. Experience suggests that budgeting is normally myopic, often based on the pattern of past funding rather than a comprehensive trade-off among competing alternatives.

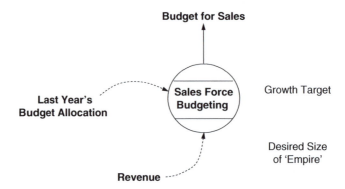

What is the rationale for allocation of revenue to different activities or organisational areas? Imagine participating in budget meetings with functional directors of Sales, Manufacturing, Product Development, each fighting for a share of the budget.

Figure 7.8   The myopic and political world of budgeting

This myopic logic is represented in two information flows. First, the total budget to cover operating expenses across all functions is assumed proportional to revenue. The more revenue generated, the bigger the total budget. Then comes the budget allocation, which is often based on past precedent so that functions normally feel entitled to receive at least last year's budget allocation. Sometimes strategic and political factors intervene (such as a growth target or desired size of 'empire') to cause departures from simple historical precedent. However, in this case precedent is assumed to be the dominant influence.

Capital Investment

Figure 7.9 shows three different approaches to capital investment, each relying on different sources of information. On the left is a finance-driven approach, while on the right is a planning-driven approach, and in the centre is an operations-driven approach. We begin on the left. A company that prides itself on rigorous financial appraisal might justify investment in terms of discounted cash flow, using information about expected revenue, machine price and a hurdle rate. Overlaid on this evaluation is the availability of funding that limits investment when the firm's pool of financial resources is low. By contrast, on the right is a forward-looking and planning-driven approach to capital investment. There are two information sources, expected demand and growth target, which are entirely different from the previous financial criteria and also much simpler. They suggest a management team whose investment is driven by a belief in a market plan or vision for the future, rather than financial performance.

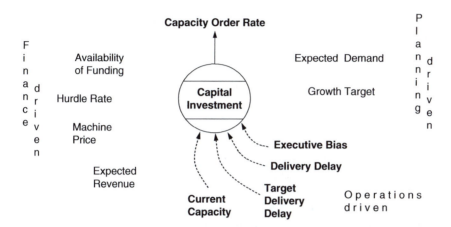

How does the company recognise the need for capacity expansion? What compromise is struck between the pressures from finance, operations and formal planning? Imagine you are participating in capital investment meetings with the Managing Director, Finance Director, Factory Manager, and Sales Manager.

Figure 7.9   The pressures and politics of capital investment

In the centre of the diagram is a reactive operations-driven approach. The information sources are different yet again. Here the top management team responsible for investment is assumed to pay particular attention to the capacity needs of the factory as reflected in current capacity, delivery delay and target delivery delay. Imagine the situation. Factory managers present their case for capacity expansion to an investment committee, arguing that current capacity is inadequate because delivery delay is too long relative to the target. The investment committee may or may not be sympathetic to the factory's case and has the discretion to fully or partially approve new investment. Such discretion is captured in the notion of executive bias and shown as a fourth influence on capital investment.

Of course in any firm all these sources of information are potential influences on investment. But that does not mean they should all be included in the modelled investment policy. Again the formulation guidelines come into play. What does the top management team responsible for investment know and really care about, and when do they know it? In this particular case, we adopt the same assumption as the original market growth model, that capital investment is operations driven and reactive. Hence, the influential information sources entering the investment policy are reduced to only three: delivery delay, target delivery delay and current capacity, overlaid by executive bias. The implied style of investment is both practical and well-grounded in facts available from the factory as seen through the eyes of cautious executives who want solid evidence of demand before committing to capacity expansion.

The perceptive modeller looks for distinctive managerial attitudes toward investment. As a practical illustration consider the visionary (some would say reckless) capacity expansion plans of Sochiro Honda in the early days of the Japanese motorcycle industry.[1] He committed the fledgling Honda company to a massive increase of capacity, equal to twice industry capacity for the whole of Japan, to be installed in only two years. This investment programme was justified on the basis of his personal belief in the importance of the motorcycle to post-war Japanese society, and the manufacturing prowess of his own organisation. Moreover, he persuaded the rest of the management team to go along with his bold plan. There was no tangible business evidence to support his view, no burgeoning delivery delay, no solid cash flow projections nor even a demand forecast based on formal market research. The point is that influences on investment vary from one firm to another, sometimes dramatically. It is the job of modellers to recognise which influences dominate. Incidentally, Honda's blinkered optimism proved to be justified and his company grew swiftly at a time when less bold rivals held back their investment. Passionate belief in a future can drive successful capital investment, but not always.

Goal Formation

At the heart of capital investment is corrective action – adding more capacity because it is deemed necessary. In this case, the trigger for investment is target delivery delay. But where does the target itself come from? It need not be a constant. In fact, it is often useful to view a management target as the output from a decision-making process of goal formation. In other words, targets and goals are a matter of policy. Recognising such fluidity naturally focuses attention on the information sources that drive goal formation. Figure 7.10 shows four potential information sources for target delivery delay.

---

[1] A description of Sochiro Honda's visionary and hugely confident approach to developing his fledgling motorcycle company can be found in a classic Harvard Business School case study entitled 'Honda (B)', Christiansen and Pascale, Case No. 9-384-050, HBS Case Services Cambridge MA. In the company's very early days he founded the Honda Technical Institute. It sounded like Bell Laboratories or Google X, but in reality it began as one man tinkering, who had a passion for engines and motorcycle racing. Yet he believed his workshop would become an Institute. The first factory was an old sewing machine plant, with plenty of space for growth. A combination of supreme self-belief coupled with technical know-how and hard work led him to take risks in capacity expansion that no other rival would dare. In all likelihood he did not perceive the risk that others did, but instead saw a vast opportunity. This attitude underpinned the company's bold capital investment policy.

How does the company establish a target for delivery delay (or any other component of product attractiveness)? What compromise is struck between pressures from the market and from operations?

Figure 7.10 Target delivery delay as the output from a goal formation policy

On the left are market-oriented factors such as competitors' delivery delay and the delivery delay expected by customers. On the right are operations-oriented factors such as the delivery delay recognised by the factory and a delivery delay management goal. Yet again the formulation criteria are important for recognising which information sources best coincide with management practice. It is highly unlikely that all four will be used. In some firms it will be possible to discern a culture of market awareness that gives priority to the factors on the left. In other firms, dominated by manufacturing, the factors on the right will be given priority. The modeller should not assume that one or other orientation is used just because prevailing wisdom or accepted theory says it should be. In this particular case, we choose the same operations-oriented formulation as found in the original market growth model.

An Information Feedback View of Management and Policy

The market growth model embodies the essence of the information feedback view of the firm. There is more to this view than feedback loops, stocks and flows – important though they are. There is also an underlying philosophy about management and policy (in all areas of business and society), which I want to reflect on now before developing the model any further. A good place to start is with Forrester's original comments about the craft of management.

In his seminal book *Industrial Dynamics* (Forrester, 1961: 93) he describes management as the process of converting information into action:

> If management is the process of converting information into action, then management success depends primarily on what information is chosen and how the conversion is executed. Moreover the difference between a good manager and a poor manager lies right at this point between information and action.

The viewpoint is cognitive but also action oriented. As Forrester (1994: 51) goes on to explain:

> A manager sets the stage for action by choosing which information sources to take seriously and which to ignore. A manager's success depends on both selecting the most relevant information and on using that information effectively. How quickly or slowly is information converted into action? What is the relative weight given to different information sources in light of desired objectives? How are these desired objectives created from available information?

Here is a parsimonious and stylised portrayal of management, entirely consistent with the principles of information feedback systems, yet capable of capturing a very wide range of managerial behaviour. Leadership, charisma and other important attributes of management (vital to business performance and explicitly addressed in the organisational and strategy literature) are represented implicitly and subtly in system dynamics through their influence on the information sources deemed important enough to justify action.

This information-processing view of management leads directly and naturally to the fundamental representation scheme in system dynamics. Again quoting from Forrester's early work:

> A simulation model is based on explicit statements of policies (or rules) that govern decision making. The decision making process consists of three parts: the formulation of a set of concepts indicating the conditions that are desired, the observation of what appears to be the actual conditions, and corrective action to bring apparent conditions toward desired conditions.
>
> **(Jay Forrester, 1961, *Industrial Dynamics*, available from the System Dynamics Society www.systemdynamics.org, originally published by MIT Press, Cambridge MA. Quotes are from Chapter 10 in the book. Reproduced by permission of Jay W. Forrester.)**

The verbal description above translates into Figure 7.11. It represents how managers make adjustments to organisational asset stocks or resources through operating policy. The policy is represented mathematically as:

$$\text{Corrective Action} = (\text{Desired Resource} - \text{Apparent Resource})/\text{Time to Correct Gap.}$$

In a simple formulation, the desired resource is constant and the apparent resource is identically equal to the actual resource.

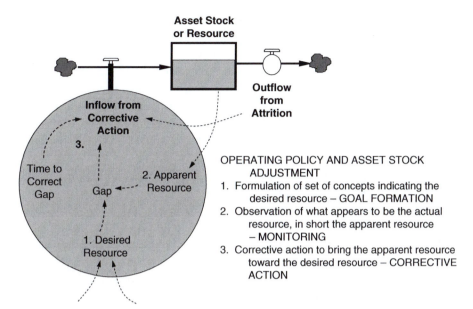

Figure 7.11   Converting information into action – an information feedback view of management

More sophisticated asset stock adjustment can be portrayed too, capturing the ambiguity of resource management found in practice. For example, the apparent resource may differ from the actual resource because of reporting delays, error or bias. In extreme cases, the condition of the actual resource may not be known at all and so cannot be managed or controlled. The desired resource need not be constant but instead varies over time, through a process of goal formation, depending on conditions elsewhere in the business. Hence, this stock adjustment formulation though compact is very versatile. Moreover, it raises lots of interesting questions about managers' ability to build and to balance organisational resources by focusing attention on: (1) whether, for each resource, there is a clear communicable goal as the basis for corrective action; (2) whether resources are accurately known or not; and (3) whether, having sensed a gap between desired and apparent resource, management react quickly or slowly to close the gap.

Information Available to Decision Makers and Bounded Rationality

According to the feedback view of management, information drives the corrective actions of organisations as they seek to build and maintain a balanced set of resources. Which information sources, among those available, are actually used by managers? This question lies behind the Baker criterion and the formulation guidelines mentioned earlier in the chapter. In principle, the state of every single resource in an organisation is relevant to every point of decision making in the organisation so that stock adjustments are fully informed. Consider, for example, a supply chain comprising customers, retailers, wholesalers, distributors and a factory. Customers buy from retailers. The retailers order from wholesalers who in turn order from distributors. The distributors then place orders with the factory. In other words, orders flow upstream, originating with customers and ending at the factory. Goods flow in the reverse direction, downstream; originating in the factory and eventually arriving at retailers for purchase by customers. What information is relevant for the factory's production planning? Obviously the factory should take account of distributors' orders because the factory supplies the distributors. The factory should also take account of its own inventory and backlog condition and much more besides. Clearly there is a lot of information in the supply chain that, theoretically at least, is relevant to production planning. For example, there is customer demand and the amount of downstream inventory and backlog at every stage of the supply chain. Compiling and making sense of all this data, however, is a huge task, beyond the abilities of normally competent people, even in an era of big data and analytics.

Usually things are much simpler. Factory managers normally pay most attention to tangible information that is available locally such as distributors' orders and factory inventory. The more general point is that decision makers typically use much less information than the total available to them. Moreover, the available information is less than is commonly presumed. One way to think about this selection process is to picture operating policy surrounded by information filters, as shown in Figure 7.12.

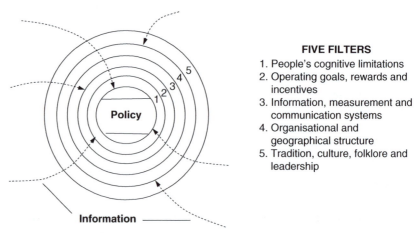

FIVE FILTERS

1. People's cognitive limitations
2. Operating goals, rewards and incentives
3. Information, measurement and communication systems
4. Organisational and geographical structure
5. Tradition, culture, folklore and leadership

Figure 7.12 The policy function, information filters and bounded rationality – behavioural decision making

The figure shows five possible filters. The first and most basic filter stems from people's cognitive limitations. It doesn't take much information for us to feel overwhelmed and so we pick the signals that seem most relevant and ignore the rest. The torrent of email and social media messages is a daily reminder of our information limits. The formal name for cognitive limitations as they affect decision making is 'bounded rationality', a term first proposed by Nobel laureate Herbert Simon. The concept was developed in the influential literature of the Carnegie School as a theory of firm behaviour and an alternative to conventional microeconomic theory (Simon, 1979; 1982).

The other filters are created by the organisation itself as it parcels out responsibilities across functional areas and departments. In a sense, the organisation compensates for individuals' cognitive limitations by placing them in a departmental structure that means they can get on with their own job without worrying about what is happening in every other department. As Simon (1976) and Barnard (1938) have pointed out, the organisation provides a psychological environment that shapes (sometimes very powerfully) how people act and it is the function of the executive to 'design' this environment so departmental efforts are coordinated. The CEO is a designer with various design tools at his or her disposal (Forrester, 1996). Most obvious are operating goals, rewards and incentives (the second filter) that direct people's attention and effort to organisational objectives. Such inducements reduce the complexity of decision making by prescribing what needs to be achieved by different departments. The potential downside is a functional mentality, though this syndrome is not necessarily a problem in a well-designed organisation, it just means people are focused (and that could be an advantage).

The next filter represents the effect of information, measurement and communication systems on decision making. Undoubtedly, computers and the internet have massively boosted the amount of information flowing around and between organisations. Again supply chains are a good example. These days it is possible for factories to hold data on retail orders at point of sale and distributors' inventory for use in production planning. However, such data are not necessarily as convenient or trusted as information gleaned from informal channels such as casual conversations, ad hoc meetings and walkabouts. Moreover, informal 'intelligence' is often more persuasive and timely than information available on the official database.

The fourth filter represents the effect of organisational and geographical structure. Organisations frequently set up or acquire a new business unit at arm's length from the existing business. A good example is the fledgling low-cost airline Go, set up by BA in the 1990s, to compete with easyJet and Ryanair in the European short-haul business. Go was deliberately made independent of BA, operating its own planes with its own staff and information systems. The whole point was to design an enterprise that could decide and act in its own right, free from the influence of parent BA. The amount of information flowing between the two organisations was much less than if they were seamlessly merged in a single airline. Another example is the MINI car division of BMW, created as an independent business unit, able to take its own decisions (under corporate guidance) on product development and capital investment in order to develop a new and distinct brand in the highly competitive global small-car market.

The fifth filter is the most subtle yet, and also the most powerful. It captures the attenuating and amplifying effect on information of tradition, culture, folklore and leadership. From a cognitive view these intangible traits shape the psychological environment in which people take decisions and act. They define what the organisation stands for and therefore what really needs attention. Consider, for example, Google and its co-founders Larry Page and Sergey Brin. Commentators have said they are intellectually obsessed with an omniscient and omnipotent algorithm for mining the world's knowledge. This belief is part of Google's culture, permeating the minds of thousands of employees and helping to coordinate their actions. Another example is MIT with its culture of technological excellence that pervades all departments including the humanities and management, shaping decisions on faculty recruitment, the curriculum and choice of students.

Nature of Decision Making and the Decision Process

An important conclusion from the discussion so far is that the feedback view of organisations incorporates behavioural decision making and assumes bounded rationality (Morecroft, 1983; Sterman, 1989). This perspective on decision making distinguishes system dynamics sharply from traditional microeconomics in which 'economic man' makes objectively rational decisions, weighing up all available sources of information to arrive at an optimal (profit maximising) configuration of resources. Figure 7.13 captures the essential philosophical stance on decision making in system dynamics. Any operating policy sits amid its filters, bombarded by information originating from all asset stocks in the system. Consistent with the Baker criterion, however, only a handful of information flows penetrate to the policy core leading to action and stock accumulation.

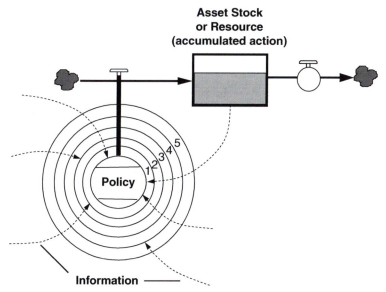

Figure 7.13   Behavioural decision making leading to stock accumulation and information feedback

A corollary is that decision making is conceived as a continuous process for converting varying information flows into signals that determine action (rates of flow). In system dynamics, a decision function does not portray a choice among alternatives, as found in a decision tree with its various discrete nodes and branches. Neither is it the familiar logic of 'if-then-else' that applies to individual decisions like whether to take a taxi or catch the bus. The crucial point is that we are viewing decision processes from a distance where discrete choices disappear, leaving only broad organisational pressures that shape action.

Choosing the proper distance from which to view and model a system is crucial. As Forrester has noted, we are not as close as a psychologist, concerned with the mechanisms of human thought, delving into the nature and sources of cognition, personality and motivation. We are not even close enough to see each separate decision, but instead observe a modulating stream of decisions. We may not be close enough to care whether one person or a group creates the decision stream. On the other hand, we are not as remote as a public stockholder who is so far from the corporation as to be unaware of the internal structure, social pressures and decision points. Modellers need to adopt an intermediate position, similar to the perspective of the Board of Directors, top management team, strategy consultant or investment banker.

Policy Structure and Formulations for Sales Growth

In the light of our discussion on decision making we now return to the market growth model to see how its various policies fit together. Figure 7.14 shows the policy structure behind the reinforcing sales growth loop that links sales force hiring, budgeting, customer ordering and order fulfilment. Before plunging into the detail of the formulations, first look at the broad pattern of connections between the grey areas that correspond to operating policies. Why should sales grow at all? Is the growth engine plausible? To investigate, we start with the sales force and trace anticlockwise. Crucially sales force hiring relies on a signal from budgeting (the authorised sales force) to guide adjustments to the sales force size. Hiring in this organisation is budget driven. Budgeting itself is quite myopic, a characteristic clearly shown in the single information link that feeds in from order fulfilment. Fundamentally, the budget is proportional to the order fill rate – it is not a complex trade-off between competing alternatives. Meanwhile, leaving aside capacity constraints, the principal pressure on order fulfilment comes from the backlog: the bigger the backlog, the greater the order fill rate. Looking down on this company from the perspective of the CEO, we can see there is a causal chain, weaving among the functions, that connects sales force hiring to the size of the order backlog. In addition, the backlog itself is an accumulation of unfilled customer orders.

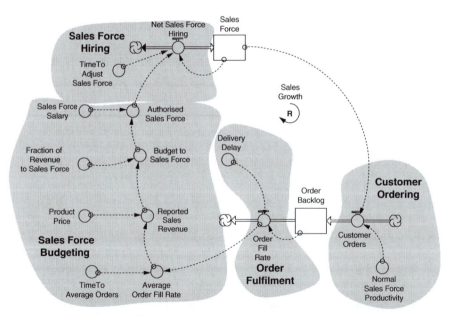

Figure 7.14   Policy structure and formulations for sales growth

Only one more link is needed to form a reinforcing sales growth loop – the link from sales force to customer orders which is likely to be strong in firms that sell high-specification technical products.

The policy structure provides a framework within which the equation formulations take shape. In other words, the architecture of the information network is defined and it now remains to explain the equations underlying each operating policy. Again we will begin with sales force at the top of the diagram and work anticlockwise through the formulations.

Sales Force Hiring – Standard Stock Adjustment Formulation

We know that sales force hiring is budget driven. An elegant way to capture this effect is with a standard stock adjustment formulation as shown in the equations below.

> Sales Force (t) = Sales Force(t – dt) + (Net Sales Force Hiring) ∗ dt
>
> INIT Sales Force = 4 {sales people}
>
> Net Sales Force Hiring = (Authorised Sales Force – Sales Force)/
> Time to Adjust Sales Force
>
> Time to Adjust Sales Force = 12 {months}

The sales force is represented as a stock that accumulates net sales force hiring. Hiring results from corrective action of the hiring policy and depends on the difference between the authorised sales force and the sales force (the gap in head count) divided by the time to adjust sales force. In this case, the head count goal of the hiring policy is the authorised sales force that comes from budgeting. The model is initialised with just four sales people and the time to adjust sales force is set at 12 months. This choice of adjustment time reflects an assumption that the company is reasonably patient in filling any head count gap. Essentially, a shortfall or excess of sales people is corrected gradually over a period of 12 months.

Sales Force Budgeting – Revenue Allocation and Information Smoothing

Budgeting is modelled as a political allocation process driven by past precedent and captured in the eight equations shown below. The authorised sales force depends on the ratio of the budget allocated to the sales force and sales force salary. This equation is simply a matter of definition. The bigger the budget, the larger the authorised sales force; whereas the higher the sales force salary the fewer sales people the budget will support. We assume that sales force salary is £4000 per sales person per month, including overhead. Note that this choice of units ensures dimensional consistency. The most important formulation is the equation representing the budget allocated to the sales force because here are embedded the assumptions about precedent and the politics of budgeting. The budget to sales force is defined as the product of sales revenue and the fraction of revenue to the sales force, in other words a fixed fractional revenue allocation. This one-line equation is surprisingly simple, but captures a lot about the typical shortcuts and compromises that characterise real-world budgets. For example, in a modelling project for BBC World Service (mentioned briefly in Chapter 3 and described more fully in an article that appears in the learning support folder for Chapter 7 – entitled 'Modelling and Simulating Firm Performance') it was found that operating funds were divided into separate components for programme making, programme support and transmission. The proportion of available funds allocated to each of these activities was 70% for programme making, 15% for programme support and 15% for transmission. These proportions, steeped in the traditions of an international radio broadcaster, were not easily changed. Similar rigidity applies to the fraction of revenue available to the sales force in the market growth model. The fraction is set at 0.1, so that 10% of sales revenue is normally allocated to fund the sales force.

> Authorised Sales Force = Budget to Sales Force/Sales Force Salary {salespeople}
>
> Sales Force Salary = 4000 {£ per sales person per month, including overhead and support}
>
> Budget to Sales Force = Reported Sales Revenue * Fraction of Revenue to Sales Force {£/month}
>
> Fraction of Revenue to Sales Force = 1 {dimensionless}
>
> Reported Sales Revenue = Average Order Fill Rate * Product Price {£/month}
>
> Average Order Fill Rate = SMTH1 (Order Fill Rate, Time To Average Orders) {systems per month}
>
> Product Price = 9600 {£ per system}
>
> Time To Average Orders = 1 {month}

Reported sales revenue is formulated as the average order fill rate multiplied by product price, which is set at £9600 per system. This equation is more or less an accounting identity that might appear in a spreadsheet model, but for one subtle change inspired by principles of information feedback and the Baker criterion. We assume that data on sales revenue must be gathered and reported before it can be used to inform decision making. Such measurement involves information smoothing. This idea is captured in the average order fill rate, formulated as a smooth (SMTH1) of the true and instantaneous order fill rate observable in the factory. (See Chapter 5 for a review of information smoothing.) The time to average orders is assumed to be one month, representing the typical amount of time required to compile a business report.

Order Fulfilment – Standard Stock Depletion Formulation

Order fulfilment controls the rate at which the factory fills customer orders. At the heart of the formulation is the order backlog, an accumulation of customer orders that have not yet been filled. We assume the product is built to order. Hence, when new customer orders arrive they are added to the backlog and stay there until filled. The average time to fill an order is called the delivery delay. Sometimes, but not always, it is reasonable to assume that delivery delay is constant, in other words the average time taken by the factory to process an order, build the product and ship it is the same no matter how large or small the volume of customer orders. Under this special condition, order fulfilment can be expressed as a standard stock depletion formulation as shown in the equations below. The order fill rate is simply the ratio of backlog to delivery delay. The larger the order backlog, the greater the order fill rate, and this proportionality always holds true given our assumption of constant delivery delay. In this particular case, the delivery delay is set at two months and the initial order backlog is 80 systems, so the order fill rate is 40 systems per month.

Order Backlog(t) = Order Backlog (t – dt) + (Customer Orders – Order Fill Rate) ∗ dt

INIT Order Backlog = 80 {the initial backlog of orders is 80 systems, which results from a customer order rate of 40 systems per month with a delivery delay of 2 months}

Order Fill Rate = Order Backlog/Delivery Delay {systems/month}

Delivery Delay = 2 {months}

More sophisticated order fulfilment formulations are common in which the order fill rate depends on factors such as available capacity, the adequacy of finished inventory or some combination of the two. We will see a good example later in the chapter when capacity is added to the model. For now, a simple stock depletion formulation proportional to backlog is adequate. Incidentally, it is important to realise that, in any of these alternative formulations, backlog does not track individual orders entering and leaving the business in the way one might observe close up in a factory or in the formulation of a queue in a discrete event simulation model. Instead, there is a volume of orders, so many orders received per week or per month. They flow into the backlog where they are mixed together with no trace of individual identity. Some orders may be for a standard version of the product and others for special product variants that take longer to make. On average, across the product range, these orders reside in backlog for a period of time defined as the delivery delay. This mixing together and resulting anonymity of orders is a good example of viewing the system from the appropriate intermediate perspective, close enough to see the build-up of unfulfilled demand and the resulting pressures on the business, but not so close as to see each individual order.

Surprisingly, the mundane notions of order backlog and order fulfilment reach quite deeply into the philosophy of system dynamics. Backlog is widely used by modellers and is a highly versatile concept broadly applicable to firms, industries and society. Any system dynamics model of supply and demand will, in principle, contain one or more backlogs of accumulated demand waiting to be satisfied. In such dynamical models, equilibrium is not presumed and so supply need not always equal demand. If, in the short to medium term, there is a supply shortage, then excess demand accumulates in backlog. From backlog arise (directly or indirectly) realistic pressures for price adjustment, capacity expansion or demand reduction, pressures that reveal the invisible hand of market forces at work, seeking to equilibrate supply and demand.

Customer Ordering

The formulation for customer ordering completes the sales growth loop. Recall that customers in this case are commercial buyers who learn about the product from a professional sales force. The bigger the sales force, the more orders. The formulation is shown below. Customer orders equal sales force multiplied by normal sales force productivity, where normal productivity is assumed to be 10 orders per sales person per month. So with an initial sales force of four people, the company wins 40 orders per month.

> Customer Orders = Sales Force * Normal Sales Force Productivity {systems per month}
>
> Normal Sales Force Productivity = 10 {system orders per sales person per month}

Policy Structure and Formulations for Limits to Sales Growth

Although the sales force is vital for generating orders, we also know that product availability is a very important consideration for buyers. Even the most successful sales force cannot sell a product that is not available.

Intuitively, we might expect customer orders to be limited by production capacity and therefore write the following equation to capture the supply constraint (where MIN is a logical function that selects the minimum value of the two expressions in parentheses).

Customer Orders = MIN (Sales Force * Normal Sales Force Productivity, Production Capacity)

However, a moment's reflection reveals this is not a good formulation. It fails the Baker criterion because it implies that customers know the factory's production capacity and ignore the efforts of the sales force the moment the limit of production capacity is reached. Figure 7.15 shows a much more realistic and subtle formulation in which customers respond to delivery delay and where delivery delay depends indirectly on both production capacity and the utilisation of capacity. The beauty of this formulation is that customers know delivery delay (from experience or rumour) and regard it as very important in their ordering decision, consistent with our earlier discussion of the customer ordering policy. Moreover, the formulation is dynamically interesting. In the short to medium term, it allows the freedom for customers to order more than the factory can produce rather than arbitrarily imposing a rigid balance of supply and demand.

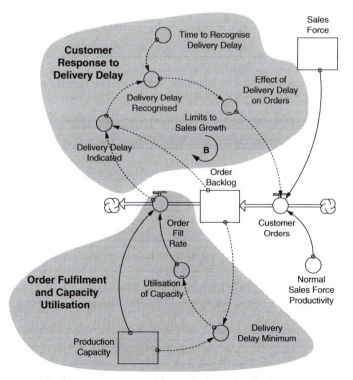

Figure 7.15   Policy structure and formulations for limits to sales growth

Customer Response to Delivery Delay – Non-linear Graphical Converter

In Figure 7.15, customer orders now depend not only on the sales force and its productivity but also the effect of delivery delay on orders. It would be reasonable to assume that the longer the delivery delay, the fewer orders are placed. What is the strength of the effect and how would you estimate it in practice? Normally, modellers sketch such relationships in consultation with the management team, either on a whiteboard or direct on the computer screen so the shape is visible for inspection and comment. Notice that the corresponding equation for the effect of delivery delay is expressed as a GRAPH where the shape of the function is contained in terms of paired coordinates that lie along the line.

> Customer Orders = Sales Force * Normal Sales Force Productivity * Effect of Delivery Delay on Orders {systems per month}
>
> Effect of Delivery Delay on Orders = GRAPH (Delivery Delay Recognised)
> (0.00, 1.00), (1.00, 0.97), (2.00, 0.87), (3.00, 0.73), (4.00, 0.53), (5.00, 0.38), (6.00, 0.25), (7.00, 0.15), (8.00, 0.08), (9.00, 0.03), (10.0, 0.02)

A plausible function is shown in Figure 7.16. The horizontal axis is delivery delay recognised (by customers) defined on a scale from zero to 10 months. The vertical axis is the effect of delivery delay on orders defined on a scale from zero to one. The numerical values in the table on the right of the figure correspond to the shape of the function. The general shape is downward sloping – gradual at first, then steep and ending gradual. For comparison, a straight dotted line is superimposed to show a linear relationship.

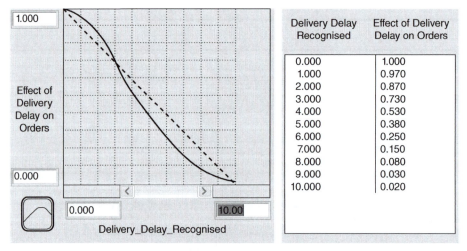

Delivery Delay Recognised	Effect of Delivery Delay on Orders
0.000	1.000
1.000	0.970
2.000	0.870
3.000	0.730
4.000	0.530
5.000	0.380
6.000	0.250
7.000	0.150
8.000	0.080
9.000	0.030
10.000	0.020

Figure 7.16   Graph for the effect of delivery delay on orders

When delivery delay recognised is less than one month then customers are satisfied and the effect takes a neutral value of one, or very close. As delivery delay rises, the effect becomes stronger. A delay of two months reduces orders to 87% of what the sales force could otherwise sell. A delay of three months reduces orders to 73% while a delay of four months reduces them to only 53%. A delivery delay of 10 months is completely unacceptable to most customers and reduces orders to only 2% of what could otherwise be sold, thereby rendering the sales force ineffective.

Customers' Perception of Delivery Delay – Information Smoothing

Delivery delay recognised represents customers' perception of delivery delay. It takes time for customers to build an impression of delivery delay from their own recent experience of deliveries and from rumours circulating in the industry. The natural formulation is information smoothing. The equation is written as a SMTH1 function of delivery delay indicated, where the time constant of the smoothing process is called the 'time to recognise delivery delay' and is set at 10 months. Think about this formulation for a moment in terms of the Baker criterion – what do customers know and when do they know it? What they know and use as the basis for ordering is delivery delay recognised. Customers form this impression by averaging, over a period of 10 months, their day-to-day experience of 'delivery delay indicated'. This measure of delivery delay is the actual time it takes the factory to fill orders, defined as the ratio of the order backlog to the order fill rate. A brief spate of late deliveries, lasting just a few weeks, will do little harm to demand and customers will continue to order in the belief that normal delivery will be resumed. However, if the factory is slow to deliver for months on end then customers begin to think it is the norm. As a result some will stop ordering and place their orders with rivals instead.

Delivery Delay Recognised = SMTH1 (Delivery Delay Indicated, Time to Recognise Delivery Delay, 2) {months}

Time to Recognise Delivery Delay = 10 {months}

Delivery Delay Indicated = Order Backlog/Order Fill Rate {months}

Order Fulfilment and Capacity Utilisation

Order fulfilment from the perspective of a customer looks like a time delay. Orders are placed with the factory and some time later the corresponding products are delivered. The factory is a black box, but step a bit closer and the operating constraints of the factory become apparent. From the perspective of a CEO or factory manager, the order fill rate depends broadly on production capacity and the utilisation of capacity. A big factory can supply more than a small one and a factory working flat out, three shifts, 24 hours a day can supply more than a factory working a single shift. These common-sense facts about factory output are captured in the equations below. The order fill rate is defined as production capacity multiplied by the utilisation of capacity. But what determines utilisation? The formulation below, taken from the market growth model, is particularly insightful. Utilisation of capacity depends on 'delivery delay minimum'. This new concept is an estimate of how long it would take to clear the order backlog if the factory were working flat out with no glitches. It can be interpreted as a measure of the load on the factory, a kind of informal metric likely to be known by experienced factory managers.

Order Fill Rate = Production Capacity * Utilisation of Capacity {systems per month}

Utilisation of Capacity = GRAPH (Delivery Delay Minimum)

(0.00, 0.00), (0.5, 0.25), (1.00, 0.5), (1.50, 0.67), (2.00, 0.8), (2.50, 0.87), (3.00, 0.93), (3.50, 0.95), (4.00, 0.97), (4.50, 0.98), (5.00, 1.00)

Delivery Delay Minimum = Order Backlog/Production Capacity

{the minimum time in months to clear the backlog if capacity were 100% utilised}

The longer delivery delay minimum, the greater is the load and the higher capacity utilisation. The relationship is shown in Figure 7.17. The horizontal axis is delivery delay minimum on a scale from zero to five months. The vertical axis is capacity utilisation on a scale from zero to one. For light loads, when delivery delay minimum is between zero and one month, utilisation increases linearly from zero to 50%.

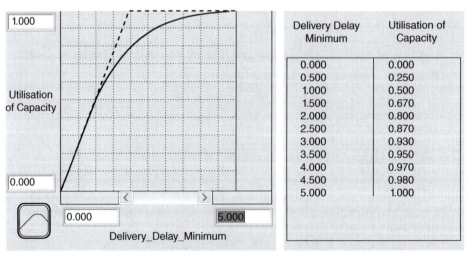

Delivery Delay Minimum	Utilisation of Capacity
0.000	0.000
0.500	0.250
1.000	0.500
1.500	0.670
2.000	0.800
2.500	0.870
3.000	0.930
3.500	0.950
4.000	0.970
4.500	0.980
5.000	1.000

Figure 7.17   Graph for capacity utilisation

The dotted line shows a continuation of this linear trend. Utilisation of 50% represents a factory working normally between one and two shifts. As the load increases to three months, utilisation continues to rise to 80%, but less quickly than before because the busier the factory the more difficult it is to squeeze out extra production. Finally, as the load increases to five months, the curve flattens out and utilisation gradually approaches its maximum numerical value of one – corresponding to uninterrupted three-shift production. The assumption is that factories very rarely work flat out and only the most extreme load can induce the managerial pressure needed to sustain such high output.

Policy Structure and Formulations for Capital Investment

At the heart of capital investment lies the question of whether the firm should expand capacity and by how much. As discussed earlier, business leaders take quite different approaches to investment decisions. Some invest according to a vision of future demand while others need hard evidence that the factory is stretched or that the financial return will be high. In this case, we represent a conservative investment policy driven by operating pressures in the factory. The policy is conceived in three parts as shown by the grey areas in Figure 7.18.

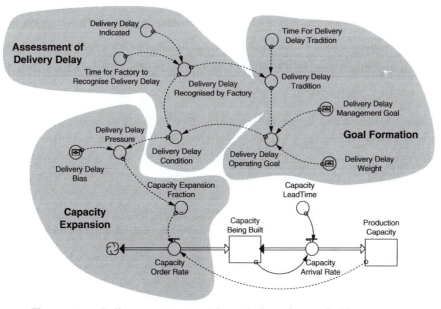

Figure 7.18   Policy structure and formulations for capital investment

There is an assessment of delivery delay that drives capacity expansion. Lying behind this assessment is a process of goal formation in which factory managers establish the company's standards for delivery performance. The corresponding formulations are described below.

Assessment of Delivery Delay

From a factory perspective, a high delivery delay is a mixed blessing. On the one hand, it suggests that a product is selling well and is popular with customers. On the other hand, it is a sign that production capacity is inadequate. So a crucial question for factory managers is whether delivery delay is too high. This managerial judgement is captured in the concept 'delivery delay condition', which is defined as the ratio of delivery delay recognised by the factory to delivery delay operating goal. If the ratio takes a value of one then delivery delay is exactly on target and no new net investment is needed. However, if the ratio takes a value greater than one then factory managers sense a need for capacity expansion. Moreover, they have the tangible evidence to justify expansion. However, it takes time to estimate whether goods are being shipped on time and so delivery delay recognised by the factory is formulated as an information smooth of delivery delay indicated, where the smoothing time is set at two months. Note that the factory is quicker to recognise changes in delivery delay than customers.

> Delivery Delay Condition = Delivery Delay Recognised by Factory/ Delivery Delay Operating Goal {dimensionless}
>
> Delivery Delay Recognised by Factory = SMTH1 (Delivery Delay Indicated, Time for Factory to Recognise Delivery Delay, 2)
>
> Time for Factory to Recognise Delivery Delay = 2 {months}

Goal Formation – Weighted Average of Adaptive and Static Goals

How does the company decide an appropriate operating goal for delivery delay? A simple formulation is a fixed goal, a target that once set does not change. But in reality organisational goals can adapt to changing circumstances. A suitable formulation is a weighted average of delivery delay tradition and delivery delay management goal that allows for either an adaptive or static goal, or a combination of both. Delivery delay tradition is performance the factory has achieved in the past, based on a long-term smooth or average of delivery delay recognised. The time constant in this information smoothing process is 12 months meaning that tradition is heavily influenced by performance achieved over the past year. Delivery delay management goal is a fixed performance target, a goal that management aspires to regardless of past performance. If delivery delay weight is set to one then the operating goal depends entirely on delivery delay tradition, and if the weight is set to zero then the operating goal depends entirely on the fixed management goal. A weight between zero and one allows for a combination of both influences.

> Delivery Delay Operating Goal = Delivery Delay Tradition * Delivery Delay Weight + Delivery Delay Management Goal * (1 − Delivery Delay Weight) {months}
>
> Delivery Delay Tradition = SMTH1 (Delivery Delay Recognised by Factory, Time For Delivery Delay Tradition, 2) {months}
>
> Time For Delivery Delay Tradition = 12 {months}
>
> Delivery Delay Management Goal = 2 {months}
>
> Delivery Delay Weight = 1 {dimensionless; delivery delay weight = 1 puts all the weight onto tradition, = 0 puts all the weight onto the fixed management goal}

Capacity Expansion – Fractional Asset Stock Adjustment

Capacity expansion is an example of asset stock adjustment. The firm adds more capacity when there is pressure to do so. However, in this formulation there is not a clear target for desired production capacity to use as a benchmark for corrective action. Rather, we are thinking of a process where factory managers argue for a proportional increase of existing capacity (requesting perhaps five or 10% more over the coming year) and then top management decide whether the case for expansion is justified. Such informal pressure-driven asset stock adjustment is quite common, especially in capital investment where there is not only ambiguity about how much investment is really needed but also competition for limited funds. Accordingly, the capacity order rate is defined as production capacity multiplied by a 'capacity expansion fraction'. This expansion fraction is a non-linear function of delivery delay pressure, in which the higher the pressure the greater the expansion approved. But pressure for expansion is a matter of opinion and the formulation cleverly allows for a difference of opinion between factory managers and the top management team who have the final say on investment. Factory managers report the delivery delay condition and the management team interprets this information according to a delivery delay bias. Delivery delay pressure is equal to delivery delay condition minus delivery delay bias. The bias is set at 0.3, which means that the management team approves less expansion than requested, reflecting a conservative attitude toward investment. The same formulation can also be used to portray an optimistic and pre-emptive attitude to investment by setting the bias to a value less than zero.[2]

Capacity Order Rate = Production Capacity * Capacity Expansion Fraction {systems/month/month)}

Capacity Expansion Fraction = GRAPH (Delivery Delay Pressure)

(0.00, −0.07), (0.5, −0.02), (1.00, 0.00), (1.50, 0.02), (2.00, 0.07), (2.50, 0.15)

Delivery Delay Pressure = Delivery Delay Condition − Delivery Delay Bias {dimensionless}

Delivery Delay Bias = 0.3 {dimensionless}

The non-linear function for capacity expansion fraction is shown in Figure 7.19. The horizontal axis is delivery delay pressure on a scale from zero to 2.5. The vertical axis is capacity expansion fraction on a scale from −0.1 to 0.15, expressed as a fraction per month. Where do you find the data to sketch such a graph? The answer lies in carefully defining the axes, identifying points that logically belong on the curve and using common sense to fill in the gaps. In this case, we define delivery delay pressure of 1 to be neutral, requiring no change of capacity. So the curve must pass through the point (1,0). Common sense suggests the function is upward sloping because the higher delivery delay pressure the greater the need for capacity expansion. The gradient of the line around the (1,0) point defines how much extra capacity expansion is approved for a given change of pressure. Everyday experience suggests that expansion of 20 or 30% per year is common and even 100% or more per year is feasible. Capacity reduction is also possible. Moreover, it is not unreasonable to argue that the gradient of the line increases the more extreme the delivery delay pressure. This kind of logical argument leads to the curve in Figure 7.19.

---

[2]An alternative formulation of delivery delay pressure is to multiply the delivery delay condition by a delivery delay bias. In such a multiplicative formulation the neutral value of the bias is one. A bias of less than one (say 0.8 or 0.9) represents management with a conservative attitude to capital investment, whereas a bias greater than one represents management with a pre-emptive attitude to investment, willing to invest in capacity ahead of demand. In the algebraic context shown, the choice of multiplication or subtraction (with an appropriately scaled bias) makes no difference to the resulting feedback structure and dynamics. A subtraction formulation is used here because it matches the formulation in Jay Forrester's original model.

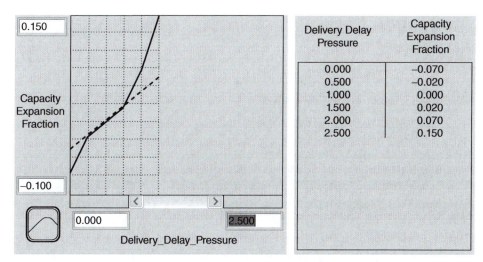

Delivery Delay Pressure	Capacity Expansion Fraction
0.000	−0.070
0.500	−0.020
1.000	0.000
1.500	0.020
2.000	0.070
2.500	0.150

Figure 7.19   Graph for capacity expansion fraction

As delivery delay pressure rises from 1 to 1.5, the capacity expansion fraction increases from 0 to 0.2 per month (24% per year). As pressure rises even further to 2 (meaning that top management believe that factory deliveries are taking twice as long as normal) the expansion fraction increases to 0.7 per month (84% per year). Extreme pressure of 2.5 leads to a fractional expansion fraction of 0.15 per month (180% per year). The reverse logic applies when delivery delay pressure is considered to be too low. As pressure falls from 1 to 0.5, the expansion fraction decreases from 0 to -0.2 per month (a capacity reduction of 24% per year). When pressure reaches zero (meaning that both demand and backlog have also fallen to zero) it is plain to the management team that demand has collapsed and drastic action is needed to shed capacity. The capacity fraction decreases to -0.7 per month leading to capacity reduction of 84% per year that, if sustained, would lead to closure in less than two years.

There is a lot of meaning packed into these few equations for fractional asset stock adjustment. Effectively, the organisation 'searches' for the right amount of capacity needed to supply the market, but without setting a specific target. In terms of the Baker criterion such a policy is myopic but also versatile. Pressure for expansion is able to filter through to those who have the power to invest. They are not concerned with the detail of investment but rather the appropriateness of the proposed expansion relative to existing capacity. Providing there is a good case, capacity expands. Interestingly, this policy leads to reinforcing feedback in capital investment. The bigger the factory, the greater the absolute investment, leading to an even bigger factory.

Production Capacity – Two-Stage Stock Accumulation

Production capacity is represented in the aggregate. It is the total output achievable by the factory, measured in systems per month, using all the available equipment. As always perspective is important. We are not so close to the factory as to see individual machines, conveyors and assembly lines, but we are not so far away as to be unaware that capacity constrains factory output and can be changed only gradually. When investment is approved there is a substantial time lag before new capacity is actually operating. Equipment needs to be built, delivered and installed. These aggregate characteristics of capacity are portrayed in a two-stage stock accumulation process shown in Figure 7.18 and captured in the equations below. Stage one is a stock of capacity being built but not yet available for production. This pipeline of latent capacity is increased by the capacity order rate and reduced by the capacity arrival rate (i.e. final delivery to the factory). The capacity arrival rate is defined as the ratio of capacity being built to capacity lead time. This ratio is a standard stock depletion formulation where the time to build new capacity is assumed to be 12 months. The bigger the pipeline, the greater the arrival rate. We assume the initial value of capacity being built is equal to the capacity order rate multiplied by the capacity lead time, in other words there are 12 months' worth of orders in the pipeline to begin with.

> Capacity Being Built(t) = Capacity Being Built (t − dt) + (Capacity Order Rate − Capacity Arrival Rate) ∗ dt
>
> INIT Capacity Being Built = Capacity Order Rate ∗ Capacity Lead Time {systems per month}
>
> Capacity Arrival Rate = Capacity Being Built/Capacity Lead Time {systems/month/month}
>
> Capacity Lead Time = 12 {months}
>
> Production Capacity (t) = Production Capacity (t − dt) + (Capacity Arrival Rate) ∗ dt INIT Production Capacity = 120 {systems/month}

Stage two is a stock of production capacity already installed in the factory and available for use. This fully operational capacity is an accumulation of the capacity arrival rate. The factory is initialised with a capacity of 120 systems per month which, at normal utilisation of 50%, is more than enough to fill customer orders of 40 systems per month generated by the initial sales force of four people. Note there is no explicit representation of obsolescence or capacity reduction. When disinvestment occurs it is treated as negative capacity arrival. Accordingly, the capacity arrival rate in Figure 7.18 is shown as a bi-flow to signify that capacity can either increase or decrease. This simplification really means that investment and disinvestment are treated symmetrically. Just as it takes time to add new capacity, so it takes time to dispose of surplus capacity once an approval for disinvestment has been agreed. Incidentally, if this kind of approximation is unsatisfactory (and results in formulations that contradict the guidelines in Figure 7.5) then capacity obsolescence and discard should be represented separately.

Multi-stage stock accumulations are widely used in system dynamics in any situation where there is a significant lead time in building organisational resources. The structure applies to capital investment of all kinds (equipment, buildings, infrastructure). It is also appropriate for skilled human resources where people take time to train, to master skills on the job and to be fully assimilated by the organisation. For example, an airline model to investigate the dynamics of service capacity might distinguish between stocks of rookie staff and experienced staff with a flow rate between the two stocks to represent on-the-job training. The training rate would be a standard stock depletion formulation defined as the ratio of rookie staff to the normal training time. Occasionally more than two stages are needed. For example, in Chapter 9 a hospital model to investigate the quality of patient care shows stock accumulations for medical students, junior doctors and consultants, with standard stock depletion formulations controlling the flow rates from student to junior doctor and from junior doctor to consultant. Intangible asset stocks can be represented in multiple stages too. A model to investigate knowledge development by firms engaged in an R&D alliance might show stock accumulations for incubating knowledge and applied knowledge, connected by a knowledge transfer rate.

Simulation Experiments

We have now reviewed all the formulations of the market growth model and are ready to conduct simulation experiments. It is common to simulate multi-loop and multi-sector models in stages in order to build a good understanding of dynamics. In this case, we start with the sales growth loop in isolation to examine the dynamics of market growth in an ideal situation where the factory can reliably supply whatever demand the sales force generates. Then, we add the customer response loop and a factory with fixed maximum capacity (but variable utilisation) to examine the dynamics of reinforcing sales growth that eventually hits a capacity limit. Finally, we add the capacity expansion loop to arrive at the complete model and to examine the dynamics of market growth and capital investment.

Note that it is good practice to conceive partial model simulations as realistic experiments whose outcome could be imagined despite the deliberately simplified conditions. For example, a simulation of the sales growth loop in isolation shows how the business would grow (or even whether it could grow) if there were no capacity constraints. A simulation in which there is a factory with fixed maximum capacity shows how growth approaches a capacity limit. These are not simply technical tests. They are opportunities to compare common sense and intuition with simulated outcomes and to build confidence in the model's structure and dynamic behaviour.

Simulation of Sales Growth Loop

Open the model called 'Sales Growth' in the learning support folder for Chapter 7 and inspect the diagram and equations. You can switch between the model and equations by using the tabs on the left of the screen. The relationships correspond exactly to the policy structure and formulations for sales growth presented earlier in the chapter. Press the button labelled 'Graph' and a blank time chart appears with customer orders on the vertical scale from zero to 4000 systems per month and time on the horizontal axis from zero to 60 months. Before simulating, sketch customer orders – the trajectory you expect to see. To begin a sketch simply move the cursor to any point inside the axes of the graph. Select and hold the mouse button and then move the mouse to draw a plausible trajectory. When you are satisfied with the shape of the line, press the 'Run' button on the left of the screen and watch customer orders unfold. Inspect both pages 1 and 2 of the graph pad, which will look like the charts in Figure 7.20.

Line 1 in the top chart shows customer orders growing steadily from 40 to 4000 systems per month in a pattern of exponential growth typical of a reinforcing feedback loop. Line 2 is my sketch of customer orders, growing optimistically to about 1500 systems per month in only 30 months and eventually rising to about 3800 systems per month after 60 months. Although I knew the simulated trajectory beforehand, my sketch shows an almost linear growth pattern to emphasise the marked difference between linear and exponential growth. As mentioned in Chapter 6, exponential growth begins slowly and gradually gathers pace as steady fractional increase translates into ever greater absolute increase.

Line 1 in the bottom chart shows the authorised sales force and line 2 shows the actual sales force. In month zero, the firm employs four sales people, but already they are generating enough sales revenue to fund an authorised sales force of 10 people. This gap leads to hiring, expansion of the sales force, additional revenue, a bigger budget and a further increase in the authorised sales force. By month 30, the sales force is 41 people while the authorised force is 80, and by month 45 the sales force is 129 people while the authorised force is 248. There is continual pressure to hire and with an ever larger sales force the firm sells more and more.

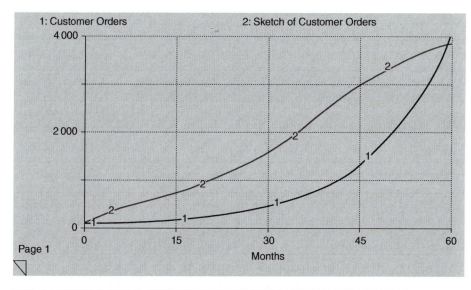

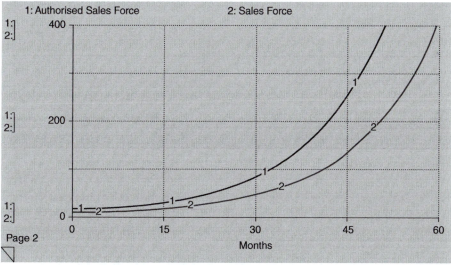

Figure 7.20   Simulation of sales growth loop in isolation

Of course no firm can grow forever, but many firms with successful products enjoy long interludes in which potential demand is far greater than realised demand. Yet even this seemingly ideal world does not always behave in quite the way one might expect. Consider, for example, the effect on sales if the product price were raised from £9600 to £10 000, an increase of 4%.

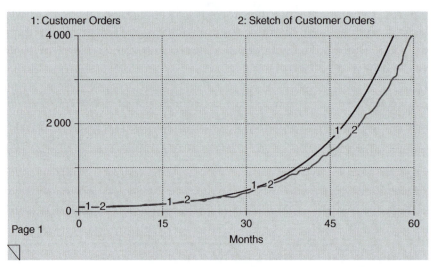

Figure 7.21   Sales growth with four per cent increase in product price

To test this price scenario return to the model, double select the icon for 'product price' and enter 10 000. Then go to page 1 of the graph, sketch your best guess of customer orders and press 'Run'. The resulting simulation is shown in Figure 7.21. My sketch of customer orders (line 2) re-traces the trajectory of customer orders in the original simulation. So I am guessing that a 4% price increase makes no difference to orders because we assumed, during model conceptualisation, that customers are not sensitive to price. Surprisingly, however, simulated customer orders (line 1) are higher than before. Between months 30 and 45, a clear gap opens between the two trajectories. The gap continues to grow, so that orders reach 4000 per month in only 57 months, three months sooner than before. The reason for the sales increase lies in the reinforcing sales growth loop shown in Figure 7.14 and easily visible on-screen in the model. In this loop, product price does not directly affect the volume of customer orders. However, when price is higher, reported sales revenue is higher in the same proportion – leading to a larger budget for the sales force and eventually to a larger sales force. With higher prices, the firm can afford a larger sales force and it is this greater power of persuasion that boosts customer orders and feeds back to reinforce itself. Note the argument is dynamic – we are saying that a price increase accelerates growth in demand, not that customers prefer high prices.

Consider another scenario in which sales force salary is increased from £4000 to £5000 per sales person per month, a 25% increase. To test this scenario, return to the model diagram. Two parameter changes are needed: first, modify the salary (from 4000 to 5000); and then reset the product price (from 10 000 back to 9600).

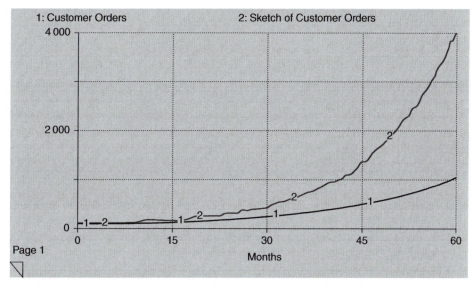

Figure 7.22   Sales growth with 25 per cent increase in sales force salary

Then go to page 1 of the graph, sketch your best guess of customer orders and press 'Run'. The resulting simulation is shown in Figure 7.22. Once again my sketch of customer orders follows the trajectory of the original simulation, but this time as a benchmark rather than an expectation. Simulated customer orders grow, but much more slowly than before, reaching only 1000 systems per month after 60 months rather than 4000. Is this outcome really credible? Why should a more expensive sales force do so much worse? The reason lies in a slight reduction in the strength of reinforcing feedback around the sales growth loop. The growth rate is diminished because any budget increase translates into 25% fewer additional sales people and the compound effect over 60 months (five years) is huge.

Strength of Reinforcing Loop

The growth rate of sales depends on the strength of the reinforcing loop, which in turn depends on the economics of the sales force. If each new sales person generates a budget surplus, a contribution to the sales budget larger than their salary, then the business will grow. If not the business will decline and the virtuous reinforcing circle will become a spiral of decline. There are four parameters around the sales growth loop that determine the budget surplus according to the following formula:

> budget surplus = (sales force productivity ∗ product price ∗ fraction of revenue to sales force) − sales force salary.

Substituting numerical values from the base case model gives a budget surplus of (10 * 9600 * 0.1) − 4000, which is £5600 per sales person per month.

Further simulation experiments reveal how these factors work individually and in combination. For example, an increase in sales force productivity boosts the surplus and accelerates growth. On the other hand, as we saw above, an increase in sales force salary stunts growth. Specifically, a salary of £9600 per month reduces the budget surplus to zero and results in stagnation. More than £9600 per month leads to decline. Intuitively, a highly paid sales force is not economic unless funded with a higher product price, a bigger slice of the budget or enhanced productivity. Any plausible combination of the four parameters that creates a healthy budget surplus leads to sustained growth. But if, for any reason, the surplus disappears then growth turns to stagnation and decline – despite the reinforcing loop and the assumption of plentiful customers.

Technically speaking a reinforcing loop generates growth when its 'steady state open-loop gain' has a value greater than one. Gain is a special measure of loop strength and is computed from the numerical values of parameters around the loop. The concept is fully explained in the Appendix of this chapter. When the steady state open-loop gain is less than one, a reinforcing loop generates a spiral of decline. When the gain is exactly equal to one then the result is stagnation. Interestingly, the gain of the sales growth loop involves the same four parameters as the budget surplus and is expressed as follows:

gain = (sales force productivity * product price * fraction of revenue to sales force)/sales force salary

A gain of one corresponds to a budget surplus of zero and is the special combination of parameters in which one extra sales person contributes just enough to the sales budget to pay his or her own salary.

Simulation of Sales Growth and Customer Response Loops

The next partial model simulation adds the customer response loop to the sales growth loop in a scenario where production capacity is deliberately held constant. This fixed capacity is much larger than initial customer orders and so initial capacity utilisation is low and there is room for growth. Intuition suggests that in the long run fixed capacity sets a limit to growth in orders. The simulation experiment tests the intuition and shows exactly how the capacity limit is approached.

Open the model called 'Limits to Growth in Sales' and inspect the diagram and equations. Move the pointer and hover over selected variables to check the starting conditions. The relationships include all the formulations in the previous model plus the extra policy structure and formulations for limits to sales growth presented earlier in the chapter. Note the customer response loop showing the effect of delivery delay on orders. Customer orders arrive at a rate of 35 systems per month, generated by a sales force of four people. Delivery delay recognised (by customers) is initially two months and, as a result, orders are reduced to 87% of what they would otherwise be (the effect of delivery delay on orders is equal to 0.87 initially). Next, press the button labelled 'order fulfilment' to see the capacity formulations. Production capacity is 200 systems per month and the initial order backlog is 80 systems. As intended the factory is far from stretched at the start of the simulation: delivery delay minimum is only 0.4 months (80/200) and capacity utilisation is 0.2 (20%) of the flat-out maximum achievable. With this modest utilisation the order fill rate is 40 systems per month (200 ∗ 0.2), slightly greater than customer orders of 35 systems per month.

Return to sales and press the button labelled 'Graph' to find a blank time chart. Before simulating, once again sketch customer orders – the trajectory you expect to see. Then press 'Run' and inspect all four pages of the graph pad. The charts in Figures 7.23 and 7.24 will appear. The top chart in Figure 7.23 shows production capacity, customer orders, and the order fill rate on a scale from zero to 400 over a period of 60 months. Note that production capacity (line 1) remains constant, as expected, at 200 systems per month throughout. Meanwhile, simulated customer orders (line 2) grow exponentially to reach the capacity limit of 200 by month 29, under the influence of the sales growth loop. Orders continue to grow for a further eight months, reaching a peak of 252 orders per month by month 37. Why is this 25% overshoot possible? Surely a company cannot sell more than the factory can produce. In an equilibrium world, such an imbalance of demand and supply is impossible, but in a realistic and dynamic world, orders can exceed factory capacity for extended periods of time. Excess orders simply accumulate in backlog, leading to an increase in delivery delay, as shown in the bottom chart. Here, delivery delay indicated (line 1) begins at two months and remains steady at that value until month 18 as the factory comfortably increases capacity utilisation to accommodate growing customer orders.

Over the next year-and-a-half to month 36 delivery delay indicated rises steadily to four months. For this entire period, customer orders (top chart, line 2) continue to rise even though customers don't want late deliveries. This apparent contradiction is explained by the lag in customers' perception of delivery delay as shown in the trajectory for delivery delay recognised (bottom chart, line 3).

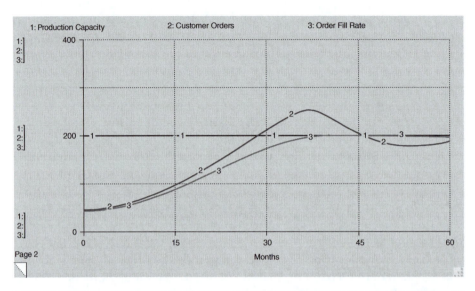

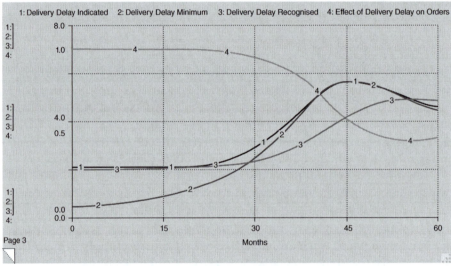

Figure 7.23   Limits to sales growth with fixed capacity

In the interval between months 18 and 36 the trajectory rises from two months to just less than three, even though the reality is that the factory is taking four months to deliver by month 36. Customers only gradually discover the true delivery situation. This inevitable myopia means that customers remain amenable to persuasion by the growing sales force, so orders exceed maximum capacity. By month 45, delivery delay recognised is 4 months and now customers are genuinely dissatisfied with chronic late deliveries. The sales force wins fewer orders and the growth engine is shut down and begins to go into reverse. Between months 36 and 45 customer orders fall from their

peak of 250 systems per month back to 200 systems per month, in line with
factory capacity. However, even this is not the end of the story. By month 45
delivery delay recognised by the customer (bottom chart, line 3) has reached
just over four months and is still rising. The supply situation is highly
unsatisfactory. The factory is working flat out and delivery delay indicated has
reached a peak of almost six months – three times normal. Orders therefore
continue to fall. Between months 45 and 60 orders remain below factory
capacity. Delivery delay gradually begins to fall. The pressure on the factory
eases slightly and a long-term equilibrium between orders and factory capacity
begins to be established. Notice in Figure 7.24 that the sales force growth
engine is neutralised. It is no longer economically attractive to hire new sales
people and so market growth is halted. Technically speaking, the gain of the
sales reinforcing loop has been reduced to one by permanently high delivery
delay of greater than four months. In Figure 7.23 the effect of delivery delay
(bottom chart, line 4) falls from 1 to 0.4, meaning that sales force productivity
is slashed by 60% ((1 − 0.4) ∗ 100) by chronically high delivery delay.

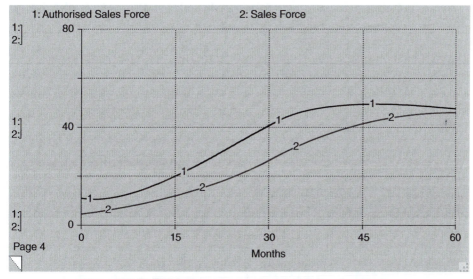

Figure 7.24   Dynamics of sales force with fixed capacity

In reality, extreme backlog pressure on the factory would lead to capacity
expansion, but our partial model shows how a capacity shortage presents
itself. The effect is subtle. There is no dramatic signal to announce when the
factory is overloaded. Arguably, overload is first apparent in the period
between months 18 and 30 when delivery delay indicated increases from two
to almost three months, but for all of that time (and bear in mind the interval
is a whole year), customer orders continue to rise steadily. One could easily
imagine people in the factory (and even in the sales force) concluding that
customers are indifferent to delivery delay. The full consequences of late

deliveries are not apparent until much later. The first clear sign is the levelling off of customer orders in month 36, fully 18 months after the first signs of capacity shortage in the factory. The delay in the effect makes a correct attribution of the cause very difficult in practice. It is not necessarily obvious, particularly at the functional level, what corrective action is most appropriate when orders begin to falter. Should the company expand capacity or expand the sales force? Should it reduce or increase product price?

Simulation of the Complete Model with all Three Loops Active – The Base Case

The complete model can shed light on these questions by probing the coordination of growth in orders, capacity and sales force. In the learning support folder, open the model called 'Growth and Investment' and inspect the diagram and equations. The picture looks just like the previous model showing the reinforcing sales growth loop and the feedback effect of delivery delay on customer orders. Select 'order fulfilment' to see the formulations for utilisation of capacity and order fill rate. The only visual difference by comparison with the previous model is in production capacity. The stock appears as a 'ghost' meaning that it is defined elsewhere in the model. To view the capacity formulations, first select the 'Sales' button to return to the opening screen and then select the 'Capacity' button. Here is the policy structure for capital investment described earlier.

Move the pointer and hover over selected variables to check the starting conditions. Production capacity starts at 120 systems per month, lower than before, but comfortably more than the 35 orders per month generated by the initial sales force of four. Capacity being built is −17 systems per month at the outset. At first glance, this negative value may seem curious, but remember the capacity formulations allow for both capacity increase and decrease. If there is pressure to reduce capacity then the pipeline being built will in fact be an amount of capacity being withdrawn or temporarily idled. Pressure to change capacity stems from an assessment of delivery delay within the investment policy. In this case, delivery delay recognised by the factory is initially two months, which is the same as the delivery delay operating goal. Hence, at the start of the simulation delivery delay condition takes a value of one, meaning that factory managers think the delivery situation is about right and, in their minds at least, there is no need to change capacity. However, delivery delay bias is set at 0.3 meaning that the top management team is reluctant to invest unless the evidence for expansion is really compelling. From their point of view, there is plenty of capacity and some room to cut back – even though factory managers would disagree. The capacity expansion fraction takes an initial value of −0.012, calling for a modest monthly capacity reduction of just over 1%. To be consistent, the initial pipeline of capacity being built is also negative. From these starting conditions the simulation unfolds.

Go to the 'graph pad' by first selecting the 'Sales' button and then the 'Graph' button. Now sketch a trajectory for customer orders you expect to see in this more complex and realistic situation with variable manufacturing capacity. Notice the time horizon is 96 months (eight years) to allow plenty of time to observe the pattern of market growth. Press the 'Run' button to create a time chart similar to Figure 7.25 showing sketched and simulated customer orders. In my sketch, I expect customer orders to grow slowly and steadily because I know the product is attractive and that both the sales force and capacity can be expanded to sustain growth. However, simulated orders are very different. Following a promising burst of growth to 125 systems per month in the first 20 months, orders stagnate and then decline. After 36 months, the company is selling only 80 systems per month. A turnaround then heralds a year-long recovery in which orders grow to almost 100 systems per month. But the recovery is short-lived and stagnation sets in once again at about month 48 to be followed by inexorable decline. At the end of the simulation, orders fall to merely 50 systems per month and, after eight years of trying, a once-promising market proves to be disappointingly small. Why? The remaining time charts help to explain.

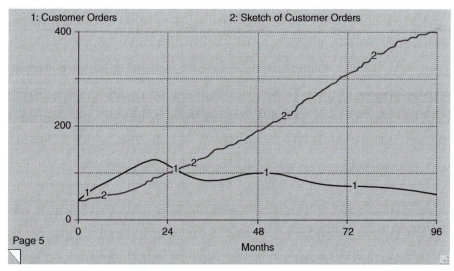

Figure 7.25   Customer orders in the base case of the full model – simulated and sketched

Figure 7.26 shows the behaviour over time of delivery delay and capacity. At the start of the simulation the factory is comfortably able to supply the fledgling market.

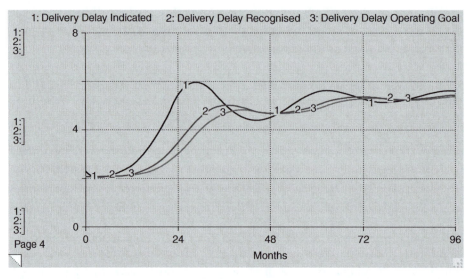

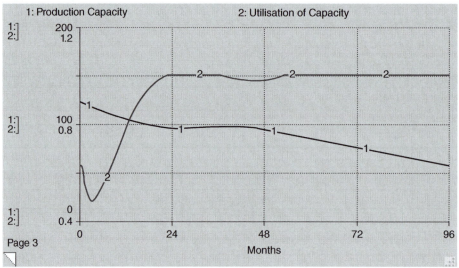

Figure 7.26 Delivery delay and production capacity in the base case of the full model

Delivery delay in the top chart begins at a value of two months, no matter which of the three different measures is chosen. However, during the first 28 months delivery delay indicated rises to a peak of almost six months as orders grow quickly and the factory becomes increasingly stretched. The situation in the factory is shown in the bottom chart. Utilisation of capacity (line 2) starts at a moderate 60% (0.6), falls briefly and then rises quickly to its maximum value of 100% (1) by month 24, where 100% utilisation means the factory is working flat out, three shifts, seven days a week. In a matter of only two years the factory becomes extremely busy. Meanwhile, orders have more than trebled (Figure 7.25, line 1). So why does capacity fall? Recall that pressure to expand capacity comes from delivery delay relative to the company's operating goal. This pressure is evident in the gap between delivery delay indicated (line 1) and delivery delay operating goal (line 3) that widens for the first 28 months of the simulation. Hence, pressure to expand capacity does indeed rise as expected. Yet the pressure is not enough, partly because the operating goal itself rises and partly because of the conservative investment bias of top management. Paradoxically, the company fails to expand capacity because it gets used to late deliveries.

Nevertheless, production capacity in the bottom chart does increase slightly for more than a year between months 24 and 40. However, this modest investment is not enough to reduce delivery delay back to its starting value of two months. As a result, customer orders decline and the pressure on the factory begins to subside. By month 38, delivery delay indicated is equal to the operating goal and top management is no longer convinced of the need for investment. Capacity cuts follow. The company is locked into a self-fulfilling spiral of decline. Reluctance to invest leads to high capacity utilisation and high delivery delay. Chronically high delivery delay eventually depresses customer orders and reduces the pressure to invest, thereby prolonging the capacity shortage. By the end of the simulation, delivery delay indicated (line 1) is more than five months and so too is the delivery delay operating goal (line 3). The company has inadvertently settled for long delivery times.

The consequences of dwindling capacity on the sales force and customers are shown in Figure 7.27. In the top chart, the sales force (line 2) adjusts towards the authorised sales force (line 1). The authorised force itself grows significantly in the interval between months four and 16 (fuelled by sales revenue), but later levels off and begins to decline as the product becomes more difficult to sell. By month 48, the authorised sales force is equal to the sales force and growth is halted. Thereafter, the sales force shrinks as sales people become less productive and no longer contribute enough to the sales budget to pay their own salaries. The gain of the reinforcing sales loop falls below one. Meanwhile in the bottom chart, customer orders (line 1) grow to begin with, reaching a peak of 124 systems per month in month 21. However, the order fill rate (line 2) does not keep pace with rising demand, causing an increase in delivery delay as already seen in Figure 7.26. As a result, customer orders decline sharply in the interval between months 20 and 34, even though the sales force continues to expand. There is a slight recovery when the order fill rate (line 2) briefly exceeds customer orders, thereby improving the supply situation, but eventually customer orders settle into steady decline through a combination of chronic high delivery delay and falling sales force.

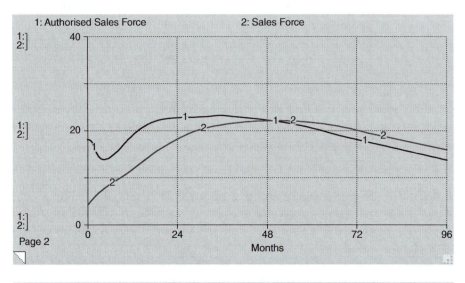

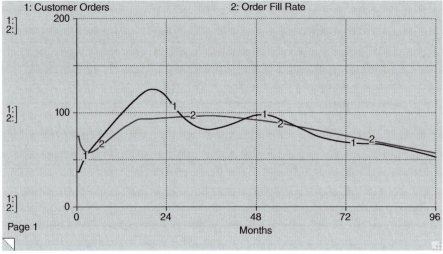

Figure 7.27   Sales force, customer orders and order fill rate in the base case of the full model

Redesign of the Investment Policy

This pattern of stagnation and decline clearly demonstrates the syndrome of growth and underinvestment mentioned at the start of the chapter. Despite huge market potential, the firm fails to achieve even modest growth. Adequate investment is simply not forthcoming. Yet the policy of capacity expansion makes sense in that it responds to realistic pressure from delivery delay. What kind of policy changes can the firm implement to dramatically improve performance and to realise the market potential?

Critics of the firm might argue it is far too inward looking. Capacity expansion relies heavily on evidence from the factory that delivery delay is too great. Surely it would be better to use a forecast of customer orders and build capacity to match. But remember, the top management team adopts a conservative attitude to investment. They listen to the evidence for expansion but downplay it. More interesting than a forecast is to explore the effect of softening this conservative attitude. What if it were replaced with an optimistic attitude to approve more investment than factory managers themselves are calling for? This change calls for a fundamental shift in top management attitude to risk – a willingness to invest in capacity ahead of demand (which is rather like believing an optimistic growth forecast). We can test this change in the model by simply reversing the sign on the delivery delay bias.

Top Management Optimism in Capital Investment

Return to the capacity diagram of the growth and investment model. Double select 'delivery delay bias' and change the value from 0.3 to -0.3. Review the implications of this parameter change in the equations for delivery delay pressure and capacity expansion fraction. Essentially, delivery delay pressure is now higher than it would have been leading to a larger capacity expansion fraction. For example, in the case where delivery condition is one (factory managers think delivery delay is OK) then delivery delay pressure now takes a value 1.3 and top management approve capacity expansion even though factory managers do not think extra capacity is essential. Return to the graph pad and before running re-sketch customer orders (line 2) to follow the trajectory of customer orders from the base case. The sketch is now a reference for comparison. Press the 'Run' button and watch the new trajectory of customer orders unfold. The time chart at the top of Figure 7.28 appears. Notice that the number of customer orders (line 1) grows. By month 48 it reaches almost 200 systems per month by comparison with 100 systems per month in the base case. Moreover, orders continue to grow, albeit slowly, reaching 250 systems per month by the end of the simulation. The reason for this gradual growth is apparent in the bottom chart. Just as in the base case delivery delay indicated (line 1) rises as the factory tries to cope with increasing orders, but crucially this rise is less than in the base case because top management approve more investment. With extra capacity, the factory settles on a delivery delay of just over four months (rather than almost five months in the base case) and this service improvement (while far from ideal) is sufficient to sustain modest growth.

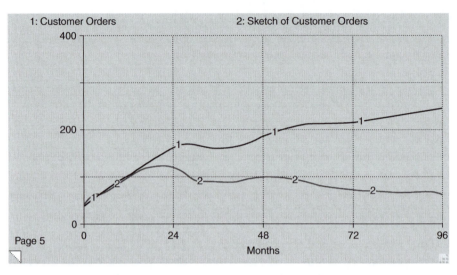

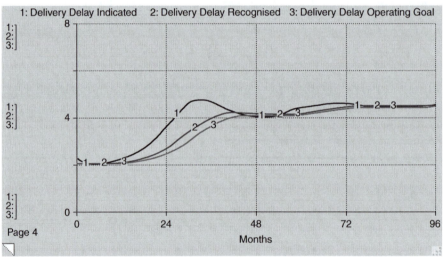

Figure 7.28   Customer orders and delivery delay with optimistic investment (sketch shows the base case)

Further analysis can be carried out by investigating the other time charts showing production capacity, utilisation, sales force and authorised sales force. However, this extra work is left as an exercise for the reader. (Note that it will be necessary to re-scale the time charts in order to see the complete 96-month trajectories.) Hence, optimistic capacity expansion pays off, at least in this case. However, the resulting market growth is still far short of potential and has been bought by abandoning a belief in prudent and conservative investment. In practice, such a change of mindset may be difficult to achieve. Some would regard investment optimism as mere speculation, akin to hunch and hope.

High and Unyielding Standards – A Fixed Operating Goal for Delivery Delay

Pressure for capacity expansion exists whenever delivery delay exceeds the operating goal. In many organisations, however, goals drift to fit what was achieved in the past. As the goal drifts then pressure to take corrective action is reduced. But what if the goal were to remain fixed? The idea can be tested in the model by changing the delivery delay weight in the formulation for delivery delay operating goal so that all the weight goes to the management goal and none to delivery delay tradition. In practice, unyielding standards originate from the leadership whose job it is to communicate expected standards of performance and to create an environment or culture where the standards are respected and adhered to.

Return to the capacity diagram and double select the icon for 'delivery delay weight'. Change the weight from one to zero and then review the formulation for delivery delay operating goal to confirm that the change sets the operating goal equal to the delivery delay management goal which is itself set at two months. Make sure delivery delay bias is reset to its original value of 0.3 (rather than −0.3). Go to page 5 of the graph pad that will still be showing the trajectories in Figure 7.28, top chart. (If these trajectories are not showing then first re-run the experiment above to test investment optimism and then repeat the instructions in this paragraph.) Press the 'Run' button and watch the trajectory of customer orders unfold. The time chart at the top of Figure 7.29 appears. For the first 26 months customer orders (line 1) follow the base case (line 2 sketch). Thereafter orders grow quickly, reaching 222 systems per month in month 48 and 400 systems per month in month 77. This sustained growth is possible because pressure for capacity expansion remains high throughout. The bottom chart tells the story. Recall that pressure for capacity expansion is proportional to the gap between delivery delay indicated (line 1) and delivery delay operating goal (line 3). The operating goal is rock steady at two months and so when (in the initial surge of growth) delivery delay indicated rises, the gap between the two trajectories widens and stays wide. As a result much more capacity is added than in the base case, despite the reinstatement of conservative investment. Extra capacity results in lower delivery delay and so the product remains quite attractive to customers. Delivery delay recognised by the customer (line 2) settles at four months. This value is still double the operating goal, but the difference ensures continued pressure for capacity expansion to satisfy the growing volume of customer orders generated by a burgeoning sales force. With this policy change the company begins to realise the huge potential of the market.

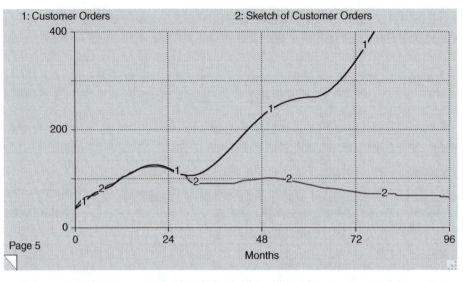

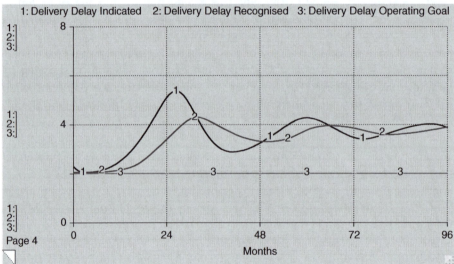

Figure 7.29   Customer orders and delivery delay with fixed operating goal (sketch shows the base case)

Unyielding standards can unlock the market, but they are not guaranteed to work. The standards the company strives for must also be appropriate for customers. This mantra may seem obvious but it raises the question of where such standards come from. Often they are deeply held beliefs of the top management team, anchored perhaps in an intuitive understanding of the market. If the intuition is wrong then the market will not materialise. The simulator vividly shows the consequences of such a mismatch. Return to the capacity diagram and set delivery delay management goal to four months.

Also check that delivery delay weight is set to zero. Return to the graph and press 'Run'. The trajectories shown in Figure 7.30 appear. In the top chart, customer orders (line 1) collapse to only three systems per month in month 24. Over the next 24 months orders stage a recovery to almost 50 systems per month but then level off and decline to end at 25 systems per month. The sketch of customer orders (line 2) re-traces the base case for comparison. Clearly a company that sets the wrong goal for delivery service performs far worse.

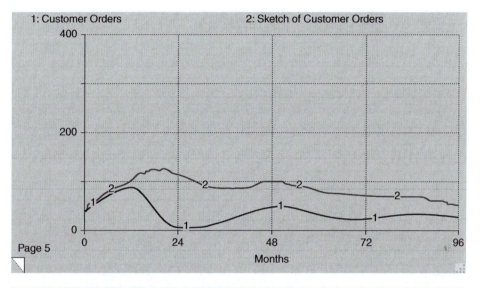

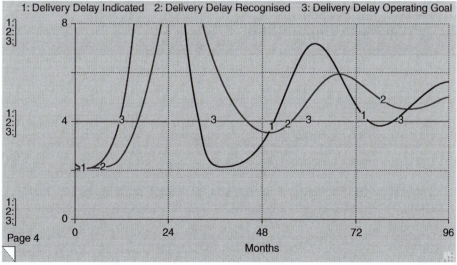

Figure 7.30   Customer orders and delivery delay with wrong fixed operating goal (sketch shows the base case)

Notice the dramatic behaviour of delivery delay in the bottom chart. Delivery delay indicated (line 1) starts at two months while the operating goal (line 3) is four months. This discrepancy signals surplus production capacity that leads to disinvestment. Capacity is decommissioned and delivery delay rises sharply, going off-scale and reaching a peak value of almost 14 months after 21 simulated months. (Note that off-scale variables can be read by moving the pointer within the axes of the time chart and then selecting and holding the mouse button. A moveable vertical cursor appears. Numbers are displayed below each variable reporting their numerical values.) Delivery delay recognised by the customer (line 2) reaches a peak of 9.5 months in month 26 making it virtually impossible for the sales force to sell the product. Subsequent re-investment reduces delivery delay and revives orders, but because the delivery delay operating goal is set at four months, the amount of investment is inadequate and customer orders continue to languish.

Policy Design, Growth and Dynamic Complexity

The dynamical issue at the heart of the market growth model is the coordination of production capacity with sales force and customer orders. The model shows that it is all too easy for companies to under-invest without realising it. By assumption, the market opportunity is large and, at first glance, it would seem impossible to fail. Hire a sales force to tap demand and build a factory to supply the customers. In reality these actions are interdependent. A management team cannot build a factory and invest the huge sums of money required without solid evidence of demand. Customers will not buy a product unless it is available, no matter how attractive it is in other respects. The marketing department cannot hire sales people without revenue, at least not in the medium to long term. Because of these interdependencies, many factors influence business growth and successful market development. Success depends on the importance customers attach to quick delivery, their patience and perceptions, on the size of the sales budget, how much sales people are paid, how quickly they can be hired, on the operating goals of the factory, the business pressures that drive capital investment, top management attitude to risk, the speed of adjusting production capacity, the flexibility in utilisation, and so on. In theory it is possible to find a combination of all these factors that ensures success – optimal growth if you like. But the practical challenge is more pragmatic – to discover those few factors that avoid stagnation and decline.

The secret of growth in this case is coordination between sales force, capacity and customer orders. The previous simulations show that sales tend to grow quickly when delivery delay is low. What does it take for the firm to achieve this condition?

We can use our knowledge of the feedback structure to make informed guesses and then test them with simulation. Delivery delay arises in the interaction between the sales growth loop and the capacity expansion loop. If capacity expansion is well matched to the expansion of the sales force then delivery delay should remain reasonably stable. Capacity expansion depends heavily on the goal formation process for delivery delay operating goal and on the investment bias applied by the top management team. The more pressure these processes bring to bear on investment the more effective is the balancing loop for capacity expansion and the more likely it is that capacity will keep pace with growth in sales. For these reasons, both delivery delay bias and delivery delay weight are high leverage parameters for sustainable growth, as earlier simulations have already shown. One might suspect therefore that combining optimistic investment (delivery delay bias = −0.3) with a well-chosen fixed operating goal (delivery delay weight = 0, delivery delay management goal = 2) will unleash even more market potential. The way to find out is to simulate, which the reader is invited to do.

The policy changes proposed so far fix the coordination problem from the supply side, by boosting investment. What can be achieved on the demand side? Our analysis suggests, paradoxically, that the firm fails to grow because its sales force is too good at winning orders – too good relative to the firm's willingness to invest. So an alternative policy might be to reduce the strength of the sales growth loop, say by reducing the fraction of revenue allocated to the sales force. In the base case this fraction is set at 0.1 (10%). Again the way to test the policy change is to simulate. Other policy changes are possible too. For example, one might test the effect of reducing the time to adjust the sales force or increasing normal sales force productivity. Combination supply side and demand side changes can also be investigated, though complex parameter juggling is best avoided because the corresponding real world policy change may be difficult to implement and the marginal performance gains small. An interesting structural change is to make product price a function of the order backlog. These and other experiments are left as exercises for the reader. Remember the objective in policy design is to find high leverage parameters that result in significant and robust performance improvements.

Conclusion

Overview of Policy Structure

The model diagrams presented earlier in the chapter (Figures 7.14, 7.15 and 7.18) are quite detailed and show all the concepts used in the equations. As mentioned in Chapter 5, sometimes it is useful to stand back from the formulation detail and compress all the symbols contained within a given policy (the grey regions in Figures 7.14, 7.15 and 7.18) into a single macro policy function. This overview of policy structure gives a feel for how dominant information flows (arising from bounded rationality and characteristic traits of decision making in the organisation) translate into feedback structure.

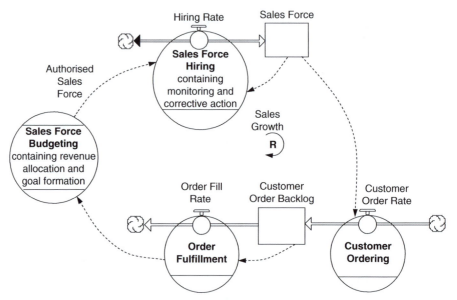

Figure 7.31 Overview of policy structure driving growth

Figure 7.31 is an overview of policy structure driving growth. It shows four main policies: sales force hiring, sales force budgeting, order fulfilment and customer ordering. The management team of any manufacturing company employing a professional sales force will recognise these processes of decision making individually and be able to discuss them in depth without the need to think algebraically. What the management team and the modeller need to discover is how these processes fit together, without losing sight of the processes themselves. This particular diagram shows clearly how the reinforcing sales growth loop arises because sales force hiring is driven by a revenue budget and customer orders are driven by sales force.

Figure 7.32 is important because it extends across the functional boundary between sales and manufacturing, covering territory that is rarely seen in a unified way. Here a useful structural insight is simply that customer ordering is linked to order fulfilment, production capacity and capacity utilisation. Orders that cannot be filled immediately accumulate in a customer order backlog. In itself this statement is just common sense, but it is important to realise that backlog sits at the strategic interface between the customer and the factory. In the diagram it is centre stage, whereas in practice it is virtually invisible,

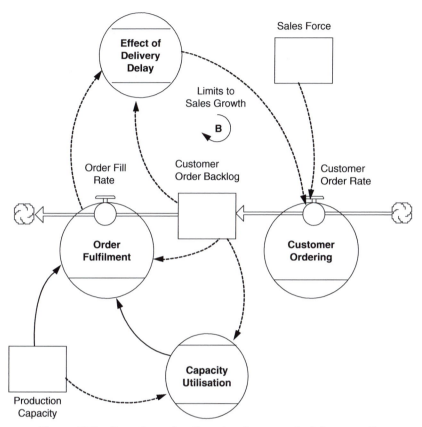

Figure 7.32   Overview of policy structure constraining growth

stored somewhere in a database and not even appearing on the balance sheet (where it might attract critical attention). This shadowy variable is the invisible hand responsible for balancing supply and demand in the medium to long term. The diagram shows its mediating role clearly. On the demand side it feeds back through delivery delay to influence customer ordering, creating the balancing loop labelled limits to sales growth. On the supply side it influences order fulfilment by exerting pressure on factory managers to increase capacity utilisation.

Figure 7.33 is an overview of policy structure for reactive capital investment. This picture takes us to the core of the coordination problem in the market growth model. It shows five operating policies: capacity ordering, assessment of delivery delay, goal formation, order fulfilment, and customer ordering. In some form or another all factories use policies like these to adjust capacity to customer demand. In a normal healthy and profitable business if demand grows then firms recognise the increase of orders and build more capacity. This economic logic applies equally to manufacturing and service firms. But how is the demand signal transmitted from customers to the group of top executives who approve investment and hold the purse strings?

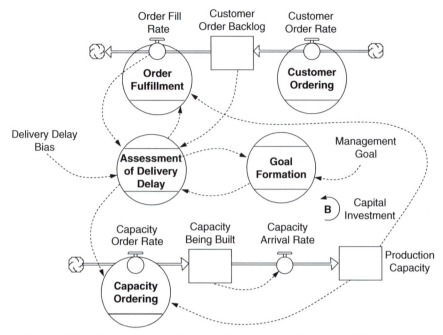

Figure 7.33   Overview of policy structure for reactive capital investment

The overview diagram addresses this question. It says that all firms define for themselves a metric for recognising whether or not there is a capacity shortage. This metric involves an assessment of the supply–demand balance and goal formation to set an appropriate standard for managing the balance. From the assessment comes a flow of information to drive capacity ordering. In this particular case, delivery delay is the metric for recognising a capacity shortage and, by comparing delivery delay with an operating goal, management is able to take corrective action leading to investment or disinvestment.

The diagram can be used to contemplate alternative information sources for accomplishing similar corrective action and to reflect on why the company has adopted its distinctive investment approach. For example, it is easy to imagine capacity utilisation (rather than delivery delay) as the metric for recognising a capacity shortage. Why doesn't the management team use this metric? What is so important about delivery delay in this company that it grabs managerial attention? What difference would it make if utilisation were the metric instead? What would be the goal formation process for 'target' utilisation?

An entirely different approach to investment is to use sales force as a proxy or leading indicator for potential demand and to gear up capacity accordingly. In this approach the goal formation process might define target capacity in proportion to sales force size. An assessment of the supply–demand balance would then be a matter of comparing target capacity with existing capacity and investing to correct any perceived gap. Would the top management team believe in a speculative estimate of demand arising from sales force size? What form would their conservative investment bias take if presented with such information?

These overviews of policy structure conclude the chapter on the market growth model. By composing models in terms of operating policies, modellers can harness a great deal of practical managerial knowledge in their quest for realistic feedback structure and plausible dynamics. Readers who wish to see another in-depth example of policy structure analysis in business are referred to the learning support folder for Chapter 7, and the subfolder c07 Archive Materials. Here you will find my working paper D-3757 Learning From Behavioral Modeling and Simulation of Business Policy.

Growth and Underinvestment at People Express?

This has been a long chapter with new and abstract concepts like bounded rationality, behavioural decision making and information filters. These concepts help modellers to identify, from the overwhelming flux of information in business and society, those few information channels that shape decision making and action in real world situations. The more finely modellers can discriminate between attention-grabbing information flows (that are truly influential in real-world decision making and action) and those information flows that managers and business leaders ignore, then the more plausible will be the information feedback structures they discover and the better the resulting models. The abstract material in this chapter is important. I have always told MBA and Executive MBA students at London Business School that if they really understand the structure, formulations and simulations of the market growth model they are well on their way to becoming a good system dynamics modeller and an effective conceptualiser of complex situations in business and society (a valuable skill in its own right).

But simply reading about these abstract concepts and experimenting with a pre-built model is not enough. It is important to practise and use the concepts in real world situations. Here I suggest readers set aside a chunk of time to return to the People Express case mentioned at the end of Chapter 6. The rise and fall of People Express can be viewed as a growth coordination problem, not unlike the situation in the market growth model. Which strategic resources get out of balance and why? If the fate of People Express is an example of growth and underinvestment then where, in the company's operating policies, is the locus of underinvestment? How did People Express achieve such spectacular growth over five years only to collapse? We can be sure that CEO Don Burr and his management team did not deliberately underinvest in any aspect of the business to cause its collapse. The company's officers wanted profitable growth, particularly the CEO. To probe this paradox, I suggest that readers first review the original Harvard Business School case study (cited in the references for Chapter 6) to formulate a dynamic hypothesis. Then use the materials and airline model components in the learning support folder for Chapter 6 to develop a personalised People Express model that is capable of explaining the company's rise and fall.

More Examples of Growth Strategies that Failed or Faltered – and One that Succeeded

Other models in the system dynamics literature also probe strategic coordination problems that lie behind failures of companies to grow as quickly as intended.[3] Two I am most familiar with come from practical applications projects. One project (reported in Morecroft, 1986) investigated periodic downturns facing a high technology materials handling company located in Salt Lake City, Utah and traced them to overexpansion of rookie rivals who undermined the industry's reputation. The feedback loops believed responsible for the company's varying fortunes were outlined in Chapter 2, Figure 2.12. The other project (reported in Morecroft, Lane and Viita, 1991) examined the faltering growth strategy of a biotechnology start-up firm located to the west of London and owned by Royal Dutch/Shell. This tiny company belonged in Shell's portfolio of promising non-traditional start-up businesses (i.e. not in oil) that Shell managers were nurturing to learn about new technologies and markets. Many of these small firms they would sell on as seedling ventures, but they hoped a few would grow in ways suited to the Shell Group. Hence, the project was an effort to understand the drivers and limits to growth. The biotechnology start-up firm (codenamed Bio-Industrial Products (BIP)) seemed to present a clear case of capital underinvestment (the same as the market growth model) but intriguingly the collective reluctance of senior management to invest stemmed from inherent uncertainty about the true operating capacity of the company's fermentation vessels (in which microbes were cultivated for use in the company's grease-eating products). Even the scientists and technologists operating the vessels did not know the factory output capacity to an accuracy any better than an order of magnitude; which is like Ford of Europe saying it does not know whether the potential output of an assembly plant is 10 000 or 100 000 cars per year! This

---

[3]Growth coordination during corporate diversification also presents important strategic management challenges that can be interpreted as variations on growth and underinvestment in a single business. This topic is explored in Gary (2000; 2005).

technological uncertainty made it difficult for BIP executives to mount a convincing case at Shell headquarters for capital investment funding.

Some growth strategies succeed. One of the earliest models in the archives of system dynamics is a study of the dynamics of corporate growth in a start-up company. This 200 equation business simulator was conceptualised by Jay Forrester to guide his thinking as an invited board member of the fledgling Digital Equipment Corporation (DEC). It is surely among the most subtle and insightful behavioural simulation models of a growth firm. Its formulations and characterisation of coordinating information flows and organisational pressures in a growing firm are well worth studying closely. Readers can view the full original documentation, by Jay Forrester and David Packer, in the learning support folder for Chapter 7, in the subfolder c07 Archive Materials. Here you will find working papers D-0433 Introduction to the Industrial Dynamics Study of Corporate Growth and D-0434 A Model for the Study of Corporate Growth.

The company was founded in 1957 by Ken Olson and Harlan Anderson, talented engineers who designed the PDP mini computers that became the foundation of a global business. As graduate students Olson and Anderson had worked on Forrester's Whirlwind Computer project at MIT's Lincoln Laboratory (Fisher, 2005; Lane, 2007). Forrester was uniquely close to the heart of the new firm and its pioneering technology and therefore able to adopt the executive view of interlocking operations so vital to perceptive modelling. Among the insights he gleaned from model simulations was a recommendation for the founders to begin operations in a Civil War era textile mill in Maynard, Massachusetts, where plenty of inexpensive manufacturing space was available to accommodate growth. The old wool mill served as the company headquarters from 1957 to 1992, when DEC was acquired by Compaq.

The ambitious boundary and scope of the corporate growth model are conveyed in the following abstract from the original documentation of the project:

> This memo describes an industrial dynamics model developed as the initial step in a continuing study of corporate growth. The model is composed of twelve sectors, each presented in one chapter of this [128 page] memo. The first sector represents the market for a firm producing complex new technology products. Company operations are described by the following six sectors: Professional Staff Sector, Professional Staff Time Allocation Sector, Production Worker Sector, Production Rate Sector, Inventory and Order-Filling Sector, and the Quality Generation Sector. The information flows in the organization and the organizational pressures which control company operations are the subject of the following four sectors, each generating a particular organizational pressure: Delivery Delay Pressure Sector, Marketing Pressure Sector, Quality Pressure Sector, and the Professional Workload Pressure Sector. A final sector tabulates the effective size of the organization, based on the size of the professional staff (engineers

and managers) and the growth rate of the organization. The last chapter contains equations which set to constants several variables used in the model but
not yet formulated. The result is an operating system with which we can study
some of the interactions which are thought to produce significant aspects of
corporate growth behavior.

Growth Strategy for New Products and Services in a Competitive Industry

So far we have said very little about rival companies, almost as though they
have no effect on the success of a firm's growth strategy. This inward-looking
assumption reflects a philosophical bias of the field. Failures of growth
strategy often arise from hidden difficulties in building and coordinating a
firm's internal resources. Competitors are not necessarily to blame. Competent
managers may pursue policies that, in their minds, appear reasonable, yet
which turn out to interact in surprising ways to undermine growth strategy. So
there is good reason to look inward.

Nevertheless it is important for executives, and therefore also modellers, to be
aware of rival firms and their competitive intentions. Sometimes rivals should
be explicitly modelled (Sterman *et al.*, 2007). As always, it is a matter of
judgement about where to set the boundary of a model and how much to
represent about competitors' behaviour and intentions in order to address the
strategic issue at hand.

Figure 7.34 provides a framework for thinking about the operational and
competitive setting for a firm's growth strategy. There are three sectors.

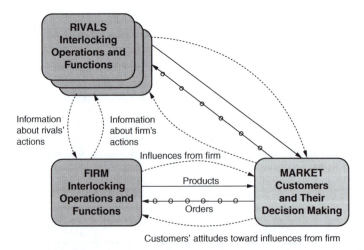

Figure 7.34 A framework for modelling the growth of new products and services in a competitive industry

In the lower left is the firm itself with its internal interlocking operations and functions. On the right is the market with customers and their decision making processes and preferences. In the upper left are rival firms, each with their own internal interlocking operations and functions. There are also numerous lines and arrows that bind together the firm, market and rivals into a closed-loop feedback representation of a competitive industry.

In the bottom half of the figure there are four arrows to represent various channels of information and action flow between the firm and the market. Orders flow from customers to the firm while products (or services) flow back. The firm and market also exchange flows of information. Influences from the firm such as sales effort, delivery delay, quality and price combine to affect customer orders. In return the firm gleans information about customers' attitudes toward its overall product or service 'offering' which managers use to control operations and investment. Equivalent interactions take place between rival firms and the market.

Finally, on the left of the figure, there are competitive interactions between the firm and its rivals. Information about rivals' actions and intentions enters the firm with the potential to influence operations and investment. For example, knowledge of a price cut by rivals may prompt the firm to reduce the price of its own products or services. Rumour of impending capacity expansion by a prominent rival may deter or delay capital investment by the firm. Reciprocal information about the firm's actions and intentions flows to rivals where, likewise, it can influence operations and investment.

It is tempting to think that any dynamic model of firm growth strategy should include sectors just like these. But such inclusivity is rarely necessary. It is unlikely that all the factors in the picture are important in a given case situation. Instead it is better to use the framework to make simplifying choices about model boundary to fit a particular growth situation.

To illustrate, consider the boundary of the Bass model from Chapter 6. Essentially it is a model of the market sector alone. In Figure 6.7, favourable word-of-mouth within the market converts potential adopters (of a new product or service) into adopters, thereby driving s-shaped growth in sales. There is no model of the firm's interlocking functions, except a stylised representation of advertising to kick-start word-of-mouth sales. There are no rivals because the focus is on the typical dynamics of adoption for any innovating firm in the industry. The resulting elegant simplicity of the basic Bass model conveys many useful insights into the timing, pace and lifecycle of sales growth in a word-of-mouth market. Rivals can be bolted on later, if necessary.

The market growth model is very different. Essentially it is a model about the interactions within and between a multi-function firm and its market. The key to sales growth is not word-of-mouth among customers but rather the firm's successful internal coordination of growth in capacity and in sales force to ensure timely delivery of product to customers. There is no explicit model of rival firms, though there is an assumption of background competition in the graph for the effect of delivery delay on orders (see Figure 7.16, earlier in this chapter). The downward slope of the graph is a stylised representation of industry competition which assumes customers will go elsewhere when they perceive that delivery times are too long.

Appendix – Gain of a Reinforcing Loop

Gain is a technical term used to describe the strength of a reinforcing loop. The procedure for calculating gain is outlined in Figure 7.35. There is a reinforcing loop A-B-C-D. What it represents is immaterial. What matters is whether the causal links amplify or attenuate a change that originates in the loop. To test this property we first imagine the loop is cut at some convenient point and then unfolded to form a linear chain or 'open loop'. In this case a cut is made in the link connecting D and A. The gain of the open loop is defined as the size of the change transmitted back to A when the value of A itself changes by one unit. Alternatively, if A changes by a small amount A, then the gain is the size of the change transmitted back to A divided by A. The calculation assumes a steady state is achieved, so enough time elapses for any stock adjustment processes to run their course. The full name for the calculation is the 'open loop steady state gain'.

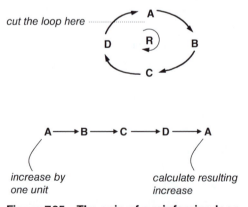

Figure 7.35   The gain of a reinforcing loop

The concept is best illustrated with a practical example. Figure 7.36 shows the sales growth loop from the market growth model, including the parameters that determine the strength of causal links.

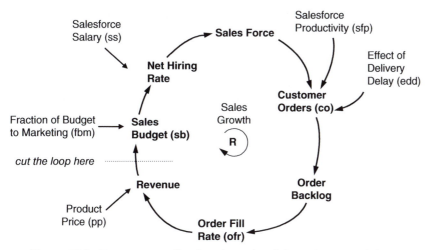

Figure 7.36   Parameters affecting the gain of the sales growth loop

In this case, imagine the loop is cut at a point in the link between revenue and sales budget. Suppose there is a small increase in the sales budget sb. The size of the change transmitted back to the sales budget is defined in the model as the change in the order fill rate (ofr) multiplied by the product price (pp) and the fraction of budget to marketing (fbm). By working back through the links we can express the change in the order fill rate ofr itself as a function of the change in the sales budget sb and so end up with an expression for gain that depends only on the parameters around the edge of the loop. The steps in the calculation are shown below:

Step 1: gain = ofr * pp * fbm/sb
Step 2: gain = co * pp * fbm/sb, since in steady state the change in the order fill rate ofr is equal to the change in customer orders co.
Step 3: gain = sf * sfp * edd * pp * fbm/sb, because the change in customer orders co is equal to the change in sales force sf multiplied by sales force productivity.
Step 4: gain = sb * sfp * edd * pp * fbm/ss * sb, since in steady state the change in sales force sf is equal to the change in the sales budget sb divided by sales force salary ss.
Step 5: gain = sfp * edd * pp * fbm/ss, cancelling the original change in sales budget sb to leave only numerical parameters.

There are five parameters that determine the open loop steady state gain: sales force productivity (sfp), the effect of delivery delay (edd), product price (pp), the fraction of budget to marketing (fbm) and sales force salary (ss). Substituting numerical values from the model gives a gain of 2.4 (10 * 1 * 9600 * 0.1/4000). Since the gain is greater than one the loop generates growth.

Notice the effect of delivery delay (edd). We assume in the calculation that it takes a neutral value of one. However in the full model the effect is variable and can take a value anywhere between one and zero, depending on delivery delay recognised by the customer (as shown in Figure 7.16). If the effect of delivery delay (edd) were to take a value of 0.4167 (which is the inverse of 2.4), then the gain would be exactly one and customer orders would remain steady and neither increase nor decline. If the effect of delivery delay were to take a value of say 0.2 then the gain would be less than one and customer orders would go into a spiral of decline. This transformation from growth to decline is exactly what happens in the base case simulation of the full model as shown in Figure 7.27.

References

Barnard, C. (1938) *The Functions of the Executive*. Boston, MA: Harvard University Press.

Fisher, L. (2005) The prophet of unintended consequences. *strategy+business*, 40, Booz & Co.

Forrester, J.W. (1961) *Industrial Dynamics*. Available from the System Dynamics Society www.systemdynamics.org; originally published by MIT Press, Cambridge MA 1961.

Forrester, J.W. (1968) Market growth as influenced by capital investment. *Industrial Management Review*, 7(1), 5–17.

Forrester, J.W. (1994) Policies, decisions and information sources for modelling. In Morecroft, J. and Sterman, J. (eds), *Modeling for Learning Organizations*. Portland, OR: Productivity Press.

Forrester, J.W. (1996) The CEO as organization designer. *McKinsey Quarterly Anthologies: Business Dynamics – overcoming the limits to growth*, 98–118.

Gary, M.S. (2000) The Dynamics of Resource Sharing in Related Diversification. PhD Thesis, London Business School, June.

Gary, M.S. (2005) Implementation strategy and performance outcomes in related diversification. *Strategic Management Journal*, 26: 643–664.

Lane, D.C. (2007) The power of the bond between cause and effect: Jay Forrester and the field of system dynamics. *System Dynamics Review*, 23(2/3): 95–118.

Morecroft, J.D.W. (1983) System dynamics: portraying bounded rationality. *Omega*, 11(2): 131–142.

Morecroft, J.D.W. (1986) The dynamics of a fledgling high technology growth market. *System Dynamics Review*, 2(1): 36–61.

Morecroft, J.D.W., Lane, D.C. and Viita, P.S. (1991) Modelling growth strategy in a biotechnology startup firm. *System Dynamics Review*, 7(2): 93–116.

Senge, P.M. (1990) *The Fifth Discipline: The Art and Practice of the Learning Organization*. New York: Doubleday.

Simon, H.A. (1976) *Administrative Behavior* (3rd edn). New York: Free Press.

Simon, H.A. (1979) Rational decisionmaking in business organizations. *American Economic Review*, 69: 493–513.

Simon, H.A. (1982) *Models of Bounded Rationality*. Cambridge, MA: MIT Press.

Sterman, J.D. (1989) Misperceptions of feedback in dynamic decisionmaking. *Organizational Behavior and Human Decision Processes*, 43(3): 301–335.

Sterman, J.D. (2000) *Business Dynamics: Systems Thinking and Modeling for a Complex World*. Boston, MA: Irwin McGraw-Hill. (See, in particular, Chapter 13, Modeling Decision Making.)

Sterman, J.D., Henderson, R., Beinhocker, E.D., and Newman, L.I. (2007) Getting big too fast: Strategic dynamics with increasing returns and bounded rationality. *Management Science*, 53(4): 683–696.

Chapter 8

Industry Dynamics – Oil Price and the Global Oil Producers

- Problem Articulation – Puzzling Dynamics of Oil Price
- Model Development Process
- A Closer Look at the Stakeholders and Their Investment Decision Making
- Connecting the Pieces – A Feedback Systems View
- A Simple Thought Experiment: Green Mindset and Global Recession
- Using the Model to Generate Scenarios
- Devising New Scenarios
- Endnote: A Brief History of the Oil Producers' Project

Previous chapters have dealt with firm-level dynamics of cyclicality, growth, stagnation and decline. In this chapter, we turn our attention to the dynamics of an entire industry, global oil, comprising thousands of firms and billions of consumers around the world. At first glance, this shift of perspective may seem ambitious, requiring an immensely large model to capture the vast web of interactions among so many players. What is really required is a shift in the unit of analysis, away from the individual firm and its functions to major groupings in the industry. Industries, as a whole, exhibit interesting and puzzling dynamics. The modeller's task is to discover feedback loops that explain observed dynamics. As always, the conceptual challenge is to adopt an appropriate perspective from which to view the situation and interpret its dynamic complexity. In this case, the model arose from a team model-building project with planners at Royal Dutch/Shell (Morecroft and van der Heijden, 1992).[1] The team wanted to develop a simulation model of global oil markets.

---

[1] The oil producers' project was part of a larger initiative at Shell International to reposition corporate planning as a process for organisational learning. This important role for planning is described by de Geus (1988) and is further developed in an influential book *The Living Company* (de Geus, 1999). Firms that successfully adapt and survive are those where important decisions and actions are embedded within an effective learning cycle.

The project was part of a broad ranging scenario exercise to explore the strategic implications of changes in the structure of the energy industry.

In Shell, scenario planning is viewed as a way to discover new concepts and language that enable the organisation to become more agile in recognising significant industry trends, defining emerging business problems and preparing the minds of senior managers to deal with such problems. Scenario planning is not a way of predicting the future. Instead it works by the development of consistent stories about alternative futures, as the basis for what-if thinking in the organisation (van der Heijden, 1996). A consistent story traces a time path into the future that forces managers and planners to think 'what would I do, within my area of business responsibility, if this future were to unfold?' The internal consistency of the stories, creating credibility and persuasiveness, is an important factor in evaluating the usefulness of scenarios – much more important than the ex-post accuracy of the time paths. Scenarios are selected on their ability to make the organisation a skilful observer of the business environment. As such they do not have to describe the most likely future, but the reasoning behind the scenarios must be plausible.

Problem Articulation – Puzzling Dynamics of Oil Price

The long-term behaviour of oil price reveals striking contrasts between periods of price stability, mild price fluctuations, dramatic price surges and equally dramatic collapses. Figure 8.1 shows world oil price spanning 142 years, from 1869 to 2011; a remarkably long time series. The vertical axis is on a scale from zero to 100 dollars per barrel in 2010 dollars. Lying behind this price trajectory is the turbulent history of the oil industry as vividly told in *The Prize: The Epic Quest for Oil Money and Power* (Yergin, 1991) and *The Quest: Energy, Security and the Remaking of the Modern World* (Yergin, 2011).

Between 1869 and 1880 there was extreme price volatility. This period corresponds to the early pioneering days of the oil industry in the Pennsylvania Oil Regions of the United States. The chaotic mix of speculators, fortune-seeking prospectors and their greedy exploitation of newly discovered reserves led to extraordinary periods of overproduction – too many wells and too much oil. The price trajectory in Figure 8.1 gyrates wildly, starting at $58 per barrel in 1869, rising to $75 per barrel by 1872, and falling to only $20 per barrel in 1874. Over the next two years to 1876, the price rose sharply to $50 per barrel before falling again to $18 in 1879. Then followed an interval of relatively low and stable oil price in the decade to 1889.

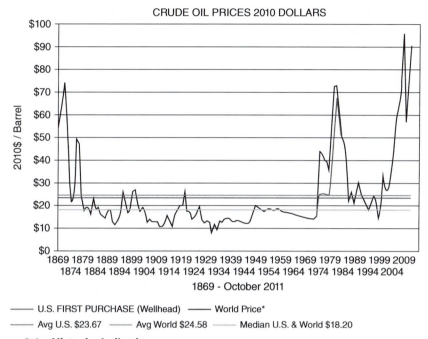

Figure 8.1 Historical oil price

Source: WTRG Economics Copyright 2011. Reproduced by permission.

This shift to stability was imposed on the industry through the vision and will of John D. Rockefeller, founder of Standard Oil. His objective was to end what he described as a cut-throat policy of making no profits and instead make the oil business safe and profitable – by controlling supply and especially refining and distribution. The long-term results of Rockefeller's efforts are evident in the relative calm between 1889 and 1939, when the price moved in a range between $10 and $25 per barrel. There is some evidence of a short-term price cycle with an interval of about four years from peak to peak. Nevertheless, there is much greater price stability than in the pioneering early days. Rockefeller's era of supply discipline, ruthlessly imposed on a naturally chaotic industry and its fledgling markets, led to the rise of the integrated oil company and the enduring legacy of the 'Seven Sisters'. (The Seven Sisters is a term credited to Italian Enrico Mattei to describe the close association of the major oil companies: the four Aramco partners – Jersey (Exxon), Socony-Vacuum (Mobil), Standard of California and Texaco, together with Gulf, Royal Dutch/Shell and British Petroleum.)

In the post-war era from 1945 to 1970, this legacy and stable industry structure remained in place – almost unchallenged – even as the Seven Sisters expanded their operations internationally on the back of colossal oil reserves in the Arabian Peninsula. Despite these huge reserves, and the rapid expansion of oil output in the post-war era, prices were remarkably stable as Figure 8.1 shows. The price tranquillity was a far cry from the chaos of the Pennsylvania Oil Regions at the birth of the industry. Throughout this era, which spanned two and a half decades, supply and demand were in almost perfect balance – an astonishing achievement when one considers the complexity of the industry, its global reach, the diversity of stakeholders (encompassing producers, consumers and nations), and the array of objectives sought by these stakeholders from their share in the oil bonanza.

Already, however, new forces were at work, stronger even than the Seven Sisters, ushering in a new era of oil supply politics. As the locus of production moved to the Middle East, so the global political power of the region was awakened, feeding on western industrial countries' appetite for Arabian oil to sustain energy-intensive economies and lifestyles. Control over Middle Eastern oil was seized by the newly formed OPEC – the Organisation of Petroleum Exporting Countries. In 1974, and again in 1978, OPEC exercised its power by withholding production and forcing up the price of oil. As Figure 8.1 shows, the price doubled and continued to rise to a peak of more than 70 dollars per barrel by 1979 – a peak not seen since the early days of the Pennsylvania Oil Regions. Hence, in the 1970s, after two decades of managed calm and predictability, chaos returned to global oil markets.

After 1979, price fell sharply to only $20 per barrel by the mid-1980s. For almost 20 years price fluctuated in the range $15 to $30 per barrel, but there were no further upheavals to match the dramatic variations of the 1970s. As the turn of the century approached, oil price was still low. In fact, many industry observers at the time believed it would remain low for the foreseeable future. However, the industry proved them wrong. Price began to rise again in 2001, reaching more than $30 per barrel by 2004 and $90 per barrel in 2009. By 2013 price had risen to more than $100 per barrel. Yet as 2014 drew to a close press reports began to appear suggesting that a new era of lower price, below $80 per barrel, was dawning.

Towards a Dynamic Hypothesis

An explanation of price behaviour lies in the feedback processes that balance supply and demand in the global oil markets. Periods of price stability correspond to times in which supply and demand are more or less in balance. Price spikes in the 1860s and 1970s correspond to times in which demand greatly exceeded supply. The gentle price roller-coaster of the early 1900s corresponds to a period in which supply sometimes exceeds and sometimes falls short of demand, but never by much. The remarkable price stability of the 1960s corresponds to a golden age of perfect supply management.

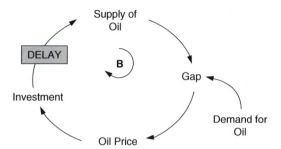

Figure 8.2   Simple balancing loop with delay in the oil industry

A useful template to begin conceptualisation of the oil industry is a balancing loop with delay as shown in Figure 8.2, the same as in Chapter 5's production and employment model, but this time conceived at the industry level and applying to upstream investment in oil rigs and platforms. Broadly speaking, if demand for oil exceeds supply then the gap (excess demand) leads to an increase in oil price that stimulates additional investment. After a delay of several years to open new oil fields, the supply of oil increases to eliminate the supply gap. Due to the long time delay in capacity expansion, it is difficult for the industry to achieve a balance of supply and demand and so oil price can be volatile. This explanation provides a preliminary dynamic hypothesis.

However, such a simple feedback loop by itself cannot explain the sustained price stability of the 1960s and 1970s. The corrective mechanism of capital investment, with its construction delay of almost five years, is simply not responsive enough to guarantee the near perfect balance of supply and demand that price stability requires. Equally, the invisible hand of balancing feedback alone cannot explain the wild price gyrations of the 1860s and 1870s, or the memorable price hikes of the 1970s and early 2010s. Reasoned commercial investment decisions should not result in oil famines and feasts with such extreme price movements. Obviously there are other feedback processes at work in the global oil system. Some must be fast-acting to prevent temporary imbalances and to short-circuit the inevitable time lags of commercial investment. Others must work to sustain imbalances, yet be powerful enough to override the natural balancing tendency of market forces and the invisible hand.

Model Development Process

There is clearly more to the global oil system than a simple balancing loop with delay. To gain more insight into the structure of the industry the project team (10 people in all) came together to share their knowledge about oil companies, oil producing nations and motives for investment and production. The team met three times for working sessions lasting three hours each. The meetings were facilitated by an experienced system dynamics modeller. One member of the team kept detailed minutes of the meetings (including copies of flip-chart notes and diagrams) in order to preserve a permanent trace of the model's conceptualisation. A sub-group of the project team met separately to develop and test a full-blown algebraic model.

Figure 8.3 shows the resulting overview of global oil producers comprising five main sectors. On the right are the independent producers making commercial investment decisions in response to the needs of the market and oil consumers. On the left are the swing producer and the opportunists that make up the oil producers' organisation OPEC. This powerful group of producers has access to very large reserves of low-cost oil. Their production decisions are motivated principally by political and social pressures, in contrast to the commercial logic of the independents. They coordinate production through quota setting. The opportunists agree to abide by quota, but will sometimes cheat by producing above quota in order to secure more oil revenues. The combined output of all three producer groups supplies the market where both price and demand are set.

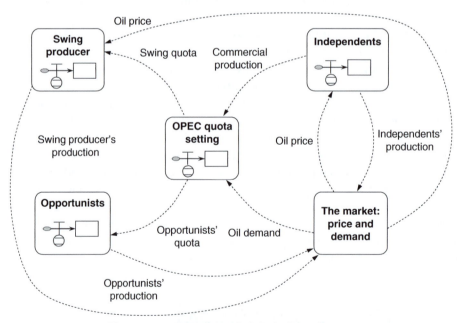

Figure 8.3   Overview of global oil producers

Price responds to imbalances in supply and demand and then feeds back to influence both demand and the behaviour of producers.

Now consider, in broad terms, how these five sectors are linked. In a purely commercial oil world there are only two sectors: the independents and the market. The market establishes the oil price and also consumers' demand for oil at the prevailing price. The oil price drives independents' investment and, eventually, leads to a change in production, which then feeds back to the market. The closed loop connecting the two sectors is none other than the balancing loop with delay mentioned earlier.

OPEC's involvement begins with quota setting. The nations of OPEC must collectively decide on an appropriate production quota. They do this by monitoring oil demand from the market and subtracting their estimate of independents' production. This difference is known as the call on OPEC and is the benchmark relative to which overall quota is set. The agreed quota is then allocated among member states. A portion called the swing quota goes to the swing producer and the rest to the opportunists. If OPEC is unified then all members follow quota, with the exception of the swing producer who makes tactical adjustments to production to ensure that oil price remains close to OPEC's target. In order to control oil price, the swing producer must closely monitor oil price and demand. Production from both the swing producer and opportunists then feeds back to the market, thereby completing the supply loop. As we shall see later there is much additional detail within each sector. For now, however, there is enough: five sectors with nine interconnecting lines to begin representing the rich and complex feedback structure of the global oil industry.

Why these five sectors? Why not lots more? Of course there is no one correct or best way to represent the industry. In reality, there are hundreds of companies and dozens of nations engaged in oil exploration and production. The project team was well aware of this detail complexity, but through experience had learned useful ways of simplifying the detail. In this case, the team agreed a unique conceptualisation of industry supply that focuses attention on the internal structure and political pressures governing a producers' organisation (OPEC) and its commercial rivals.

Models that fit the needs of executives and scenario planners do not have to be accurate predictive models. They should, however, have the capability to stimulate novel thinking about future business options. Moreover, models that are used to construct consistent stories about alternative futures need to be understood by the story writers (often senior planners) in order to be communicated effectively to corporate executives and business unit managers. A black-box predictor will not lead to the desired result, even if it has a good record of predictive power. These criteria help explain the style of modelling adopted – the need for a comparatively simple model, the relatively closed process (the project did not make direct use of other world oil market models or enlist the aid of world oil market experts as consultants) and the intense participation of senior planners in model conceptualisation. The project was not intended as an exercise in developing another general model of the oil trade to forecast better. The project team wanted to model their understanding of the oil market. Within the group, there was an enormous amount of experience, reflecting knowledge about the actors in the oil market and observations about market behaviour. But the knowledge was scattered and anecdotal, and therefore not very operational. The group also recognised that the interlinkages in the system were complex. The desire of the group was to engage in a joint process through which their knowledge could be pooled in a shared model and used to interpret real events. Most of the group members were not professional modellers. To them, other existing energy models were non-transparent black boxes, useful as a reflection of other's views, but quite unsuitable for framing their own knowledge.

A Closer Look at the Stakeholders and Their Investment Decision Making

To uncover the feedback structure of the oil industry the modeller led a discussion of the investment decision making of each main producer group. The same formulation principles introduced in Chapter 7 apply once again, including the Baker criterion, fit to industry practice, robustness and recognition of bounded rationality. For example, what do executives in commercial oil companies know and pay attention to as they make their upstream investment decisions? What information really matters to OPEC oil ministers as they agree quotas and set production targets? Which organisational, social and political factors shape and filter the signals used by different producer groups and their leaders to justify investment and production decisions? The diagrams that follow are similar to the flip-chart drawings from team meetings in which all these questions, and more, were thoroughly explored. Three versions of the model are described that differ only in their assumptions about the available pool of commercial reserves and development cost per barrel. The first version of the model reflects conditions starting in 1988, during the Soviet era, when the oil market excluded communist areas. The second version reflects conditions starting in 1995 when Russian oil was trading in the world market. The third version reflects conditions starting in 2010 when Russia had become the world's largest oil producer and when hydraulic fracturing technology, 'fracking', had been successfully adapted to begin exploiting large shale oil reserves (particularly in the US). A selection of equation formulations is included in the description that follows. Full documentation of the equation formulations can be found in the file named Oil World 1988 Equation Description in the learning support folder for Chapter 8.

Investment by the Independent Producers

The independents are all those producers – state-owned oil companies, the majors and other private producers – who are not part of OPEC and who expand crude oil output on the basis of commercial criteria. This category includes international oil companies such as BP Amoco, ExxonMobil and Shell, and non-OPEC nations such as Norway. The independents are assumed to produce at economic capacity all the time. Their production rate is therefore dictated by available capacity. The rationale for capacity expansion is dominated by commercial factors as shown in Figure 8.4. The circular symbol represents independent producers' upstream investment or capacity expansion policy – often known as 'capex'. The independents add new capacity when they judge it is profitable to do so.

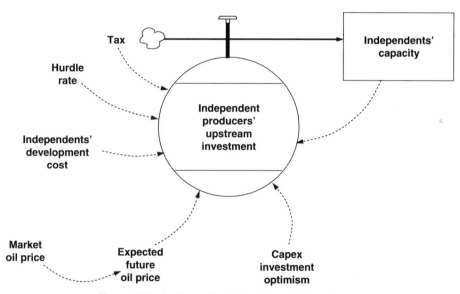

Figure 8.4   Independents' upstream investment

The figure shows the main information inputs to upstream investment decisions used to calculate the average profitability of potential projects. Independents estimate the development costs of new fields and the expected future oil price over the lifetime of the field. Knowing future cost, oil price, the likely size of a new field and the tax regime, financial analysts can calculate the future profit stream and apply a hurdle rate to identify acceptable projects. In reality, each project undergoes a thorough and detailed screening, using well-tried upstream investment appraisal methods. The greater the estimated profitability, the more projects exceed the hurdle rate and the greater the recommended expansion of capacity. There is a scale effect too represented by information feedback from independents' capacity. The more capacity, the bigger are the independents and the more projects in their portfolio of investment opportunities.

Executive control of recommended expansion is exercised through capex investment optimism that captures collective investment bias among top management teams responsible for independents' investment (rather like 'delivery delay bias' in the market growth model of Chapter 7). Optimism can be viewed on a scale from low to high. High optimism means that oil company executives are bullish about the investment climate and approve more capacity expansion than financial criteria alone would suggest. Low optimism means executives are cautious and approve less expansion than recommended. It is important to appreciate the distance from which we are viewing investment appraisal and approval. We are not concerned with the detail of individual oil field projects. Rather, we are seeing investment in terms of commercial pressures that lead to fractional growth of existing capacity, where the growth rate is typically between 5 and 10% per year but can be up to 25% per year when profitability is exceptionally high. The formulation is explained in more detail later.

Development Costs

Development costs in Figure 8.5 are experts' views of industry marginal costs as a function of remaining undeveloped reserves (excluding OPEC reserves). In 1988, experts estimated remaining reserves to be 580 billion barrels of oil.

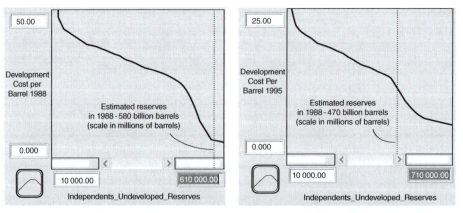

Figure 8.5   Estimated development costs in 1988 (left) and in 1995 (right)

Of this quantity, about 30 billion barrels (in the decreasing range 580 to 550 on the graph) were believed to be low-cost reserves recoverable at less than $9 per barrel. Once these low-cost reserves are used up there is a steep shoulder to the cost profile. Development cost rises from $9 per barrel to $26 per barrel as reserves fall from 550 billion to 450 billion barrels. Then the cost profile stays quite flat, rising gently to 40 dollars per barrel as reserves fall from 450 billion to 100 billion barrels. Thereafter, the cost rises gently to 44 dollars as reserves fall to 50 billion barrels. Cost rises sharply to 1000 dollars per barrel as reserves are exhausted reflecting an assumed finite supply of commercially viable oil.

By 1995, experts' views had changed. Remaining reserves were now thought to be about 470 billion barrels – down by more than 100 billion barrels from the 1988 estimate of 580 billion barrels due to usage. However, the cost is much lower and the profile is flatter than before meaning that cost is expected to rise less steeply with depletion. Cost rises gently from 12 dollars per barrel to 20 dollars per barrel as reserves fall from 470 to 100 billion barrels. Moreover, there is a new possibility of replenishing low cost reserves by adopting 225 billion additional barrels of Russian oil. For this reason the scale for reserves runs out to 710 billion barrels. The process of adoption is described later in the section entitled 'The Rise of Russian Oil'. The overall effect is to further flatten development cost. The reserve and cost assumptions for the model that starts in 2010 are also described later in the section entitled 'The Shale Gale'.

Technology can undoubtedly be expected to lower cost as more efficient production and recovery methods are devised. In both the 1988 and 1995 models the effect of technology on cost starts at a neutral value of 1 as shown in Figure 8.6.

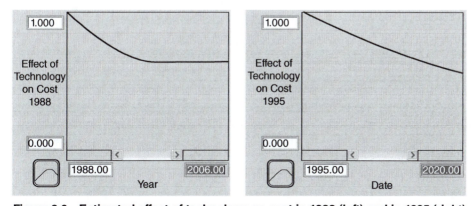

Figure 8.6   Estimated effect of technology on cost in 1988 (left) and in 1995 (right)

In 1988, experts anticipated that technology would improve rapidly over the decade 1988 to 1998, so the effect of technology on cost falls to a value of 0.64 by 1998. This fall means that technology improvements were expected to cut development cost by 36% (1–0.64) over the decade. Interestingly, the experts in 1988 were very conservative beyond a 10-year technology horizon, anticipating no further efficiency improvement. Hence, after 1998 the effect of technology on cost remains constant at 0.64. By 1995, experts' views of technology were more optimistic for the long term and they were prepared to look across a 25-year horizon. The effect of technology on cost falls steadily to a value of 0.5 by 2020. This fall means that technology improvements were expected to cut development cost by a further 50% relative to the advances already made by the end of 1995. For the model that starts in 2010 there is a less optimistic view of technology improvement. The effect of technology falls steadily to a value of 0.74 across a 25-year horizon to 2034.

Policy Structure and Formulations for Upstream Investment – Fractional Asset Stock Adjustment

More detail about the formulations behind the investment policy is shown in Figure 8.7. Notice the two-stage accumulation for capacity that distinguishes capacity in construction from independents' capacity in operation. The annual onstream rate is assumed to be a quarter of capacity in construction to represent an average construction delay of four years. Independents' production is exactly equal to production capacity, reflecting an important assumption that commercial producers fully utilise capacity once it comes onstream.

The grey region contains all the variables used to operationalise the investment policy. Capacity initiation (the rate of approval of new upstream investment) is a fractional asset stock adjustment formulation, similar to capital investment in the market growth model in Chapter 7, but driven by financial rather than operational pressures. The units of measure are millions of barrels per day, per year. The equation is written as the product of independents' capacity, viable fractional increase in capacity and capex optimism.

Capacity Initiation = Independents' Capacity ∗ Viable Fractional Increase in Capacity ∗ Capex Optimism {millions of barrels/day/year}

Upstream investment projects are deemed attractive when the profitability of new capacity exceeds the hurdle rate. In the equation below this condition is met when the profitability ratio is greater than 1. The hurdle rate is set at (0.15) 15% per year, a high value that reflects the inherent risk of upstream investment. The profitability of new capacity depends on the total profit expected from a new oil field in relation to its development costs.

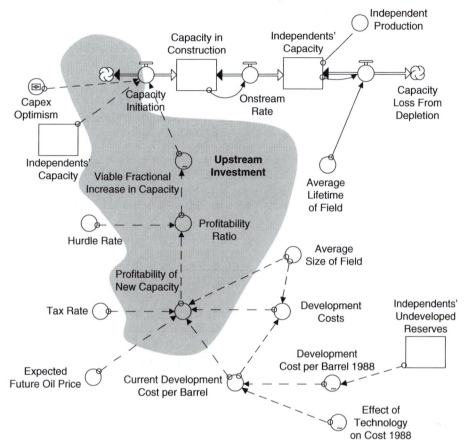

Figure 8.7   Policy structure and formulations for independents' upstream investment

Total profit is defined as the difference between expected future oil price and current development cost per barrel multiplied by the average size of a field in millions of barrels. This gross profit is adjusted for tax according to the expression (1 – tax rate). The ratio of total profit to overall development cost then yields profitability expressed as a fraction per year.

Profitability Ratio = Profitability of New Capacity/Hurdle Rate
{dimensionless}
Profitability of New Capacity = (1 – Tax Rate) * (Expected Future Oil Price
– Current Development Cost per Barrel) * Average Size of
Field/Development Costs {fraction/year}

The profitability ratio determines the viable fractional increase in capacity through the non-linear function in the equation below. When the profitability ratio takes a value of 1 the fractional increase in capacity is a modest 6% per year (0.06). The function is upward sloping. When the profitability ratio is 1.5, the fractional increase in capacity is 18% per year. At even higher profitability the function levels off at a fractional increase of 25% per year, which is assumed to be the maximum rate of capacity expansion achievable in the industry.

Viable Fractional Increase in Capacity = GRAPH(Profitability Ratio)
(0.00, 0.00), (0.1, 0.00), (0.2, 0.00), (0.3, 0.00), (0.4, 0.00), (0.5, 0.00), (0.6, 0.00), (0.7, 0.01), (0.8, 0.02), (0.9, 0.04), (**1.00, 0.06**), (1.10, 0.08), (1.20, 0.1), (1.30, 0.12), (1.40, 0.15), (1.50, 0.18), (1.60, 0.2), (1.70, 0.22), (1.80, 0.24), (1.90, 0.25), (2.00, 0.25)

Oil Price and Demand

It is common to think that market forces simultaneously determine price and demand. But in dynamical models it is important to capture the separate processes that adjust price and demand and the information on which they depend.

Figure 8.8 shows demand for oil as a stock that accumulates change in demand. Similarly market oil price is a stock that accumulates change in price. The influences on these two processes of change were the focus of attention in conversations with the project team.

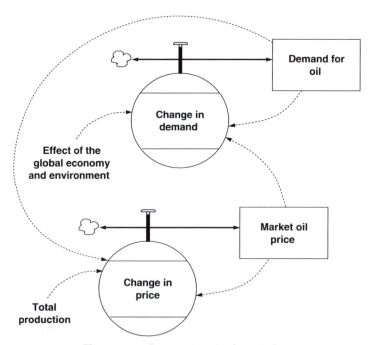

Figure 8.8   Demand and price setting

Change in demand responds to market oil price, the effect of the global economy and environment, and to the level of demand itself. In the short to medium term, the basic rationale behind demand changes is straightforward. When price goes up, demand goes down and vice versa. In reality, there are more subtle dynamics of demand. For example, if there is a shock price increase, the resulting reduction in demand will be greater than if the same price increase were spread over a few years. Consumers modify demand quickly in the short run by conservation and easy substitution. But they can also continue adjusting in the long run by making improvements in energy efficiency – with more fuel-efficient cars, or more heat-efficient homes.

Price sensitivity combines short- and medium-term dynamic effects. A numerical example illustrates the idea. Suppose price is steady at $60 per barrel, then rises suddenly to $90 per barrel and settles at this new and higher value. The model assumes that consumers faced with this 50% price hike set out with the intention of reducing demand by 20%. Yet radical cuts in consumption are slow to implement. It takes years for people to switch to more fuel-efficient cars or better insulated homes. In the meantime, they get used to a higher oil price and the pressure to reduce consumption declines. What began as an intention to reduce demand by 20% is much diluted as time passes, to 5% or less. Effectively, people are hooked on oil, and consumption depends not on the absolute oil price but on the difference between the current oil price and the price people are used to.

In the long term, there are broad societal and global pressures on demand, captured in the effect of the economy and environment. This effect is formulated as a bias so that indicated demand for oil is either magnified or diminished relative to current demand. For example, in the period between 1990 and 2008 the global economy grew strongly, led by China and India, resulting in steady upward pressure on demand for oil. On the other hand, if, in response to global warming, society curbs its use of fossil fuels, then there will be steady downward pressure on demand for oil. These long-term pressures are superimposed on the price effect.

In the lower half of Figure 8.8 the change in market oil price responds to differences between demand and total production. If demand exceeds total production then there is persistent pressure for price to rise. A fractional formulation is used in which the change in price is a fraction of the current market oil price. Therefore, as long as a demand surplus persists, price will move steadily upwards. Conversely, if production exceeds demand, there is persistent pressure for price to fall. Note there is no pre-defined ceiling or floor on oil price and the development cost of oil does not directly influence change in price. Only when demand and production are exactly equal does the change in price become zero. Hence, oil price can drift across a wide range of values, far removed from the underlying development cost incurred by commercial producers. A numerical example, based on the formulations used in Oil World 1988 and Oil World 1995, reveals the sensitivity of the modelled oil price to production and demand imbalances. When there is a shortfall of 2 million barrels per day, price is assumed to increase at a rate of 4% per month. The rate of increase rises to 7.5% per month if the shortfall reaches 4 million barrels per day. There are corresponding rates of price decline resulting from a glut of production. These numbers produce plausible price profiles in the simulator. Note that the sensitivity of price change has been deliberately reduced in Oil World 2010 to compensate for the fact that both oil price and total oil production were much higher by then than they were in the 1980s and 1990s.

The Swing Producer

The role of the swing producer is to supply just enough oil to defend OPEC's intended price, known in the industry as the 'marker price'. A producer taking on this role must have both the physical and economic capacity to increase or decrease production quickly, by as much as 2 million barrels per day or more in a matter of weeks or months, in order to absorb unexpected variations in demand (due say to an unusually mild winter) or to compensate for cuts in the output of other producers. The model makes the important assumption that the swing producer always has adequate capacity to meet any call. The project team felt this assumption was reasonable given the large capacity surplus of Saudi Arabia, estimated at 5 million barrels per day under normal supply conditions. A similar surplus remains today. As long as Saudi maintains this huge surplus then there is no need to model explicitly the capacity expansion policy of the swing producer, since capacity is never a constraint on output. Instead, the focus switches to the rationale for changes in crude oil production.

The swing producer (Saudi Arabia) operates in either swing mode or punitive mode. Most of the time Saudi is in swing mode, abiding by and supporting the production quotas set by OPEC. Occasionally, Saudi switches into punitive mode, by abandoning agreed quotas and rapidly cranking up production in order to discipline the other producers.

Figure 8.9 shows the factors influencing Saudi production policy when operating in normal swing mode. Production responds to pressure from both quota and oil price. There are two stock adjustment processes operating simultaneously. Saudi ministers change production in order to meet the swing producer's quota, but they also take corrective action whenever the market oil price deviates from the intended price that OPEC members collectively wish to achieve. When the price is too low, Saudi production is reduced below quota thereby undersupplying the market and pushing up the market price.

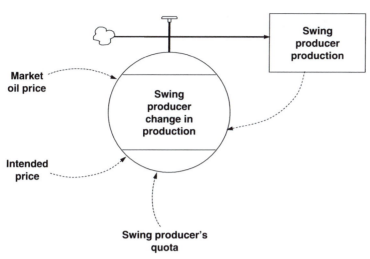

Figure 8.9   Swing producer in swing mode

Similarly, when the price is too high, Saudi production is increased above quota to oversupply the market and reduce price to the level OPEC is trying to defend. Such willingness to adjust production in the short term is in sharp contrast to the independent producers and is a defining characteristic of any swing producer.

In punitive mode, Saudi oil ministers feel that production is inadequate and they are not getting a fair share of the market. They decide to re-establish a strong position by increasing production regardless of the price consequences, thereby also punishing the other producers. The resulting punitive production policy is shown in Figure 8.10. The swing producer sets a minimum threshold for share of global demand (estimated to be 8%) and will not tolerate anything less. Whenever market share falls below the threshold the volume of production is increased rapidly in order to flood the market with oil and quickly lower the price.

The team spent some time discussing the detail of punitive behaviour. For example, how does the swing producer decide on the volume of punitive production, and when do policymakers switch back to swing mode? The team's proposal was to include a punitive price, a low target price, for teaching a lesson to the other producers. Punitive production continues to expand until market oil price reaches the punitive price, or until the swing producer regains an acceptable market share (which is the signal to return to swing mode). The switch to punitive mode can send a powerful price signal to discipline the other producers. It is an act of last resort, however, because in this mode the swing producer has abandoned the role of price regulator – essentially the market is no longer managed.

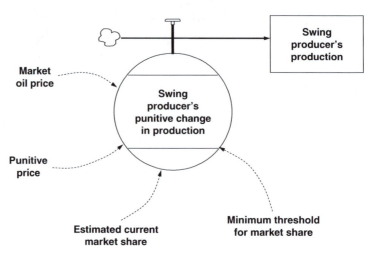

Figure 8.10   Swing producer in punitive mode

Quota Setting

Quota setting takes place in two stages. First, OPEC members agree on a quota for the cartel as a whole. Then, member states negotiate individual quotas by allocating the total quota among themselves.

How much should OPEC produce? The main influences are shown in Figure 8.11. The members need to form a view of the likely 'call on OPEC' over the time period covered by the quota agreement.

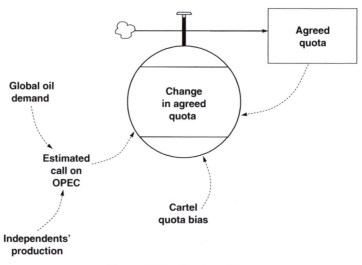

Figure 8.11   Quota setting

To do this, they estimate both global oil demand and the independents' production. The difference between these two quantities is the estimated call on OPEC which is just a best guess of the volume of OPEC oil required to balance supply and demand. But the estimate need not be spot-on. In practice, it could differ from the actual call by as much as 1 or 2 million barrels per day. The swing producer will compensate for any mis-estimation by OPEC through swing changes to production. More important than spot-on estimation of the call is for OPEC members to agree on whether to set an overall quota that is deliberately less than the estimated call, or deliberately more. By setting a quota that is less than the call, the member states are pursuing a policy aimed at increasing market prices. Their decision to over- or under-produce is politically and economically motivated and is represented by the scenario parameter 'cartel quota bias'.

Quota negotiation, shown in Figure 8.12, allocates OPEC's agreed quota among members. In reality, the negotiation is a highly political process, though a benchmark allocation is established based on objective criteria that include member states' oil reserves, production capacity and population. In the model, quota is allocated in proportion to each member's share of OPEC's total operating capacity. Although this formulation is a simplification, it does capture the flavour of political bargaining by making the members' bargaining strength proportional to capacity share.

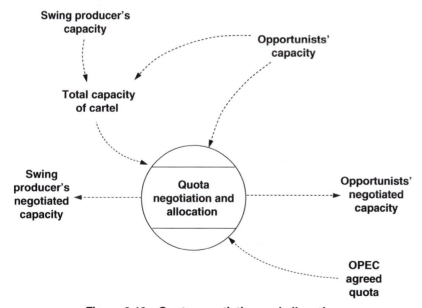

Figure 8.12   Quota negotiation and allocation

The Opportunists

The opportunists are all the other member states of OPEC besides the swing producer. The list of countries includes Algeria, Iran, Kuwait, Nigeria and Venezuela. Some of the opportunists are known to adhere strictly to quota, so their production policy is straightforward – it is simply equal to negotiated quota. Other countries, however, have a huge appetite for oil revenue to support their growing populations and developing economies. This need for revenue, coupled with underutilised production capacity, provides opportunists with the motivation to exceed quota and to strengthen their quota negotiating position by deliberately over-expanding capacity.

Figure 8.13 shows the main influences on opportunists' production and capacity. First, focus on change in capacity shown in the lower half of the figure. Generally speaking, opportunists aim for surplus capacity, at least 2 or 3% more than negotiated quota, partly to provide flexibility, but also to improve their bargaining position in future quota negotiations. The size of the surplus depends on a scenario parameter called capacity bias, which represents the tendency of opportunists to overbuild capacity. Opportunists' change in capacity is formulated as an asset stock adjustment process where the effective target for capacity is equal to negotiated quota multiplied by the capacity bias.

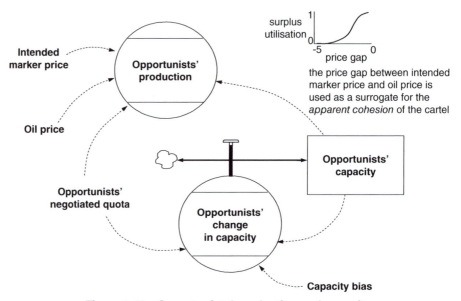

Figure 8.13   Opportunists' production and capacity

Now consider opportunists' production shown in the upper half of the figure. When opportunists are fully cooperating within the framework of the cartel they produce at a rate equal to the negotiated quota. But there is always the temptation for opportunists to exceed quota and fully utilise capacity – if only they can get away with it. How do opportunists know whether conditions are right for utilising surplus capacity and quota busting? The project team felt that the 'apparent cohesion' of the cartel would be an important factor. Cohesion is high when the market oil price is close to the intended marker price – in other words, when OPEC is successfully defending its intended price. Under these price conditions, quota busting may go unnoticed. Cohesion is low when the intended marker price is greater than the market price. Under these price conditions, quota busting is likely to be visible and to incur the wrath of the other member states, especially the swing producer. Figure 8.13 shows that both the intended marker price and oil price influence opportunists' production, and the inset on the upper right shows the assumed shape of the relationship between the price gap and surplus utilisation. When the price gap is in the range minus \$4 to minus \$5 per barrel surplus utilisation is zero. As the price gap diminishes surplus utilisation rises, slowly at first and then more rapidly. When the price gap is zero then opportunists fully utilise surplus capacity.

The Rise of Russian Oil – Incorporating Unforeseen Political Change

No scenario planning exercise has perfect foresight and the oil producers' project was no exception. The model was originally built in 1988 and then updated some years later to fit the global oil industry of the mid-to-late 1990s. The most significant political change during the interval was the break up of the Soviet Union. Before the Soviet break-up, oil companies and scenario planners ignored oil production from communist areas. This assumption was justified on the grounds that little if any such oil was traded outside the communist block. However, President Gorbachev's perestroika and peaceful restructuring eventually brought Russian oil to world markets. Moreover, Russian reserves are huge – estimated at the time to be about 225 billion barrels, almost 6% of proven global reserves and more than 50% of non-OPEC reserves. Freely-traded Russian oil can therefore have a big impact on the global balance of supply and demand.

A member of the original scenario modelling team helped revise the model to include Russian oil. A key issue was how to classify Russian reserves – do they fall within the influence of OPEC, or are they best viewed as purely commercial reserves? After careful thought, the industry expert recommended that all Russian oil should be added to independents' reserves. In other words, in his view, the oligarchs controlling Russian oil have commercial rather than political instincts. They prefer to develop reserves in response to market forces rather than OPEC political pressure. Profit matters. However, the industry expert also recognised that Russian reserves are not instantly available for commercial exploitation, even if the economics look favourable. There is still a political dimension to Russian oil representing the time it takes to build the trust required for long-term commercial contracts and to agree rights in the key Russian oil regions.

When viewed in this quasi-commercial way, Russian oil adds two new stock accumulations and six new concepts to the original model – only a small increase in complexity for such an important structural change in the oil world.

Figure 8.14 shows the change exactly as it appears in the revised oil producers' model. A huge pool of risky Russian reserves, approximately 225 billion barrels, is available to commercial producers. Gradually, over time, these reserves come to be viewed by investors as secure. Secure Russian reserves are then adopted by commercial producers into the pool of independents' undeveloped reserves. The pace of adoption depends on the time to agree rights, which is set at three years.

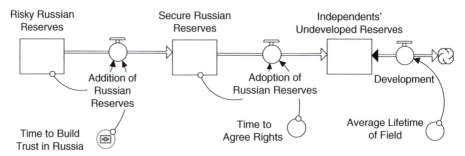

Figure 8.14   Replenishing independents' reserves with Russian reserves

The crucial limiting process for commercialisation is the rate at which investors reclassify risky reserves. This rate depends on a vital scenario parameter called 'time to build trust in Russia', which can be anywhere in the range 5–40 years. If the time is short (say 10 years), then Russian oil fields are commercialised quickly. If the time to build trust is very long (say 40 years), then Russian oil, though economically attractive, is commercialised slowly.

The Shale Gale – Incorporating Unforeseen Technological Change

The existence of 'tight oil' reserves, trapped in oil-bearing shale rocks, has been known about for centuries. Patented extraction processes date from the late 1600s and extraction industries became widespread during the 19th century. However, the industry shrank and virtually disappeared in the 20th century following the discovery of large reserves of cheaper and more easily extracted conventional oil. Tight oil was no longer commercially viable.

Recently the shale industry has staged a remarkable comeback through a combination of radical technology change and high oil price. Around 2008 specialist commercial oil producers began adapting the new technologies of hydraulic fracturing and horizontal drilling first used to tap shale gas. This technology breakthrough lowered the breakeven cost of tight oil below $70 per barrel, making it competitive with some of the more expensive conventional oil from offshore fields. As a result, between 2008 and 2013 shale oil production in the US rose swiftly from 0.5 to 3.5 million barrels per day, a 'shale gale' that surprised the industry and was entirely unforeseen in the original oil producers' project.

What difference might commercially abundant shale oil make to the structure of the global oil industry and to long-term oil price dynamics? The oil producers' model has been further updated to investigate this important question, using publicly available information on reserves and production gleaned from the internet and the business press. The updated model starts in 2010 at the end of a decade in which the oil price had risen dramatically. This extended period of rising price unleashed the shale gale. Shale oil brings extra commercial reserves to the independent producers, a bit like Russian oil in the mid-1990s, but without the commercialisation delays stemming from political risk and the economic uncertainty it engenders. Independents' undeveloped reserves are initialised in 2010 at 300 billion barrels of discovered oil, including shale reserves. A particularly significant change to the model is a boost to independents' capacity made possible by shale oil. Capacity starts at 47 million barrels per day in 2010, more than 50% of global oil demand, and poised to grow still further as swathes of new commercial upstream capacity projects are approved and developed, many of them for shale oil. The initial growth rate of capacity is 4% per year, a rate destined to increase as swelling capacity in construction (26 million barrels per day in 2010) comes onstream.

Three versions of the oil producers' model are available in the learning support folder for Chapter 8: Oil World 1988, Oil World 1995 and Oil World 2010. Readers are invited to browse the models and find the parameter and formulation changes used to capture the rise of Russian oil and the resurgence of shale oil. A tour of the icons in the Independents sector will reveal many of the changes. Simulations of these three models later in the chapter show the impact on industry dynamics of surprise political and technological changes that have each released vast new reserves of oil. At the start of the oil producers' project in 1988 nobody in the industry expected these extra reserves to become available in world oil markets.

Connecting the Pieces – A Feedback Systems View

As we have seen, the project team supplied their knowledge and opinions on the pieces of the global oil industry. Now let's see how the pieces fit together. Figure 8.15 shows the main concepts necessary to describe the industry. Take a few minutes to inspect this scatter list of words and phrases. Altogether, there are 37 phrases on the page which record shared vocabulary developed from team dialogue. Some phrases are specialised industry jargon such as intended marker price, call on OPEC, agreed quota, negotiated quota, and cartel quota bias. As a list for describing a large and complex industry it is short, but as nodes of a web it is quite daunting. Potentially, there are an enormous number of ways to connect 37 concepts. In fact, the team's knowledge of industry structure greatly reduced the raw combinatorial problem. The modelling process pinned down, with some confidence, eight feedback loops that capture (at least for team members) the essence of the industry's enduring feedback structure and the basis of its dynamic complexity.

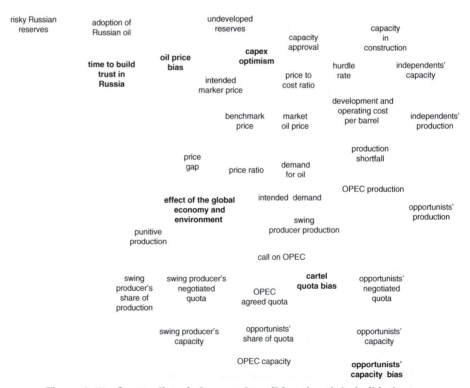

Figure 8.15   Scatter list of phrases describing the global oil industry

Two Invisible Hands and More

Figure 8.16 shows six feedback loops within and between the independents' and market sectors. (By the way, you can create your own industry web by photocopying Figure 8.15 and then drawing the connections.) Our review starts with commercial supply loop B1. A production shortfall stimulates a rise in market oil price and an increase in the price to cost ratio which, through capacity approval and construction, leads to expansion of independents' capacity and production. Extra production corrects the shortfall and completes loop B1 – the first invisible hand. A new loop B2 arises from reserve depletion. The price to cost ratio is influenced by development and operating cost per barrel, which rises as undeveloped reserves fall. Reserves are depleted by capacity approval, thereby completing the new balancing loop B2 that captures the economics of finite global oil reserves as described earlier in Figure 8.5.

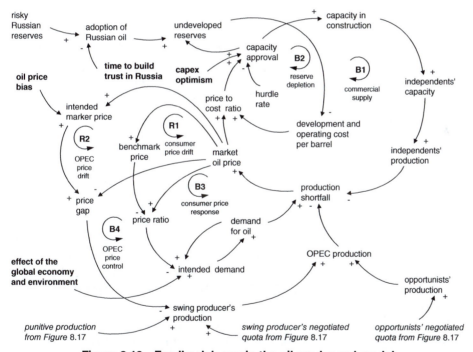

Figure 8.16   Feedback loops in the oil producers' model

In the 1995 version of the model, reserves are replenished by the adoption of Russian oil. The rate of adoption depends on the magnitude of risky Russian reserves and the time to build trust in Russia which is a scenario parameter. Time to build trust can take a value anywhere in the range 5–40 years. If the time is short (say 10 years), then Russian oil fields are commercialised quickly, giving rise to a surge of commercial development and production exploiting the favourable economics of Russian oil regions. If the time to build trust is very long (say 40 years), then Russian oil, though economically attractive, is commercialised slowly.

Now we turn to the demand side to find a second invisible hand. The production shortfall is the difference between demand for oil and the sum of independents' and OPEC production. Demand for oil falls as price rises and vice versa. But consumers take time to adapt and to some extent they are addicted to oil. These behavioural factors are captured in loops B3 and R1. Demand for oil adjusts with a time lag to consumers' intended demand. Intended demand responds to the price ratio and the effect of the global economy and environment (a link we return to shortly). As the price ratio goes up, intended demand goes down. The price ratio itself combines factual and behavioural information. It depends directly on the market oil price, thereby completing loop B3 representing consumer price response. The ratio also depends on the benchmark price, which is the price consumers are used to. This benchmark adapts with a time lag to the market oil price to form loop R1 that captures price drift in consumer behaviour. The combination of feedback loops B3 and R1 is very common in business and social systems. The structure is known as an eroding goal archetype (Senge, 1990: Appendix 2) and represents the tendency in any goal-seeking, purposive enterprise for the goal itself to adapt to current conditions. In this case, consumers facing high oil prices eventually get used to them and carry on consuming – they are hooked on oil.

The effect of the global economy and environment is a scenario parameter. It sits on the edge of the feedback structure representing pressures on demand that are not directly attributable to price. It is an enormously versatile parameter. It is a single number (confined in the range −0.1 to 0.1), yet it can portray scenarios as different as a green world or an Asian boom and bust. When the parameter is set to its neutral value of 0, then price alone drives intended demand. Market forces prevail on the demand side. When the parameter is set to a value less than 0 there is continual pressure from consumers to reduce demand, independent of market forces (though market forces are of course still at work). Such downward pressure might correspond to environmental awareness (a green mindset), the effects of an economic recession or steady increase in the efficiency of energy-consuming devices from technological progress. The exact cause need not be modelled in detail. Whether driven by the global economy or the environment, the effect is to suppress demand below what it would otherwise be on the basis of price alone. Conversely, when the parameter is set to a value greater than 0, there is continual pressure on consumers to increase demand, due to boom times and general optimism about the future.

The Visible Hand of OPEC

Loops B4 and R2 complete Figure 8.16 and show OPEC's control of oil price exercised by the swing producer. OPEC production in the bottom right of the figure is the sum of swing producer production and opportunists' production. When the member states are in harmony they produce to quota, so in each case production depends on negotiated quota. Two circumstances can cause the swing producer to depart from negotiated quota. One is punitive action, but this is quite rare and occurs only when the swing producer's share of production is too small (see next section on 'webs of intrigue'). The most common circumstance is a short-term tactical adjustment of production to manage price – a legitimate and important role for the swing producer. In Figure 8.16, swing producer production is influenced by the price gap, which is the difference between intended marker price and market oil price. This connection to market oil price closes a balancing feedback loop B4 that passes back through production shortfall and OPEC production before reconnecting with swing producer production. This fast-acting balancing loop represents OPEC's price control and is capable of creating prolonged periods of price stability, as seen in the 1960s. When market price falls below the intended marker price, due to a temporary supply glut, the swing producer quickly cuts production below negotiated quota to bring price back in line with the target or marker. The loop acts quickly because the swing producer is willing to make capacity idle – a process that takes only a month or two. Similarly, when market price rises above the intended marker price, due to a temporary demand surge, the swing producer quickly re-activates idle capacity to increase supply and bring price down. Despite the popular bad-guy image of Saudi Arabia, the swing producer is in fact a benign and calming influence in global oil markets, boosting or curtailing production in order to maintain stable prices. As we shall see, this benign role only becomes sinister and threatening when OPEC as a whole agrees quotas that deliberately undersupply or oversupply the global oil market, or when the swing producer is provoked into punitive mode.

The intended marker price itself changes over time. It depends on the recent history of market oil price. This adaptive connection from the market price to the marker price completes a reinforcing loop R2 (OPEC price drift) that combines with loop B4 to form another eroding goal archetype.

Webs of Intrigue – Inside OPEC's Opulent Bargaining Rooms

Figure 8.17 shows feedback loops within OPEC's quota agreements and quota negotiations. The starting point is the call on OPEC, which is the difference between demand for oil and independents' production.

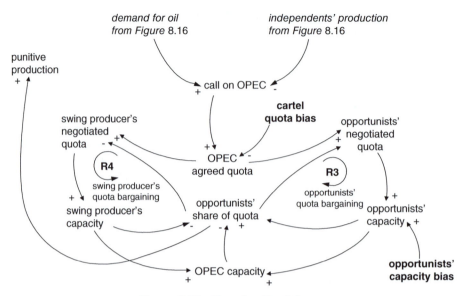

Figure 8.17   More feedback loops

OPEC member states use the call as a first-cut guide to their agreed quota. This approach makes sense because when quota equals call then OPEC is exactly filling the supply gap between global demand and independents' production. But OPEC can manipulate quota above or below the call depending on political and social motives reflected in the cartel quota bias. Quota bias is a scenario parameter that can be set to represent an OPEC supply squeeze or even political turmoil in OPEC. When the parameter is set to its neutral value of 0, then agreed quota is equal to the call. When the parameter is negative, say −0.1, then agreed quota is 10% less than the call and there is a sustained supply shortage or squeeze (as happened in the 1970s). When the parameter is positive, say +0.1, then agreed quota is 10% greater than the call and there is a supply glut (as happened in the late 1990s).

Agreed quota is allocated between the swing producer and the opportunists through negotiation and hard bargaining. Opportunists' negotiated quota depends on agreed quota and opportunists' share of quota. Negotiated quota then drives opportunists' production and also justifies expansion (or contraction) of opportunists' capacity. Capacity is a surrogate for bargaining power. The more capacity OPEC members bring to the bargaining table, the stronger is their case for a bigger share of quota. This bargaining logic is captured in opportunists' share of quota that depends on opportunists' capacity relative to OPEC capacity as a whole and completes reinforcing loop R3 in which successful quota negotiations lead to more capacity, more bargaining power and so on. OPEC capacity is simply the sum of opportunists' capacity and swing producer's capacity, where capacity is defined (for the purposes of bargaining) as operating capacity excluding any idle capacity. Loop R4 is the mirror image bargaining process of the swing producer. Here, negotiated quota depends on OPEC agreed quota and the complement of opportunists' share of quota. As before, quota drives capacity, which affects bargaining power and share of quota.

The combination of loops R3 and R4 is a common feedback structure known as the success-to-the-successful archetype (Senge, 1990: Appendix 2). This archetype occurs repeatedly in business and social systems where rivalry is at play. A successful player reinforces its competitive position at the expense of rivals. The phenomenon is well-known in battles between competing industry standards such as Betamax versus VHS in videos, or Google versus Yahoo in search engines. The dominant standard attracts more followers, which increases its dominance. Similarly, in quota bargaining, the actions of the successful negotiator strengthen future bargaining position while the rival becomes ever weaker.

Opportunists are easily tempted to boost their bargaining power by covert additions to capacity. For some member states of OPEC, the temptation is huge. They are developing economies with large populations, inadequate infrastructure and endless possibilities for revenue-consuming development such as social investment programmes in education, health, housing, road building and so on. In the model covert capacity comes from opportunists' capacity bias.

Capacity bias is the last of the scenario parameters in the model. It is used to invoke scenarios such as political turmoil in OPEC and quota busting. When the parameter is set to its neutral value of 0, then opportunists adjust capacity to match negotiated quota. When the parameter is positive, say +0.1, then opportunists covertly add 10% capacity more than quota alone could justify in the expectation that the extra capacity will bring them more bargaining power. This covert investment provides the opportunists with surplus capacity above quota.

If opportunists' share of quota becomes too large then the swing producer takes punitive action by greatly expanding production and abandoning quota. The result is a temporary supply surplus which drives market price down. If market price falls significantly below the intended marker price then this price gap is a clear signal for opportunists to stop using their surplus capacity and to fall back in line with quota.

The scatter list of 37 phrases in Figure 8.15 has become a network of more than 50 interconnections and eight dynamically significant feedback loops in Figures 8.16 and 8.17. This web embodies a slice of dynamic complexity from our modern industrial society with its intricate membrane of stakeholder interdependence. The best way to investigate this complexity is through simulation. Before presenting simulations, however, first imagine how the web might work by conducting a thought experiment.

A Simple Thought Experiment: Green Mindset and Global Recession

What if consumers were gripped by a collective green mindset (leading to a reduction in the use of fossil fuels) and, at the same time, there was a global economic recession? Intuitively one might expect this combination of forces to damage the industry. What does the industry web tell us? Demand would fall due to strong downward pressure from the effect of the global economy and environment. A supply surplus would appear and simultaneously a fall in the call on OPEC. From this starting condition numerous alternative futures can unfold depending on OPEC solidarity, the cost of commercial reserves and the psychology of consumers. If OPEC is disciplined, and its members in harmony, then the quota system absorbs the full impact of a downturn in global oil demand with little or no disturbance to the market oil price – the managed tranquillity of the 1960s. We can trace the effect in Figures 8.16 and 8.17. As the call on OPEC declines then OPEC agreed quota falls leading to a prompt reduction of output which removes the original supply surplus and restores the balance of supply and demand. Oil price remains stable and the independent producers carry on investing as though nothing had changed. OPEC absorbs the revenue loss for the industry as a whole.

However, a more complex chain reaction is possible leading to a different, less tranquil future. If OPEC's revenue loss is significant and sustained (for example, it eats into budgets for social programmes funded by oil), then cracks can appear in OPEC's solidarity. Opportunists begin to cheat, expanding output and revenue at the expense of the swing producer (loops R3 and R4). For a time the swing producer absorbs the additional loss. But dwindling quota share, idle capacity and diminishing power will eventually provoke the swing producer to punish the industry. Output rises dramatically and oil price plummets. Now the market is in turmoil. Price is low and volatile. OPEC member states suffer chronically low revenues and commercial producers report low or negative profits. Many green-minded consumers question the need for conservation in the face of an oil glut. Turmoil continues until discipline returns to OPEC or until independent producers reduce output by depleting existing fields (a 10-year wait!).

Using the Model to Generate Scenarios

Having described the conceptual building blocks and feedback loops of the oil producers' model we are now ready to simulate scenarios. The key to effective scenario modelling is to unfold several alternative futures (each an internally consistent story, but with a different plot and a different ending) in order to challenge conventional wisdom and to encourage users to think how they would act if this future were to unfold. It is important to remember that such simulated futures are not predictions of oil price, supply or demand, nor do they represent official company forecasts. Two archive simulations are presented below. Each covers a 25-year period from 1988 to 2012 using the version of the model without Russian oil, developed before the fall of the Soviet empire. The model, called 'Oil World 1988' can be found in the learning support folder for Chapter 8. I have deliberately chosen to include these archive scenarios in order to show simulations exactly as they were originally presented to the project team. However, it is also instructive to repeat the simulations under the same scenario conditions in 'Oil World 1995'. This model runs over a 25-year period from 1996 to 2020 and shows the profound effect of Russian oil reserves on the global oil market and long-term price dynamics.

Archive Scenario 1: 10-Year Supply Squeeze Followed by Supply Glut

Imagine that in 1988 OPEC had followed a policy in which quotas were set 10% lower than the call on OPEC (the difference between total demand for crude oil and the independents' production). The policy is successfully enforced for 10 years until 1998, and then reversed. Hence, in the remaining 15 years of the simulation, from 1998 to 2012, quotas are set 10% higher than the call. The result is a 10-year supply squeeze followed by a supply glut. Assume that OPEC maintains quota discipline throughout the squeeze and glut, so there is no cheating on quota by any member of OPEC. Also assume that non-price pressures on crude oil demand from the global economy and the environment are neutral so that, in the absence of price changes, demand would stay constant at 50 million barrels per day.

To run this scenario for yourself, open 'Oil World 1988'. The initial screen displays a blank time chart and the simulator controls for creating scenarios, as shown in Figure 8.18. Set 'cartel quota bias' to −0.1 by moving the slider to the left. This change brings about an OPEC supply squeeze. All the other controls should remain in their default positions.

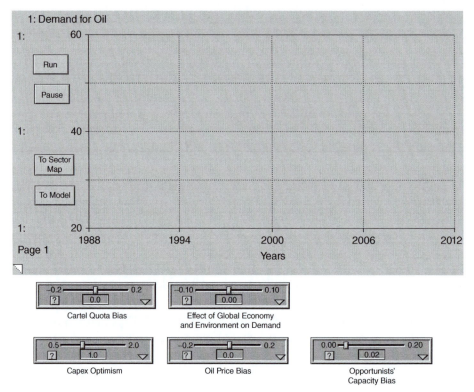

Figure 8.18   Opening screen of Oil World 1988 showing simulator controls for scenarios

Press the 'Run' button and simulate for five years and then press the 'Run' button once more to simulate for a further five years to 1998. At this point, reset the 'cartel quota bias' to +0.1 by moving the slider to the right in order to bring about an OPEC supply glut. Run the simulation out to 2012 and inspect the time charts. There are four pages available to view by selecting the 'page' tab symbol at the bottom left of the graph pad. The time charts are described below.

Figure 8.19 shows profiles of demand and production for the squeeze-then-glut scenario. Demand in the top chart begins at 50 million barrels per day in 1988 and falls gradually to about 45 million barrels per day during the decade of supply squeeze. As OPEC switches policy from squeeze to glut in 1998, demand begins to rise and maintains a steady growth to about 52 million barrels per day by the end of the simulation in 2012. The lower half of the figure shows how demand is shared among the different producers. In 1988, the independents are producing 26 million barrels per day (line 1), the opportunists 17 million barrels per day (line 2), and the swing producer 7 million barrels per day (line 3).

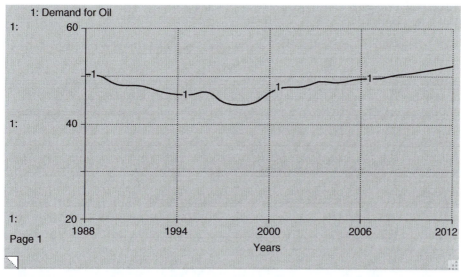

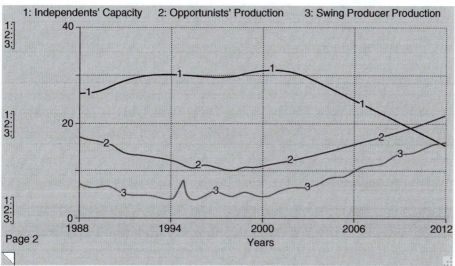

Figure 8.19   Demand and oil production in an archive scenario: OPEC squeeze then glut without Russian oil

As the supply squeeze begins to bite OPEC's output gradually falls. By 1993 the opportunists have cut production by 5 million barrels to 12 million barrels per day, while the swing producer's output has fallen to 4 million barrels per day. Meanwhile the independents' production has risen to compensate.

In 1994 and 1995 there is a temporary surge in production as the swing producer switches to punitive mode to prevent further loss of market share. At this point, the policy of supply squeeze is almost exhausted because the swing producer is unwilling to sacrifice further market share. The burden of any additional OPEC supply reductions is carried mainly by the opportunists. In 1997, there is another small burst of punitive production by the swing producer. Then in 1998, OPEC reverses policy, changing a supply squeeze into a supply glut. Gradually OPEC's output begins to rise. Opportunists' production increases from a low of 10 million barrels per day in 1998 to 21 million barrels per day in 2012. Meanwhile, the swing producer's output rises from 4 million barrels per day to 16 million barrels per day in 2012. It is interesting to note that OPEC's policy change from squeeze to glut has no immediate impact on independents' production. At the time of the policy change in 1998, the independents are producing 30 million barrels per day. Their combined output then rises to 31 million barrels per day by the year 2001. By 2003, five years after the policy change, independents' output is still 29 million barrels per day. Thereafter it declines steadily to 15 million barrels per day by the end of the simulation in 2012.

The impact of OPEC's policy on market oil price is shown in the top half of Figure 8.20. Oil price (line 1) begins at $15 per barrel in 1988. Broadly speaking, during the supply squeeze price rises to a peak of $30 per barrel in 1998, then falls during the supply glut back to about $15 per barrel. Within the rising and falling trend there is much interesting detail in the movement of price that arises from the interplay of feedback loops that balance supply and demand. The reader can view the state of supply and demand by comparing the trajectory of demand minus production (line 2) with the horizontal grid line denoting equilibrium. When line 2 is above the grid line, demand exceeds supply. When line 2 is below the grid line there is a supply surplus and supply exceeds demand.

From 1988 to 1990, price rises sharply to $20 per barrel as the supply squeeze takes hold. Demand exceeds supply as shown by line 2. Price then declines slightly between 1990 and 1991 as falling demand creates a temporary supply surplus (despite OPEC's policy). Then as the supply squeeze bites once more, price rises steadily to the next peak of $25 per barrel during 1994. Price dips sharply in 1995 as the swing producer switches into punitive mode and rapidly expands production, creating a supply surplus. After the pulse of punitive production OPEC sharply curtails production which causes price to rise sharply during 1996 to a peak of $33 per barrel. The oil price is maintained around $30 per barrel for a period of three years. The era of moderately high price ends during 1998 as the swing producer once more switches into punitive mode and price falls rapidly to $20 per barrel. Over the next two years, the price level recovers slightly to a peak of about $24 per barrel in 2001 before settling into a slow and gently fluctuating decline to its final value of $15 per barrel as OPEC's new policy of excess supply takes effect.

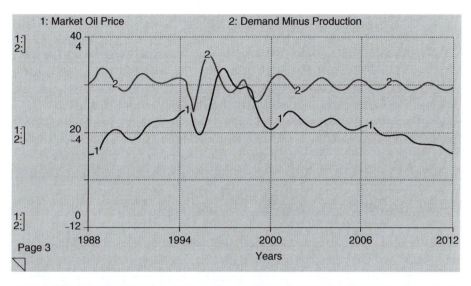

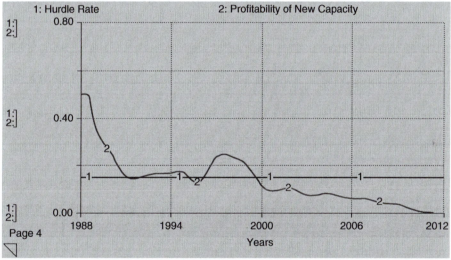

Figure 8.20   Oil price and profitability of independents' capacity in an archive scenario: OPEC squeeze then glut without Russian oil

The lower half of Figure 8.20 shows the changing investment incentives for independent producers that helps explain the rise and fall of independents' production. The hurdle rate for upstream investment projects (line 1) is assumed to remain constant at 15% (0.15). At the start of the simulation, when the oil price is $15 per barrel, the profitability of new capacity (line 2) is 50% (0.5), reflecting the initial low cost of reserves. It is financially very attractive to add new capacity, but over the three-year interval to 1991, profitability falls sharply to equal the hurdle rate. This fall in profitability occurs despite the rise in oil price from $15 to $20 per barrel, because the development cost of new reserves is rising even faster (the independents are operating on the steep shoulder of the cost profile). As price rises to its second peak of $25 per barrel in 1994, the profitability of new capacity increases slightly above the hurdle rate. The price plateau of $30 per barrel between 1996 and 1998 creates an attractive era for investment in which the profitability of new capacity rises to 25%, well above the hurdle rate. Then, as the swing producer generates a pulse of punitive production, and as OPEC changes policy, profitability falls quickly to only 10% in the year 2000. The investment climate continues to deteriorate throughout the remainder of the simulation. By the year 2011, the profitability of upstream investment has fallen to zero, meaning that the price of oil is now equal to independents' development costs. In the final year of the simulation, profitability actually goes negative.

Changing profitability drives independents' capacity as shown in Figure 8.19, but only after a lag that represents the time to develop a new field. The lag effect is most obvious following the attractive investment era between 1996 and 1998.

Independents' capacity is static at 30 million barrels per day (actually declining slightly) during the high price plateau. Then as profitability declines sharply between 1998 and 2000, independents' capacity rises gradually to 32 million barrels per day as new fields, approved earlier, begin to come on stream.

Archive Scenario 2: Quota Busting in a Green World

Imagine a world in which there are environmental pressures to reduce oil consumption – a green world. In the absence of price changes, these pressures are assumed to be sufficient to cut consumption by 10% per year. Imagine too that the opportunist producers in OPEC are inclined to cheat on quota. They deliberately plan to build capacity 10% greater than quota, and secretly use the excess capacity to produce more than quota whenever the opportunity arises. Assume that OPEC adopts a neutral quota policy, setting quotas that exactly match its estimate of the market call on OPEC. To create these scenario conditions set the effect of 'global economy and environment on demand' to −0.1 and the 'opportunists' capacity bias' to +0.1. Also, make sure to reset the 'cartel quota bias' to its default value of zero. The other sliders should remain at their default values.

Figure 8.21 shows profiles of demand and production for this scenario of quota busting in a green world. In the top half of the figure, demand begins at 50 million barrels per day in 1988 and falls gradually to a final value of 44 million barrels per day by 2012. The decline is due to the assumption of a green world. Despite the *ceteris paribus* green assumption of a 10% cut in consumption per year, demand falls by only 6 million barrels per day over 25 years due (as we will see) to the compensating effect of lower price resulting from conservation and quota busting.

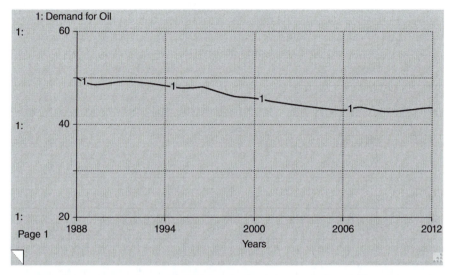

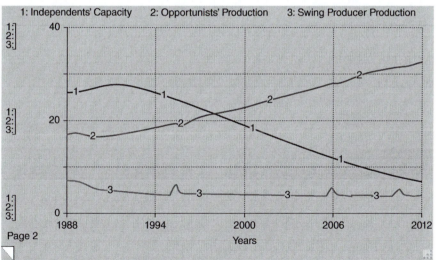

Figure 8.21   Demand and oil production in an archive scenario: Quota busting in a green world without Russian oil

In the bottom half of the figure, the opportunists' propensity to cheat pays off as they expand capacity and increase their bargaining strength in quota negotiations. Their production rises steadily from a starting value of 17 million barrels per day to a final value of 33 million barrels per day. Most of this expansion comes at the expense of the independent producers who see their output fall from a starting value of 26 million barrels per day to only 7 million barrels per day at the end of the simulation. The swing producer too is squeezed by the opportunists at the start of the simulation, as output falls from 7 million barrels per day in 1988 to 4 million barrels per day in 1994. However, beyond 1994, and for the rest of the simulation, the swing producer uses mild pulses of punitive production to maintain market share and hold production at 4 million barrels per day. The first pulse occurs in 1995. The next pulse of punitive production occurs in 2006 and again in 2011.

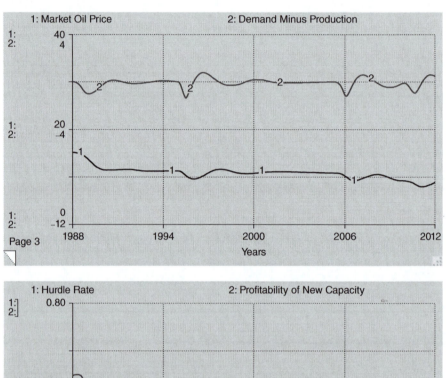

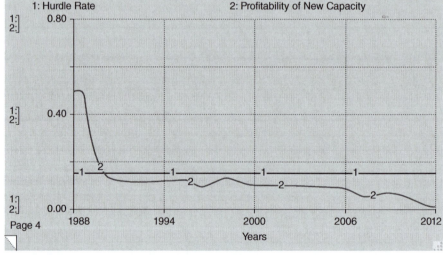

Figure 8.22   Oil price and profitability of independents' capacity in an archive scenario: Quota busting in a green world without Russian oil

The top half of Figure 8.22 shows market oil price (line 1). Price drops quickly from its starting value of $15 per barrel in 1988 to $11 per barrel in 1990 as demand falls in response to green conservation pressures. After this initial sharp drop, price falls very gradually during the rest of the simulation (with minor fluctuations caused by the swing producer's bursts of punitive production) to a final value of $8 per barrel by the end of the simulation. Needless to say, the sustained run of low oil price generates a bleak environment for independents' upstream investment. In the lower half of Figure 8.22, the profitability of new capacity quickly falls below the hurdle rate of 15%. By 1991, profitability is at 11%, and continues to fall throughout the simulation to a final value of about 1% in 2012.

With no financial incentive for new investment, the independents' capacity (lower half of Figure 8.21) gradually declines as existing fields are depleted. Quota busting in a green world leads to a rapid demise of the independent producers. They end the simulation with no new capacity in the pipeline, a gloomy investment climate, and a market share of only 16% (down from 52% at the start of the simulation, and still declining).

Scenario from the Mid-1990s to 2020: Asian Boom with Quota Busting, Cautious Upstream Investment and Russian Oil

The previous simulations were archive scenarios created before the fall of Communism in an era when the expectation among industry experts was that Russian oil would never be globally traded. Circumstances then changed. The next scenario runs from 1996 to 2020 and includes Russian oil. The scenario assumes steady upward pressure on oil demand arising from a sustained Asian boom in the giant developing economies of China and India. In this climate of growth, opportunist producers within OPEC are assumed to engage in quota busting while independent producers take a cautious approach to upstream investment, approving development of only the most profitable new fields.

To run this scenario for yourself, open 'Oil World 1995'. The initial screen is identical to Oil World 1988 in Figure 8.18 except that the time chart spans the period 1996 to 2020. There is also one extra control called 'time to build trust in Russia' that determines the rate at which commercial confidence builds to develop Russian reserves. To mimic demand pressure from an Asian boom, move the slider 'effect of global economy and environment on demand' to the far right so it takes a value of 0.1. This setting means that consumers collectively want to use more oil. To activate quota busting within the OPEC cartel move the slider 'opportunists' capacity bias' to the right so it takes a value of 0.1. Also set the 'cartel quota bias' to a value of −0.05 to enact a deliberate policy of moderate undersupply by OPEC. Finally, to represent cautious upstream investment by independents reset 'capex optimism' to 0.6.

This setting has the effect of authorising only the most profitable 60% of the upstream development projects whose estimated financial return exceeds the hurdle rate. The remaining two sliders ('time to build trust in Russia' and 'oil price bias') can remain at their default settings.

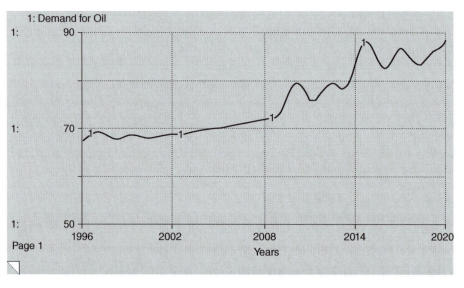

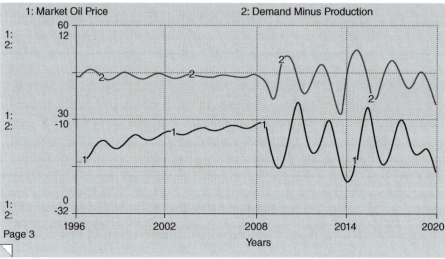

Figure 8.23   Demand and oil price in a scenario from the mid-1990s to 2020: Asian boom with quota busting, cautious upstream investment and Russian oil

Press the 'Run' button to see this scenario play out in five-year intervals resulting in the time charts shown in Figures 8.23, 8.24 and 8.25. Remember that any scenario shows time paths that are internally consistent with the assumptions about conditions in the industry. These time paths do not

necessarily fit history or point-predict the future. In Figure 8.23, demand for
oil starts at 68 million barrels per day in 1996 and over the decade to 2006
rises gradually to 71 million barrels per day. The increase in demand is
modest, only 4% over 10 years despite steady upward pressure on demand
from the assumed growth in Asian economies. The reason that demand does
not grow more quickly is that oil price (shown in the bottom half of
Figure 8.23) rises from $16 per barrel to almost $30 per barrel – practically
doubling over the simulated decade. Such a large price increase evokes greater
fuel efficiency in the global economy.

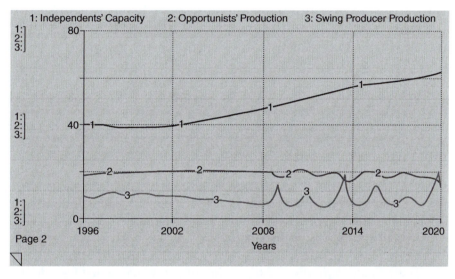

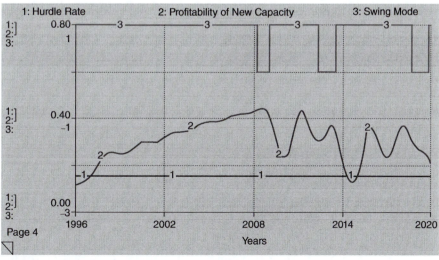

**Figure 8.24   Production profiles and profitability of independents' capacity in a
scenario from the mid-1990s to 2020: Asian boom with quota busting, cautious
upstream investment and Russian oil**

In the remainder of the simulation, from 2006 to 2020, demand grows swiftly and is also far more volatile. In only two years, from 2008 to 2010, demand surges from 72 to 79 million barrels per day, a 10% increase, as global economic growth combines with a dramatic drop in oil price (from $30 to $15 per barrel) to unleash vast additional consumption. As we will see later the price drop is caused by a temporary burst of punitive production by the swing producer that floods the market with oil. When punitive production ends the oil price rapidly rises to $35 per barrel by late 2010 leading to a slight reduction of demand, despite the continued pressure of economic growth. Thereafter, demand continues on an upward trajectory with intermittent upturns and downturns, reaching almost 90 million barrels per day by 2020. The ups and downs stem from volatility in oil price as the oil industry enters an era of OPEC-induced supply instability between 2008 and 2020.

The supply story can be seen in Figure 8.24. The top chart shows the production profiles of the three main producer groups – the independents (line 1), the opportunists (line 2) and the swing producer (line 3). In the interval between 1996 and 2002, independents' capacity (and therefore production) is steady at almost 40 million barrels per day. Over the same six years, opportunists' production increases gently from 18 to 20 million barrels per day as opportunists take advantage of demand pressure and stable oil price to engage in limited quota busting. Meanwhile, the swing producer's production fluctuates gently and then settles into a downward trend resulting from the deliberate policy of undersupply and the need to compensate for quota busting by opportunists. The overall picture in the early years of the scenario is restrained production by the industry as a whole that leads to the near doubling of oil price already seen in Figure 8.23. High price creates a favourable environment for commercial upstream investment as shown by the trajectory for the profitability of new capacity in the bottom half of Figure 8.24. Profitability (line 2) begins at 12% (0.12), just below the hurdle rate (line 1) of 15% (0.15) in 1996 and rises steadily to 43% (0.43) by 2008. As a result, more and more upstream projects are approved and independents' capacity (line 1 in the top chart begins to rise) reaches 47 million barrels per day by 2008 and 56 million barrels per day by 2014. Independents take an increasingly large share of demand and this relative growth puts pressure on the OPEC cartel. The swing producer is increasingly marginalised and finds production falling to only six million barrels per day by 2008 despite growth in demand.

This unsatisfactory condition of chronic low output provokes the swing producer into punitive production starting in early 2008. The indicator for swing mode (line 3 in the bottom chart) moves from one to zero and swing producer production surges upward reaching 14 million barrels per day in 2009. As we saw previously, oil price plummets, unleashing latent growth in demand. Meanwhile, the opportunists cease quota busting and their production takes a temporary dip between 2009 and 2010. By 2010, the swing producer ceases punitive production having regained market share. Opportunists resume quota busting under the cover of rising oil price and booming demand. Notice that independents' capacity continues to grow over the interval 2008 to 2010 and beyond despite a steep decline in profitability of new capacity from 44% (0.44) to 23% (0.23) in 2010. Even so, the financial return from new upstream projects comfortably exceeds the hurdle rate and there is lots of new capacity in the pipeline from the previous decade of investment.

In the remaining years of the simulation to 2020 the relentless expansion of independents' capacity creates periodic crises within OPEC, leading the swing producer to renewed bouts of punitive production that induce volatility in oil price and demand. This instability of supply in the period 2008 to 2020 restricts oil price to a range between $10 and $35 per barrel. Moderate, though volatile, oil price is conducive to greater consumption in a growing global economy and consequently demand rises. The resulting upstream investment climate remains mostly favourable (with the exception of a notable downturn in profitability in 2014) and so the independent producers continue to expand capacity and to grab most of the extra global demand.

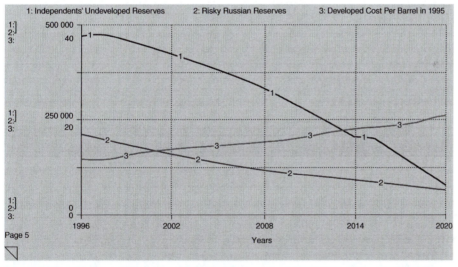

Figure 8.25   Commercial reserves and development cost in a scenario from the mid-1990s to 2020: Asian boom with quota busting, cautious upstream investment and Russian oil

Figure 8.25 shows the effect on commercial reserves of the Asian boom scenario with quota busting. Independents' undeveloped reserves (line 1) begin at 471 billion barrels in 1996 (471 000 million on the vertical scale), while risky Russian reserves (line 2), known to exist but not yet adopted by any major commercial producer, begin at 210 billion barrels (210 000 million on the vertical scale). Over time, risky Russian reserves steadily fall as confidence builds among commercial producers to exploit more and more Russian oil. These risky reserves are essentially transferred into independents' undeveloped reserves. The rate of transfer is governed by the parameter 'time to build confidence in Russia' which is set at 20 years in the scenario. By 2008 risky reserves are down to 115 billion barrels and by 2020 to 63 billion barrels, barely a quarter of the initial amount. The transfer of almost 150 billion barrels of Russian oil replenishes independents' undeveloped reserves and extends their lifetime. Nevertheless, independents' reserves decline steadily throughout the simulation because the rate of development of new commercial oil fields exceeds replenishment. Reserves fall to 329 billion barrels by 2008 and to 202 billion barrels by 2014. Notice that in the period 2014 to 2015 independents' reserves are virtually stable at 200 billion barrels despite production of 56 million barrels per day. This plateau corresponds to a brief period in which replenishment of reserves (through adoption of risky Russian oil) exactly balances new development in the wake of a dip in new upstream projects caused by low oil price. Thereafter, reserves continue to fall, declining to 75 billion barrels by 2020.

Figure 8.25 also shows development cost per barrel. This trajectory merits close investigation. Development cost starts quite low at $12 per barrel in 1996. It rises steadily over the 25-year simulation to $21 per barrel in 2020. This increase is modest considering that total non-OPEC reserves have fallen from 681 billion barrels in 1996 (the sum of independents' undeveloped reserves and risky Russian reserves) to 138 billion barrels in 2020. Almost 80% of known commercial reserves are used over this period. Surely such extensive depletion means that remaining recoverable reserves will be much more expensive to extract. However, escalation of development cost is curtailed by two factors. First, known Russian reserves, available at modest cost, are steadily replenishing commercial reserves as independent producers build confidence in Russian oil. Second, recovery technology is advancing throughout the quarter-century scenario period, as reflected in the downward sloping technology cost curve shown on the right of Figure 8.6. If this particular technology assumption is broadly correct, then it means that recovery costs in 2020 for a given oil field are only 55% of their 1996 value. So far, technology has delivered on this efficiency assumption.

A High Price Scenario from the Mid-1990s to 2020: How to Push Oil Price Over $60 per Barrel

In 2006, oil price was almost $70 per barrel and the pump price of petrol in the UK was very nearly £1.00 per litre. This price level is much higher than achieved in the simulated scenario above. So what scenario conditions are needed to push oil price into this realm? Apparently buoyant demand alone is not enough, although it is certainly an important scenario ingredient. The model suggests that it is difficult to invoke high oil price because OPEC oil is cheap and even non-OPEC oil can be extracted for less than $25 per barrel under quite aggressive assumptions about growth in global demand. If oil price exceeds $40 per barrel then commercial production is highly profitable and, sooner or later, adequate supply will be forthcoming. Conditions that would cause chronic undersupply are an Asian boom coinciding with restricted supply from OPEC; but is OPEC undersupply plausible in light of quota busting by opportunist producers? The answer is yes if a combination of political uncertainty, economic sanctions and military conflict in the Middle East conspire to reduce OPEC output so much that opportunist quota busting is cancelled out.

The scenario parameters in Oil World 1995 can be adjusted to capture the political uncertainty that would curb OPEC output. Two changes are required relative to the previous scenario. Opportunists' capacity bias is reduced to zero meaning that collectively opportunist producers are unable to engage in quota busting because oil exports for some are curtailed through sanctions or war. In addition, capex optimism is reduced to its minimum value of 0.5 to represent extreme caution in the investment decision of independent producers because of assumed political volatility and conflict in the Middle East. Otherwise, all the other scenario parameters remain at the same settings as in the previous scenario, including of course the assumption of an Asian boom driving global economic growth.

Figure 8.26 shows a simulation of this modified scenario. Only two time charts are displayed, but additional charts can be inspected by running Oil World 1995 with the parameter settings described. Oil price (line 1, bottom chart) rises steeply from $16 per barrel in 1996 to $40 per barrel in 2008, increasing still further to $63 per barrel in 2016 and $68 per barrel in 2020. There is also considerable volatility in price, with peaks of more than $60 per barrel and troughs of $30 per barrel. This volatility is caused by an interaction between the swing producer (as price regulator) and consumers. Demand growth is curtailed by high price despite the assumption of an Asian boom. Demand for oil rises from 68 million barrels per day in 1996 to 74 million barrels per day in 2020.

The simulation shows that it is possible for oil price to rise very high even when development costs remain at less than $20 per barrel (as they do in this particular scenario). High price is sustained by a combination of demand pressure and politically induced restriction in OPEC supply. Even so, the simulator cannot fully match the price peak of 2006.

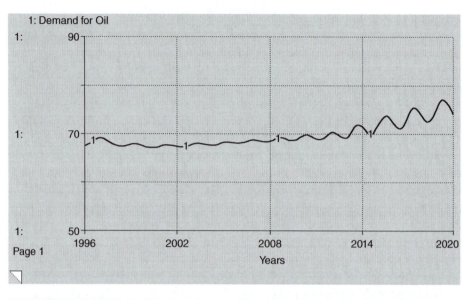

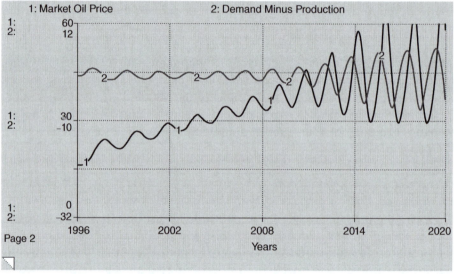

Figure 8.26 Demand and oil price in a high price scenario from the mid-1990s to 2020: Asian boom with OPEC undersupply, very cautious upstream investment and Russian oil

Most likely, this shortcoming is because the model does not fully represent oil stocks, hoarding and speculation in oil markets; short-term factors that make oil price particularly sensitive to political uncertainty in the Middle East. Nevertheless, the simulator clarifies the enduring economic and political forces driving long-term supply, demand and price in the oil industry.

A 2010–2034 Scenario: Subdued Global Oil Economy with Shale Gale and OPEC Supply Boost

By 2010 conditions in the oil industry had changed significantly by comparison with the mid-1990s. Global oil demand had surged to almost 90 million barrels per day in the wake of an Asian economic boom and oil price was more than $100 per barrel. Meanwhile Russia had become the world's biggest oil producer and output of shale oil was rising in the US. The updated model 'Oil World 2010' captures these changes.

Imagine now a scenario, starting in 2010, in which the Asian boom has ended, global economic growth is moderate, and there is increasing environmental pressure to curtail the use of fossil fuels. The result is a subdued global oil economy in which the world's growing appetite for oil is curbed, though not eliminated. Let's also assume that shale oil is rapidly exploited and that OPEC expands production through a combination of quota busting and deliberate oversupply. To explore this scenario open 'Oil World 2010'. The initial screen shows a blank time chart for the period 2010 to 2034 with a vertical axis set up to show Demand for Oil. The scenario controls are below the time chart, just as they were in 'Oil World 1995'.

The settings and parameters to generate the three main features of the intended 2010–2034 scenario are as follows:

1 The assumption of a subdued global oil economy is captured in the default value of 0 for the slider labelled 'effect of global economy and environment on demand'. This setting means that for 25 years, from 2010 to 3024, there is no upward pressure whatsoever on oil demand, unless it comes from falling oil price. In other words, in the absence of price change, oil demand remains constant. If there is economic growth, as seems likely, then its upward effect on oil demand is presumed to be cancelled by oil substitution from non-fossil fuel sources (such as pure electric vehicles for transportation or nuclear power/solar for home heating) and from improvements in energy efficiency (such as hybrid vehicles for transportation or improved insulation for home heating).

2 A shale gale happens without the need to make any slider adjustments. The effect plays out through a variety of parameter assumptions that boost the capacity and output of the independents' sector. These assumptions were described earlier in the chapter. They include extra reserves, a high initial oil price, and an attractive commercial investment climate.

3 An OPEC supply boost is created by moving the sliders for 'cartel quota bias' and 'opportunists' capacity bias'. First set 'cartel quota bias' to +0.05 by moving the slider to the right. This change causes OPEC to deliberately oversupply the market by agreeing a collective quota for member states that is 5% higher than the call on OPEC. Then set the slider f or 'opportunists' capacity bias' to 0.1. This change activates quota busting within OPEC as individual member states attempt to boost vital oil exports and revenues.

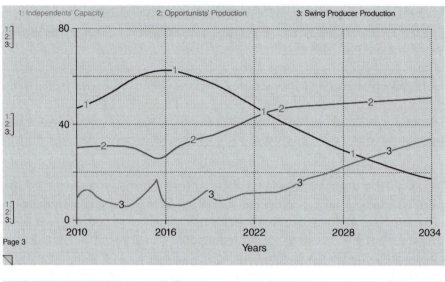

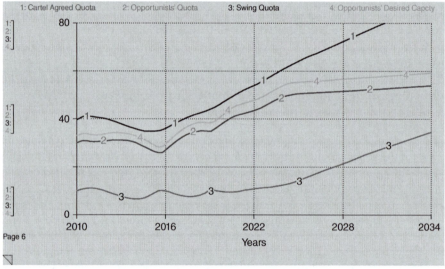

Figure 8.27   Production and OPEC quotas in a 2010–2034 scenario: subdued global oil economy with shale gale and OPEC supply boost

All the other sliders remain in their default positions.

Press the 'Run' button to generate the time charts shown in Figure 8.27. The shale gale is evident in the trajectory for independents' capacity (line 1, top chart) which grows rapidly in the period between 2010 and 2016 from 47 million barrels per day to 63 million barrels per day; a huge increase of more than 30%. This expansion puts a severe squeeze on OPEC, forcing a decline in the cartel's agreed quota (line 1, bottom chart) from 41 million barrels per day in 2010 to only 34 million barrels per day in 2015. As a result the swing producers' production (line 3, top chart) falls by 50% between 2010 and 2013 while opportunists' production (line 2, top chart) remains level at 31 million barrels per day – despite opportunists' quota busting.

The squeeze on OPEC invokes retaliation within the cartel. Starting in late 2013 the swing producer temporarily abandons the quota system and increases production far above quota in order to regain lost market share and to punish other producers for pumping too much oil. By early 2015 the swing producer's production (line 3, top chart) peaks at 17 million barrels per day. By comparison the swing quota peaks at only 9 million barrels per day (line 3, bottom chart). This surge of punitive production fails to quell the shale gale. Independents' capacity (line 1, top chart) remains above 60 million barrels per day from early 2014 to late 2017, reaching a peak of 63 million barrels per day in 2016 – one year later than the peak in swing production. The market is flooded with oil. Only the opportunists reduce production (line 2, top chart) from 30 million barrels per day in late 2013 to 25 million barrels per day in mid-2015. This modest reduction is too small to offset the supply glut.

After 2016, and over the next two decades, the oil world changes almost beyond recognition. There is a gradual long-term decline in independents' capacity (line 1, top chart) from its peak value of 63 million barrels per day in 2016 to only 18 million barrels per day in 2034. The shale gale is over and conditions are now ripe for expansion of OPEC. The cartel's agreed quota (line 1, bottom chart) rises almost linearly from 34 million barrels per day in 2015 to 80 million barrels per day in 2030, partly to fill the supply gap left in the wake of the shale gale and partly as a result of sustained quota busting by opportunists overlaid on OPEC's deliberate policy of oversupply. Opportunists' quota (line 2, bottom chart) doubles from 25 million barrels per day in 2015 to 54 million barrels per day in 2034 while the swing quota (line 3, bottom chart) more than trebles in the same period.

If this future were to unfold the upstream businesses of big commercial producers like ExxonMobil and Shell would be reduced by two-thirds (just a shadow of their former selves) and the world would be more reliant than ever on oil from the Middle East.

How could such radical change happen? The answer lies in the geology and economics of the oil industry with its vast low-cost reserves concentrated mainly in the Middle East and its modest high-cost reserves spread around the globe, trapped in awkward-to-reach places at the bottom of deep oceans, or in shale rocks and tar sands. If, as assumed in the 2010 scenario, global oil demand is subdued for more than two decades then OPEC may be tempted to compete on price and use its reserves to drive commercial producers out of business or at least curtail their market power.

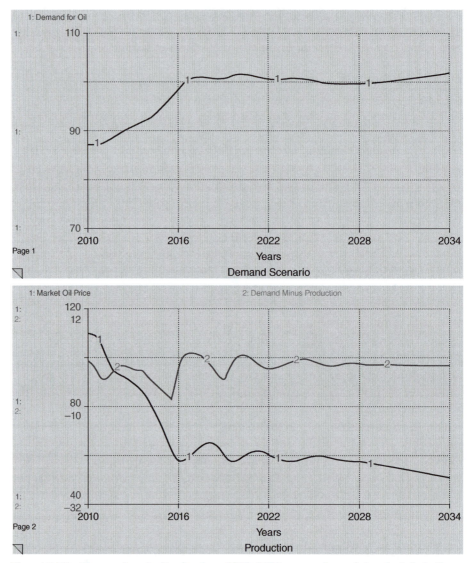

Figure 8.28   Demand and oil price in a 2010–2034 scenario: subdued global oil economy with shale gale and OPEC supply boost

The resulting demand and price story can be seen in Figure 8.28. Demand (line 1, top chart) starts at 87 million barrels per day in 2010 and rises to 101 million barrels per day in 2017. Thereafter demand remains steady, hovering around 100 million barrels per day for the rest of the simulation out to 2034. An increase in demand may seem surprising given the scenario assumption of a subdued global-oil economy. However there is a glut of oil during the first seven years of the scenario which causes a rapid decline in market oil price (line 1, bottom chart). As oil price falls from $110 per barrel to just under $60 per barrel then oil consumption is stimulated, despite environmental pressure to use less fossil fuel. For example, new hybrids or pure electric vehicles will be much more difficult to sell if the pump price of gasoline plummets and stays low.

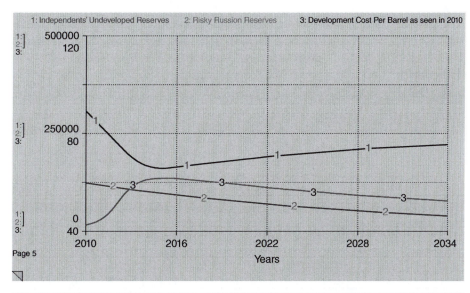

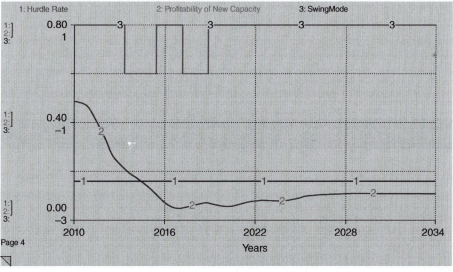

Figure 8.29   Independents' reserves, development cost and profitability in a 2010 scenario: subdued global oil economy with shale gale and OPEC supply boost

Figure 8.29 shows just how unfavourable upstream oil economics can become if OPEC adopts a hostile stance toward commercial producers in the wake of the shale gale. Independents' undeveloped reserves (line 1, top chart) fall swiftly in the period 2010 to 2015 as already-approved commercial oil fields are developed and come onstream. Meanwhile the profitability of new upstream capacity (line 2, bottom chart) declines sharply and by late 2014 has fallen below the hurdle rate (line 1, bottom chart) due to the pincer movement of oil price and development cost per barrel (line 3, top chart). Projects to develop new oil fields that would previously have been profitable are now rejected. Upstream investment is halted and remains unprofitable all the way out to 2034. For 20 years no new capacity is added by upstream commercial producers. Commercial output dwindles and OPEC fills the supply gap. It is cold comfort for the independents that their undeveloped reserves (line 1, top chart) rebuilt gradually between 2016 and 2034 as risky Russian reserves are deemed suitable for future development – if and when there is a financial incentive to do so.

Modified 2010–2034 Scenario: Subdued Global Oil Economy with Shale Gale and Punitive Saudi Supply Control

A subdued global oil economy leaves no room for long-term growth of the West's commercial upstream oil industry. So a sustained OPEC supply boost as described above, lasting 25 years, is not necessarily a wise policy for OPEC to adopt. It shifts too much market power to OPEC and emaciates the independents. Instead imagine a more pragmatic policy in which the cartel agrees quotas sufficient to meet, but not exceed, the call on OPEC (the difference between global demand and independents' production). Also imagine that Saudi Arabia exerts punitive control over supply by deploying its surplus capacity to pump extra oil, above the swing quota. The result of such Saudi intervention is a deliberately lower oil price intended to punish excess production by the other producers.

To examine this modified scenario reset the sliders for cartel quota bias and opportunists' capacity bias to their default values. Also confirm that all other sliders are set at their default values. Then press the 'Run' button to obtain the two time charts shown in Figure 8.30. For brevity I have chosen to exhibit only two pages (3 and 6) from the full set of simulated time charts. Readers can view all the other pages and trajectories (including oil demand and oil price) by using the 'page' tabs at the bottom left of the charts.

Once again, independents' capacity (line 1, top chart) surges upward between 2010 and 2017 as new capacity, including shale, comes onstream, justified by high oil price. In response the cartel pragmatically lowers its agreed quota (line 1, bottom chart). However by 2013, after three years of quota accommodation, the swing producer switches into punitive mode, in an

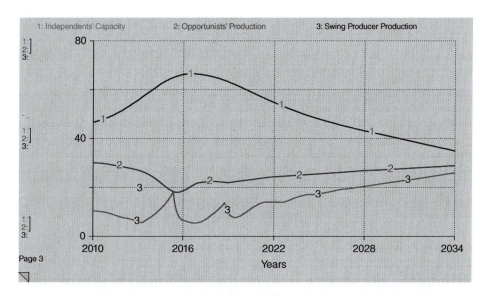

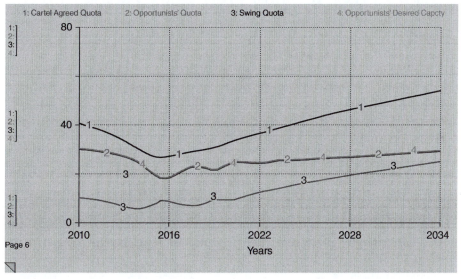

Figure 8.30　Production and OPEC quotas in a modified 2010–2034 scenario: subdued global oil economy with shale gale and punitive Saudi supply control

attempt to quell the shale gale. Swing production (line 3, top chart) rises sharply and greatly exceeds swing quota (line 3, bottom chart), to reach a peak of 18 million barrels per day in 2015, before subsiding close to swing quota of 8 million barrels per day in 2016. This burst of punitive production, followed by another brief burst in 2018, lowers oil price enough to discourage further investment by the independents (see pages 2 and 5 of the simulated time charts for price and profitability trajectories). As a result, capacity (line 1, top chart) gradually declines throughout the rest of the simulation to year 2034.

However, unlike the previous scenario, OPEC no longer attempts to drive the independents out of business. The cartel's agreed quota (line 1, bottom chart) rises only gradually to fill the supply gap left by the independents; ending in 2034 at 54 million barrels per day and split almost equally between opportunists' quota (line 2, bottom chart) and swing quota (line 3, bottom chart). Note that during OPEC's long period of gentle growth there is no need for further punitive production by the swing producer. From 2018 onwards the cartel works harmoniously within the framework of the quota system.

2010–2034 Thought Experiment: Subdued Global Oil Economy with a Shale Gale and Mooted US Supply Control – The 'Saudi America' Hypothesis

The final simulation experiment tests an intriguing hypothesis advanced by some oil economists and reported in *The Economist* magazine (February 2014). A reprint of the original article can be found in the learning support folder for Chapter 8. The argument is that shale oil production is much more responsive to world prices than conventional oil due to the short lifetime of tight oil wells. Oil flows sluggishly through impermeable shale rock by comparison with the much freer movement of oil through porous rocks that make up conventional reservoirs. As a result the area that can be tapped with a shale well is much smaller than the area for a conventional well and, as pumping commences, production declines quite rapidly for the first few years (typically by 30% a year by comparison with only 6% a year for a conventional well). So when oil price rises, tight oil producers quickly drill more holes and ramp up supply. When price falls they simply stop drilling and production soon declines. From this geological difference arises the 'Saudi America' hypothesis which suggests that as US shale production expands, and the US becomes one of the world's largest producers, then America will replace Saudi Arabia as the swing producer.

 To test the hypothesis it is first necessary to manually adjust the model parameter called 'Average Lifetime of Field Wells' in Oil World 2010. Re-open Oil World 2010 and press the button labelled 'To Model' in the bottom left of the time chart on the opening screen. A diagram of the Independents sector appears. (Note: If the 'Map' tab is selected on the left of the diagram then, before proceeding, be sure to select the 'Model' tab instead.) Double select the icon for the 'Average Lifetime of Field Wells' in the top right of the diagram. Change the parameter value from 10 years to 5 years. Then press the button labelled 'To Charts' and rerun the simulator with all the sliders set at their default positions, just as they were for the modified 2010–2034 scenario above.

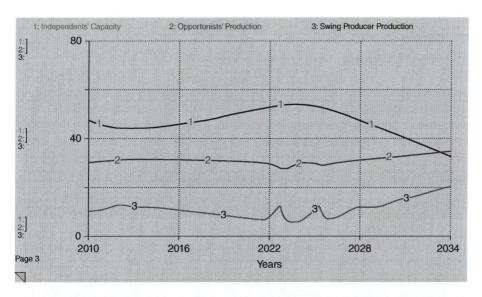

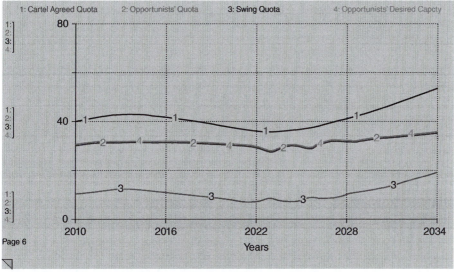

Figure 8.31 Production and OPEC quotas in a 2010 thought experiment: subdued global oil economy with shale gale and mooted US supply control; the 'Saudi America' hypothesis

Locate the two time charts shown in Figure 8.31 and compare the trajectories with those shown in Figure 8.30.

There is a noticeable change in dynamics. Independents' capacity (line 1, top chart) remains quite flat all the way to 2028 and only then begins to decline gradually. The distinctive capacity hump of the shale gale, clearly visible in

Figure 8.30, has disappeared. Meanwhile swing producer production (line 3, top chart) closely matches the swing quota (line 3, bottom chart) meaning that Saudi Arabia no longer needs to exert supply control through bursts of punitive production. Moreover, the cartel's agreed quota (line 1, bottom chart) remains relatively stable for almost two decades, from 2010 to 2028, suggesting the cartel's influence on supply (or need to influence supply) is diminished, consistent with the 'Saudi America' hypothesis. Meanwhile oil price (shown on page 2 of the graph pad) remains above $100 per barrel for most of the simulation. This high and relatively steady price stabilises demand for oil (shown on page 1 of the graph pad), which settles at or just below 90 million barrels per day; a pattern that now fits well with the scenario assumption of a subdued global oil economy. Also, the profitability of new capacity (shown on page 4 of the graph pad) remains above the hurdle rate all the way out to 2034 (despite shrinking reserves and rising costs). So, unlike previous shale gale scenarios, there is always a financial incentive, albeit diminishing, for independents to invest in new capacity.

So perhaps the Saudi America hypothesis is true and the locus of power in the oil world will shift from Saudi Arabia and OPEC to the US in coming decades. However the simulator suggests there is only a grain of truth in the hypothesis. The main reason is that only a small fraction of independents' overall capacity is in shale oil, which is anyway relatively expensive to develop. There is lots of conventional oil capacity too in Russia's medium-cost oil fields, and in conventional deep-sea fields rendered profitable by high oil price. With all this commercially viable non-shale output already in the industry it is extremely unlikely that shale producers in the US can, by themselves, enforce production cuts big enough to stabilise price in the way the hypothesis suggests. It would take remarkable discipline by entrepreneurial frackers in the biggest US tight-oil production basins (such as Bakken and Eagle Ford) to withhold production for months on end, or even years, in the hope that the oil price will rise. Meanwhile, conventional oil producers will continue to pump oil from their long-life wells, unable to match the production cuts in nimble tight-oil fields. Moreover, some shale oil producers will surely behave opportunistically, drilling new wells to sustain their output even as other shale producers cut back – rather like the opportunist producers in OPEC. So the most likely outcome for independents' output as a whole is a partial production cut, much shallower than imagined in the Saudi America hypothesis.

The true aggregate situation can be represented in the simulator by a smaller reduction in the average lifetime of field wells from (say) 10 years to 7 years (rather than 5 years). When this more realistic assumption is used then the main dynamic features of the modified 2010 scenario reappear. The capacity hump of the shale gale returns, prompting bursts of punitive Saudi production that in turn causes a significant drop in oil price. Of course it is important to bear in mind, as with all scenarios, that the trajectories are internally consistent stories, not accurate point predictions of future oil price and production. Nevertheless there is a strong message in the 2010 simulations. Unless there is another global economic boom, then we are entering an era of lower oil price, ushered in by a shale gale that re-ignites the smouldering power of OPEC.

Devising New Scenarios

You can devise new scenarios by varying the slider settings in any of the three versions of the oil producers' model: 'Oil World 1988', 'Oil World 1995', or 'Oil World 2010'. The sliders, which can be seen in Figure 8.18, correspond to the parameters marked in bold in Figures 8.16 and 8.17. The default settings represent a benign oil industry in which demand is stable and OPEC cooperates with independents to fully supply the market. The meaning of each slider is explained below. By understanding the sliders it is possible to create a very wide range of plausible scenarios from low-price to high-price, from stable to volatile, and from OPEC-dominated to independent-dominated.

Effect of Global Economy and Environment on Demand

The effect of global economy and environment is a parameter representing pressure on oil demand from the global economy or from environmental policy to limit carbon emissions. The effect can vary from −0.1 to 0.1 with a default value of zero. When the effect is zero long-term demand is normally stable. Moving the slider to the right results in growing oil consumption because, at constant price, intended demand (in Figure 8.16) exceeds demand. Conversely, moving the slider to the left results in falling oil consumption. With this versatile slider an Asian boom is portrayed by setting the slider to its maximum value of 0.1, whereas a green world (committed to reducing carbon emissions and using fewer fossil fuels) is portrayed by setting the slider to its minimum value of −0.1.

Cartel Quota Bias

Cartel quota bias captures the tendency of OPEC to deliberately oversupply or undersupply the market by setting a collective quota that differs from the call on OPEC (the difference between demand and independents' production). The effect can vary from −0.2 to 0.2, with a default value of zero. When the effect is zero OPEC agrees a quota exactly equal to the call. Moving the slider to the left causes an OPEC supply squeeze, a deliberate undersupply of oil that can be as much as 20% of the call. Moving the slider to the right causes an OPEC supply glut, a deliberate oversupply of oil.

Opportunists' Capacity Bias

Opportunists' capacity bias represents the propensity of some OPEC member states to over-expand capacity and exceed their allocated quota. There is always a temptation for OPEC producers to cheat on quota, particularly oil nations with underdeveloped economies and large populations that desperately need oil revenues to support social welfare and infrastructure projects. Capacity bias is defined on a scale from zero to 0.2 where zero means no quota busting. The default value is assumed to be 0.02 on the presumption that, no matter how hard OPEC strives for quota discipline, there is naturally some propensity to cheat and over-expand capacity. Moving the slider to the right amplifies this natural propensity up to a maximum where opportunists strive for capacity at a level 20% (0.2) above allocated quota.

Oil Price Bias

The oil price bias is a parameter that captures any inclination of OPEC to intentionally increase oil price by setting a target (marker) price higher than the current oil price. The default value is zero and the parameter can be moved in the range −0.2 to 0.2. Moving the slider to the right creates a condition in which OPEC's target price exceeds the current oil price by up to 20%. There is no presumption, however, that OPEC will always pursue a policy of price escalation. Moving the slider to the left creates a condition in which OPEC's target price undercuts the current oil price. Incidentally, the oil price bias does not (and cannot) directly influence oil price. It acts indirectly to restrict or to boost the swing producer's production.

Capex Optimism

Capex optimism represents the collective investment optimism of senior management in commercial oil companies. It is defined on a scale of 0.5–2 and has a default value of 1. Capex optimism influences the amount of upstream investment undertaken by the independents. When optimism is set to 1, senior managers approve all recommended investment projects, in other words all those that satisfy the hurdle rate. Moving the slider to the left makes management more cautious and they approve fewer investment projects than recommended, as little as 50% fewer (0.5 or half the recommended). Moving the slider to the right makes managers more optimistic and less cautious and they approve more investment projects than recommended.

Time to Build Trust in Russia (in Oil World 1995 and 2010)

As mentioned earlier, Russian reserves are huge, with an initial value of 225 billion barrels in Oil World 1995 and 137 billion barrels in Oil World 2010 (after 15 years of commercial exploitation). They amount to almost 50% of total non-OPEC reserves. Time to build trust in Russia controls the rate at which commercial oil companies adopt risky Russian reserves into their undeveloped reserve portfolio. The parameter is defined on a scale of 5–40 years. When the time to build trust is at its default value of 20 years commercial companies are assumed to adopt 1/20 (5%) of risky Russian reserves per year. In other words, the value of the slider setting (20 years) defines the denominator (1/20) in the adoption rate. Moving the slider to the right captures the effect of a less trusting climate for exploration and production. Adoption of risky Russian reserves slows to as little as 1/40 (2.5%) per year at the slider's maximum setting of 40 years. Moving the slider to the left increases adoption to as much as 1/5 (20%) per year at the slider's minimum setting of five years.

Endnote: A Brief History of the Oil Producers' Project

There have been five phases in the life of the oil producers' project. The first phase was the original model development, which happened in the period 1988–1989 as an input to Shell's 1989 scenario round (Shell Group Planning, 1989). This work took place under the guidance of Kees van der Heijden who was then head of the scenario team at Shell International, London, within a department known (at the time) as Group Planning. Model conceptualisation was led by John Morecroft and the model development team included Kees van der Heijden, Ged Davis (a member of the 1989 scenario team) and Andrew Davis (who had been seconded to the team from the business consultancy department of Shell UK).

The second phase was translation of the model into a microworld for internal Shell management training programmes, in the period 1990–1992. The original interface design was carried out by Linda Morecroft in a language called Microworld Creator (Diehl, 1992). The integration of the microworld into the training programmes was carried out by John Morecroft in collaboration with Brian Marsh, a senior member of Group Planning. Samples of the interface and experiences from the training programmes are reported in Morecroft and Marsh (1997).

The third phase was the use of the oil producers' model in Paul Langley's PhD dissertation at London Business School, in the period 1993–1995. The purpose of the thesis was to study user learning in gaming simulators (Langley, 1995). The research required a completely new graphical interface suitable for controlled experiments on user learning. Paul Langley collaborated closely with Erik Larsen (then a research fellow at London Business School) to develop the interface in Visual Basic before going on to design and execute his experiments. He also simplified the user controls. Originally there were the five sliders depicted in Figure 8.18. The thesis microworld had just one control – the capacity approval decision.

The fourth phase, in the period 1995–1997, involved revisions to the original oil producers' model to take account of structural changes in the oil industry since 1988. The most dramatic and significant change, as mentioned earlier in the chapter, was the opening up of Russian oil fields to global markets, stemming from the break-up of the Soviet Union and the fall of Communism. It was fortunate that Ged Davis, a member of the original model development team, was by then back at Shell Centre and able to offer expert advice on how best to incorporate Russian oil into the model. The result was a new model (called Oil World 1995 to distinguish it from the original Oil World 1988) that captured Russia's vast oil reserves as an extension of the commercial reserves available to independent (non-OPEC) producers. Though Russian oil was treated in the model as commercial oil, there were nevertheless political strings attached to the timing of its exploitation. Ged Davis' conceptualisation of Russian oil fields fit very well within the model's existing architecture. The necessary changes required the addition of only six new equations to the existing 100 equations portraying industry structure.

The fifth model development phase took place in 2014 as I prepared the second edition of the book. Although by this time more than a quarter century had passed since the creation of the original model, it nevertheless seemed that key feedback structures from the 1988 model were still present in the new oil world of the 21st century. Indeed I was intrigued by the idea that the model contained a practical example of 'enduring feedback structure', thereby illustrating a principle central to the modelling philosophy of system dynamics. In particular, the OPEC cartel was intact with a swing producer and opportunists following much the same operating policies as in the 1980s and 1990s for quota setting, price control and punitive production. It remained to add the changes brought about by the exploitation of shale oil which were mostly concentrated in the Independents sector. These changes were introduced by adjusting parameter assumptions for reserves and development costs, using data available from public sources such as BP's Statistical Review of World Energy and articles in the business press of the time, such as the report on 'cheaper oil' in *The Economist* (2014b). I also updated the initial oil price numbers in the model to match the real world price of $110 per barrel in 2010.

References

BP Review (2014) BP Statistical Review of World Energy http://www.bp.com/en/global/corporate/about-bp/energy-economics/statistical-review-of-world-energy.html (accessed 14 October 2014).

de Geus, A. (1988) Planning as learning. *Harvard Business Review*, March–April: 70–74.

de Geus, A. (1999) *The Living Company*. London: Nicholas Brealey.

Diehl, E. (1992) Managerial microworlds as learning support tools. *European Journal of Operational Research*, 59(1): 210–215.

Langley, P.A. (1995) An Experimental Study of the Impact of Online Cognitive Feedback on Performance and Learning in an Oil Producers' Microworld. PhD thesis, London Business School, November.

Morecroft, J.D.W. and van der Heijden, K.A.J.M. (1992) Modelling the oil producers. *European Journal of Operational Research*, 59(1): 102–122.

Morecroft, J.D.W. and Marsh, B. (1997) Exploring oil market dynamics. In Bunn, D. and Larsen, E. (eds) *Systems Modelling for Energy Policy*. Chichester: John Wiley & Sons, pp. 167–203.

Senge, P.M. (1990) *The Fifth Discipline: The Art and Practice of the Learning Organization*. New York: Doubleday.

Shell Group Planning (1989) *Scenarios, challenge and response*. Group Planning Publication, PL 89 S12. London: Shell International Petroleum Company.

The Economist (2014a) The economics of shale oil: Saudi America. *The Economist*, 15 February 2014, pp. 33–34.

The Economist (2014b) Cheaper oil: winners and losers. *The Economist*, 25 October 2014, pp. 65–67.

van der Heijden, K.A.J.M. (1996) *Scenarios: The Art of Strategic Conversation*. Chichester: John Wiley & Sons.

Yergin, D. (1991) *The Prize: The Epic Quest for Oil, Money and Power*. London: Simon and Schuster.

Yergin, D. (2011) *The Quest: Energy, Security and the Remaking of the Modern World*. London: Allen Lane.

Chapter 9

Public Sector Applications of Strategic Modelling

- Urban Dynamics – Growth and Stagnation in Cities
- Medical Workforce Dynamics and Patient Care
- Fishery Dynamics and Regulatory Policy
- Conclusion
- Appendix – Alternative Simulation Approaches

Many system dynamics models have been built to address public policy issues. The topics read like a list of political speeches: health care reform, prison overcrowding, drug-related crime, transportation, urban renewal, environmental policy, energy policy and fisheries regulation. In this chapter, we sample three topics from this manifesto to illustrate how models and simulators are used in public policy and their impact on political debate. We begin with *Urban Dynamics* (Forrester, 1969), a classic system dynamics study of stagnation and economic decline in cities. Then we turn to health care reform and a model that examines the impact on patient care of changes to the working practices of junior hospital doctors. Finally, we return to fisheries, with a simulator to explain the paradox of over-fishing and to examine regulatory policy.

While describing these applications, I will take the opportunity to review basic modelling principles. The urban dynamics model illustrates the art of model conceptualisation. Although we touch just lightly on the model, the elegance of the conceptual model will be apparent. The medical workforce dynamics model illustrates formulation principles, the modelling of intangibles and the interpretation of simulations. The fisheries policy model provides more examples of formulation principles and the modelling of behavioural decision making. It also demonstrates traditional practice in system dynamics for policy design and interpretation of policy simulations.

Urban Dynamics – Growth and Stagnation in Cities

The year 2007 was a momentous point in world history when, for the first time, urban dwellers outnumbered those living in rural areas (Urbanization, 2003). Alongside this rise in urban population, there has also been an increase in the number and size of very large cities, bringing both benefits and problems of urban growth. Figure 9.1 shows the population of London over 200 years from 1800 to 2000. The city was already large at the start of the 19th century with more than one million inhabitants. Over the next hundred years, throughout the Victorian era, London's population grew steadily to reach seven million people by the early 1900s, before peaking around eight million in the 1940s and gently declining back to seven million in the remaining 60 years up to 2000 (although the Home Counties surrounding London continued to grow). Since the turn of the millennium the city's population has grown once more, reaching just over eight million in 2011.

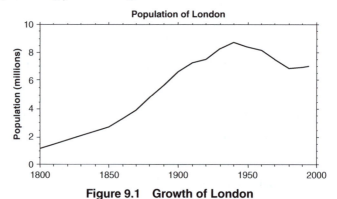

Figure 9.1   Growth of London

City growth and stagnation is a dynamic phenomenon well suited to modelling and simulation. Why do cities grow? What factors limit their growth and economic success? Why is the standard of living in some cities much higher than others? Why do cities that were once successful fall into periods of stagnation and decline? How do you turn around a failing city? These kinds of questions faced Jay Forrester in the creation of the Urban Dynamics model. The story of the model's development is told in 'The prophet of unintended consequences' an article about Forrester's life and work by Lawrence Fisher (2005: 8):

> When John F. Collins, a former mayor of Boston, took a temporary appointment at MIT as a visiting professor, he was assigned the office next door to Professor Forrester's. It was 1968, riots had broken out in cities across America, and the two instructors naturally fell into conversations about solving the stagnation and unemployment that plagued many cities. 'Collins was very much a man of action', Professor Forrester recalls. 'I suggested enlisting researchers – not urban studies students, but people who knew the real urban world – for a half day a week for as long as it would take to extract a dynamic picture of the problem.

Collins's immediate answer was: "They'll be here Wednesday afternoon"'. With Mr Collins's clout, the two quickly assembled a team of high-level advisers from politics and business to research the dynamics of urban poverty. After four months, Professor Forrester had the basis for a new book, *Urban Dynamics*, with a startling assertion: the harder a policymaker tried to relieve poverty, the more that poverty would increase.

('The Prophet of Unintended Consequences' by Lawrence M. Fisher, excerpted with permission from the Fall 2005 issue of *strategy+business magazine*, published by PwC Strategy & LLC. © 2005 PwC. All rights reserved. PwC refers to the PwC network and/or one or more of its member firms, each of which is a separate legal entity. Please see www.pwc.com/structure for further details. www.strategy-business.com.)

Urban Model Conceptualisation

We will return to the policy implications later. Now I want to concentrate on the model's conceptualisation that captures a fundamental interaction between urban development and the ageing of urban infrastructure. The dynamic hypothesis recognises that under favourable conditions, the interplay between the parts of a new urban area causes it to develop. As the area grows and its land area fills, the processes of ageing cause stagnation. As the urban area moves from the growth phase to the equilibrium phase, the population mix and the economic activity change. Unless there is continuing renewal, the filling of the land converts the area from one marked by innovation and growth to one characterised by ageing housing and decline. This verbal hypothesis is shown as causal loops in Figure 9.2.

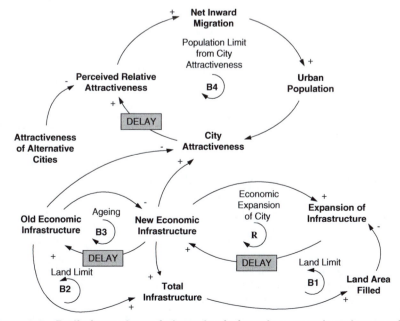

Figure 9.2   Preliminary dynamic hypothesis for urban growth and stagnation

Growth and stagnation arise from reinforcing and balancing loops. The reinforcing growth process (R) is economic expansion of the city in which the existence of new economic infrastructure encourages further expansion of infrastructure and so on. This process continues until the available land area is filled, as represented by loops B1 and B2. Meanwhile new economic infrastructure gradually ages to become old infrastructure in loop B3. Ageing infrastructure combined with rising population eventually lead to city stagnation by making the city less attractive thereby reducing net inward migration in loop B4.

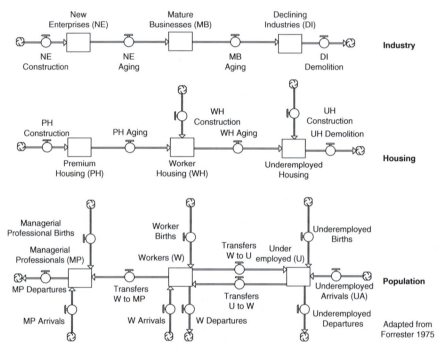

Figure 9.3 Stocks and flows in urban dynamics model
Source: Forrester, 1975. Figure 1 from 'Systems Analysis for Urban Planning', Chapter 11 of *Collected Papers of Jay W. Forrester*, available from the System Dynamics Society www.systemdynamics.org. Reproduced by permission of Jay W. Forrester.

This intriguing hypothesis, inspired by meetings between the urban advisers and the modeller, was fleshed out to yield the stock and flow diagram in Figure 9.3. In particular, the concept of economic infrastructure took on a specific and concrete meaning in terms of nine stock accumulations or levels grouped into three subsystems. Forrester (1975: 178–179) describes these sectors in the following way:

> Across the top the industrial sector contains commercial buildings in three categories distinguished primarily by age. Across the centre are residential buildings in three categories, also distinguished by age and condition. Across the bottom are three economic categories of population.

Even though the information linkages are not shown in this figure it nevertheless begins to show possible reasons for urban decline. Continuing Forrester's interpretation:

> The age of a building tends to determine the character of its occupants. A new commercial building is occupied by a healthy successful commercial organisation that uses relatively more managers and skilled workers than unskilled workers. As the building ages, it tends to house a progressively less successful enterprise with lower employment skills. In addition to the changing employment mix as the industrial building ages, there is a tendency for total employment per unit of floor space to decline. On the other hand, as residential buildings age, there is a tendency for occupancy to increase as well as to shift to a lower economic category of population. One then perceives a condition in which the aging of buildings in an urban area simultaneously reduces the opportunities for employment and increases the population. The average income of the community and standard of living decline.
>
> (Forrester, 1975 *Collected Papers of Jay W. Forrester*, Chapter 11, from: System Analysis for Urban Planning, Available from the System Dynamics Society www.systemdynamics.org. Reproduced by permission of Jay W. Forrester.)

Figure 9.4 shows the same nine system levels and one of the 22 flow rates. This single flow rate depends on the factors or conditions in a city that urban experts believe are likely to attract underemployed people from other regions of the country, thereby causing inward migration. For authenticity, the abbreviated variable names from the original model are shown. However, full names are given for all variables that directly affect inward migration through the Attractiveness Mobility Multiplier (AMM). The dotted lines are the information linkages from the system levels to control the one flow rate – here the arrival of underemployed population into the urban area. The various levels of the system combine to create a composite attractiveness that determines the inflow rate to the area. If the area is more attractive than those from which people might come, a net inward population flow occurs. If the area is less attractive, an outward flow dominates. Five components of attractiveness are shown in the figure, which are now described – starting at the top of the diagram and working downwards. In the upper right corner is the underemployed job multiplier (UJM), which relates the population to the available jobs and represents the income-earning attractiveness of the area. The circle UAMM (Underemployed Attractiveness from Mobility Multiplier) generates the attractiveness created by upward economic mobility. In other words, an area with high upward economic mobility is more attractive than one offering no hope of advancement. The circle UHM (Underemployed Housing Multiplier) relates the underemployed population to the available housing. The area becomes more attractive as housing becomes more available. UHPM (Underemployed Housing Programme Multiplier) represents the attractiveness of a low-cost housing programme if one exists. In the lower right corner, PEM (Public Expenditure Multiplier) is the influence on attractiveness of public expenditure per capita. Rising per capita expenditure means better public services, better schools and higher welfare budgets.

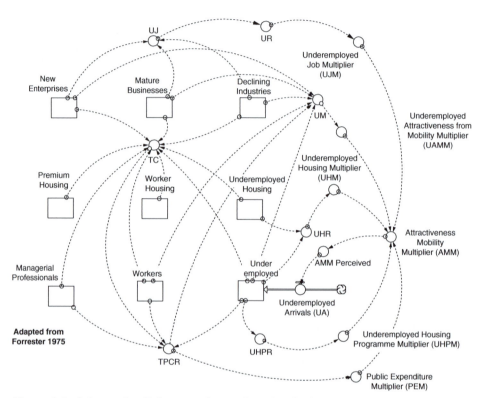

Figure 9.4   Information links to underemployed arrivals

Source: Forrester, 1975. Figure 2 from 'Systems Analysis for Urban Planning', Chapter 11 of *Collected Papers of Jay W. Forrester*, available from the System Dynamics Society www.systemdynamics.org. Reproduced by permission of Jay W. Forrester.

The concept of attractiveness is fundamental to the population flows. All the characteristics that make an area attractive – these five and many more – combine to influence migration. An attractive area draws people. But almost every component of attractiveness is driven down by an increase in population. If there is an excess of housing, the area is attractive, but a rising population crowds the housing. If there is an excess of jobs, the area is attractive, but the incoming flow of people fills those jobs. In other words, migration continues until the attractiveness of the area falls and becomes equal to that of all other places from which people might come.

Urban Dynamics challenged conventional wisdom that urban problems are caused by economic and social forces beyond the control of cities. On the contrary, cities' own policies determine their economic success and the quality of life of their citizens as illustrated by the base run of the model in Figure 9.5, which is a reproduction of an original simulation made in 1968. Notice the healthy development of the city over the first 100 years when labour, managers, worker housing, premium housing and new enterprises grow strongly. Meanwhile, declining industry and underemployed housing remain small. Over the next 50 years social and economic conditions in the city deteriorate. Declining industry rises and new enterprise shrinks. The number of underemployed rises swiftly, peaking in year 120 and premium housing ages to become underemployed housing. The city gradually settles into an equilibrium characterised by chronic underemployment, run-down housing and reduced enterprise.

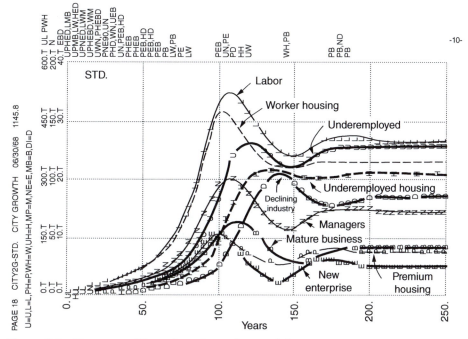

Figure 9.5 Base run of the urban dynamics model

Source: Forrester, 1975. Figure 3 from 'Systems Analysis for Urban Planning', Chapter 11 of Collected *Papers of Jay W. Forrester*, available from the System Dynamics Society www.systemdynamics.org. Reproduced by permission of Jay W. Forrester.

The model's message to policymakers was counterintuitive. Poverty cannot be solved by welfare spending – at least not in the long run. Simulations suggested that an increase in low-income housing exacerbates the decline of the central city by attracting low-skill workers. Similarly, government-sponsored job programmes for the underemployed were found to be ineffective because they too attract low-skill workers and trap them in declining businesses and inadequate housing. Instead, to help cities return to economic health, spending should be allocated to incentives that stimulate new businesses and that speed the demolition of declining business structures and derelict housing. Another surprise result from simulations was that external financial aid to the city, to supplement local spending, eventually forces up local taxes. The reason is that the natural tax base gradually erodes as more and more underemployed people arrive in the city seeking government handouts.

These controversial recommendations sparked much political and academic debate at the time. *Business Week* reported: 'Urban Dynamics is an unsettling, complex and ground-breaking new book about our cities and the decay that afflicts them.' In addition, *Fortune* magazine noted: 'Urban Dynamics has become the subject of heated debate even prior to publication. It has captured the imagination of politicians and managers in the public domain, and it has been furiously attacked by social scientists.' It remains a classic model in the system dynamics literature and a potent reminder of the ability of models to influence the thinking of political and business leaders.

Medical Workforce Dynamics and Patient Care

On 1 August 2004, the European Working Time Directive (EUWTD), a measure intended to limit the working week to 48 hours for all workers within the European Union (EU), became mandatory for junior doctors working for the National Health Service (NHS) in Britain. The intuition behind this piece of health and safety legislation was to reduce the fatigue experienced by junior doctors by limiting doctors' working hours and so improve the quality of patient care. This rationale, though compelling, does not address the non-clinical effects of the EUWTD, in particular, the fundamental change that the Directive has on doctors' working patterns, in-service training and work–life balance.

These concerns were of personal and professional interest to Dr Mark Ratnarajah, a paediatric specialist registrar based in London, who, at the time, was also enrolled on the Executive MBA programme at London Business School. He decided to conduct a project to consider the effects of the Directive on junior doctors' career decisions and the consequences of these decisions on the medical workforce and quality of patient care. Based on his experience and knowledge of the UK National Health System (NHS), he developed a system dynamics model to consider the broad implications of the Directive and to explore alternative courses of action. His work is summarised below.[1]

[1] I am grateful to Dr Ratnarajah for permission to use this material, which is based on the management report he wrote as part of the Executive MBA degree at London Business School. The report (Ratnarajah, 2004) received the Student Prize of the UK Chapter of the System Dynamics Society in 2005.

Background

Since the inception of the NHS over 60 years ago, junior doctors have formed the backbone of the service. Medical cover at night is provided by the junior ranking doctor, who remains resident in the hospital overnight with senior support from the consultant specialist in charge (who usually consults from home and is available to be called into hospital if the need arises). Traditionally, a junior doctor would be expected to work a full day, followed by an overnight period on-call and then work the following day (up to 32 hours resident in the hospital). Although this work schedule accounts for only one and a half days of doctor cover, it constitutes over half the 48 weekly working hours permissible under the EUWTD. The Directive also stipulates that there must be a minimum of 11 hours' rest between continuous periods of work and no doctor working a night duty will be allowed to work at any time during the previous or following daytime. As a consequence of the restrictions, junior doctors will be expected to adopt a full-shift pattern of work involving shorter, more frequent, serial periods of work, usually covering the day/evening and night separately. This transition presents a major challenge for NHS hospitals. Traditionally, junior doctors have worked a 72-hour week. When the 48-hour week and full-shift system is fully implemented, the number of hours of doctor cover lost will be between 208 296 and 476 638 hours, which is the equivalent of 4300–9900 junior doctors. These numbers are based on estimates published by the British Medical Association.

A system dynamics model was developed to examine the consequences of the working time directive on the UK medical workforce and junior hospital doctors in particular. The project was conducted in two stages. In stage one, a workforce planning model was built to explore how hospitals will cope with the expected loss of junior doctor cover and the transition to full-shift work patterns. This model focuses on the tangible effects of the Directive on the total hours available from junior doctors. In stage two, the model was extended to include intangible effects of the working time directive on the work–life balance and morale of junior doctors and potential knock-on consequences to doctors quitting the medical profession. The models' structure was derived from the modeller's own decade of personal experience as a physician trained in the NHS. Parameters were gleaned from government health care policy documents and from journal articles about the medical profession. These publications are listed in the footnote below as a practical example of the use of formal information sources for model building.[2]

---

[2]Information sources for parameters in the medical workforce model:

Source 1: 'Hospital Doctors – The European Working Time Directive', May 2004, British Medical Association.

Medical Workforce Planning Model

Hospitals are professional service organisations that rely on teams of highly trained doctors and nurses to deliver patient care. To achieve high standards of care it is important for hospitals to maintain the right balance of personnel. The medical workforce planning model represents the number of medical students, junior doctors and specialist doctors working in the National Health Service and examines how this balance will change over time under the provisions of the European Working Time Directive. As mentioned above, the Directive will reduce medical cover by the equivalent of 4300–9900 junior doctors (see footnote 2, source 1). The model examines how hospitals will adapt to this shortage through a combination of additional training and overseas recruitment.

Figure 9.6 shows the composition of the medical workforce in terms of specialist doctors, junior doctors, non-UK resident doctors and medical students. The dynamic hypothesis is that the Working Time Directive will alter the balance of medical professionals, which in turn will affect the service capacity of hospitals and patient care. The hypothesis was conceptualised directly in terms of stocks and flows of doctors (rather than causal loops) as this seemed a natural way to think about service capacity. In the top half of the figure is a commonly used stock and flow network known as an

Source 2: 'Medical schools delivering doctors of the future', Department of Health Report, March 2004.

Source 3: Review Body on Doctors and Dentists Remuneration, 33rd Report 2004.

Source 4: Trevor W. Lambert, Jean M. Davidson, Julie Evans and Michael J. Goldacre. Doctors' reasons for rejecting initial choices of specialties as long-term careers. *Medical Education*, 37(4): 312–318.

Source 5: S. Chesser, K. Bowman and H. Phillips (2002). The European Working Time Directive and the training of surgeons. *British Medical Journal Careers Focus*, 31(8): 69–70.

Source 6: 'The future healthcare workforce', Discussion paper 9. February 2002. BMA Health Policy and Economic Research Unit.

Source 7: 'An organisation with a memory', Report of an expert group on learning from adverse events in the NHS. 2000, Department of Health.

Source 8: C. Mann and H. Guly (1998). Is the emergency (999) service being misused? A retrospective analysis. *British Medical Journal*, 316: 437–438.

Source 9: Patients' Charter, Department of Health, revised 1996.

Source 10: C. White (1998). The loss of doctors can be stemmed. *British Medical Journal*, 316: 1851; C. White (2004). Why do doctors leave the profession? BMA Health and Economic Research Unit, April.

Source 11: Survey of SAS doctors and dentists report, Health policy and Economic Research Unit, July 2004.

Source 12: P. Burn, 'EUWTD, the European dimension'. Royal College of Physicians, Nov 2002.

experience chain (or ageing chain). Medical students are recruited into medical schools where they spend time in training to become junior doctors. They then undergo further specialist training to take lifetime appointments as specialist doctors (or consultants) before eventually retiring. Along the way, some junior doctors take non-hospital appointments as general practitioners and others leave the medical profession altogether. In equilibrium, the rate of medical student recruitment is exactly equal to the rate at which doctors of all types are leaving hospitals (the sum of the rates of non-hospital appointments, junior doctor attrition and specialist doctor retirement).

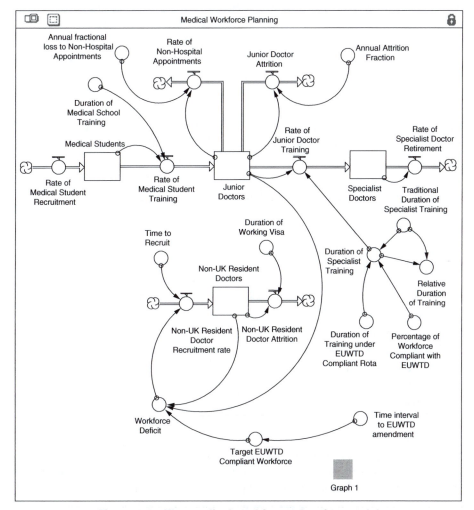

Figure 9.6   The medical workforce planning model

A characteristic of experience and ageing chains is that they are slow to achieve an equilibrium or appropriate balance among the different categories represented in the chain. If one were starting a hospital from scratch, with only a handful of newly graduated medical students, then it would take decades to build a cadre of specialist doctors and achieve the kind of consultant-led care typical of hospitals in developed nations. In the meantime, the hospital would run with a relatively inexperienced medical workforce. Similarly, if, through policy change, one were to alter the proportion of trained doctors needed at a point in the chain then it would take hospitals years to re-establish an appropriate balance of professionals. Such re-balancing is one important consequence of the EUWTD as it will require hospitals to employ a larger proportion of junior doctors in order to achieve the same medical cover as in the past. Incidentally, a similar slow process of category balance is observed in the urban dynamics model, which contains two linked ageing chains: one for housing and another for business. City growth is characterised by a high proportion of new buildings and enterprises. The transition from growth to equilibrium results in a larger proportion of old houses and declining businesses, with a consequent decline in the quality of urban life.

Consider now the factors determining the flow rates of doctors in Figure 9.6 and the composition of medical staff. We will start with medical students and trace the influences throughout the experience chain all the way to specialist doctors. We will also consider the balancing effect of non-UK resident doctors shown in the lower half of Figure 9.6.

The number of medical students recruited each year from secondary schools or as mature students is determined by the Department of Health. The inflow is treated as an exogenous variable, beyond the control of individual hospitals and independent of the EUWTD. Historically, medical school places in the UK increased by more than 50% in the seven-year period 1997–2004. This growth was achieved through expansion of existing medical departments and the building of entirely new medical schools. By 2004, the intake reached approximately 6000 medical students per year according to a report from the Department of Health (see footnote 2, source 2). At the time of the study, no further capacity expansion was planned and therefore the model was parameterised with a static recruitment rate of 6000 medical students per year, a number which applies across the model's 15-year time horizon.

It requires, on average, five years for a medical student to qualify as a doctor in the UK and take a junior post in a hospital. This delay is captured in the duration of medical school training that controls the outflow from the level of medical students. A typical depletion formulation is used in which the rate of medical school training is the ratio of medical students to the duration of training. The flow of trained students then accumulates in the pool of junior doctors. From this pool, a significant annual percentage will choose a career path in general practice or primary health care, away from hospital medicine.

Others will leave the medical profession. The proportion lost to general practice (shown in Figure 9.6 as the annual fractional loss to non-hospital appointments) is currently 2% per year (see footnote 2, source 3). Those who quit medicine are represented by the junior doctor attrition rate, which is estimated in the medical literature to be 1.2% annually. The outflows are simple depletion formulations, proportional to the number of junior doctors, where the proportionality depends on the annual percentages quoted above (see footnote 2, source 4). Note that we assume the attrition rate is unaffected by working environment changes, an assumption broadly consistent with the thinking behind the Working Time Directive. This assumption is relaxed in the stage two model, where the attrition rate depends also on junior doctors' morale.

Doctors' postgraduate training in recent years has undergone a process of formalisation. Prior to the introduction of the EUWTD, it had taken an average of nine years for a junior doctor to achieve consultant status. The Directive is set to increase this period for reasons that are now explained and are represented by the influences on the duration of specialist training in Figure 9.6. Although most postgraduate education takes place through autonomous learning at work, formal clinical in-service training (for instance in surgical specialities) and seminars can only occur under direct senior supervision during normal working hours. Hence, any reduction in the number of working hours or increase in the number of shifts worked outside of normal working hours will have the effect of extending the time required to train. The duration of specialist training is formulated as a weighted average of the traditional duration of training (nine years) and the duration of training under the EUWTD (11.45 years), where the weighting is defined by the percentage of workforce compliant (which gradually increases from an initial value of 57% to 100% over two years). The extra 2.45 years of training is a result of an estimated 79% reduction in the number of daytime hours worked under a full shift system assuming a 48-hour working week (see footnote 2, source 5).

The final influence on the composition of the medical workforce comes from non-UK resident doctors. The high quality of training and service offering within the National Health Service has consistently attracted overseas doctors wishing to undertake sabbatical periods of work and for some to train towards attaining permanent residency in the United Kingdom. More recently, with the relaxation of workforce transfer among European Union member states and an inherent delay in satisfying any required expansion of the health care workforce with domestically trained doctors, increasing numbers of overseas doctors are being recruited to make up the shortfall. Effectively, they are a source of spare medical 'capacity'. The rate of non-UK resident doctor recruitment is influenced by the workforce deficit and the time to recruit (an example of a standard stock adjustment formulation). The workforce deficit is the difference between the target workforce and current aggregate workforce consisting of UK trained junior doctors and non-UK doctors. The target workforce grows as more hospitals become compliant with the Working Time Directive. The time to recruit is assumed to be six months (0.5 years) from the time of advertising the post to successful candidates passing the prerequisite admittance exams for starting work in a UK hospital. Once recruited, overseas doctors are assumed to take a temporary post of four years (limited by the length of a UK working visa) and do not undertake specialist training during their period of employment. Hence, the attrition rate is formulated as the ratio of non-UK resident doctors to the duration of a working visa.

Specialist doctors (consultants) are replenished by the rate of junior doctors training and diminished by senior consultants retiring. The rate at which senior consultants retire depends on the average tenure of consultants, which is assumed to be 32 years. Although concerns have been raised about consultants choosing to retire early, the number of them that have decided to do so is currently insignificant and so is not included in the model.[3]

Quality of Patient Care

There are many factors that may influence the quality of patient care. The two most pertinent to current medical practice, and presumed to be under the influence of the EUWTD, are clinical error rate and patient–doctor ratio or work schedule pressure. Both are shown in Figure 9.7.

---

[3]The role of consultants in this particular hospital model is rather passive. They simply accumulate at the end of the medical personnel chain and spend their time in the stock of specialist doctors until they retire, without any particular effect on the delivery of patient care. Clearly, in real life, consultants play a vital role in service delivery and junior doctor training that the model overlooks. This simplification might be justified on the grounds that the model's dynamic hypothesis focuses on the changing work patterns and number of junior hospital doctors as a consequence of EUWTD and that the number of consultants and their activities is relatively stable under EUWTD and therefore not dynamically significant. However, this hidden assumption could (and perhaps should) be tested, particularly in the way it affects junior doctor training. The present formulation assumes that the duration of specialist training will increase because junior doctors' working hours decrease and so there are fewer opportunities in a typical working week for them to interact with consultants. However, it is common in models of service organisations also to represent the feedback effects from the number of senior/experienced personnel on the rate at which on-the-job training can be delivered. The lower the proportion of senior/experienced personnel in an organisation the more thinly their time is spread and the less on-the-job training takes place. An example, as it applies to hospitals, is presented in Winch and Derrick (2006) and readers are invited to modify the hospital model in the learning support folder for Chapter 9 to include the supervision of junior doctors by consultants and the feedback effects on flow-through of doctors (and possibly patient care). Sample formulations of on-the-job training in a service organisation can be found in the staff sector of the airline model in the learning support folder for Chapter 6 – but these formulations will need to be modified for a hospital.

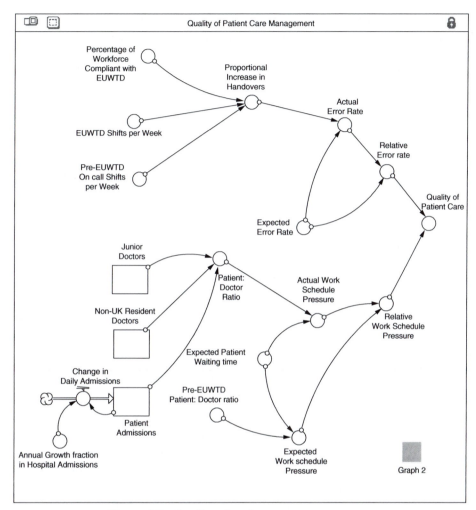

Figure 9.7   Quality of patient care management

Clinical errors often stem from confusion about a patient's condition. This causal effect is represented in the top half of Figure 9.7. Dissemination of patient information among clinical professionals is vital to the continuation of the highest level of medical care and assurance that an individual patient's clinical progress is followed. The medical handover is the keystone of this process and an important part of continuous professional learning. Doctors who have finished a shift provide detailed verbal and written communication to the next shift of doctors about their patients' clinical status and progress. Under the EUWTD, the number of shifts per week will need to increase, as will the number of handovers between shifts. As the pressure of time keeping increases, in order to stay compliant with the maximum duration of a shift, handovers are likely to become hurried and less detailed in content (see footnote 2, source 6). Therefore, we hypothesise that the change in the handover process under the EUWTD will cause the actual error rate (benchmarked against the expected error rate prior to the introduction of the EUWTD) to increase in proportion to the relative increase in the number of handovers (see footnote 2, source 7).

The other determinant of the quality of patient care is the patient–doctor ratio shown in the bottom half of Figure 9.7. The patient–doctor ratio is used to calculate a work schedule pressure, which acts as a crude measure of organisational stress. The work schedule pressure represents the amount of work expected by each doctor and is calculated by the ratio of the number of acutely admitted patients per year (growing by 8.9% annually; see footnote 2, source 8) to the sum of junior and non-UK trainee doctors per year, and multiplied by the expected maximum patient waiting time, which, according to the Department of Health's Patients' Charter, is three hours (see footnote 2, source 9).

The effect of the error rate and patient load on the quality of patient care is calculated by deriving equally weighted, normalised ratios for current to expected work schedule pressure and the relative error rate.

Base Run – Changing Composition of the Medical Workforce

Figure 9.8 is the base run of the medical workforce planning model and shows the changing composition of the medical workforce during and after the implementation of the European Working Time Directive. The simulation runs for 15 years, which represents the average time for a doctor to be trained from medical student to clinical specialist. The gradual ramping up of medical students (line 2) reflects the throughput effect of planned capacity expansion of medical schools by the Department of Health over the previous seven years. By year 7.5, the total number of medical students levels off at 30 000 (a maximum of 6000 students per year in each of the five years at medical school).

The effect of the increase in medical student recruitment is reflected in the gradual rise in numbers of junior doctors (line 1), as the inflow of newly graduated junior doctors is greater than the combined outflow of junior doctors leaving the profession, becoming general practitioners or specialists. In addition, the prolongation of junior doctors' postgraduate training under the EUWTD contributes to the rise in the number of junior doctors.

Specialist doctors remain in post longer than other medical personnel in training (medical students and junior doctors), on average 32 years before retirement. The number of specialists swells over time as the rate of junior doctors completing their training is greater than the specialist retirement rate.

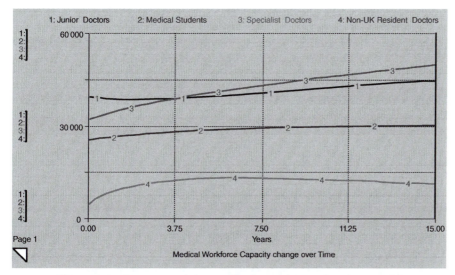

Figure 9.8   Base run of the medical workforce planning model

During the simulation the perceived workforce deficit is smoothed over the five years running up to the EUWTD amendment, which was due to take effect in 2009, in order to emulate the prospective behaviour of workforce planners in preparing for the expected shortfall in the medical workforce. As a consequence, the number of non-UK resident doctors (Figure 9.8, line 4) increases over the first five years and then gradually declines as UK trained junior doctors begin to make up an increasing proportion of the workforce. Therefore, the non-UK resident doctors act as a sort of 'swing' workforce provider, because of their short time to recruitment and limited duration of service. Note that the EUWTD amendment referred to above reduces working hours from an interim target of 58 hours per week to the final target of 48 hours per week.

In summary, the simulation shows a gradual adjustment in the composition of the UK medical workforce in response to changes in junior doctors' work patterns. There is a temporary rise in overseas doctors that gradually subsides as more UK-trained junior doctors become available through the training pipeline of medical schools. The number of specialist doctors rises steadily over the entire 15-year horizon, reflecting both the increased supply of junior doctors and an initial shortage of specialists in the National Health Service.

Base Run – Quality of Patient Care

The two determinants of the quality of patient care affected by the introduction of the EUWTD are the relative clinical error rate and relative work schedule pressure. In Figure 9.9, the quality of patient care (line 3) steadily declines to approximately half its initial value over the 15 years of the simulation under the influence of the EUWTD. Much of the early decline in quality of patient care is due to a rise in the relative error rate (line 2). The trajectory matches the shape of EUWTD compliance, reflecting a gradual transfer of junior doctors to full-shift working and more frequent handovers that cause errors.

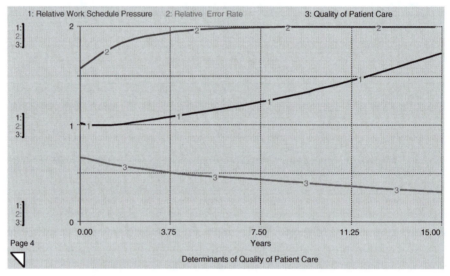

Figure 9.9   Quality of patient care in the base run

The continuing decline in quality of patient care is due to growth in relative work schedule pressure (line 1). The total number of non-specialist doctors does not keep pace with the assumed 8.9% annual growth in the number of patient admissions. An imbalance arises because recruitment of non-UK resident doctors is aimed at maintaining 24-hour doctor cover in hospital, rather than maintaining a fixed and effective patient–doctor ratio. This lack of coordination between medical staff and patients may seem surprising when viewed from the reader's detached perspective outside the National Health Service. Ambiguity in the patient–doctor ratio, however, is entirely plausible at the sharp end of hospital practice due to the inertia of the experience chain and the added complexity of staff administration caused by the Working Time Directive itself. Bear in mind that the total number of hospital doctors grows substantially during the simulation, from almost 75 000 to 104 000 – a rise of nearly 40%. Against this backdrop of staff growth, a decline in quality of patient care will, in practice, appear anomalous.

Intangible Effects of the European Working Time Directive

The base case model assumes that the effects of the working time directive on hospitals are fully captured in the time budget of junior doctors. If each junior doctor works fewer hours a week then there will need to be more of them to provide the same level of cover. This balancing act may be dynamically complex but essentially if the time budget is restored then quality of patient care will not be diminished, except for the increase in clinical errors due to more frequent medical handovers. What if new work patterns also have indirect effects on the morale of junior doctors due to changes in their work–life balance, duration of training and other working conditions? Dr Ratnarajah was in no doubt that these intangible effects existed and was curious to investigate their potential impact. The quest to represent and test intangibles led to a second stage of modelling that retained all the structure and relationships of the base case model and added the new concept of doctors' morale and the various influences on it.

Modelling Junior Doctor Morale

In the extended model, morale is an integral part of junior doctors' decision-making process to either stay or leave medical training, and is influenced by changes in junior doctors' working conditions (in the base case junior doctors were considered resilient to any working environment change). The level of morale has a direct impact on the rate of junior doctor attrition: the lower the morale, the higher the rate of junior doctor attrition. The equation formulation is simply a variant of standard stock depletion in which the attrition rate depends on the product of junior doctors and the annual attrition fraction, multiplied by the inverse of morale.

> Junior Doctor Attrition = Junior Doctors * Annual Attrition Fraction *
> (1/Morale)

Here morale is conceived as a dimensionless index that runs on a scale from zero to one (though strictly speaking the minimum value is slightly greater than zero). Morale is initialised at a value of one which is taken to be the normal state of morale prevailing in the pre-EUWTD era. A change in morale is represented as an asset stock adjustment process brought about through a difference in indicated morale and the previous level of morale, as shown in Figure 9.10. Indicated morale is an equally weighted multiple of the key factors, as reported within the profession itself, that contribute to junior doctors' morale. The factors include the quality of patient care, relative duration of junior doctor training, relative work–life balance, flexibility of the rota and aggregate pay discrepancy (see footnote 2, source 10).

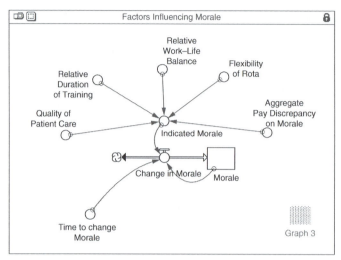

Morale(t) = Morale(t - dt) + (Change in Morale) * dt
INIT Morale = 1
Change in Morale = (Indicated Morale - Morale)/Time to change Morale
Indicated Morale = Aggregate Pay discrepancy on Morale * Flexibility of Rota * Quality of Patient Care * Relative Work–Life Balance * Relative Duration of Training
Time to change Morale = 1 {year}

Figure 9.10 Factors influencing the change in morale of junior doctors

Each of these morale factors is defined as a dimensionless index with a normal value of one. So, for example, the relative duration of training is equal to the ratio of the duration of specialist training (under EUWTD) to the traditional duration of specialist training (pre-EUWTD). The factors are combined in a multiplicative formulation as shown in the equations at the bottom of Figure 9.10. The reason for multiplying the determinants of indicated morale, rather than applying an additive formulation, is that each determinant has a spill-over effect on the other determinants of morale and, therefore, should not be considered as independent effects. The change in morale is represented as a bi-flow because morale can go up as well as down, depending on the prevailing conditions. The timescale for junior doctors' morale to change is estimated to be approximately one year.

Such multiplicative formulations, involving dimensionless indices normalised at one, are common whenever there is a need to combine the effects on a flow rate of two or more co-dependent variables. A similar formulation is used in the urban dynamics model to combine the five components of city attractiveness that control the arrival of underemployed population into an urban area. Multiplication of normalised indices can result in a surprisingly low resultant value if several determinants in the expression fall below their normal value of one. For example, if each determinant of morale takes a value of 0.8 (20% below normal) then indicated morale, which in this case would be equal to the fifth power of 0.8, falls to only 0.328 (two-thirds or almost 70% below normal).

Overview of the Complete Model

The complete model represents the workplace pressures behind junior doctor morale and adds several new feedback loops in the representation of medical workforce dynamics. The resulting sector map is shown in Figure 9.11. On the left is medical workforce planning and on the right is quality of patient care management – the two sectors already described. In addition, there are new sectors for work–life balance, doctors' remuneration and factors influencing morale. The light shaded region shows how the boundary of the model has been expanded. The new module neatly overlays the base case model and allows us to examine the incremental impact of morale and junior doctor attrition on the implementation of the working time directive.

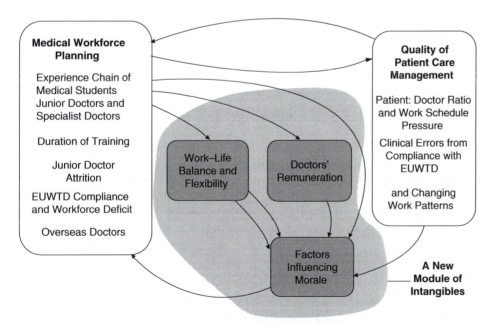

Figure 9.11 Sector map of the complete medical workforce dynamics and patient care model

The Formulation of Work–Life Balance and Flexibility

Results from a longitudinal cohort study of doctors who graduated from UK medical schools, carried out by the British Medical Association, suggest that the current generation of junior doctors view their commitment to the NHS very differently to that of their predecessors. While prepared to fulfil a reasonable contract, the current crop of young doctors also demands time for self-fulfilment and family life. For those doctors who choose to leave the NHS (15–20% of domestically trained doctors will not be working for the NHS a few years after graduation), the majority cite issues with work–life balance, risk of litigation, flexibility, remuneration, quality of training and workload as their reasons for resigning. Therefore, despite the fact that the implementation of the EUWTD has reduced absolute numbers of hours worked per week, there may be unforeseen consequences that are unacceptable to the current generation of junior doctors and that may yet manifest as changes in the junior doctors' attrition rate and quality of health service provision.

Work–life balance in the model is a measure of the number of social hours available after each shift. Under EUWTD, shift work eats into social activity. The main assumption is that post-shift-work recovery time is often incompatible with social activity. These ideas are represented in the concepts linking average shifts per week to relative work–life balance in Figure 9.12. A typical pre-EUWTD 1:6 rota (one shift worked every six days) allows 8 social hours per shift whereas an EU-compliant rota of three or more shifts per week allows 6 or less social hours per shift. Relative work–life balance is formulated as the ratio of social hours available under EUWTD to social hours available pre-EUWTD.

Flexibility of shift work is also of concern to junior doctors. More flexibility is better. The pre-EUWTD rota allowed for 24-hour shifts to be swapped among co-workers on the same rota with relative ease, because of the discrete nature of the working pattern and the relatively long working week. By introducing a full-shift system, under the Working Time Directive, the process of swapping shifts becomes more complex. There are additional restrictions from adhering to the minimum rest requirement between shifts and through having to work a pattern of serial night/day shifts (for many doctors the introduction of a EUWTD-compliant rota will result in having designated periods of annual leave). In the model, the measure of flexibility (shown as flexibility of rota in the lower-right of Figure 9.12) is formulated as the ratio of the average number of shifts worked per week under EUWTD to the number of shifts worked pre-EUWTD.

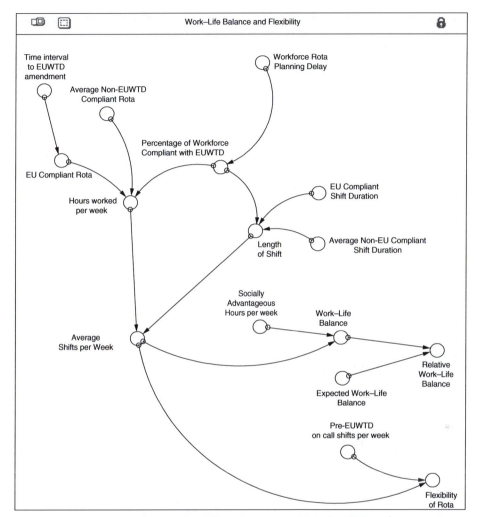

Figure 9.12 Work–life balance and rota flexibility

Simulations of the Complete Model

As in the base case, simulations were run over a time horizon of 15 years. It should be remembered that the simulator is not intended to be an accurate forecast of the future, but merely to provide a recognisable and compelling story for the possible outcomes of various policy decisions and assumptions within an internally consistent framework. This caveat is particularly relevant to the interpretation of junior doctor morale with which we begin.

Figure 9.13 shows an exponential decline in morale from a value of one to only 0.1 over the first five years of the simulation. Contributing to this precipitous fall are increases in both the relative duration of training and relative error rate, together with declines in the quality of patient care, work–life balance and rota flexibility. Junior doctors come under increasing pressure as the five determinants of indicated morale take their toll. Intuitively the exponential decline in morale fits with the notion that its determinants have a combined effect much stronger than each individual effect in isolation. Of course, we are only seeing the implications of our assumptions, which may be overstated or incomplete. Nevertheless, the simulation gives pause for thought and challenges us to explain why apparently reasonable descriptions of junior doctors' working conditions, supported by evidence from the medical profession's own journals, produce such a detrimental effect. The extreme outcome is not implausible. When one considers that historically individual doctors have had little direct influence in effecting change in their working conditions, one can surmise that an inability to respond to onerous working conditions would contribute to a pattern of sustained decline in morale.

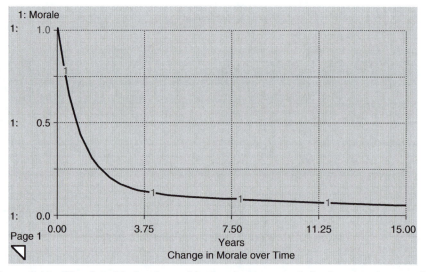

Figure 9.13   Simulated behaviour of junior doctor morale in the complete model

Anecdotally, a recent medical workforce questionnaire has shown a sustained decrease in the levels of job satisfaction after graduation. Over half of the 2500 doctors surveyed in a recent British Medical Association study reported that morale had declined over the past five years (see footnote 2, source 11).

If we accept the simulated behaviour of junior doctor morale then what are the knock-on consequences for hospitals? Simulations of the complete model allow us to explore this scenario. First, though, consider what you think would happen to the number and composition of hospital doctors and the quality of patient care if morale were to plummet. The base runs in Figures 9.8 and 9.9

are useful benchmarks for this preliminary thought experiment. Relative to the base case we now make just one additional assumption – that low morale accelerates junior doctor attrition. The ramifications are far reaching.

Figure 9.14 shows the number of junior doctors (line 1) is significantly eroded by the increasing attrition rate from low morale. At the start of the simulation there are about 40,000 junior doctors and by the end there are only 20,000 – a 50% reduction over 15 years. Some reduction is to be expected under the circumstances. What is more surprising is the resilience of hospitals in the face of this mass exodus of talent – at least in the short run. The number of non-UK resident doctors (line 4) increases over the first five years to make up for the shortfall in the numbers of junior doctors and the target workforce. By year 4 of the simulation, the number of non-UK resident doctors exceeds the number of UK trained junior doctors – despite the fact that the number of UK medical students (line 2) follows exactly the same trajectory as in the base run.

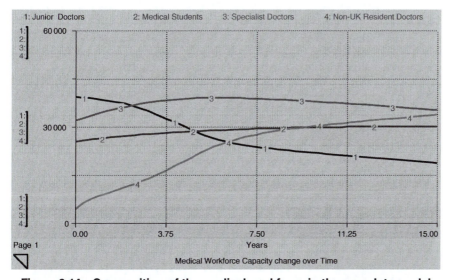

Figure 9.14   Composition of the medical workforce in the complete model

The shifting composition of junior doctors has serious long-run consequences for the supply of specialist doctors. Initially, the stock of specialist doctors (line 3) rises because the inflow of trained junior doctors is greater than the outflow of specialist doctors retiring. However, as the number of junior doctors undertaking specialist training declines, due to the increasing attrition rate, the rate at which specialist doctors retire eventually exceeds the rate of junior doctor training and so by year 8 the population of specialist doctors also begins to decline. The rate of junior doctor attrition is gradually stemmed by year 5 through a more gradual decline in morale. The change is due to the slight increases in flexibility and work–life balance brought about by the reduction in the number of hours and reduced frequency of shifts worked per week under the amended EUWTD.

The quality of patient care is shown in the top half of Figure 9.15. For comparison, the equivalent chart from the base run is shown in the bottom half of the figure. In both charts, quality of care (line 1) declines throughout the simulation due to a rise in both the clinical error rate and work schedule pressure. Again the total number of non-specialist doctors does not keep pace with the assumed 8.9% annual growth in patient admissions, as shown by the rising patient–doctor ratio (line 2), which ends up slightly higher in the complete model than in the base run.

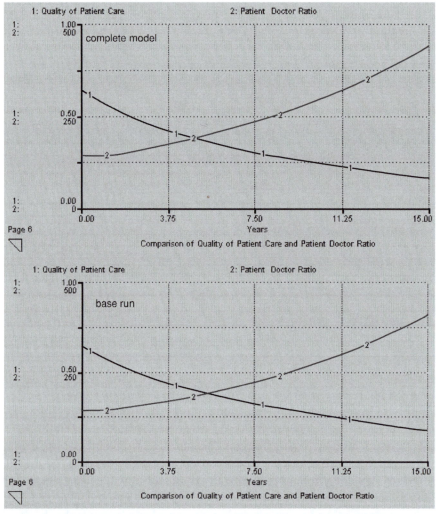

Figure 9.15   Quality of patient care and patient–doctor ratio. A comparison of the complete model (top chart) with the base run (bottom chart)

Conclusions from the Medical Workforce Study

The purpose of the modelling project was to examine the effects of the European Working Time Directive on junior doctors' career decisions and the consequences of these decisions on the medical workforce and quality of patient care. The use of system dynamics provided a framework within which to consider these possibilities and a useful tool to explore alternative courses of action.

The results of the base run demonstrate that the target medical workforce (required to fulfil 24 hours' continuous hospital cover, compliant with the EUWTD) can be achieved under current UK recruitment practices and that the non-UK resident doctors serve to temporarily fill any workforce deficit. This outcome implicitly assumes that UK trained junior doctors are resilient to changes in their work environment in the sense that the fraction who eventually quit the medical profession remains constant. Hence, any increase in medical student intake or in the target workforce numbers serves to increase the long-term numbers of UK trained junior doctors.

Given that the planned capacity expansion of UK medical school intake has already been achieved, the patient–doctor ratio will continue to rise as the numbers of acute patient admissions grow year on year while the size of the medical workforce remains static. The consequences are likely to be higher demands placed on the existing medical workforce and a continual erosion in the quality of patient care as the service pressure mounts on already over-stretched hospital staff.

This issue of work schedule pressure can only really be addressed by further workforce expansion in line with increases in patient admissions or improvements in the efficiency of in-patient management. For instance, focusing resources on primary care, to manage non-urgent cases in the community, would reduce the burden on accident and emergency departments. In addition, re-assigning routine clinical and administrative tasks to suitably trained health care professionals would free junior doctors to treat more patients and undertake more appropriate tasks relative to their level of training.

When the level of junior doctors' morale is factored into the complete model, the simulation demonstrates a precipitous decline in the numbers of UK trained junior doctors brought about by an increasing attrition rate. The fall in morale is caused by the decline in the quality of patient care, work–life balance, rota flexibility and an increase in the duration of specialist training. Interestingly, the perception of remuneration in the form of the aggregate pay discrepancy has little effect on junior doctors' attrition rate, as relative pay remains almost constant over time. This outcome reinforces the notion that pay plays a less important role in junior doctors' career decision-making processes than other work and lifestyle-related factors.

As a consequence of low morale, there is an increase in junior doctor attrition and a progressive loss of junior doctors in exchange for non-UK resident doctors, who not only make up the shortfall in the target workforce numbers but also constitute an increasing majority of the overall junior doctor workforce. The fall in the number of UK trained junior doctors is contrary to the base run and to policymakers' optimistic expectations about the effects of the EUWTD.

There remains a question mark over what the service impact will be of having fewer UK trained doctors. In the model, no value judgement has been made about the relative competence of non-UK trained versus UK trained junior doctors. Nevertheless, unless more non-UK trained doctors are recruited as specialist trainees (rather than only for service provision) or the loss of UK trained junior doctors is stemmed, there will be a long-term reduction in consultant specialists and the ability of the NHS to deliver a consultant-led service.

Sensitivity analyses on the complete model suggest an inevitable decline in junior doctor numbers irrespective of policy changes in the level of recruitment of medical students or delays in implementation of the EUWTD amendment. This result suggests that quantitative policy changes alone are insufficient to ensure a sustainable workforce. Without consideration of the qualitative effects of the EUWTD on junior doctors' morale, it would appear that the introduction of the EUWTD is unlikely to result in a successful outcome.

Ultimately, time will tell as to what the effects of the EUWTD will be on junior doctor attrition and the medical workforce. However, there are a number of areas highlighted by the simulator that are worth pursuing further. First, more accurate data about the relative weight or importance of the determinants of morale would build more confidence in the model's intangible sectors and provide a cross-check to attitudes held by junior doctors in the NHS. Second, there needs to be active collaboration between policymakers and the medical workforce to address important lifestyle and training issues affected by the EUWTD. Third, other European member states that have already been operating under the EUWTD would be a valuable source of information and experience. The implementation of EUWTD policy in the UK may benefit from sharing best practices and areas of concern with other EU countries. In particular, Denmark and the Netherlands have fully implemented the EUWTD and, for the most part, within their current workforce capacity (see footnote 2, source 12). Despite the demographics and population distribution of these countries being different to the UK, it may be useful to identify the critical success factors in managing the medical workforce to effectively implement policy.

Finally, in an attempt to minimise the impact of the EUWTD on extended specialist training, alternatives need to be actively pursued to allow for the most effective training while working under a full-shift system. One possible solution, which has been considered by the Royal Colleges, is the introduction of hospital resident consultants, who could streamline in-patient management and be available for teaching throughout the shift. In addition, the patient–doctor ratio for acute admissions would be reduced if consultants are considered to be directly involved in managing acute patients rather than consulting from home.

Fishery Dynamics and Regulatory Policy

To conclude this review of public sector applications we return to the topic of fisheries from Chapter 1. The dynamics of fisheries are reflected in collapsing fish stocks, idle fishing fleets and impoverished fishing communities. The economic and social costs of these dynamics are enormous. It has been estimated that on a global scale, the loss of economic rents (profits) due to mismanagement of fisheries may easily amount to 50% or more of the global landed value of the fish catch of some 100 billion US dollars annually.[4] If present trends continue then the industry's future is bleak. A report by a team of scientists and economists estimates that by the year 2048, fish stocks in all the world's main fishing regions will be close to extinction (Worm *et al.*, 2006). Already one-third of fisheries have biologically collapsed and stocks could take decades to recover, even with a complete moratorium on fishing. It is a sobering thought that in less than 50 years there may be no commercial sea-fishing industry and no wild fish to eat on the table. The paradox of the fishing industry is that fishermen do not appear to act in their own best interests. They overexploit a renewable resource to the point of destruction, yet their livelihoods depend on a sustainable catch. It need not be that way.

Fisheries Management

Fisheries management is fundamentally a control and regulation problem, ensuring that collective fishing effort is well-balanced with available fish

---

[4]When, in the mid-2000s, global landings from ocean fisheries were about 84 million metric tonnes per year, the average landed value of fish was close to 1.20 US dollars per kg, giving an annual landed value of the entire global catch equal to 100.8 billion US dollars. Various empirical studies of fisheries around the world typically suggest loss of potential profits of some 50% of the value of landings.

stocks and fish regeneration. Without any regulation fisheries tend towards bloated fishing fleets, excess effort, fish stocks that are too small, low profitability and low personal incomes. At worst, fisheries collapse entirely. But why? An information feedback view suggests that fishermen do not receive a clear feedback signal from the fishery to tell them when to stop investing in ships and gear.[5] This signal should be strong and credible at the point in time when collective effort (and therefore the catch) is approaching the highest regeneration rate the fishery can support (the so-called maximum sustainable yield). Regulatory policy should therefore be aimed at generating a 'correct' feedback signal to curtail overinvestment and to ensure, with appropriate sanctions, that fishermen take notice and restrict the catch size.

In the following sections, we augment the simple fisheries model from Chapter 1 to illustrate the origins of the fisheries management problem and the feedback principles that lie behind effective regulation. The analysis involves a sequence of models that illustrate the challenges in coordinating fish stocks with the fleet size (and fishing effort). We begin with a simple model of fish population dynamics for a single species and demonstrate that sustainable catch increases with fleet size until a critical tipping point is reached. We then add a behavioural model of investment in ships to show the tendency towards overexploitation in unregulated fisheries. Finally, we add a new module to represent the monitoring, control and surveillance of fish stocks as the basis for regulation.

Economists have also studied the overexploitation of fisheries. They explain the paradox of bloated fishing fleets in terms of the 'common property problem' (Arnason, 2005, 2007; Hardin, 1968; Ostrom, Poteete and Janssen, 2010; Ostrom, 2009). Ocean fish stocks have traditionally been arranged as common property resources, meaning that anyone with nets and a boat is able to harvest the resources. Under this arrangement it can be shown there are financial incentives to expand the fishing fleet (and effort) until costs equal revenues. At this special equilibrium point there are no profits left in the industry and the fish stock is depleted well below the biological optimum (and often dangerously close to collapse). Although this economic analysis does not investigate the dynamics of fish population and fleet expansion (focusing instead on feasible equilibria), it nevertheless sheds light on the decision

---

[5]The relationship between managerial investment decision making and firm performance is examined in Kunc and Morecroft (2010) based on classroom experiments with the popular fisheries gaming simulator Fish Banks (Meadows, Fiddaman and Shannon, 2001) that was mentioned in Chapter 1. Teams of MBA students were asked to manage the growth of rival fishing firms as profitably as possible. Collectively the rival teams (and their simulated firms) overinvest in ships and collapse the fishery. Moreover the paper shows there are significant differences in teams' investment decisions and resulting firm performance that are relevant to fisheries management and to resource-based theory of competitive strategy.

making of fishermen that leads them, collectively, to excess fishing effort. Regulatory policy is then seen as the design of fishing restrictions, quotas, property rights or taxes to inhibit investment and limit the catch. With appropriate incentives and sanctions an ideal equilibrium is envisaged in which the catch is sustainable and fishery profit is maximised.

Improving the management of fisheries is a big task but it can yield huge social and economic benefits. Ragnar Arnason (2007), an economist from the University of Iceland and expert in fisheries management, notes that:

> While mismanagement characterises the global fishery as a whole, it is important to realise that there are fisheries, sometimes quite sizeable fisheries, that do not adhere to this general pattern and are both biologically sustainable and highly profitable. These fisheries, which comprise such diverse marine conditions as those of New Zealand, Falkland Islands and Iceland, are in no way different from the other fisheries which exhibit declining stocks and negative profits. The only thing they have in common is good management. Generally, this management is based on high quality and well enforced property rights.

Here we take a similar view that good fisheries management is vital to their long-term success, but we approach the topic dynamically from an information feedback perspective (Moxnes, 1998).

A Simple Harvested Fishery – Balancing Catch and Fish Regeneration

Cast your mind back to the very first simulator in the book. There we examined the dynamics of a simple natural fishery, free from human intervention – just fish in the sea with no fishermen or ships. The result, over a period of 40 years, was smooth S-shaped growth, as shown in Figure 9.16.

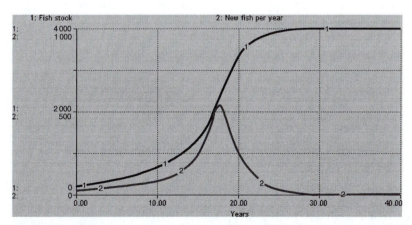

Figure 9.16   Simulation of a natural fishery with an initial population of 200 fish and maximum fishery size of 4000

A small initial population of 200 fish (scaled for numerical convenience) grows exponentially for 18 years. Then, over the next decade, as the fish stock approaches its maximum sustainable value of 4000, growth is halted and the fishery settles into a long-term equilibrium.

Now imagine a harvested fishery. Ships arrive in the previously pristine sea and cast their nets. The total catch depends both on the number of ships and their productivity (how many fish each ship catches in a typical trip). Common sense suggests that if you add a few more ships to a small fleet then the catch will increase. Equally, there must come a time when there are too many ships competing for a limited number of fish. We can use simulation to investigate the relationship between catch and fish population as fleet size varies.

A simple model of a harvested fishery is shown in Figure 9.17 involving a fish stock, an inflow of new fish per year and a harvest rate. The corresponding equations appear below the diagram. Net regeneration is a non-linear function of fish density as indicated by the graph. The fish stock is depleted by a harvest rate, equal to the catch and proportional to the number of ships at sea.

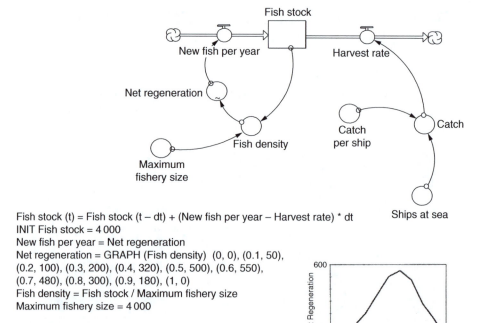

Fish stock (t) = Fish stock (t − dt) + (New fish per year − Harvest rate) * dt
INIT Fish stock = 4 000
New fish per year = Net regeneration
Net regeneration = GRAPH (Fish density) (0, 0), (0.1, 50), (0.2, 100), (0.3, 200), (0.4, 320), (0.5, 500), (0.6, 550), (0.7, 480), (0.8, 300), (0.9, 180), (1, 0)
Fish density = Fish stock / Maximum fishery size
Maximum fishery size = 4 000

Harvest rate = Catch {fish/year}
Catch = Ships at sea * Catch per ship {fish/year}
Catch per ship = 25 {fish per ship per year}

Figure 9.17   A simple harvested fishery

Consider a scenario spanning 40 years in which the fleet size starts at zero and then grows in stepwise bursts to reach a maximum of 30 ships. The productivity of these ships is identical. Bear in mind this is a scale model which can be calibrated to fit a realistic fishery without changing the pertinent dynamics. Each ship can catch 25 fish per year and for clarity we assume there is no stochastic variation in productivity. At the start there are 4000 fish. The fishery is full and the population is in equilibrium. Then, in year four, 10 ships sail into the pristine fishery and set about harvesting for the next 12 years. The simulated result is shown in Figure 9.18. The catch (line 3) rises from zero to 250 fish per year. As a result, the fish stock (line 1) begins to fall. Then something dynamically interesting happens. The fishery is less heavily populated, and, hence, fish regenerate faster (as defined by the non-linear regeneration graph). As the years pass the number of new fish added to the population each year approaches ever closer to the harvest rate (and the catch) and so, by the end of year 15, the fish stock (line 1) settles into a sustainable harvested equilibrium.

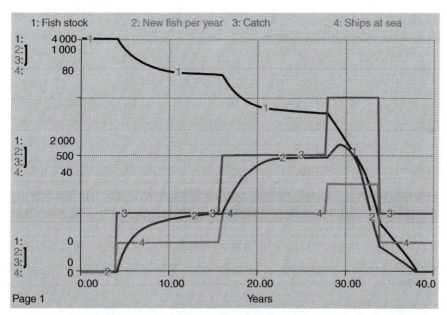

Figure 9.18   Simulation of a harvested fishery with stepwise changes in fleet size

This pattern of bountiful adjustment is repeated as 10 more ships are added in year 16. The catch (line 3) once again increases, this time reaching a value of 500 fish per year, just below the maximum sustainable yield. Gradually the regeneration rate rises to equal the catch bringing the fishery into a new and higher harvested equilibrium with a population of about 2700 fish. However, in year 28, when a further 10 ships are added to the fleet, the extra expansion pushes the catch beyond a tipping point that causes a rapid decline in the regeneration rate and the fish stock. The tipping point occurs at the peak of the non-linear relationship between net regeneration and fish density as depicted in Figure 9.17.[6] Before the peak, any reduction in fish density boosts regeneration. After the peak, however, any further reduction in fish density inhibits regeneration. The effect is clearly visible in the behaviour of new fish per year (line 2) which, shortly before year 30 and after more than two decades of growth, suddenly falls sharply to a value far below the catch (line 3). Even though the fishing fleet is later reduced to only 10 ships in year 34 (a fleet size that had previously yielded a sustainable catch), it is too late to reverse the fishery's decline and the fish stock collapses completely. Here in this dramatic switch of dynamic behaviour, from a robust sustainable catch to a fragile and declining catch, lies the key to the fisheries paradox.

A Harvested Fishery with Endogenous Investment – Coping with a Tipping Point

Investment in ships is a collective decision-making process (or policy) representing, in aggregate, the judgements of those people most closely involved (fishermen in this case) and the information sources on which their decisions are based. Such decision-making processes are behavioural in the sense that they capture the broad intention of investment without necessarily assuming decision makers have perfect information or perfect foresight. As we saw in Chapter 7 (the market growth model) typical investment policy has three main parts: a goal for the intended capacity, monitoring of current capacity, and corrective action to bring capacity in line with the goal. This process of 'asset stock adjustment' applies equally well to investment in fishing fleets.

Figure 9.19 shows the investment policy for fleet adjustment in the fisheries model. Notice that connections between variables are depicted as dotted lines denoting flows of information. The connections are not 'hardwired' as they were for the natural fishery. They are discretionary and reflect the information available and deemed most relevant to investment. The desired fleet size (the goal) depends on the number of ships at sea and the propensity for growth. Specifically the desired fleet size is equal to ships at sea multiplied by a growth factor denoted as (1+ propensity for growth). We assume that the normal propensity for growth is 0.1, so the desired fleet size is 10% larger than the current fleet size. In other words, fishermen normally and collectively want a bigger fleet than they now have, an attribute of human nature – bigger is

---

[6]A thorough explanation of tipping points and the dynamics of 'quantity-induced' crises is to be found in Rudolph and Repenning (2002).

better, growth is inherently attractive. This is an important behavioural assumption and recognises that fishermen lack the information (or even the inclination) to agree an optimal fleet size. They just want more and better ships. As we will see later the propensity for growth also depends on conditions in the fishery, a poor catch will dampen enthusiasm for a larger fleet, despite an underlying bias toward growth.

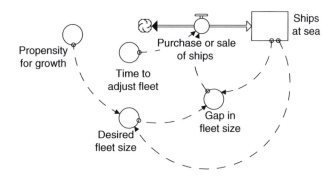

Ships at sea (t) = Ships at sea (t - dt) + (Purchase or sale of ships) * dt
INIT Ships at sea = 10 {ships}
Purchase or sale of ships = Gap in fleet size/Time to adjust fleet {ships/year}
Gap in fleet size = Desired fleet size – Ships at sea {ships}
Desired fleet size = Ships at sea * (1 + Propensity for growth) {ships}
Propensity for growth = …. See Figure 10.20 for this important formulation, for now just assume that normally the propensity for growth is positive and non-zero
Time to adjust fleet = 1 {year}

Figure 9.19   Fleet adjustment in a harvested fishery

The rest of the asset stock adjustment formulation is standard and straightforward, just like the formulations for inventory control and for employee hiring in Chapter 5. The gap in fleet size is the difference between the desired fleet size and ships at sea. If there is a large positive gap then conditions for investment are favourable. The purchase or sale of ships closes the gap over an assumed time span of one year, which is the time taken to adjust the fleet (including ordering, construction and delivery).

A crucial formulation in the model is the propensity for growth and the factors that determine it. As mentioned above, fishermen do not know the optimal fleet size and so they prefer, more simply and pragmatically, to grow the fleet until there is compelling evidence to stop. In a real fishery, the most persuasive information is catch per ship. Fishermen know this number from each fishing trip and it is vital to their livelihood. Significantly they do not know the fish population or the fish regeneration rate – because the fish are under water. Moreover, they do not believe scientific estimates of low fish stocks unless confirmed by the catch. Such practical considerations suggest that propensity for growth is curbed by low catch rather than by objective evidence of fish stocks. As a result, investment is boundedly rational, sensing only indirectly the true state of the fish population on which the long-term sustainability of the fishery depends.

Figure 9.20 shows one possible formulation that captures the essential limited information characteristic of fishermen's boundedly rational decision making. Propensity for growth depends on the normal propensity for growth multiplied by the curbing effect of catch per ship. This curbing effect is non-linear and captures another typical human tendency: to ignore bad news until it is really bad. If catch per ship falls from 25 fish per year to 15 per year (a 40% decline), propensity for growth falls from 0.1 to 0.09 (a decline of only 10%). Thereafter, the effect becomes much stronger. If the catch per ship falls to 10 fish per year (less than half the normal value) then propensity for growth falls to zero and fishermen stop purchasing ships. If the catch falls still further then the propensity for growth becomes negative and fishermen sell ships because collectively they sense it is futile to retain a large and unproductive fleet.

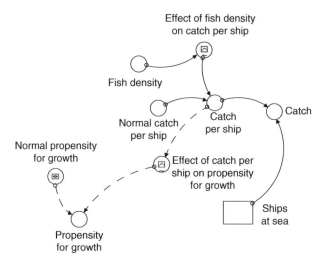

Catch = Ships at sea * Catch per ship {fish/year}
Catch per ship = Effect of fish density on catch per ship * Normal catch per ship {fish per ship/year}
Normal propensity for growth = 0.1 {fraction}
Propensity for growth = Normal propensity for growth * Effect of catch per ship on propensity for growth
Effect of catch per ship on propensity for growth = GRAPH (Catch per ship)
(0.00, -0.48), (2.50, -0.45), (5.00, -0.37), (7.50, -0.27), (10.0, 0.00), (12.5, 0.64), (15.0, 0.9),
(17.5, 0.995), (20.0, 0.995), (22.5, 1.00), (25.0, 1.00)
Effect of fish density on catch per ship = GRAPH (Fish density)
(0.00, 0.00), (0.1, 0.4), (0.2, 0.68), (0.3, 0.8), (0.4, 0.88), (0.5, 0.96), (0.6, 1.00), (0.7, 1.00),
(0.8, 1.00), (0.9, 1.00), (1, 1.00)

Figure 9.20   Formulation of propensity for growth and catch per ship

Catch per ship is essentially a measure of ships' productivity and is modelled here as a deterministic function of fish density. The scarcer the fish, the lower the productivity, but the relationship is non-linear. For moderate to high fish density (between 0.5 and 1) catch per ship remains close to normal. The assumption is that fishermen do not really notice a difference in the catch if the sea is teeming with fish or only half-teeming with fish, because fish tend to school or cluster. Catch per ship is still 68% of normal when the fish density is only 0.2, or in other words when the fish population is 20% of the maximum sustainable. Thereafter, however, catch per ship falls quickly to zero as schools of fish become increasingly difficult to find and are hotly contested by rival ships.

An overview of the model with endogenous investment is shown in Figure 9.21. In the top left quadrant is the natural fishery with its non-linear reinforcing loop depicting population dynamics. In the lower right quadrant is the fishing fleet. Investment is represented as a stock adjustment process in which a balancing loop adjusts the number of ships at sea and a reinforcing loop drives the desired fleet size. Fish biology and capital investment are linked through a dynamically complex non-linear feedback structure that involves the catch, harvest rate, fish stock, fish density, catch per ship and propensity for growth.

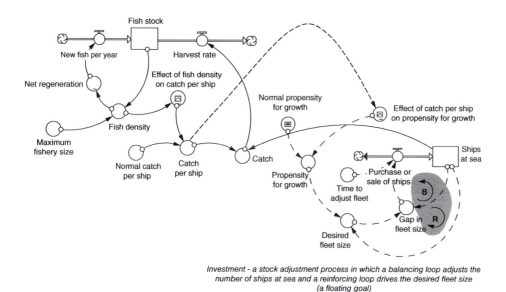

Investment - a stock adjustment process in which a balancing loop adjusts the number of ships at sea and a reinforcing loop drives the desired fleet size (a floating goal)

Figure 9.21   Overview of a simple fisheries model with endogenous investment

Simulated Dynamics of a Harvested Fishery with Endogenous Investment

The model is initialised in a sustainable equilibrium with 10 ships and 3370 fish, resulting in a catch of 250 fish per year and equivalent net regeneration of 250 fish per year. This harvest rate is below the maximum sustainable yield to allow room for growth and to investigate the dynamics of boundedly rational investment. In order to start the model in equilibrium, the normal propensity for growth is artificially held at zero during the early years of the simulation. It is as though a 'small-is-beautiful' mindset has temporarily taken hold of ship owners. Then, in year 10, propensity for growth returns to its normal value of 0.1, or 10% of the current fleet size. The results are shown in Figure 9.22. The reader can recreate this chart by running the model called 'Fish and Harvesting – Endogenous Investment' in the learning support folder for Chapter 9. Set to zero the slide bar representing the normal propensity for growth. Then press the 'Run' button to see the first five years of equilibrium. Press the 'Run' button again to extend the equilibrium to 10 years. Now reset the normal propensity for growth to its standard value of 0.1 by pressing the 'u' symbol in the lower left of the slide bar. Then run the simulation all the way to 40 years.

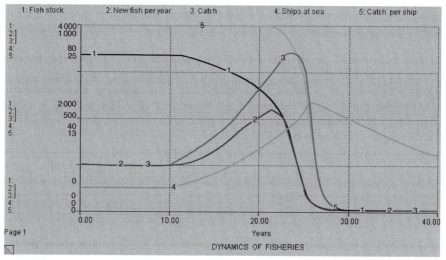

Figure 9.22   Simulation of a fishery that starts in equilibrium, grows with investment and then unexpectedly collapses

Starting in year 10 the number of ships at sea (line 4) increases steadily. For 14 years, the catch rises. Meanwhile, the catch per ship (line 5) remains steady, suggesting that continued investment is both feasible and desirable. Below the waves conditions are changing, but remember these conditions cannot be directly observed by fishermen. The regeneration rate of fish (new fish per year, line 2) rises, just as one would expect in a well-harvested fishery. The fish population falls, but that too is expected in a harvested fishery.

Signs of trouble appear underwater in year 21 when, for the first time, regeneration (new fish per year, line 2) falls. This reversal of replenishment is a signal that the fishery has passed the tipping point of the non-linear regeneration curve. The decline in the fish stock begins to accelerate.

Interestingly, however, the catch (line 3) continues to rise for fully three more years, until year 24, and the catch per ship (line 5) remains close to normal. From the viewpoint of growth-oriented fishermen floating on the waves it is business as usual. The fleet continues to grow until year 26 when it reaches a size of 46 ships. By then the catch per ship (line 5) has fallen to less than one-third of normal (only 8 fish per ship per year instead of 25), which is sufficiently low to curb further investment.

By now, the hidden fish stock (line 1) has fallen to only 300, less than one-tenth of its initial value. With so few fish in the sea, the regeneration rate is precariously low at only 30 new fish per year, well below the catch of around 300 fish per year. Fishermen are now well aware of the underwater crisis and respond accordingly by selling ships. The fleet size (ships at sea, line 4) falls from a peak of 47 ships in year 26 to 39 ships in year 30. But it is too little action too late. The boundedly rational investment policy fails to reduce the fleet quickly enough to halt the decline of the fish stock. By year 30 there are only four fish left in the sea and regeneration has fallen practically to zero. The fishery has collapsed and is left with a huge excess of relatively new ships owned by fishermen reluctant to sell and still dependent on the fishery for their livelihood. The feedback structure of an unregulated fishery leads to boom and bust in the catch.

Control and Regulation – Policy Design for Sustainable Fisheries

The purpose of regulatory policy is to persuade fishermen to reduce their fishing effort when the population of fish is deemed to be too low. But how? This question is explored in Figure 9.23, which shows the policy structure behind fishing effort. The fishing fleet is disaggregated to show both ships at sea and ships in harbour. A corresponding distinction is drawn between investment policy (whether to purchase ships) and deployment policy (whether to go fishing or to deliberately idle some ships in harbour). The concentric circles around these policies represent information filters, indicating that fishermen, as normal boundedly-rational decision makers, simplify complex (and often conflicting) information about the state of the fishery. Like everyone else, they act on the basis of evidence from their own experience, paying most attention to signals that suit their local interests. (For a reminder on information filters and bounded rationality, review Chapter 7.) We therefore continue to assume that investment decision making is myopic, driven by the normal propensity for growth and the catch per ship as described above. Even when there is scientific information available about the fishery (shown in the grey region), it is not easy to inject this evidence into commercial decision making. Incidentally, if you think this is an unreasonable assumption then consider the difficult task for climate scientists in convincing us to travel less, or to turn down our thermostats, if we are to halt global warming. Like fisheries, global warming is a problem of managing the commons. Like fishermen, we are reluctant to take scientific advice because the need to take immediate action is not compelling and the required changes in behaviour threaten our lifestyle.

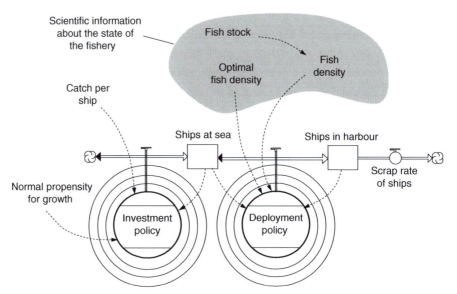

Figure 9.23   Policy design in fisheries

Regulation acts principally through deployment policy by requiring fishermen to reduce their fishing effort and/or to be selective in what they catch. In practice, there are a variety of different approaches to regulation. For example, there are biological restrictions such as mesh size regulations, total allowable catch, area closures and nursery ground protection. Alternatively, there are economic restrictions on days at sea, fishing time and transferable quotas. Here we will focus attention on economic restrictions. In Figure 9.23, deployment policy takes information, supplied to regulators by marine scientists, about fish density and optimal fish density. The regulators use this information to determine, on average, how many ships from the total fleet should be at sea and how many should be kept in harbour. This policy can be interpreted either as a limit on days at sea or a daily limit on fishing time.

Will fishermen, however, pay any attention to these restrictions and the scientific information on which they are based? There is no particular reason why they should unless violations are noticed and punished. Effective fisheries management requires credible surveillance of ships' activities and strict enforcement of the rules backed by a judicial system capable of issuing sanctions to violators (Arnason, 2005; Dudley, 2008). Only then will scientific information about the state of the fisheries penetrate the filters of behavioural decision making in Figure 9.23 and lead to a more appropriate deployment of ships. Under schemes such as limited fishing days and closed areas it is necessary to monitor the fishing vessels' actual days at sea and their location when out fishing. The labour and equipment needed for such surveillance at sea is very expensive. In fact, regulatory economists have estimated that the management costs of fisheries can be as much as 25% of the value of landings. In short, a great deal of administrative effort lies behind successful fisheries management to ensure that valid scientific information is brought to bear, both forcefully and fairly, on fishing activity.

Formulation of Deployment Policy

Figure 9.24 extends the previous model of a harvested fishery to include the deployment of ships. The original formulations for fish population, fish regeneration, ships at sea and investment policy are shown on the left of the diagram. The new formulations for deployment and for ships in harbour are shown on the right. Deployment policy is subdivided in two stages: there is a recommended fleet size (shown as the shaded region on top) and there is surveillance of ships and enforcement (the shaded region below).

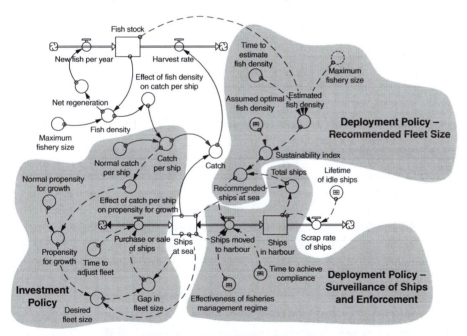

Figure 9.24   Overview of fisheries policy model

The equations for deployment policy are shown in Figure 9.25. The recommended fleet size is defined as the product of total ships and the sustainability index. The idea is to restrict the number of ships at sea if marine scientists think fish stocks are too low. Of course, nobody knows for sure the actual number of fish in the sea. There are only estimates of fish density.

Recommended Fleet Size
Recommended ships at sea = Total ships * Sustainability index {ships}
Sustainability index = GRAPH (Estimated fish density / Assumed optimal fish density)
(0.00, 0.00), (0.1, 0.00), (0.2, 0.00), (0.3, 0.00), (0.4, 0.005), (0.5, 0.03), (0.6, 0.1), (0.7, 0.3),
(0.8, 0.76), (0.9, 0.92), (1, 1.00), (1.10, 1.00), (1.20, 1.00)
Estimated fish density = SMTH1(Fish stock / Maximum fishery size, Time to estimate fish density)
   {dimensionless}
Maximum fishery size = 4 000 {fish}
Time to estimate fish density = 0.5 {years}
Assumed optimal fish density = 0.6 {dimensionless}

Surveillance of Ships and Enforcement
Ships moved to harbour = (Ships at sea – Recommended ships at sea) *
   Effectiveness of fisheries management regime / Time to achieve compliance {ships/year}
Total ships = Ships at sea + Ships in harbour {ships}
Effectiveness of fisheries management regime = 1 {dimensionless}
Time to achieve compliance = 0.5 {years}

Ships at Sea, Ships in Harbour and Scrap Rate
Ships at sea(t) = Ships at sea(t - dt) + (Purchase or sale of ships – Ships moved to harbour) * dt
INIT Ships at sea = 10 {ships}
Ships in harbour(t) = Ships in harbour(t - dt) + (Ships moved to harbour – Scrap rate of ships) * dt
INIT Ships in harbour = 0 {ships}
Scrap rate of ships = Ships in harbour/ Lifetime of idle ships {ships/year}
Lifetime of idle ships = 5 {years}

Figure 9.25   Equations for deployment policy and ships

Imagine that marine biologists monitor the fish population to arrive at an estimated fish density. In practice, this is likely to be a time-consuming process of compiling sonar data collected by biologists during missions at sea. It is modelled with a smoothing function (SMTH1) where the scientific measurement of density is captured in the ratio of fish stock to maximum fishery size, and the time to estimate fish density is half a year. Armed with this sample evidence biologists then need to establish if the density is high enough to ensure a sustainable catch. If not, then they will recommend limits on fishing. The benchmark for comparison is the assumed optimal fish density, which is set at 0.6, corresponding to the peak of the regeneration curve in Figure 9.17. The sustainability index depends, non-linearly, on the ratio of the estimated fish density to the optimal fish density. When the ratio is in the range 1 to 1.2 (or more) the index takes a neutral value of one and there are no restrictions on the active fleet size. As the density ratio dips below 1, the index falls; gradually at first, but then very swiftly. For example, if the density ratio is 0.8 (meaning that the estimated fish density is 80% of the optimal) then the index takes a value of 0.76 (meaning that the recommended fleet size is 76% of the total ships). If the density ratio falls to 0.5, however, (meaning that the estimated fish density is only half the optimal) then the index takes a value of 0.03 (meaning that all but 3% of the fleet is supposed to be idled). This aggressive cutback acknowledges the fragility of the fishery around the tipping point.

Surveillance of ships and enforcement together capture the pressures on fishermen to act on scientific advice. However, compliance may not be timely or complete and this inevitable foot-dragging is recognised in the equations. The number of ships moved to harbour is driven by the difference between ships at sea and recommended ships at sea. Hence, if there are more ships at sea than recommended, the surplus is supposed to be idled. Some fishermen may cheat and ignore the recommendation. The scope for cheating is captured in the effectiveness of the fisheries management regime, a number that multiplies the surplus fleet. The parameter is set at 1 in the base case model, meaning that fishermen are completely honest. However, the parameter can be varied on a scale from zero to 1 to explore the implications of weak management regimes in which only a fraction of surplus ships are idled. Even when the regime is presumed to be strong, redeployment does not happen instantly. In a given week or month, only a fraction of the surplus ships are brought into harbour, according to the time to achieve compliance. This parameter is set at 0.5 years in the base case. For example, if there are 10 surplus ships (ships at sea – recommended ships at sea = 10) and no cheating (effectiveness of fisheries management regime = 1), then ships are moved to harbour at an initial rate of 20 ships per year (10/0.5), which is roughly two ships per month.

Stock and Flow Equations for Ships at Sea, Ships in Harbour and Scrap Rate

The remaining equations in Figure 9.25 define the stock and flow network for ships. Ships at sea are represented as a stock that accumulates the difference between the purchase or sale of ships and ships moved to harbour. Initially, there are 10 ships at sea. Ships in harbour are represented as a stock that accumulates the difference between ships moved to harbour and the scrap rate of ships. Initially, there are no ships in harbour because, in the beginning, fish are abundant and the fishery is underexploited. The scrap rate of ships is formulated as the ratio of ships in harbour to the lifetime of idle ships. We implicitly assume that older ships are idled first and can be kept seaworthy for years. The lifetime of idle ships is set at five years in the base case.

Simulated Dynamics of a Regulated Fishery – The Base Case

To run the base case open the model called 'Fish and Harvesting – Policy Design' in the learning support folder for Chapter 9. The opening screen is shown in Figure 9.26. Notice the four slide bars at the bottom of the diagram that together determine the regulatory regime. Consider the base case settings. The assumed optimal fish density is 0.6, which is equal to the biological optimum. This is the benchmark against which fish density is compared when setting the recommended fleet size. The effectiveness of the fisheries management regime is 1, which means there is no cheating on restrictions to the number of ships allowed at sea (or the equivalent days at sea). The time to achieve compliance is half a year. Finally, the lifetime of idle ships is set at five years. To inspect the model press the button labelled 'To Model'. To return to the opening screen press the tab labelled 'Interface' on the extreme left of the page.

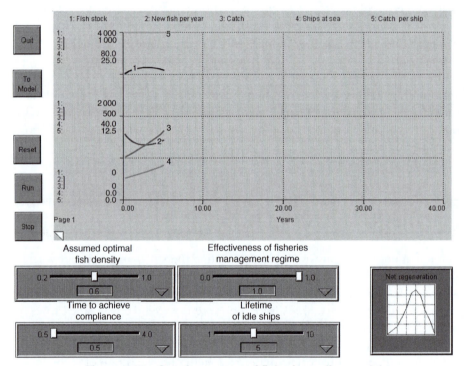

Figure 9.26   Opening screen of fisheries policy model

Press the 'Run' button once to generate the time chart in Figure 9.26 (which is deliberately truncated to show just the first five simulated years). Study the trajectories and then imagine how the future will unfold. To begin with the regulatory regime is dormant because the fishery is underexploited.

Growth-oriented investment leads to a steady rise in ships at sea (line 4) and the catch (line 3). Meanwhile, the fish stock (line 1) remains steady and plentiful. Select the 'page' tab in the lower left corner of the chart to see three more time charts. These charts provide more information than can be displayed here in the book. Page 2 shows the deployment of ships, recommended ships at sea and the sustainability index. Page 3 shows the purchase of ships, ships moved to harbour and the scrap rate. Page 4 shows fish density, the assumed optimal fish density and the sustainability index.

Press the 'Run' button again to see the next five years, and so on to year 40. The results are shown in Figure 9.27. With regulation the fishery is sustainable, as indicated in the top chart. Surprisingly there is considerable volatility in the catch (line 3), the fish stock (line 1) and ships at sea (line 4). In the early years of the simulation, the catch grows in exactly the same way as it would in an unregulated fishery (compare with Figure 9.22, during the growth phase). By year 12, the catch reaches 800 fish per year and there are 33 ships at sea. Meanwhile, the onset of regulation can be traced in the bottom chart. In year 11, biologists notice that fish density (line 1) falls below the assumed optimal fish density (line 2). This is the tipping point.

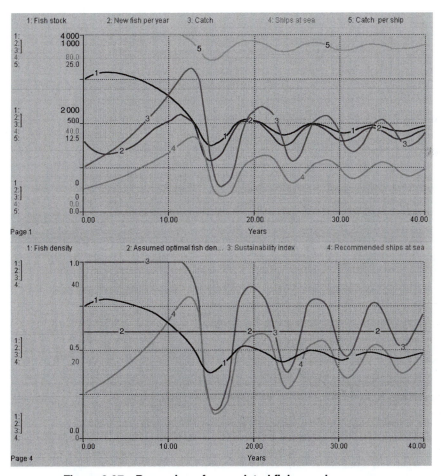

Figure 9.27 Dynamics of a regulated fishery – base case

But it takes time for the regulatory machinery to work. In year 12, the sustainability index (line 3) begins to fall sharply leading to a decline in recommended ships at sea (line 4). By year 13, the regulators recommend 30 ships at sea, by year 14 they recommend 15 ships, and by year 15 only five ships, which is far below the peak fleet of 33 ships in year 12. Fishermen reluctantly move their ships to harbour. The process of idling ships is not instantaneous, but it is swift (reflecting the assumption that the time to achieve compliance is only half a year). By year 14, there are 25 ships at sea and 12 ships in harbour (see page 2 of the time chart to confirm this deployment). By year 16 there are just six ships at sea and 25 in harbour. Note also that two idled ships have been scrapped.[7]

The highly effective regulatory regime cuts the catch dramatically. By the third quarter of year 14, the catch is 280 fish per year, down by almost two-thirds from its peak of 800 in year 12, and equal to the regeneration rate of new fish per year.

Thereafter, the fish stock is gradually replenished as further reductions in fishing effort and the catch take effect. By year 18, the fish density is restored to 0.5, which is slightly below optimal. The sustainability index recovers, thereby allowing a relaxation of regulatory restrictions, and the number of recommended ships at sea rises to 20. Fishermen re-activate their idled ships and the catch rises, reaching a new peak of 588 fish per year in year 21. From its original peak in year 12, the regulated fishery has been through a complete cycle of decline and recovery spanning almost a decade. Although a collapse of the fishery has been averted, the economic fortunes of the fishing community have varied widely in this period with a six-fold difference between the lowest catch and the highest. Moreover, further change is in store because, by year 21, the catch once again exceeds the regeneration rate of new fish per year, causing fish density to fall and invoking another round of regulation. In the remaining years of the simulation, the fishery settles into a pattern of fluctuating catch and fleet size, a pattern which is clearly sustainable

---

[7]Here is another example of traditional simulation analysis in system dynamics. This distinctive style involves close inspection and careful narrative interpretation of trajectories, stage-by-stage, of features such as magnitude and relative timing. The purpose of this 'analytic prose' is to build a coherent story of why simulated dynamics happen and how behaviour over time is related to structural and behavioural assumptions in the model. When you see how much can be written about simulated trajectories then you realise why, in system dynamics, it is deemed inadequate to present time charts as though they contain self-evident answers from the computer. They do not. Various advanced quantitative methods such as pattern recognition and eigenvalue analysis can also be used to interpret dynamics and better understand the link between a model's structure and behaviour. Such methods are beyond the scope of this book. Thorough coverage is provided in an edited volume by Rahmandad, Oliva and Osgood (2015).

but with a fish density (line 1, bottom chart) that is well below the assumed optimal fish density (line 2). This enduring biological discrepancy suggests the productivity of the fishery is too low and that fleet size regulation (even when implemented effectively) fails to maintain adequate fish stocks.

Policy Design – A Higher Benchmark for Fish Density

To improve fishery productivity it is necessary for regulators to set a benchmark for fish density that is higher than the biological optimum (Roughgarden and Smith, 1996). At first glance, this suggestion may seem counterproductive since crowding of fish inhibits their reproduction. In practice, however, a conservative benchmark is essential to counteract the growth bias of fishermen and the inevitable administrative delays in regulation.[8]

Figure 9.28 shows the effect on fishery performance of increasing the assumed optimal fish density from 0.6 (the theoretical biological optimum for the model's harvested fishery in equilibrium) to 0.8 (a pragmatic benchmark for the same fishery). To run this simulation, press the 'Reset' button, move the slider for assumed optimal fish density to 0.8, and then press 'Run'. Everything about the fishery is stabilised – the fish stock, the catch, ships at sea, fish density and the sustainability index. Moreover, in the medium to long term, the catch is higher than in the base case. This beneficial transformation happens because overfishing is nipped in the bud. As before, the fleet size starts at 10 ships and grows.

---

[8]Clover (2004: Chapter 7) exposes the fatal practical flaw, in fisheries management, of rigidly applying the scientific concept of 'maximum sustainable yield' (MSY). 'The pursuit of maximum sustainable yield encouraged fishermen to drive down the original population to a lower level – taking up to half of the total spawning stock every year – in the belief that this would boost the productivity of the population ... To decide what level of catches approached the magic figure of MSY there was little room for error. Scientists needed accurate figures for fishing mortality (i.e. fishermen must not cheat by misreporting catches or discards) and natural mortality. There were also dangers of missing or misinterpreting environmental forces or unforeseen predator effects.' The result was overfishing. 'A near-definitive demolition of MSY as a concept was written in 1977 by the Canadian biologist Peter Larkin. His short poem on the topic is better known:

Here lies the concept MSY
It advocated yields too high
And didn't spell out how to slice the pie
We bury it with best of wishes
Especially on behalf of fishes.'

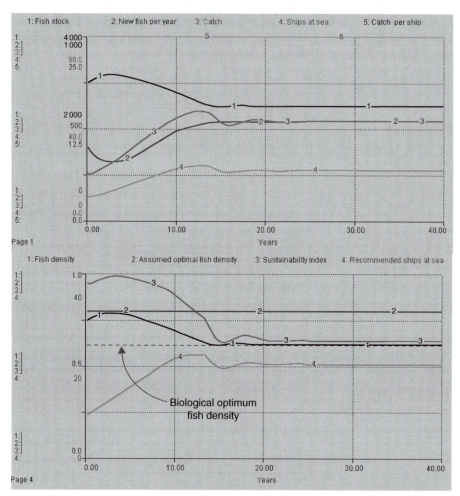

Figure 9.28 The stabilising effect of a higher benchmark for fish density

However, by year 10, the number of ships at sea (line 4, top chart) already begins to level out. This cautious deployment stems from an early recognition by regulators that fish density (line 1, bottom chart) is below the new assumed optimal (line 2). By year 12 there are only 24 ships at sea (line 4, top chart) and the catch (line 3) is 590 fish per year. Compare these figures with a fleet of 33 ships and a catch of 800 fish per year at the same time in the base case. Because the catch is reduced the fish stock falls only gently and the regeneration rate (new fish per year, line 2) continues to rise until, in the second quarter of year 14, it equals and slightly surpasses the catch. At this point the fishery is in a stable equilibrium. By coincidence the fish density (line 1, bottom chart) settles at the biological optimum density, which is below the regulators' benchmark or assumed optimal. It is precisely this discrepancy, however, that creates and maintains the regulatory pressures on fishermen to restrict fishing effort and to keep more ships in harbour. The outcome is a win–win compromise for regulators and fishermen alike.[9]

Dynamics of a Weakly Regulated Fishery

So far we have optimistically assumed that all fishermen will abide by the regulatory rules. However, what if the regulatory regime is perceived to be weak and fishermen find ways to evade surveillance or believe that violations will not be punished? To explore this scenario first press the 'Reset' button. Notice that the assumed optimal fish density returns to its original value of 0.6, as in the base case. Now reduce the effectiveness of the fisheries management regime from its default value of 1 to 0.5. This change means that, whenever the fleet size is larger than recommended, fishermen intend to move only half the surplus ships to harbour. Then, to further weaken regulation, increase the time to achieve compliance from 0.5 years to 1 year. This change means that it takes regulators a year to implement restrictions on fleet size, even for those fishermen who intend to comply. Press the 'Run' button to create the time charts shown in Figure 9.29. As before ships at sea (line 4, top chart) and the catch (line 3) grow from the outset. At the start of year 11, the fish density (line 1, bottom chart) falls below the assumed optimal density (line 2). However, due to measurement delays by biologists, administrative inertia of regulators and evasion of rules by fishermen the number of ships at sea (line 4, top chart) continues to grow until midway through year 13. Two years of overfishing causes a sharp decline in the fish stock (line 1, top chart). As a result, by year 15 the sustainability index falls to zero, leading regulators to call for a total ban on fishing by setting recommended ships at sea to zero (line 4, bottom chart). However, weak regulation means that the ban is widely

---

[9]Performance improvement through policy design is an important topic in system dynamics. The approach used here, for fisheries policy design (and policy design elsewhere in the book), is pragmatic and behavioural. It is the established and traditional approach in the field. The essential idea is to test *incremental* change to *existing* feedback structure that improves (rather than optimises) system performance. There is practical merit in such a 'satisficing' (or nudge) approach to policy design. It looks for performance improvement relative to a base case simulation. It takes-as-given the enduring feedback structure that underlies the dynamics of the base run and seeks at least one high leverage point in the system where a small and understandable change in an operating parameter yields big improvements in performance, while leaving the vast majority of the already-established policy structure intact. Policy design can also be conducted with optimisation methods that are often sophisticated and quite technically demanding. For example Anderson and Joglekar (2015) describe the use of optimal control theory with deterministic dynamic models while Rahmandad and Spiteri (2015) introduce differential games. A middle-ground of sophistication can be found in Moxnes (2015) who talks of 'optimisation in policy space' as a practical way to bridge the gap between traditional system dynamics and optimisation. He shows that optimisation of non-linear dynamical models is computationally feasible (with tailored, user-friendly software) and can yield interesting benchmarks for performance. In particular he describes a framework to optimise policy structure using a Monte-Carlo ensemble of simulations which is tested on a fisheries simulation model.

ignored. By the end of year 15 there are still around 18 ships at sea, and even two years after the start of the ban, at the end of year 16, 10 ships remain surreptitiously at sea. By this time the fish stock is severely depleted and the catch is down to 170 fish per year, just 20% of its peak value.

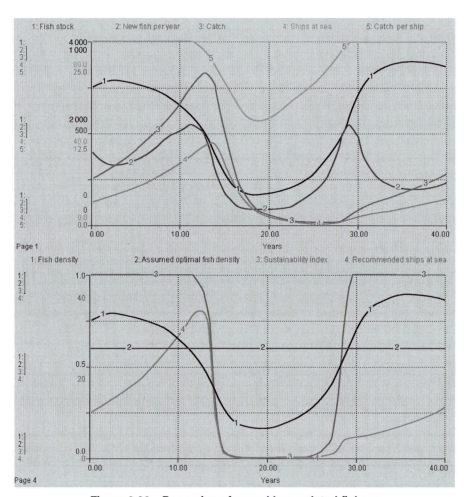

Figure 9.29   Dynamics of a weakly regulated fishery

It is not until midway through year 18 that the catch (line 3, top chart) finally falls below the regeneration rate (new fish per year, line 2) and the fish stock (line 1) begins to edge upwards. From such a low base it takes the fishery a whole decade to recover. By year 27 the fish density (line 1, bottom chart) is nearing the assumed optimal density and conditions are, at long last, suitable to allow fleet expansion. Ships at sea begin to increase, along with the catch. By the end of the simulation, in year 40, the fleet size and catch are right back to where they started in year 0 and the stage is set for another cycle of boom and bust. The weakly regulated fishery survives, but only just. Moreover, its output (average catch) is severely depressed by comparison with either the stable and conservatively managed fishery in Figure 9.28 or the cyclical base case fishery in Figure 9.27. Because of interlocking feedback loops and non-linearities the productivity of fisheries is sensitive to the regulatory regime and output deteriorates quickly if surveillance and/or sanctions are perceived to be weak.

Incidentally, marine scientists have noted that richly diverse fisheries, supporting many different species, are more robust and less prone to collapse than fisheries with only a few dominant species. One theory is that interlocking species are better able to self-regulate their fecundity or collective fertility. We can test this proposition in the simulator by flattening the hump in the curve for net regeneration. Press the 'Reset' button. Then double select the graphical input device labelled 'net regeneration' and the characteristic hump-shaped graph will appear. The maximum net regeneration is 550 fish per year at a fish density of 0.6. Re-draw the graph so it is flatter in the region to the left of the maximum point. However, for logical consistency, be sure the line still passes through the (0,0) point. Select 'OK' to return to the main interface and move the sliders back to the settings for a weakly regulated fishery (effectiveness of fisheries management regime = 0.5 and time to achieve compliance = 1 year). Then press 'Run'. The resulting time charts are similar to the base case (Figure 9.27) and exhibit cyclicality in the catch, fish stock and ships at sea. The implication is that stable fecundity improves fisheries management to such an extent that even weak regulation works. Flattening the hump in fecundity simplifies the fishery's feedback structure (by effectively removing a non-linearity) and makes it easier for regulators to maintain a sustainable balance of ships, fishing effort and fish.

Policy Design – Lower Exit Barriers Through Quicker Scrapping of Idle Ships

The hardship caused to fishing communities by collapsing fish stocks has led many governments to introduce social support schemes. For example, Canada's Atlantic Fisheries Adjustment Package paid minimum income support of $400 per month to fishers and plant workers who had lost their jobs in the 1990s. The total cost of the package was $4 billion over 10 years. Such schemes have been criticised as a pointless waste of money because they prolong excess capacity. The argument is that subsidised fishermen and their vessels remain too long in the industry.

An alternative approach is to pay fisherman to scrap their idle ships and to leave the industry permanently. The rationale is to lower the exit barriers from the industry and to remove excess capacity more quickly, once and for all. We can test this policy in the simulator. Press the 'Reset' button. Then move the slider for the lifetime of idle ships from its default value of five years to two years to represent an increase in the scrap rate of surplus ships. This change optimistically assumes that a suitable financial incentive can be devised to boost the scrap rate. Given a successful incentive, then what outcome would you expect? Obviously there will be fewer ships, but will there be an improvement in the performance of the fishery? Take a few moments to reflect. Then press the 'Run' button to create the time charts shown in Figure 9.30.

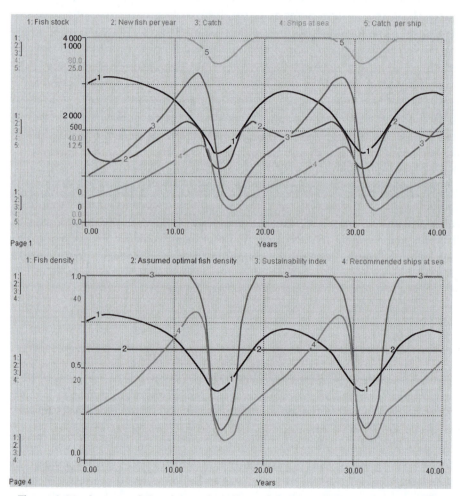

Figure 9.30   Lower exit barriers – the effect of quicker scrapping of idle ships

If you were expecting improved stability of the catch and fish stock then you will be surprised. The fishery remains strongly cyclical with periods of boom and bust. Why? Note that the first 16 years of the simulation are almost identical to the base case in Figure 9.27. A decline of fish density triggers regulatory restrictions leading to a sharp reduction of ships at sea and the catch, but the recovery phase of the fishery is much different. In the interval between years 16 and 22, the number of ships at sea (line 4) grows much more slowly than in the base case. In fact, there is a distinct flattening of the fleet trajectory in year 18, caused by accelerated scrapping of idle ships – exactly as intended by the fast exit policy. Moreover, with fewer ships at sea the fish stock (line 1) rebuilds to a higher level than in the base case, reaching a peak of almost 3000 in year 22 by comparison with a peak of only 2000 in year 18 of the base case.

Then a surprise is sprung. The abundance of fish leads to a relaxation of regulatory restrictions. Although old ships have left the industry permanently, fishermen have not. When times are good they return and buy new ships. So the cycle of fleet expansion and overshoot begins again, driven by the assumed natural propensity for growth. Ironically, because the fish stock recovers to a higher level than in the base case there is scope for greater fleet expansion, leading to a bigger catch followed by a sharper decline. Essentially lower exit barriers elongate and amplify the harvesting cycle in a regulated fishery. Whenever fish are plentiful there will always be ships and fishermen to harvest them.

A closer look at ship deployment and the scrap rate shows why cyclicality persists despite lower exit barriers. Figure 9.31 is a simulation made under the same condition as before in which the lifetime of idle ships is reduced to two years instead of five. However, the horizontal time axis of the two charts is magnified to show years 10 through 30, and different variables are plotted. These variables can be viewed in the simulator itself by selecting the 'page' tab in the bottom left of the chart and advancing to pages two and three. Also the time axis can be modified by double selecting any chart to open a window called 'define graph'. At the bottom of the window are two boxes, labelled 'from' and 'to', that set the length of the display. By inserting the values 10 and 30 (then pressing 'OK') the graph is redrawn to show the trajectories in the truncated interval from year 10 to year 30, rather than the full interval from year 0 to year 40.

The bottom chart takes us deep inside the fishermen's world as they decide to purchase ships, move them to harbour or scrap them. The top chart shows the effect of these decisions on the deployment of ships and the size of the fleet. During years 10 to 14 fishermen invest steadily in new ships as the fishery enters the final years of its long growth phase. The purchase or sale of ships (line 1, bottom chart) remains almost constant at about three ships per year. A positive value for this variable indicates purchases and a negative value indicates sales. In the third quarter of year 11 there is a rise in ships moved to harbour (line 2) as regulatory restrictions are applied.

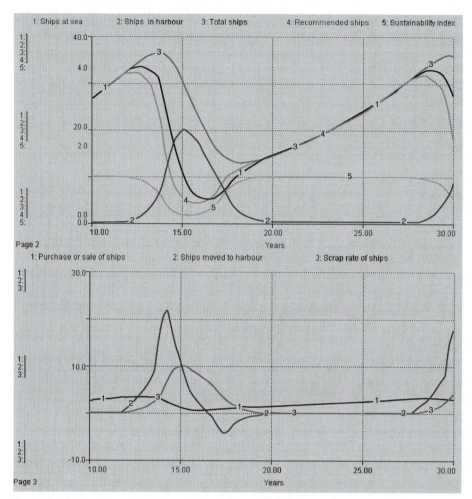

Figure 9.31 Lower exit barriers – a closer look at ship deployment and scrap rate, over 20 years

The restrictions are minor to begin with but quickly gather pace, reaching a peak of 22 ships per year in year 14. This rapid rate of idling of the fleet leads to a dramatic fall in ships at sea (line 1, top chart) and a corresponding rise in ships in harbour (line 2, top chart). Notice that during the early years of this redeployment fishermen continue to purchase new ships. This persistent investment, in the face of regulatory pressure to reduce fishing effort, reflects the growth bias of fishermen and their reluctance to believe bad news about the declining fish stock. Of particular interest is the scrap rate of ships (line 3, bottom chart) which rises to a peak of 10 ships per year in year 15 and then gradually declines back to zero by year 20. This surge in scrapping is a direct consequence of the short lifetime of idle ships. Capacity leaves the industry as intended and the total ships in the fishery, at sea and in harbour (line 3, top chart), falls from a peak of 37 in year 14 to 13 in year 18, a reduction of almost two-thirds in only four years. If regulators were to achieve such a drastic reduction in fleet capacity their policy of lowering exit barriers would surely be deemed a success. With a much reduced fleet the sustainability index (line 5, top chart) returns to a healthy value of one by year 20, and remains high for eight years. But the replenished fishery attracts new vessels. Over the same eight year interval, from year 20 to year 28, the purchase or sale of ships (line 1, bottom chart) remains positive. All the new ships go to sea, and none are scrapped or moved to harbour. By year 28 the active fleet size is back to its previous peak of 33 ships at sea and the stage is set for another round of regulatory restrictions and scrapping of idle ships.

Sustainability, Regulation and Self-Restraint

The model shows that regulation of fishing effort works and that catastrophic collapse of fish stocks can be avoided by establishing scientifically credible benchmarks for fish density and by putting in place surveillance and judicial systems to enforce the benchmarks. Even so, the result is not necessarily a stable catch. A regulated fishery may be sustainable but strongly cyclical (as in Figures 9.27 and 9.29), with wide fluctuations in the fish stock and the catch as well as large variations in economic output and the standard of living of the fishing community. Fisheries are highly non-linear, multi-loop feedback systems and managing them can be tricky. Setting a conservative benchmark for fish density (as in Figure 9.28) stabilises the fishery and raises overall productivity – assuming the benchmark can be enforced.

Other policy options can be imagined. The reader is invited to run more experiments with the fisheries policy simulator by adjusting the sliders that represent policy variables. Regulatory policy is obviously important, but so too are the biological attributes of the fishery and the aspirations of fishing communities. Regulation is never perfect. Nevertheless, even gentle regulation can work well in a robust and ecologically diverse fishery – as we discovered earlier by flattening the net regeneration curve. Gentle regulation also works if people moderate their growth expectations, a change that can be investigated in the simulator by reducing the propensity for growth.

Conclusion

We have reviewed three distinctive public policy applications of strategic modelling that have taken us from decaying cities, to overstretched hospital doctors and idle fishing fleets. These applications are just a sample of public policy modelling that also spans topics such as environmental management (Ford, 2010), energy policy (Bunn and Larsen, 1997; Naill, 1992) and global warming (Fiddaman, 2002; Sterman *et al.*, 2013) to name just a few. Health care in particular is an area where system dynamics has proved effective and where managers welcome the joined-up thinking it provides (Hirsch *et al.* (eds), 2015). Studies that involve patient flows and money flows at a strategic level of aggregation are well suited to system dynamics modelling. Good examples are to be found in 'Health and Health Care Dynamics' (Dangerfield and Roberts, 1999) and in the *Leading Edge* series of the National Health Service confederation (Wolstenholme, 2006). System dynamics has also been applied to medical workforce planning, training and career pathways. One example is a strategic review of the dental workforce in England conducted by the Centre for Workforce Intelligence and reported in Cave *et al.* (2014). In other areas of healthcare there is noteworthy work by Hamid (2009) about obesity management and by Thompson and Tebbens (2007) on poliomyelitis control.

What unites all these important, practical problems is aptly captured in Jay Forrester's concise definition of the field:

> System dynamics deals with how things change through time which includes most of what most people find important. It uses modelling and computer simulation to take the knowledge we already have about details in the world around us and to show why our social and physical systems behave the way they do. System dynamics demonstrates how most of our own decision-making policies are the cause of the problems that we usually blame on others, and how to identify policies we can follow to improve our situation.
>
> (This quote originally appeared in the System Dynamics Society Listserve on April 22, 1997 as a response to a request for an 'elevator definition' of system dynamics.)

Appendix – Alternative Simulation Approaches

These days simulators are everywhere. They are widely used to help 'designers' (architects, urban planners, engineers, military strategists, pharmacologists) understand all sorts of complex things. Simulators as thinking tools include virtual buildings, highway simulators, models of nuclear power stations, water-supply simulators, aircraft flight simulators, virtual battlefields and even virtual human hearts. Popular video games like SimCity, Tomb Raider, Formula One, Grand Theft Auto and The Sims all contain simulation engines that control what happens on the screen and animate the vivid and detailed images.

Simulators are of three main types that each use different concepts and building blocks to represent how things change through time. Besides system dynamics, there is also discrete-event simulation and agent-based modelling. Associated with each of these simulation approaches are thriving communities of academics and practitioners and a huge repertoire of models they have developed. There are frequent overlaps in the problem situations to which different simulation approaches are applied. Hence, it is useful for system dynamics modellers (which includes anyone who has reached this point in the book) to be aware that other 'simulationists' exist and to appreciate their worldview.

From Urban Dynamics to SimCity

As a start consider SimCity, a popular yet serious videogame that 'makes you Mayor and City Planner, and dares you to design and build the city of your dreams ... Depending on your choices and design skills, Simulated Citizens (Sims) will move in and build homes, hospitals, churches, stores and factories, or move out in search of a better life elsewhere' (www.simcity.com). The central concept of city attractiveness that lies behind SimCity (even its most recent versions) is reminiscent of *Urban Dynamics*. A city's attractiveness depends on the quality of its infrastructure and plays a central role in drawing residents (Sims) to the city, or making them leave.[10] However, the detailed visual and spatial representation of city infrastructure (with individual icons for commercial and residential buildings, roads, mass transit, police stations, fire departments, airports, seaports and stadiums as shown in Figure 9.32) point to a very different underlying simulation engine whose concepts and equations are far more disaggregated – not unlike an agent-based model. I stop short of saying that SimCity is a true agent-based model or cellular automata as I have never inspected its equations and, as far as I know, they are not accessible to game players. Hence, I use SimCity simply to show that dynamic phenomena can be dressed in a variety of computational clothing.[11]

---

[10] It is no accident that, conceptually, SimCity resembles *Urban Dynamics*. As the game's creator, Will Wright, explains: 'SimCity evolved from Raid on Bungling Bay, where the basic premise was that you flew around and bombed islands. The game included an island generator, and I noticed after a while that I was having more fun building islands than blowing them up. About the same time, I also came across the work of Jay Forrester, one of the first people to ever model a city on a computer for social-sciences purposes. Using his theories, I adapted and expanded the Bungling Bay island generator, and SimCity evolved from there' (quote from Friedman, 1995).

[11] I will not pursue agent-based modelling any further here and refer the interested reader to Robertson and Caldart (2009) for an informative review of agent simulation of firms and industries.

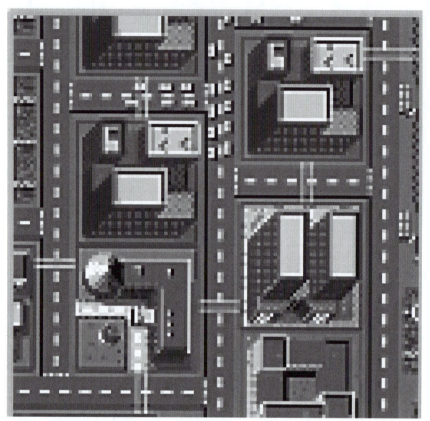

Figure 9.32 Screen shot from the original 1989 SimCity showing a spatial representation of city infrastructure

Source: Screen shot from 1989 SimCity by Maxis, © Electronic Arts EA, http://simcity3000unlim ited.ea.com/us/guide/

Discrete-event Simulation and System Dynamics

To probe how other simulationists view time-dependent problems I turn to a comparison of discrete-event simulation and system dynamics,[12] drawing on work by Morecroft and Robinson (2005; 2014).[13],[14] Figure 9.33 shows a comparison of two models of a natural fishery. Readers are already familiar

---

[12]Discrete-event simulation is a big subject in its own right and readers can find out more from Pidd (2004), Robinson (2004; 2005).

[13]These two models were developed independently by the authors (one an expert in system dynamics and the other an expert in discrete-event simulation), based on facts and data in the briefing materials for Fish Banks, Ltd (Meadows *et al.*, 2001). Each of us adopted the normal model conceptualisation and formulation conventions of our respective fields so the resulting models would be a valid comparison of the two approaches.

[14]My thanks to Stewart Robinson for permission to include in this appendix the discrete-event models and simulations that come from his part of our joint project.

with the system dynamics model on the right (which was presented in Chapter 1). On the left is an equivalent discrete-event model. Here the fish stock is represented as a queue that is fed by the annual process (cycle of 1 year) of fish replenishment. New fish are sourced from outside the model by the 'source' on the left of the diagram. Initially, there are 200 fish in the sea and the maximum size of the fishery is assumed to be 4000 fish, which are the same numerical values used in the system dynamics model. Fish regeneration is represented as a linear, but random, function of the number of fish in the sea. Fish grow at an average rate of 20% per year, varying according to a normal distribution with a standard deviation of 2%. The limit to growth of 4000 is represented as a discrete cut-off, which does not allow the fish population to exceed this limit.

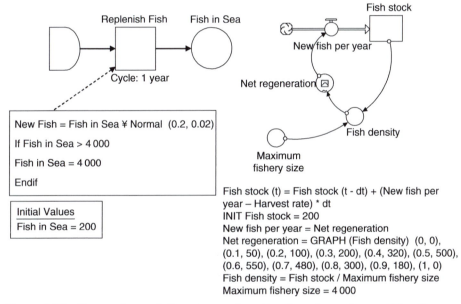

Figure 9.33   Comparison of discrete-event and system dynamics models of a natural fishery

There are some clear differences in the two representations. The system dynamics model uses stocks and flows while the discrete-event model uses queues and processes. Nevertheless, despite the new symbols, there is a clear equivalence between stocks and queues on the one hand, and between flows and processes on the other. Significantly, the feedback structure is visually explicit in the system dynamics model but hidden within the equations of the discrete-event representation. The discrete-event model deliberately includes randomness in the regeneration of fish as this is seen as a process that is subject to variability, but which is not present in the system dynamics version. Meanwhile, the relationship between fish stocks and fish regeneration is non-linear in the system dynamics model, but linear in the discrete-event model.[15]

Time charts from the discrete-event simulation model are shown in Figure 9.34. This chart is the output from a single replication (a run driven with a specific stream of random numbers). If the random number seeds were changed to perform further replications, the exact pattern of growth and fish regeneration would alter. Figure 9.34 shows s-shaped growth similar to the pattern from the system dynamics model, but with two distinct differences. First, the growth is not as smooth due to the randomness within the regeneration process. This extra variability is clear to see in the trajectory of new fish. Second, the system dynamics time chart shows an asymptotic growth towards the limit of 4000 fish, while the discrete-event model hits the limit sharply. Both of these differences in simulated behaviour are of course a result of the model formulations which in turn reflect more fundamental differences in the approach to conceptualising a fishery. For simple models of a natural fishery, the trajectories look quite similar. But the differences become greater as we move to a harvested fishery where the interactions are more complex.

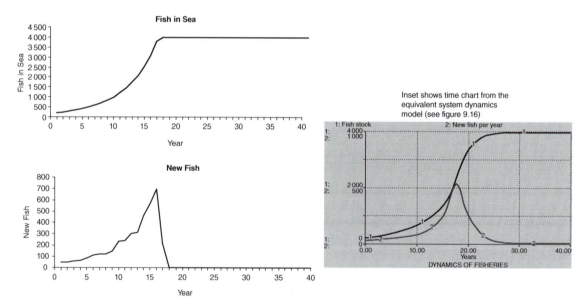

Figure 9.34   Dynamics of a natural fishery from a discrete-event simulation model

Figure 9.35 shows a discrete-event model of a harvested fishery, which should be compared with the system dynamics model in Figure 9.17. The left side of

---

[15]For such tiny models as these it is possible in principle to make the formulations identical, but that would contradict the intended independence in the work of the two modellers as outlined in footnote 10.

the process flow diagram is the same as for the natural fishery in Figure 9.33. However, a second process 'Catch Fish' is now added, which represents the catching of fish that are then sent to the sink on the right side of the diagram. The formula for the number of fish caught consists of two parts. The first sees the catch as an increasing proportion of the fish in the sea, a proportion that increases with the number of ships. The formula is non-linear, giving a reduced catch per ship with increasing numbers of ships. It is envisaged that as more ships are fishing in the same area their productivity will fall. The second part of the formula (Normal 1, 0.1) is the modelling of randomness.

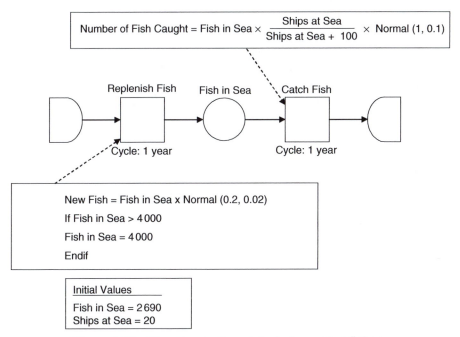

Figure 9.35   Discrete-event model of a harvested fishery

The modelling differences identified for the natural fishery apply equally to this case of a harvested fishery: the method of representation, the explicitness of the feedback structure and the inclusion of randomness. Interestingly, the discrete-event model represents the number of fish caught as a non-linear and stochastic function of the number of ships, while the system dynamics model represents this effect as a deterministic linear relation. Further, there is an implied feedback structure in the discrete-event model where the catch is related to the number of fish. A similar feedback is to be found explicitly in the system dynamics model with endogenous investment shown in Figure 9.21. Perhaps the most important distinguishing feature of the discrete-event model, however, is that it now contains two interacting random processes (one in the regeneration of fish and the other in the catch). Discrete-event modellers are well aware that puzzling and counterintuitive dynamics arise when two or more random processes are linked (Robinson, 2004: Chapter 1). These stochastic dynamics are rarely investigated by system dynamics modellers whose interest is feedback dynamics.[16]

Figure 9.36 shows the results from a simulation of the discrete-event harvested fishery, now with randomness included for the catch and regeneration of fish. As there is 'complex' randomness in the model, the simulation has been replicated 10 times, using different random number streams, the results showing the mean of the replications. The use of multiple replications is standard practice in discrete-event simulation modelling for determining the range of outcomes and the mean performance of a system (Law and Kelton, 2000; Robinson, 2004). The time charts show the catch and the number of fish in the sea over a 40-year period. Notice the variation in the annual catch with the mean shifting between just above 400 to just below 500. Similarly, there is some variation in the fish stock, peaking at about 2800 and falling to about 2600. Such variation is not surprising given the randomness in the model.

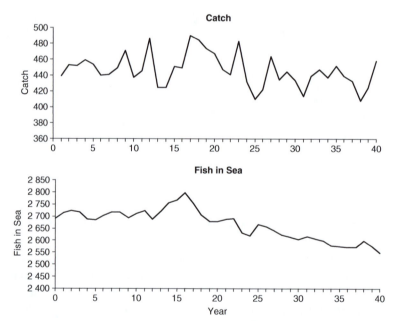

Figure 9.36   Dynamics of a harvested fishery from a discrete-event simulation model

---

[16]System dynamics models are not entirely devoid of random processes. For example, it is common in factory and supply-chain models to add randomness to demand in order to invoke cyclical dynamics, as demonstrated in Chapter 5's factory model. But system dynamicists do not normally set out to explore surprising bottlenecks and queues (stock accumulations) that stem from interlocking streams of random events.

It would be difficult to predict the interconnected effect of variations in fish regeneration and fish catch without a simulation.[17]

The discrete-event model of a harvested fishery was initialised to yield a perfect equilibrium if the two random processes were to be temporarily switched-off at the start of the simulation. This special condition was achieved by setting the initial number of fish at 2690 which yields an inflow of new fish per year that exactly balances the annual catch of 20 ships. The observed variations in fish stock therefore stem entirely from interlocking streams of random events. There is no direct analogy to Figure 9.36 for the equivalent system dynamics model of a harvested fishery, because when the fleet size is fixed then any simulation that begins in equilibrium (so the inflow of new fish is exactly equal to the catch) remains in equilibrium. The time charts are flat lines that say nothing about fishery dynamics. Not so in a discrete-event world, where seemingly equilibrium conditions can yield puzzling variations in performance. The catch can rise and fall significantly for stochastic reasons.

A very different kind of equilibrium test, that examines multiple equilibria and tipping points, applies to the system dynamics model of a harvested fishery. We have already seen an example of such a test in Figure 9.18, which shows a simulation of stepwise changes in fleet size. Here we learn something surprising about the properties of a non-linear dynamical system. There are multiple equilibria of fish stock and ships at sea in which the equilibrium catch is progressively higher as more ships are added to the fishery. Then, at a critical fleet size of around 30 ships, the fish stock and the catch begin to collapse. Thereafter, a reduction to 20 ships or even 10 does not halt the collapse.

Stochastic variability and tipping points in the catch are two different dynamical phenomena. Yet they are both compatible with real-world data from fisheries. If we look once more at the time series for the Pacific sardine catch and the North Sea herring catch, we see in Figure 9.37 evidence that could support either type of model. The Pacific sardine catch looks like tipping-point dynamics, while the North Sea herring catch looks like extreme stochastic variability.[18]

---

[17]Close inspection of the graph for fish in the sea reveals a downward trend, a trend which is confirmed by longer simulations. The phenomenon is explained in Morecroft and Robinson (2005 and 2014).

[18]The visual fit between time series and simulations is more compelling when each model includes endogenous investment in ships, as in Figure 9.22. There is not the space here to present the equivalent discrete-event model but details can be found in Morecroft and Robinson (2005 and 2014).

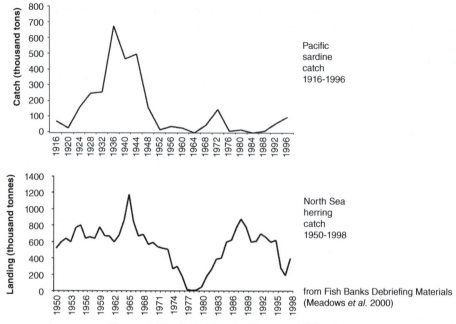

Figure 9.37   Puzzling dynamics of fisheries

Conclusions on Alternative Approaches to Simulation Modelling

What does this fisheries comparison say more generally about alternative simulation methodologies and discrete-event simulation in particular? First it shows there are alternative approaches that can each provide insight into puzzling dynamics. This is not news, but is useful to include in a book that otherwise concentrates on system dynamics. The comparison also lifts the curtain, at least a few centimetres, on the world of discrete-event simulation. There are important differences not only in technique (queues and activities versus stocks and flows, discrete versus continuous time, stochastic versus deterministic) but also in worldview. System dynamics deals with 'deterministic complexity'. Puzzling dynamic behaviour is explained by feedback structure, which implies that the unfolding future is partly and significantly pre-determined. Within this worldview, problematic situations are investigated by first identifying feedback loops (and their underlying stock accumulations, policies and information flows) and then re-designing policies to change this feedback structure in order to improve performance. Discrete-event simulation deals with 'stochastic complexity'. Puzzling dynamic behaviour arises from multiple interacting random processes, which implies that the unfolding future is partly and significantly a matter of chance. Within this worldview problematic situations are investigated by first identifying interlocking random processes (and their underlying probability distributions, queues and activities) and then finding ways to change or better manage this 'stochastic structure' to improve performance.

A corollary of these differences is that discrete-event simulation is well suited to handling operational detail. Stochastic processes are a concise and elegant way to portray detail within operations. A factory can be conceived as a collection of interacting stochastic machines that process a flow of products. A hospital can be conceived as a collection of stochastic medical procedures that process a flow of patients. Moreover, because of the way random processes release a stream of individual entities (just like individual fans entering a football stadium) then factory models can readily depict detail movement and queues of individual products, and hospital models can track the movement and waiting times of individual patients. This ability to handle detail was not exploited in the fisheries models, but detail is a vital characteristic of most discrete-event models that carries through to their visual interactive interfaces. The resulting look-and-feel of such entity-driven models is very different from system dynamics models with their aggregate stock accumulations and coordinating network of feedback loops. A system dynamics factory model (as in Chapter 5) portrays inventory, workforce and pressure-driven policies for inventory control and hiring – a distant view of operations. In contrast a discrete-event factory model shows machines, conveyor belts, storage areas and shipping bays and if-then-else decision rules that determine the movement of product and usage of machines, all because it tends to focus on a close-up view of operations. But precisely because of its distance from operations, a system dynamics model clearly depicts feedback loops that weave between functions and departments. In contrast a discrete-event model hides such connections or does not attempt to include them at all because it focuses on just one or two functions/departments. The characteristic scope, scale and detail of factors included in a model therefore arise naturally from the modellers' chosen worldview.

Clans are territorial. Their models look so different, and hence it is not surprising that proponents of system dynamics and discrete-event simulation rarely talk. However, communication will improve as understanding grows, and may even spark joint projects. There is also an opportunity for better three-way communication between agent-based modelling, discrete-event simulation and system dynamics.[19]

---

[19]Lomi and Larsen (2001) have edited an informative collection of academic papers that illustrate the wide range of ways in which simulation methods have been applied to understanding dynamic phenomena in organisations.

References

Anderson, E.G. and Joglekar, N.R. (2015) Using optimal control theory with dynamic models, Chapter 11 in Rahmandad, H., Oliva, R. and Osgood, N. (eds) (2015) *Analytical Methods for Dynamic Modelers*. Cambridge MA: MIT Press.

Arnason, R. (2005) Property rights in fisheries: Iceland's experience with ITQs. *Reviews in Fish Biology and Fisheries*, 15(3): 243–264.

Arnason, R. (2007) Fisheries management. In Weintraub, A., Romero, C., Bjørndal, T. and Epstein, R. (eds), *Handbook on Operations Research in Natural Resources*, International Series in Operations Research & Management Science, Vol. 99.

Bunn, D. and Larsen, E. (eds) (1997) *Systems Modelling for Energy Policy*. Chichester: John Wiley & Sons.

Cave, S., Darvill, H., Gioe, D. *et al.* (2014) The use of system dynamics in a strategic review of the English dental workforce, Online Proceedings of the International Conference of the System Dynamics Society, Delft, The Netherlands, July 2014, Available at http://www.systemdynamics.org/conferences/2014/proceed/papers/P1151.pdf (accessed 17 November 2014). See also a report from the Centre for Workforce Intelligence entitled A Strategic Review of the Future Dentistry Workforce, December 2013.

Clover, C. (2004) *The End of the Line*. London: Ebury Press.

Dangerfield, B. and Roberts, C. (eds) (1999) Health and health care dynamics. *System Dynamics Review*, 15(3): 197–199.

Dudley, R.G. (2008) A basis for understanding fishery management dynamics. *System Dynamics Review* 24(1): 1–29.

Fiddaman, T. (2002) Exploring policy options with a behavioral climate-economy model. *System Dynamics Review*, 18(2): 243–267.

Fisher, L. (2005) The prophet of unintended consequences. *strategy+business*, 40: 1–12.

Ford, A. (2010) *Modeling the Environment*. (2nd edn) Washington DC: Island Press.

Forrester, J.W. (1969) *Urban Dynamics*. available from the System Dynamics Society www.systemdynamics.org, originally published by MIT Press, Cambridge MA, 1969.

Forrester, J.W. (1975) Systems analysis for urban planning. In *Collected Papers of Jay W. Forrester*. Available from the System Dynamics Society www.systemdynamics.org, originally published by Wright-Allen Press, Cambridge MA, 1975.

Friedman, T. (1995) Making sense of software: computer games and interactive textuality. In Jones, S.G. (ed.) *Cybersociety*. London: Sage. (See also http://www.duke.edu/~tlove/simcity.htm.)

Hamid, T.K.A. (2009) *Thinking in Circles About Obesity: Applying Systems Thinking to Weight Management*. New York: Springer.

Hardin, G. (1968) The tragedy of the commons. *Science*, 162: 1243–1248.

Hirsch, G., Homer, J. and Tomoaia-Cotisel, A. (eds) (2015) System dynamics applications to health care. *System Dynamics Review*, Virtual Issue, January 2015.

Kunc, M.H. and Morecroft, J.D.W. (2010) Managerial decisionmaking and firm performance under a resource-based paradigm, *Strategic Management Journal*, 31 1164–1182.

Law, A.M. and Kelton, W.D. (2000) *Simulation Modeling and Analysis* (3rd edn). New York: McGraw-Hill.

Lomi, A. and Larsen, E.R. (2001) *Dynamics of Organizations: Computational Modeling and Organization Theories*. Cambridge, MA: MIT Press.

Meadows, D.L., Fiddaman, T. and Shannon, D. (2001) Fish Banks, Ltd. Micro-computer Assisted Group Simulation That Teaches Principles of Sustainable Management of Renewable Natural Resources (5th edn). The FishBanks Ltd. game was developed by Professor Dennis Meadows, co-author of 'Limits to Growth'. The board game kits which include the game software, PowerPoint slide sets for introducing and debriefing the game, instructions for playing the game, the role description, game board, and pieces are sold through the System Dynamics Society www.systemdynamics.org. Email: office@systemdynamics.org.

Morecroft, J.D.W. and Robinson, S. (2005 and 2014) Explaining puzzling dynamics: comparing the use of system dynamics and discrete-event simulation. Proceedings of the International System Dynamics Conference, Boston, July 2005. Available at www.systemdynamics.org and subsequently published in *Discrete-Event Simulation and System Dynamics for Management Decision Making* (editors Brailsford and Dangerfield), Chapter 9, 165–198, John Wiley & Sons, 2014.

Moxnes, E. (1998) Not only the tragedy of the commons: Misperceptions of bioeconomics. *Management Science*, 44(9): 1234–1248.

Moxnes, E. (2015) Optimization and system dynamics as complements, Chapter 8 in Rahmandad, H., Oliva, R. and Osgood, N. (eds) (2015) *Analytical Methods for Dynamic Modelers*, Cambridge MA: MIT Press.

Naill, R. (1992) A system dynamics model for national energy policy planning. *System Dynamics Review*, 8(1): 1–20.

Ostrom, E. (2009) Beyond Markets and States: Polycentric Governance of Complex Economic Systems. Prize lecture, Nobel Memorial Prize in Economics, www.nobelprize.org/nobel_prizes/economics/laureates/2009/ostrom-lecture.html.

Ostrom, E., Poteete, A. and Janssen, M. (2010) *Working Together: Collective Action, the Commons, and Multiple Methods in Practice*. Princeton, NJ: Princeton University Press.

Pidd, M. (2004) *Computer Simulation in Management Science* (5th edn). Chichester: John Wiley & Sons.

Rahmandad, H., Oliva, R. and Osgood, N. (eds) (2015) *Analytical Methods for Dynamic Modelers*, Cambridge MA: MIT Press.

Rahmandad, H. and Spiteri, R. (2015) An introduction to differential games, Chapter 12 in Rahmandad, H., Oliva, R. and Osgood, N. (eds) (2015) *Analytical Methods for Dynamic Modelers*. Cambridge MA: MIT Press.

Ratnarajah, M. (2004) How might the European Union Working Time Directive, designed to limit doctors' hours, contribute to Junior Doctor attrition from the British National Health Service and can desirable outcomes be achieved within these constraints? Executive MBA Management Report, London Business School.

Robertson, D.A. and Caldart, A.A. (2009) *The Dynamics of Strategy: Mastering Strategic Landscapes of the Firm*. Oxford: Oxford University Press.

Robinson, S. (2004) *Simulation: The Practice of Model Development and Use*. Chichester: John Wiley & Sons.

Robinson, S. (2005) Discrete-event simulation: from the pioneers to the present, what next? *Journal of the Operational Research Society*, 56: 619–629.

Roughgarden, J. and Smith, F. (1996) Why fisheries collapse and what to do about it. *Proceedings of the National Academy of Science*, 93(10): 5078–5083.

Rudolph, J.W. and Repenning, N.P. (2002) Disaster dynamics: understanding the role of quantity in organizational collapse. *Administrative Science Quarterly*, 47: 1–30.

Sterman, J., Fiddaman, T., Franck, T. *et al*. (2013) Management flight simulators to support climate negotiations. *Environmental Modelling and Software*, 44: 122–135.

Thompson, K.M. and Tebbens, R.J.D. (2007) Eradication versus control for poliomyelitis: An economic analysis. *The Lancet*, 369(9570): 1363–1371.

Urbanization (2003) *Times Comprehensive Atlas of the World* (11th edn). London: Times Books, pp. 42–43.

Winch, G. and Derrick, S. (2006) Flexible study processes in 'knotty' system dynamics projects. *Systems Research and Behavioral Science*, 23(4): 497–507.

Wolstenholme, E.F. (2006) 'The Potential of System Dynamics', Future Health Care Network, document 10, 1–8, Leading Edge Series. London: NHS Confederation.

Worm, B., Barbier, E.B., Beaumont, N. *et al.* (2006) Impacts of biodiversity loss on ocean ecosystem services. *Science*, 314: 787–790.

Chapter 10
Model Validity, Mental Models and Learning

- Mental Models, Transitional Objects and Formal Models
- Models of Business and Social Systems
- Tests for Building Confidence in Models
- Model Confidence Building Tests in Action: A Case Study in Fast-moving Consumer Goods
- Model Structure Tests and the Soap Industry Model
- Equation Formulation Tests and the Soap Industry Model
- Tests of Learning from Simulation
- Summary of Confidence Building Tests
- Conclusion – Model Fidelity and Usefulness
- Endnote: The Loops of Feedback

In an episode of a popular television programme called Changing Places a computer gaming enthusiast, who had clocked up thousands of simulated hours on a PlayStation driving imaginary high performance cars, was invited to drive a real racing car around Silverstone (a major race circuit in England, home of the British Grand Prix and the birthplace of Formula 1). The experience was sobering. He spun off. Even when he stayed on the track he failed to achieve competitive lap times.

This story is quite revealing about the purpose, limitations and use of models and simulators. A common view is that models are representations of reality intended to be useful to someone charged with managing and participating in that reality.[1] In this case reality has a well-defined meaning (the real racing car

---

[1]In Chapter 1 of Systems Modelling (Pidd, 2004) Mike Pidd describes a spectrum of modelling approaches ranging from those where models are intended to be a shared representation of the real world to those where models are a representation of concepts relevant to the real world. The former

on the track at Silverstone) and it is clear that the computer model falls short of reality in some important ways. The natural temptation for the model user is to demand a better model – one that represents a racing car more accurately. More realism is better.

However, there are several problems with high-fidelity modelling. The most obvious is that realism requires ever more detail. The model can become so large and complex that no one really understands it or has confidence in it. Slightly less obvious is that realism itself is often subject to debate if the system being modelled is ill-defined (suppose we're not really sure, before the event, whether the Silverstone challenge is to drive a car or a motorcycle). Finally, the elusive quest for realism can obscure the value of having some kind of tangible model (even if it is much simplified) versus no formal model at all.

To appreciate the value of a deliberately simplified model, it is useful to reconsider some positive aspects of the Silverstone racing experience. Most basically, the opportunity to 'change places' and drive a real racing car at Silverstone would never have arisen without the gaming simulator. The gaming enthusiast was passionate about motor racing and knew much more about the sport than the average person. He had learned a lot from a few thousand hours with the simulator. He was familiar with the car's instrumentation and controls, he knew Silverstone's layout, he had acquired some expertise in cornering technique (even though he later spun off), and he knew competitive lap times.

Mental Models, Transitional Objects and Formal Models

The would-be racer's success (albeit limited) calls for a new or expanded definition of a model. A model is a tangible aid to imagination and learning, a transitional object to help people make better sense of a partly understood world. This definition focuses particular attention on the interaction that takes place between the model that someone carries in their head of the way something works (their mental model) and a formal model. To illustrate, consider a very different example provided by mathematician and computer scientist Seymour Papert 1980 in his remarkable book *Mindstorms: Children,*

---

characterise hard OR, which provides tools for routine (though important) decision making. The latter characterise soft OR, which provides tools for thinking and for making sense of messes/wicked problems.

Computers and Powerful Ideas. He begins the book with an engaging personal recollection entitled 'The Gears of My Childhood', a story of how he came to better understand the working of complex sets of gears and ultimately abstract ideas in mathematics (p. vi):

> Before I was two years old I had developed an intense involvement with auto-mobiles. The names of car parts made up a very substantial portion of my vocabulary: I was particularly proud knowing about the parts of the transmis-sion system, the gearbox and most especially the differential. It was of course many years later before I understood how gears worked: but once I did, playing with gears became a favorite pastime. I loved rotating circular objects against one another in gearlike motions and naturally, my first 'erector set' project was a crude gear system.

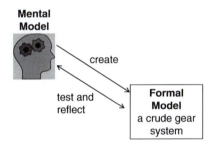

interaction of formal model and individual mental model (through creation, testing and reflection) to improve personal understanding – a learning process

Figure 10.1   Formal model as transitional object for individual learning – 'gears of childhood'

Source: From *Systems Modelling – Theory and Practice*, Edited by Mike Pidd, 2004, © John Wiley & Sons Limited. Reproduced with permission.

Figure 10.1 shows the role of the formal model (in this case a crude gear system) in a learning process. On the left is the child's mental model of a gear system depicted as gears in the mind. On the right is the formal model – a tangible set of gear parts that can be assembled, broken apart and re-assembled in lots of different ways. At the start, the child's mental model is primitive and naïve, but the activity of repeatedly playing with the gear set leads to a much more sophisticated understanding and deeper appreciation of gear-like motions. The mental model goes through a series of 'transitions' from naïve to more sophisticated through repeated use of the gear set as a transitional object. Papert (1980: vi) fondly recalls his early learning experience:

> I became adept at turning wheels in my head and at making chains of cause and effect: 'This one turns this way so that must turn that way so ...' I found

particular pleasure in such systems as the differential gear, which does not follow a simple linear chain of causality since the motion in the transmission shaft can be distributed in many different ways depending on what resistance they encounter. I remember quite vividly my excitement at discovering that a system could be lawful and completely comprehensible without being rigidly deterministic. I believe that working with differentials did more for my mathematical development than anything I was taught in elementary school. Gears, serving as models, carried many otherwise abstract ideas into my head.

(From the Foreword of Papert, S., 1980, *Mindstorms: Children, Computers and Powerful Ideas*. Basic Books, New York.)

Note that the definition of 'model-as-transitional-object' suggests a formal model achieves its value principally through creation and use (Morecroft, 2004). Moreover, tangibility is an important attribute of a transitional object somehow different from adequacy of representation. As Papert comments, gears serving as models not only enabled him to think more clearly about gear-like motion, but also to understand abstract ideas about mathematics.

Models of Business and Social Systems

The significance of viewing formal models as transitional objects is the emphasis placed on aiding understanding rather than replicating reality. The idea that there is a singular and objective world out there to be modelled is replaced with the softer notion that a formal model can help to improve mental models. It is through mental models that we interpret and make sense of the world around us. In business and social systems, mental models shape decisions and actions. As Forrester (1975: 213) noted of social systems:

> The mental image of the world around us that we carry in our heads is a model. One does not have a city or government in his head. He has only selected concepts and relationships which he uses to represent the real system. A mental image is a model. All our decisions are taken on the basis of models. All laws are passed on the basis of models. All executive actions are taken on the basis of models. The question is not to use or ignore models. The question is only a choice among alternative models.

Figure 10.2 shows the alternative mental models of a management team. Like Papert's gears in the mind, each member of the management team carries around an image of the organisation taken from the real world. Individuals' mental images vary according to their experience, responsibilities, power, ambitions and objectives, represented by different shades of grey in the boxes surrounding each head. A formal model is an instrument to elicit these different mental models with the objective of improving the quality of the decisions and actions taken by the team.

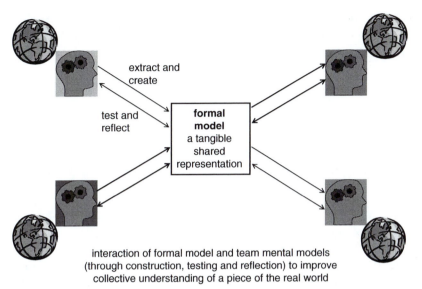

interaction of formal model and team mental models
(through construction, testing and reflection) to improve
collective understanding of a piece of the real world

Figure 10.2   Formal model as transitional object for team learning
Source: From *Systems Modelling – Theory and Practice*, Edited by Mike Pidd, 2004, © John Wiley &
Sons Limited. Reproduced with permission.

The kind of formal model created depends on the strengths and weaknesses of
mental models and common deficiencies in our ways of thinking about
business and social systems. System dynamics assumes that competent
management teams are good at describing the operating structure of their
organisations – how the different decision rules, functions, divisions and
regions work individually. Where teams need help and where mental models
are deficient are in: (1) seeing how the pieces fit together (taking an overview;
seeing the forest while not losing sight of the trees) and (2) determining the
performance over time (the dynamic consequences) when the parts of the
organisation interact with each other. Like Papert's gear-set, the formal model
enables the management team to test, reflect and learn something new about
their world – in this case to improve their understanding of the relationship
between the organisation's feedback structure and its performance over time.

Tests for Building Confidence in Models

The fluid nature of models in the social sciences has led system dynamicists
(and other social system modellers) to adopt a broad and pragmatic view of
model validity as a process of confidence building among those who will use
the model (Forrester and Senge, 1980). Confidence building involves a variety
of different tests to assess the quality of both the model and the model building

process. Here I present three categories of tests that have proven particularly useful in practice: tests of model structure, tests of model behaviour and tests of learning. Other tests are also used, but they are beyond the scope of this book. Readers who wish to know more are referred to the comprehensive treatment of model validation and testing in Sterman (2000: Chapter 21).

- Tests of model structure are intended to assess whether the feedback structure and equation formulations of the model are consistent with the available facts and descriptive knowledge of the real-world system. These tests apply to both the conceptual model and the algebraic model and are very important in system dynamics practice because they draw attention to whether modellers are making effective use of both formal and informal information sources for modelling. Often people expect model development to require large data-gathering exercises to compile facts and figures about a firm or industry from written and numerical data bases. However, as Figure 10.3 illustrates, there is also a vast amount of relevant data about social systems that resides in the minds of experienced people (their collective mental database). This information about the inner workings of the organisation, its procedures, priorities and even culture is rarely found in either formal numerical or written databases, yet is vital to a good representation of structure.[2]

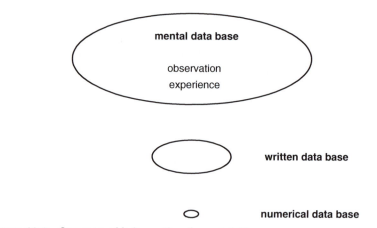

Figure 10.3   Sources of information for modelling
Source: Jay Forrester, 1994, Policies, Decisions and Information Sources for Modelling, in *Modelling for Learning Organizations*. Productivity Press. Reproduced by permission of Jay W. Forrester.

- Tests of model behaviour are intended to assess the fit of simulations to observed real system behaviour. They serve a similar purpose to conventional

---

[2]One might argue that the internet, with its vast store of searchable information, has changed the relative size of the three 'data base ovals' and even blurred the categories. However, the three-ovals diagram should not be lightly discarded. It is a clear and powerful image about the nature of data in system dynamics modelling. It suggests that behavioural modellers, in their search for structural clues about interlocking operations, will always need tacit organisational information gleaned predominantly from the minds of experienced stakeholders,

goodness-of-fit tests in statistics and econometrics. However, behaviour tests are typically less formal than regression methods or statistical tests of significance in that they often rely on visual criteria to gauge goodness-of-fit such as the shape, scale and timing of simulated trajectories relative to actual time series data. Unlike regression methods, behaviour tests do not involve statistical estimation of parameter values to achieve a best fit with time series. The parameter values in the model are obtained from numerical facts in the case, independent of time series data. Any adjustments to parameter values made to improve fit with time series must remain plausibly close to the independent numerical facts (unless of course the facts themselves prove to be wrong or misleading).

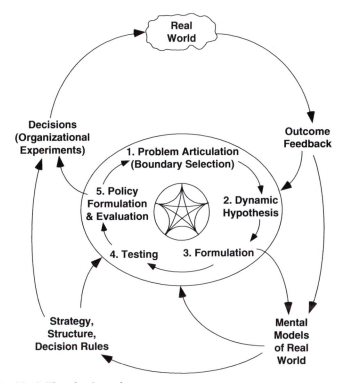

Figure 10.4   Modelling for learning

Source: Sterman, J.D., *Business Dynamics: Systems Thinking and Modeling for a Complex World*, © 2000, Irwin McGraw-Hill, Boston, MA. Reproduced with permission of the McGraw-Hill Companies.

- Tests of learning are intended to assess whether model users have gained new insight about system structure or learned something new about real system behaviour. These tests draw attention to the interaction between mental models and formal models during a modelling project. They differ from the other tests because they focus on soft aspects of modelling – not so much the fit of the model with the real world but rather its ability to influence the way model users interpret their world. Learning can occur at any stage of the modelling process from problem articulation to model formulation and testing as Figure 10.4 illustrates. Here the modelling process interacts with a larger organisational process of strategic change involving mental models, decisions and outcome feedback. The learning cycle in the outer loop is slow and imperfect because organisational experiments take a long time to conduct and mental models are resistant to change. Moreover, outcome feedback is patchy and tricky to interpret. Formal models can accelerate this learning cycle by providing new insight into both system structure and likely dynamic behaviour.

Model Confidence Building Tests in Action: A Case Study in Fast-moving Consumer Goods

To illustrate confidence building tests, we examine a model developed with the management team of a company in fast-moving consumer goods. The modelling project was part of a doctoral thesis at London Business School (Kunc, 2005).[3] For confidentiality reasons, the case is disguised as the UK personal care market involving soap products that readers know well. The fictitious name of the client firm is the 'Old English Bar Soap Company'. The purpose of the project was to help the management team think through the launch of a new liquid soap product that had been developed as an alternative to its popular traditional bar soap in a premium quality segment of the market.[4] Although the real-life product was not soap at all, the strategic innovation was similar to a change from bar soap to liquid soap.

Soap Market Overview

Before the introduction of liquid soap, the personal cleansing market had been divided between bar soaps and shower gels. As Figure 10.5 shows, bar soap was the product leader with more than 70% market share throughout the late 1980s and early 1990s. However, shower gels (which Old English did not make) had gained market share in the late 1990s pushed by aggressive marketing campaigns and changes in lifestyle. This substitution process was occurring in a market whose sales volume had been stable for many years due

---

[3]I am grateful to Martin Kunc for permission to adapt the case study in his PhD thesis for use in this chapter. I have also used text excerpts and diagrams from a book chapter based on the thesis, reported in Kunc and Morecroft (2007), Chapter 7 in *Supporting Strategy* © John Wiley & Sons Limited. Reproduced with permission and also available to readers as an electronic document in the learning support folder for Chapter 6.

[4]The project sparked many enjoyable conversations with Martin about modelling and problem structuring. It also brought into focus the interpretive stance of system dynamics during model conceptualisation, as neatly illustrated in the contrast between the preliminary and refined models of the soap industry described later in this chapter. My thanks to Gail Hohner for setting up the project.

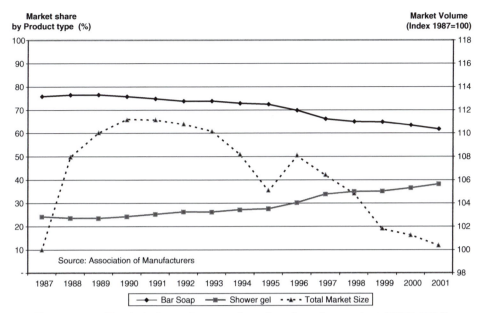

Figure 10.5   Total market volume and market share by product (1987–2001)

to high penetration of demographic segments and low population growth. Indeed, total market size was gradually declining throughout the 1990s as the dotted line in Figure 10.5 illustrates. Meanwhile, bar soap firms introduced variations on their traditional product in an attempt to increase sales value. These variations were stimulated by consumers' willingness to buy premium soaps (instead of cheaper alternatives) as well as demographic and lifestyle changes. In spite of these developments, the general trend was away from bar soap towards shower gels.

The prospect of stagnation and declining profitability in their traditional bar soap business prompted Old English to launch an entirely new premium product, liquid soap, intended to halt the erosion of soap sales and to boost the profitability of its core business in the mature soap market.

The Modelling Project

The study was undertaken about three years into the launch of liquid soap, at an early stage of market development. The modelling team consisted of two system dynamics professionals and an internal consultant of the company. The management team consisted of senior managers from marketing, sales and manufacturing. The project ran for one year with intermittent team meetings to extract and validate the information required for the model. The model was designed to answer the following questions for the management team. How can we grow and sustain the new liquid soap in the face of stiff competition? What set of policies can help us to avoid the revenue losses being incurred by the bar soap business? The project methodology followed the five steps outlined in Chapter 5 (see Figure 5.1 and also Figure 10.4), beginning with problem articulation and ending with policy formulation and evaluation.

Model Structure Tests and the Soap Industry Model

Model structure tests build confidence in the model by demonstrating that its concepts and relationships are consistent with observations about structure and policies from the mental database of people who know the business well – in this case the senior managers from marketing, sales and manufacturing. These tests are particularly important in system dynamics because structure is central to understanding dynamic behaviour. As previously mentioned, much of the data for identifying structure resides in the mental database, where it is accompanied by other kinds of system-related data as Figure 10.6 illustrates. The figure distinguishes three different types of information in the mental database: observations about structure and policies; expectations about system behaviour; and actual observed system behaviour.

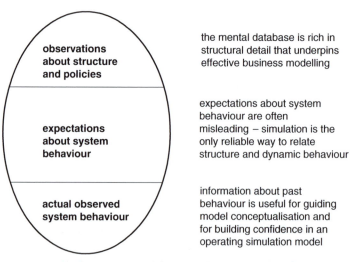

Figure 10.6   Role of the Mental Data Base in Modelling and Confidence Building

Source: Jay Forrester, 1994, Policies, Decisions and Information Sources for Modelling, in *Modelling for Learning Organizations*, Productivity Press. Reproduced by permission of Jay W. Forrester.

The mental database is particularly rich in structural detail about operations at a functional level. For example, at Old English the marketing manager could explain promotional price discounts and their impact on consumers. The factory manager knew the plant intimately and appreciated the practical difficulties in shifting capacity from bar soap to liquid soap. Collectively, the management team holds a wealth of information about causal links, operating procedures, decision rules and the relative priority of information flows – all of which underpin effective business modelling.

The mental database also contains information about system behaviour (past trends and patterns in key variables) that is useful for guiding model conceptualisation and for building confidence in simulations. In this case, the decline in bar soap volume was well known and easily cross-checked with time series data. However, not all information in the mental database is reliable for modelling. In particular people's expectations about system behaviour are often misleading because they cannot infer cause and effect. Simulation is the only rigorous way to relate the structure and dynamic behaviour of business and social systems.

Bearing in mind the contents of the mental, written and numerical databases, there are five main tests of model structure as listed below. The first two tests apply to conceptual models and the remaining tests apply to algebraic models.

- Boundary adequacy – are the important concepts for addressing the problem endogenous to the model?
- Structure verification – is the model structure consistent with descriptive knowledge of the system?
- Dimensional consistency – are all equations dimensionally correct without the use of parameters that have no real world counterpart?
- Parameter verification – are parameters consistent with descriptive and numerical knowledge?
- Extreme conditions – does each equation make sense even when its inputs take on extreme values?

Boundary Adequacy and Structure Verification Tests Applied to a Simple Soap Model

The stock and flow network shown in Figure 10.7 was sketched during the first meeting with the management team. It is a simple conceptual model that was subsequently refined and improved, but it is worth careful consideration as a transitional object leading ultimately to better understanding of the market. Notice there are two conceptually separate market segments.

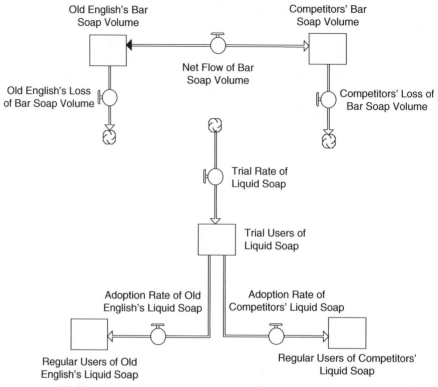

Figure 10.7 Management team's first conceptual model of soap market
Source: From *Supporting Strategy: Frameworks, Methods and Models*, Edited by Frances O'Brien and Robert Dyson, 2007, © John Wiley & Sons Limited. Reproduced with permission.

At the top of the figure is the bar soap segment, containing bar soap volume for Old English on the left and for competitors on the right. These volumes are represented as stock accumulations to capture the typical inertia of consumer buying habits. Volume lost to other product types is shown as outflows. Volume exchanged through competition is shown as a net flow of bar soap volume between Old English and competitors. Notice also there are no inflows to the two stock accumulations, reflecting an important assumption that the market is mature. So far, so good – this part of the model is compact and captures several realistic features of the bar soap market.

At the bottom of the figure is the new market segment for liquid soap in which trials of the new product lead to an accumulation of trial users who then adopt either Old English's liquid soap or competitors' liquid soap. Adoption results in an increasing number of regular users represented by two stock accumulations. Note that managers expected to attract and retain loyal customers in the new premium liquid soap market as there is no flow from regular users of Old English's liquid soap to regular users of competitors' liquid soaps.

Figure 10.7 reveals three interesting weaknesses in the initial conceptualisation of the strategic initiative in liquid soap. First, the management team perceived the bar soap and liquid soap market segments as disconnected from each other, even though when pressed they would acknowledge the markets are linked. Second, users of bar soap were lost to 'somewhere' in the personal care market, through the outflow 'Loss of Bar Soap volume'. In fact, much of this loss was to shower gel, but since Old English's management had neither a special interest nor the capabilities to compete strongly in shower gel, the slow draining of customers to gels was not clearly recognised or at least its cumulative effect was thought to be small. This blind spot may have influenced Old English's subsequent innovation. Third, the market for the new product was believed to be a one-off simple adoption process. Old English's management would convince bar soap consumers to trial the new product. These potential consumers, in the stock labelled 'Trial Users of Liquid Soap', would remain an uncertainty until they decided to adopt Old English's or a competitor's liquid soap. The strategic problem would be solved for Old English when trial users became regular users of liquid soap, protected by first-mover advantage – since management believed that Old English had a significant head-start in the technology required to produce liquid soap. In other words, the strategic intent was to contain competitors in the bar soap segment while the company built its leadership in the liquid soap segment. Then, liquid soap users would remain isolated from competitors' actions because of first-mover advantage.

Although this diagram was a useful start, and reflects the way the management team first talked about the product launch, it fails both the structure verification and boundary adequacy tests. The portrayal of rivals is inconsistent with management's own descriptive knowledge of the soap market. In fact, there are two main branded competitors (Old English with 26% market share and Global Personal Care with 31% market share). In addition there are supermarkets that collectively hold 16% market share with private label soaps. Together these rival groupings account for most of the market in value terms. However, Global Personal Care and supermarkets cannot simply be aggregated into a monolithic rival, because they are very different businesses with distinct goals and objectives.

Besides an overly-simplistic representation of rivals the conceptual model does not endogenously represent the flow rates that determine sales and market share of liquid soap. When these drivers are added to the model the interdependencies in the business become more apparent (such as cannibalism of bar soap by liquid soap, the effect of capacity on cost and price, the interplay between marketing and performance targets and the impact of rivals). An appreciation of these interdependencies sharpened management's understanding of the realistic growth prospects of the liquid soap business. All this factual information about rivals and internal operations was well known by the management team but was missing from the initial conceptual model.

A Refined View of the Market

After a presentation of the initial model and discussion with senior managers, their specific knowledge of competitors was incorporated into the modified model of the market shown in Figure 10.8. The three distinct rivals are now clearly represented, each with bar soap and liquid soap products. On the left is Old English with its established product 'Traditional English Bar Soap' and its new product 'Antibacterial Liquid Soap'. On the right is Global Personal Care with its established product 'Moisturising Bar Soap' and its new product 'Creamy Liquid Soap'. In the middle are supermarkets with their established product 'Me Too Bar Soap' and their new product 'Me Too Liquid Soap'.

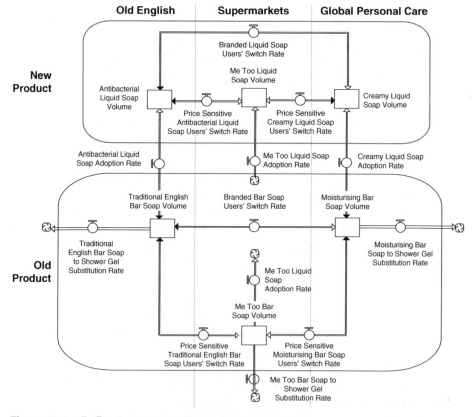

Figure 10.8 Refined conceptual model of soap market
Source: From *Supporting Strategy: Frameworks, Methods and Models*, Edited by Frances O'Brien and Robert Dyson, 2007, © John Wiley & Sons Limited. Reproduced with permission.

This new picture illustrates structure verification and also the kind of learning that happens during model conceptualisation. It reveals more clearly than before the complex situation facing the main players in the bar soap market. Each player has to balance the attractiveness of their established products, taking account of three different forces simultaneously influencing their customers. The first force is traditional inter-firm rivalry in the bar soap market from consumer promotions and advertising, aimed at maintaining market share in bar soap. This rivalry is depicted in the flow rates between the three bar soap stocks in the bottom half of Figure 10.8. For example the bi-flow labelled 'Branded Bar Soap Users' Switch Rate' represents competition in bar soaps between Old English and Global Personal Care. Similarly, the bi-flow labelled 'Price Sensitive Traditional English Bar Soap Users' Switch Rate' represents competition in bar soaps between Old English and supermarkets.

The second force influencing customers is the development of the liquid soap market represented as the set of three stocks in the top half of Figure 10.8 ('Antibacterial Liquid Soap volume', 'Me Too Liquid Soap volume' and 'Creamy Liquid Soap volume') and the corresponding adoption rates. The third force is the attractiveness of shower gels – a substitute product – represented as outflows from bar soap volume in Figure 10.8. For example, the outflow 'Traditional English Bar Soap to Shower Gel Substitution Rate' represents the loss of Old English bar soap volume to shower gel. Interestingly, the refined view of the market still implies a simple and incomplete perception by management of the shower gel market. Shower gel is effectively outside the model boundary and remained that way because the management team was not expecting to develop a presence in the market.

Since this is a mature market with a high level of penetration, there are no inflows to increase total volume. In other words, the development of the market is essentially a zero-sum game between brands and varieties – and in soaps this game is played against the backdrop of gradual volume loss to shower gels. While managers' intention at Old English was to move users from bar soaps into liquid soaps (and focus groups suggested that bar soap users would indeed adopt liquid soaps) they nevertheless faced a dynamically complex problem. The company needed to persuade bar soap users to adopt liquid soap without losing market share, while also improving profitability and avoiding costly price wars. Essentially they were managing a growth business (liquid soap) alongside a declining business (bar soap) against strong and diverse rivals.

Boundary Adequacy and Sector Map of the Complete Soap Industry Model

The refined market sector was an improvement on the first conceptual model, but it still does not pass the boundary adequacy test since it says nothing at all about the internal operations of the rival firms. Nevertheless, it is an important piece in the jigsaw because it tells the modeller a great deal about the shapes of the other missing pieces. In fact, the market sector became literally the centrepiece of a fully endogenous model whose boundary included the operational factors that control the movement of sales volume between the three main rivals and between bar soap, liquid soap and shower gel.

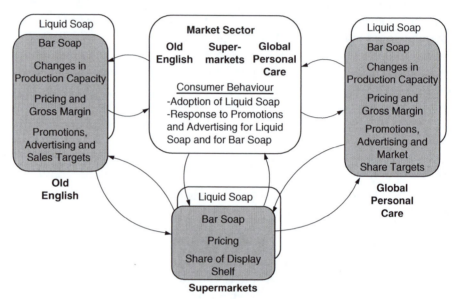

Figure 10.9   Sector map of the soap industry model

A sector map of the complete model is shown in Figure 10.9. The market sector is in the centre and includes formulations for consumer behaviour to represent both the adoption of liquid soap and response to promotions and advertising for liquid soap and for bar soap. On the left are two sectors representing Old English. The company is conceptually divided into bar soap and liquid soap operations each containing formulations for changes in production capacity, pricing, gross margin, promotions, advertising and sales targets. A similar approach is taken to representing Global Personal Care in the two sectors on the right. At the bottom of the diagram are two sectors representing supermarkets, again divided into bar soap and liquid soap, each sector containing formulations for pricing and share of display shelf.

I should stress that the conceptual separation of bar soap and liquid soap in the two branded manufacturers and in the supermarkets is a modelling convenience – a way of interpreting the complexity of the business that makes sense for the problem at hand. The separation does not imply that bar soap and liquid soap were organised as two distinct divisions; far from it. In Old English, a single factory produced both bar and liquid soaps, and product pricing was handled centrally as were promotions and advertising. These six sectors interact with each other and with the market sector in the centre to yield a rich feedback structure indicated by the arrows in Figure 10.9.

Managerial Decision-making Processes in the Old English Bar Soap Company

The majority of the model was devoted to representing managerial decision-making processes inside the three rival organisations that, directly or indirectly, influence consumer behaviour. These decision-making processes control changes in production capacity, pricing, promotions, advertising and the management of display shelf – the factors shown in the sector map. The corresponding formulations run to more than one hundred equations. They were constructed from concepts and facts gathered in many hours of meetings and sketched on a diagram occupying 12 A4 pages. There is not the space here to document each and every equation in detail. Instead, a brief verbal description of the formulations is presented below that gives a feel for the range of concepts included within the boundary of the model.

Production capacity is the responsibility of the manufacturing manager. The technology of liquid soap production is entirely different from bar soap and requires new equipment. Hence, the manufacturing manager faced a strategic dilemma about how quickly to build capacity for the new product and how quickly to retire capacity for the old product. The decision-making process for changes in production capacity is essentially driven by market size. The larger the expected sales volume the more capacity is needed and vice versa. Economies of scale are important too. The greater capacity, the lower unit cost and the lower price (at a given margin), leading to more sales and eventually to more capacity. The same process also works in reverse. When sales fall, cost per unit increases due to a combination of low capacity utilisation, high fixed cost and fewer scale economies. As a result, retail price increases too, unless the firm reduces gross margin to maintain sales. The model captures the interplay of manufacturing cost dynamics arising from the growth of liquid soap capacity and the simultaneous decline of bar soap capacity.

Promotions and advertising are adjusted to achieve a sales performance target. In Old English, the target is past sales. So the logic of the decision-making process is as follows. If current sales volume is much less than past sales volume then the company increases promotions (by offering bigger price discounts) or initiates new advertising campaigns to boost sales. On the other hand, if current sales volume is much greater than past sales volume then the company reduces promotions and advertising in order to dampen sales and also to improve operating cash flows. Small differences between current and past volumes tend to be ignored. The management response function is shown in Figure 10.10 and was calibrated by comparing observed volume changes with the historical behaviour of retail prices and the intensity of advertising campaigns. Paradoxically, this formulation of promotions and advertising implies that Old English's managers ignore competitors' actions when assessing which marketing actions to take. Instead, they focus myopically on their own sales volumes rather than benchmarking against Global Personal Care or supermarkets.

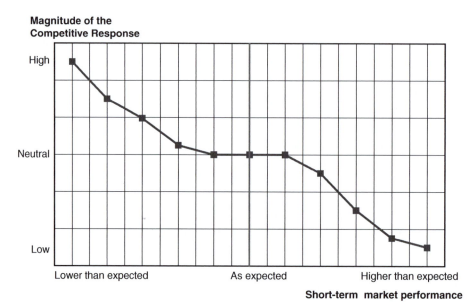

Figure 10.10 Function determining the strength of Old English's competitive response to market performance

Source: From *Supporting Strategy: Frameworks, Methods and Models*, Edited by Frances O'Brien and Robert Dyson, 2007, © John Wiley & Sons Limited. Reproduced with permission.

Managerial Decision-making Processes in Global Personal Care

The management team felt that Global Personal Care's decision-making processes were broadly similar to Old English. Therefore, Global Personal Care was modelled by replicating the formulations for Old English while modifying information flows or parameters to capture important differences of managerial emphasis. For example, it was assumed that Global Personal Care focuses its competitive actions on managing market share rather than sales volume. Hence, in Global Personal Care, promotions and advertising increase when market share falls below its historic value. Sales volume plays no significant role. Similarly, Global Personal Care's adjustment to mark-up or gross margin is formulated as a function of long-term market share instead of sales volume. It was also assumed that Global Personal Care offers a slightly higher trade margin than Old English in order to obtain an adequate share of shelf space despite lower market share.

Managerial Decision-making Processes in Supermarkets

Supermarkets' pricing is much different than Old English and Global Personal Care for a number of reasons. First, supermarkets do not aspire to be market leaders. Rather they participate in the market enough to bargain effectively with existing branded manufacturers. Second, supermarkets do not manufacture or own capacity. Instead, they buy from manufacturers that specialise in private label products. Third, supermarkets do not promote their product through advertising. They compete on price only.

Supermarkets' pricing is intended to boost income from display shelf. The decision rule for supermarkets' pricing is influenced by trade margin received and by product sales – the two main sources of retailers' income. The income received from branded products in the form of trade margin is compared with the historical trade margin. If income from branded products falls, either as result of a reduction in branded manufacturers' trade margin or market share, then supermarket managers reduce own-label retail price for two reasons. First, they want to expand supermarket sales to substitute for income lost from manufacturers. Second, they want to force an improvement in the trade margin. However, as supermarkets expand their market share, the income from branded products will decline even more (if manufacturers of branded products do not offer higher trade margins), and supermarkets will further reduce their prices.

An extreme outcome of this interaction between manufacturers and retailers is that supermarkets will dominate the market through continuous price reductions (as happened with Wal-Mart in some market segments of fast-moving consumer goods). Pricing decisions that respond to income from trade margin are embedded in a reinforcing feedback loop in which price spirals downwards. Although there is a lower limit to price, it depends on the sourcing cost of supermarket products and the actual trade margin obtained from branded manufacturers. However, supermarket managers usually prefer to set a target market share that is low enough to maintain bargaining power without pushing branded manufacturers out of the market. This policy introduces an additional balancing feedback loop that halts the spiral decline in price.

Display shelf is negotiated between retailers and branded manufacturers. Share of the display shelf is fiercely contested in fast-moving consumer goods, no matter how large or small the store. While big stores can offer lots of shelf space, it is easily filled by the huge proliferation of available products, thereby improving the bargaining position of retailers. The task of branded manufacturers' sales managers is to negotiate a significant share of display shelf at low cost in order to enhance daily sales and to increase the effectiveness of advertising campaigns. Conversely, retailers' management teams try to maximise the income received for allocated space by assigning the greatest share to the most profitable items. The decision-making process for changes in display shelf depends on trade margin and market share. The more market share or the greater trade margin then the larger the display shelf. This decision logic is embedded in a reinforcing feedback loop where the more shelf space, the greater sales volume, the higher market share and the more shelf space. If unchecked, this reinforcing loop enables branded manufacturers to dominate the market. However, retailers use private label products to retain some control.

That concludes the review of the model's main sectors and the underlying conceptual model. It should be clear that there were many opportunities to test the consistency of the model structure with descriptive knowledge of the business.

Equation Formulation Tests and the Soap Industry Model

Equation formulation tests build further confidence in the model by demonstrating that equations and numerical parameters in the model are consistent with available facts and data from the mental, written and numerical databases.

There are three common tests, mentioned earlier, and for convenience repeated here:

- Dimensional consistency – Are all equations dimensionally correct without the use of parameters that have no real-world counterpart?
- Parameter verification – Are parameters consistent with descriptive and numerical knowledge?
- Extreme conditions – Does each equation make sense even when its inputs take on extreme values?

To illustrate the tests, we review a selection of equation formulations describing consumer behaviour which are taken from the market sector of the soap industry model.

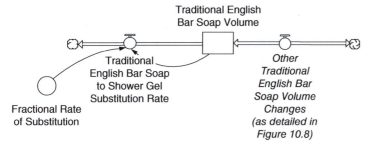

Traditional English
Bar Soap Volume

Traditional
English Bar Soap
to Shower Gel
Substitution Rate

*Other
Traditional
English Bar
Soap Volume
Changes
(as detailed in
Figure 10.8)*

Fractional Rate
of Substitution

Traditional English Bar Soap Volume (t) = Traditional English Bar Soap Volume (t-dt)
+ (Other Traditional English Bar Soap Volume Changes)
− (Traditional English Bar Soap to Shower Gel Substitution Rate) * dt
INIT Traditional English Bar Soap Volume = 12.69 *{thousands of tonnes per month}*

Traditional English Bar Soap to Shower Gel Substitution Rate =
　　Traditional English Bar Soap Volume * Fractional Rate of Substitution
　　{thousands of tonnes per month per month}

Fractional Rate of Substitution = 0.005 *{proportion per month or 1/month}*

Figure 10.11　Equations for bar soap volume and substitution by shower gel

Substitution of Bar Soap by Shower Gel

The substitution rate of bar soap by shower gel is expressed as the product of Traditional English Bar Soap volume and the fractional rate of substitution, as shown in Figure 10.11. The equation is a standard stock depletion formulation algebraically similar to the workforce departure rate in Chapter 5's simple factory model and to independents' capacity loss in the oil producers' model. Identical formulations apply to the substitution rates of Moisturising Bar Soap and Me Too Bar Soap. The fractional rate of substitution is defined as a fixed proportion, 0.005 per month, of bar soap volume. This proportion captures two shared beliefs among managers: one is that remaining bar soap consumers will gradually convert to shower gels (unless they first adopt liquid soap); and the second is that all players in bar soap are experiencing a similar substitution process. Note that the equation is dimensionally balanced, though it requires careful consideration of the units of measure to demonstrate the balance. On the right, the units of bar soap volume are thousands of tonnes per month, which is a measure of demand. On the left, the units of the substitution rate are thousands of tonnes per month per month, which is a measure of the rate of change of demand. To achieve a balance it is necessary to introduce an extra parameter on the right-hand side of the equation called the fractional rate of substitution. This parameter has a real-world meaning. It corresponds to the fraction of remaining bar soap demand substituted each month by shower gel. Its unit of measure is 'proportion per month' (or 1/month, since the proportion itself is a dimensionless quantity). Therefore, the dimensions of the multiplicative expression on the right reduce to thousands of tonnes per month per month, which balances with the left. The management team were aware of consumers' gradual conversion to shower gels and, when pressed to think hard about the process, were able to estimate an annual loss rate of about 6% per year, which re-scales to the monthly figure of 0.005 per month shown.

Brand Switching Between Competing Bar Soap Products

Brand switching is driven by promotions and advertising. However, management believed that the personal care market is commoditised with little long-term loyalty except the inertia of buying habits. Hence, although promotional price discounts and advertising campaigns win customers, any volume gains are reversible if (as usually happens) rivals respond with equivalent or better discounts and more advertising. In Figure 10.12, this to-and-fro of consumer demand is shown as a bi-flow, called the 'Branded Bar Soap Users' Switch Rate', and is formulated as the sum of two independent terms: volume change due to price promotions and volume change due to advertising. Note that the units of measure of the users' switch rate are thousands of tonnes per month per month – identical to the units of the substitution rate mentioned above, because both belong in the same stock and flow network.

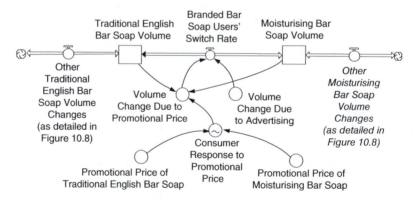

Branded Bar Soap Users' Switch Rate = Volume Change Due to Price Promotions + Volume Change Due to Advertising *{thousands of tonnes per month per month}*

Volume Change Due to Price Promotions = IF (Consumer Response to Promotional Price <= 0) THEN (Moisturising Bar Soap Volume * Consumer Response to Promotional Price) ELSE (Traditional English Bar Soap Volume * Consumer Response to Promotional Price)

Consumer Response to Promotional Price = GRAPH (Promotional Price of Traditional English Bar Soap/Promotional Price of Moisturising Bar Soap) *{proportion per month or 1/month}*

Figure 10.12 Equations for brand switching

An identical formulation is used for brand switching between liquid soaps. The formulation can also be adapted for consumers switching between branded and private label soaps by simply removing the term for volume change due to advertising (since Me Too products are not advertised and tend to attract price sensitive consumers who pay close attention to relative prices).

Consumers' responses to promotions and advertising are important assumptions in the model. Are the formulations plausible? In this case, a combination of descriptive knowledge and numerical data was used to build confidence in the equations. For brevity we will focus on the formulations for promotions and leave aside the independent effect of advertising. How do promotions work? Despite the wide variety of soaps on offer, Old English's management team believed the differences between each player's soaps were small and that consumers' choice between two brands is based on relative price including promotions. To capture this effect, the model uses the concept of 'consumer response to promotional price', which is formulated in Figure 10.12 as a function of the ratio of the promotional price of Traditional English Bar Soap to the promotional price of Moisturising Bar Soap. In this formulation the promotional price of one brand is used as a reference point for comparison with the other brand, which is an empirical generalisation often used in modelling consumer choice (Meyer and Johnson, 1995).

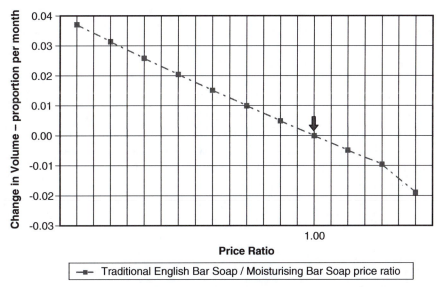

Figure 10.13   Consumer response to promotional price in branded bar soaps

The price ratio affects volume change according to the graphical function shown in Figure 10.13. The function was calibrated using time series data for relative price and volume obtained from A.C. Neilsen's report of volumes and sales by distribution channel – a reliable and well-respected source of information in fast-moving consumer goods. For confidentiality reasons, the scale of the horizontal axis is suppressed. Nevertheless, it is clear than when the price ratio takes a value '1', meaning that competing branded products are priced the same as Old English, then the change in volume is zero, as expected (unless the Old English brand has a higher reputation among consumers, leading them to pay a premium, which is represented as a price ratio greater than 1). Also the function is downward sloping as common sense would suggest. Hence, when the price ratio is less than '1' (Traditional English Bar Soap is priced below Moisturising Bar Soap) the function takes a value greater than zero and there is a net flow of volume into Traditional English Bar Soap. Moreover, this volume change is proportional to the stock of Moisturising Bar Soap volume since a price discount on Traditional English Bar Soap attracts consumers of Moisturising Bar Soap. Conversely when the price ratio is greater than '1' (Traditional English Bar Soap is priced above Moisturising Bar Soap) the function takes a value less than zero and there is a net flow of volume in the opposite direction into Moisturising Bar Soap. In this case, the volume change is proportional to the stock of Traditional English Bar Soap volume. The switch in the stock that drives volume change is formulated as a logical if-then-else function.[5]

Equivalent downward sloping functions were used to depict competition between branded and private label products. The effect of different value perceptions for competing products can be deduced from the relative slope of the functions shown in Figure 10.14. For example, the slope of the dashed line for two products with similar perceived value (Traditional English and Moisturising Bar Soaps) is much steeper than the slope of either of the solid lines for two products with different perceived value (Traditional English and Me Too Bar Soaps or Moisturising and Me Too Bar Soaps). Consumers are more likely to switch between two products perceived similarly than two products perceived differently, which implies that supermarkets need to sustain bigger price differentials with respect to branded products in order to lure customers from branded products or to avoid losing customers. The relative slopes made sense to the management team and coincided with their judgemental knowledge of the market, thereby helping to build their confidence in the formulations.

---

[5]It is unusual to find if-then-else equation formulations in system dynamics models of decision making. In fact, such formulations should normally be avoided since they suggest the modeller is adopting a perspective on the problem situation that is too close to operational detail and therefore in danger of missing the flux of pressures that come to bear on operating policy. In this case, an if-then-else equation formulation seemed unavoidable and the modeller accepted a pragmatic compromise. (Review the comments in Chapter 7 about the modeller's quest to view the firm from the perspective of the CEO or member of the board.)

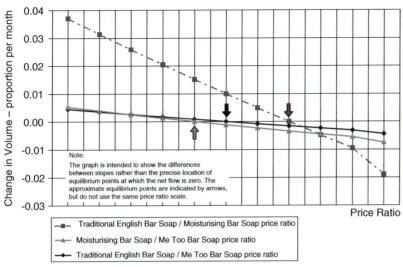

Figure 10.14   Consumer response to promotional price in branded and private label soaps

Source: From *Supporting Strategy: Frameworks, Methods and Models*, Edited by Frances O'Brien and Robert Dyson, 2007, © John Wiley & Sons Limited. Reproduced with permission.

A similar price response curve was devised for liquid soap and is shown in Figure 10.15. For comparison, the equivalent curve for bar soap is shown as a dotted line. Once again the relative slopes made sense to the management team.

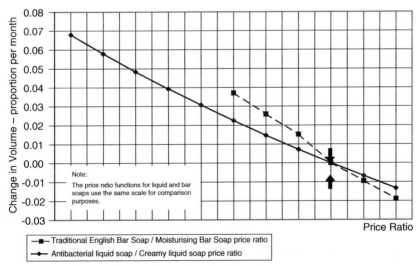

Figure 10.15   Consumer response to promotional price for bar and liquid soaps

Source: From *Supporting Strategy: Frameworks, Methods and Models*, Edited by Frances O'Brien and Robert Dyson, 2007, © John Wiley & Sons Limited. Reproduced with permission.

To summarise, this review of formulations for consumer behaviour illustrates how a combination of mental, written and numerical data helps to build confidence in the model's equations, even among people who do not normally think about their business algebraically. Wherever possible, the same process of grounding was used with the other equations. The parameterised model was then simulated and anomalous behaviour rectified by modifying equations and parameters while ensuring they were still consistent with the available judgemental and factual information. The model was then ready for evaluating the new product strategy.

At this stage of a modelling project a great deal has been accomplished. A complex situation has been represented in a visual conceptual model and in matching equations. The individual equations have been calibrated to be consistent with available knowledge. If all this work has been carried out with integrity, rigour and professionalism then confidence in the model will already be well established.

Model Behaviour Tests and Fit to Data

Model behaviour tests help to assess how well a model reproduces the dynamic behaviour of interest. The proper use of such tests is to uncover flaws in the structure or parameters of the model and to determine whether they matter relative to the model purpose. A useful starting point is to ask whether model simulations fit observed historical behaviour. One way to assess goodness-of-fit is to devise formal metrics. Intuitively, such metrics compute, point-by-point, the discrepancy between simulated and real data and then take an average over the relevant time horizon (Sterman, 1984). An example is the mean absolute error (MAE) defined as the sum of the absolute differences between model generated data points X_m and actual data points X_a divided by the total number of data points n. Division by n ensures the metric is normalised.

$$\text{MAE} = \frac{1}{n} * \sum_{i=1}^{n} |X_m - X_a|$$

The lower the mean absolute error, the better the fit. Hence, if the simulated data perfectly matches the actual data, point-by-point, then the mean absolute error is zero. If the simulated data is displaced in any way from the actual data (systematically or randomly) then the mean absolute error takes a positive value. Of course the temptation is to ask 'what is a good number for MAE?', but there is no simple answer to this question. In practice it is best to use the metric alongside visual comparisons of actual and simulated data as a way to assess whether or not fit is improving when parameter and structural changes are made to the model.[6]

An alternative metric is the mean square error (MSE), defined as the sum of the squares of the differences between the model generated data points X_m and actual data points X_a divided by the total number of data points n.

$$\text{MSE} = \frac{1}{n} \sum_{i=1}^{n} (X_m - X_d)^2$$

The lower the mean square error the better the fit. There is no particular criterion for deciding which of these two metrics, MAE or MSE, is better. Either can help modellers to objectively assess whether the fit of a given model to data is improved or worsened as its parameters are varied within plausible bounds. However, the mean square error has the advantage that it can be usefully decomposed into three separate components, known as Theil's Inequality Statistics (Theil, 1966), which correspond to informal visual measures of fit that modellers often use. The inequality statistics measure how much of the mean square error between simulated and actual trajectories can be explained by: (1) bias U^M resulting from a difference between means; (2) unequal variation or 'stretch/shrinkage' U^S due to a difference in standard deviation; and (3) unequal covariation U^C caused by phase shift or unexplained variability. The components can each be expressed in terms of standard statistical measures as shown below and are defined in such a way that their sum ($U^M + U^S + U^C$) is identically equal to 1:

$$U^M = (\bar{X}_m - \bar{X}_a)^2 / \text{MSE}$$

The unequal mean or bias statistic U^M is the square of the difference between the mean of model-generated data points $\bar{X}_m$ and the mean of the actual data points $\bar{X}_a$, divided by the mean square error MSE.

$$U^S = (s_m - s_a)^2 / \text{MSE}$$

---

[6]Formal statistical estimation techniques can also be used to compare the outcomes of model simulations against observed data, and change the model parameters to minimise the discrepancy between the two. Estimation techniques that work reliably in non-linear dynamic models require the use of more advanced statistical methods than one finds in conventional linear regression The reason is that the interlocking equations in feedback systems violate standard assumptions that lie behind linear regression, such as independence and normality of errors and homoscedasticity. Full treatment of parameter estimation in dynamic models is beyond the scope of this book. Readers who are interested in the topic are referred to Rahmandad, Oliva and Osgood (2015) which includes five chapters that address different methods and considerations in the statistical estimation of model parameters in dynamic models.

The unequal variation or stretch/shrinkage statistic U^S is the square of the difference between the standard deviation of the model-generated data points s_m and the standard deviation of the actual data points s_a, divided by the mean square error MSE.

$$U^C = (s_m * s_a) * 2(1 - r)/MSE$$

The unequal covariation statistic U^C is the product of the standard deviation of model-generated data points s_m and the standard deviation of actual data points s_a multiplied by double the complement of the correlation coefficient $(1 - r)$, divided by the mean square error MSE.

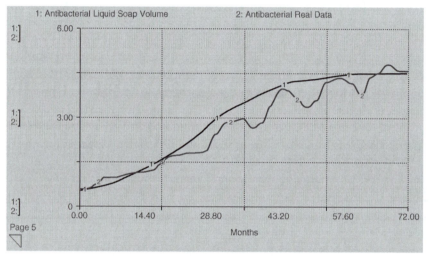

Figure 10.16   Comparing actual and simulated data

Consider the inequalities between the two trajectories shown in Figure 10.16, which are taken from the soap industry model. Line 1 shows model-generated behaviour, while line 2 is actual time series data for the same variable plotted on a scale from zero to six over a 72-month time horizon. A visual comparison suggests the two lines follow a similar path of growth and saturation. However, the actual time series contains a short-term cycle that is absent from the simulation. Also, the simulated line has a slight upward bias. The mean square error (MSE) between the two trajectories is 0.2, reflecting the broad similarity in the shape and timing of the growth trajectories. Using the Theil inequality statistics to decompose the error we find the following results. The bias U^M is 0.39, so 39% of the mean square error arises from the difference of means, reflecting the upward displacement of the simulated data points. The stretch U^S is 0.04, so only 4% of the mean square error arises from stretch or shrinkage, as there is no discernable cyclicality in the simulated data points to mimic, at smaller amplitude, the cycle in the actual data. The unequal covariation U^C is 0.58, which means that 58% of the mean square error arises from point-by-point differences caused by the unexplained cyclicality in the data. We will return later to an interpretation of the practical significance of these differences.

Qualitative tests of fit are also widely used in practice – eyeballing the magnitude, shape, periodicity and phasing of simulated trajectories and comparing to past behaviour. Such tests may appear ad hoc at first glance, but they are well suited to situations in which observations about real-world behaviour arise from a patchwork of mental, verbal and written data sources. In many modelling projects, time series data is sparse and incomplete. However, it is still possible to build confidence in model fit by ensuring that simulated trajectories are correctly scaled, pass through recognised data points, have the appropriate periodicity and relative phasing and are consistent with reliable anecdotal information about past behaviour.

An interesting example of such confidence building with limited data is provided by the World Dynamics model mentioned in Chapter 1. Part of the model's purpose was to understand the long-term dynamics of population in a world of limited resources and the problems facing humanity when industrial activity exceeds the finite carrying capacity of the earth. The time horizon of the study was two hundred years, from 1900 to 2100, and the model contained highly aggregated stock variables such as population, natural resources, capital investment, quality of life and pollution as well as a host of other interlocking auxiliary variables. The behaviour over time of population was central to the model's arguments, so it was important that its historical behaviour looked realistic. The simulated trajectory of population was calibrated using just two data points and a logical argument about the dynamics of reinforcing feedback. The following quote from World Dynamics illustrates the reasoning:

> Taking a world population of 1.6 billion in 1900 (the start of the simulation) and a world population of 3.6 billion in 1970 (at the time of the study), the cumulative growth rate has averaged 1.2 per cent per year. This is the difference between the birth rate and the death rate which we will here take as the difference between the coefficients BRN (birth rate normal) and DRN (death rate normal). A value of 0.04 for BRN (meaning that the annual birth rate is 4 per cent of the population) and a value of 0.028 for DRN (2.8 per cent of the population per year) would satisfy this 1.2 per cent difference and would be compatible with observed demographic rates for the first three-quarters of the 20th century. The reciprocal of death rate normal DRN of 0.028 implies a life expectancy at birth of 36 years (including infant mortality).

Effective calibration of the population trajectory was achieved with sparse but reliable data. By knowing population at two widely separated points in time it was possible to estimate the net growth rate of population. Then, by choosing plausible coefficients for the birth rate and death rate (the two parameters that control exponential growth), it was possible to ensure that the behaviour of population was realistic and correctly scaled over the entire historical period of the simulation from 1900 to 1970.

Tests of Fit on Simulations of the Soap Industry Model – The Base Case

No simulation model of a business or social system will ever replicate historical data perfectly. Nevertheless, if reliable time series data are available they should be used to scale the model as accurately as possible and to correct erroneous or poorly known parameter estimates and inappropriate assumptions. The objective should be to remove discrepancies that are important to the model's purpose. Any remaining discrepancies (and there will always be some) are those the model cannot explain. Remember, too, that the aim of the model is to provide an endogenous structural explanation of behaviour. Hence, it is not acceptable to 'introduce fudge factors or exogenous variables whose sole function is to improve the historical fit of the model' (Sterman, 2000: Chapter 21).

The soap industry project used historical data to build confidence in the base case simulations. The base case replicates the decision-making processes followed by the management team during the development of the liquid soap business. For comparison there was monthly data available on sales volume and price by product and by company over a period of six years. The intention in showing the base case to managers was to help them understand how their normal way of running the business led to the actual situation they were facing. In other words, the simulation moved them from actors in the business to spectators of their strategies, similar to re-playing a video of the performance of a football team after a match. Hence, it was important to compare the simulations with real data.

Figure 10.17 shows the simulated and actual sales volume for branded liquid soaps over a period of 72 months. Although the trajectories do not match perfectly, the magnitude and main trends are similar. Old English's new Antibacterial Liquid Soap volume (line 1) grows quickly during the first 36 months, as actually happened (line 2) and as the management team had hoped. From the simulator we can infer that this growth is due to two managerial actions: trialling and price reductions. The trialling effort is complemented with a large reduction in the retail price of liquid soaps that boosts the adoption rate. Meanwhile, the branded competitor's new Creamy Liquid Soap volume (line 3) grows much more slowly, as also happened in real life (line 4).

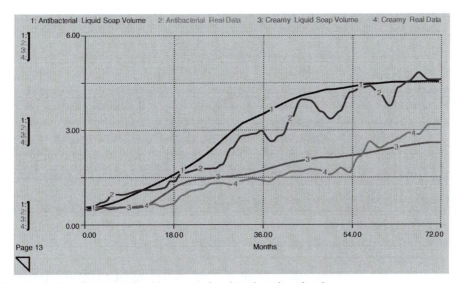

1: Antibacterial Liquid Soap Volume   2: Antibacterial Real Data   3: Creamy Liquid Soap Volume   4: Creamy Real Data

Page 13

Months

Figure 10.17   Branded liquid soaps simulated and real volumes
Source: From *Supporting Strategy: Frameworks, Methods and Models*, Edited by Frances O'Brien and Robert Dyson, 2007, © John Wiley & Sons Limited. Reproduced with permission.

After month 36, two factors reduce the growth rate of Antibacterial Liquid Soap. First, Old English's management stops reducing the price of the new product due to the early success of the launch. Sales volume after three years matches the expected market size and managers do not want to further erode the revenues from liquid soap. Second, the steady reduction in the number of bar soap users begins to slow market growth, despite the intensity of marketing actions.

It is clear from the comparison of simulated and actual data that the model realistically captures the growth trend in sales volume during the early years of liquid soap and the subsequent levelling off. These were strategically important features of the developing liquid soap market with practical lessons for management. One lesson from the simulation is that Old English's managers might have been able to further exploit the potential of the new market with more intense marketing actions at the beginning of the process. A corollary is that later marketing action is much less effective.

However, the model cannot explain everything about movements in the sales volume of liquid soaps. There is more volatility in the actual time series (lines 2 and 4) than in the simulated time series (lines 1 and 3). Specifically, the real data for Antibacterial Liquid Soap volume (line 2) contains cyclicality with a period of about one year superimposed on S-shaped growth. In contrast, the simulation exhibits smooth S-shaped growth. However, failure to capture the short-term cycle is not a serious deficiency, because the model's purpose is to examine long-term growth strategy.

In principle, the fit could be improved by adjusting the model's parameters, but in practice the model had been carefully tuned, and so the remaining discrepancies show the limited scope, in a well-grounded model such as this, for modellers to alter trajectories. Remember that important parameters such as consumers' response to promotional price (in Figures 10.14 and 10.15) have been obtained from reliable sources, independent of the time series data. These relationships cannot be modified simply to improve the fit between simulations and data. They are part of the feedback structure of the model that pre-determines its dynamic behaviour and limits the range of trajectories it can generate. Good fit is not easy to achieve in closed-loop models and is not merely a matter of twiddling parameters.

Continuing with the base case, Figure 10.18 shows simulated and real retail prices in the branded liquid soap market. Old English reduces price at an early stage to stimulate growth (lines 1 and 2). Some time later, Global Personal Care also reduces liquid soap price as a reaction to erosion of market share (lines 3 and 4). Global Personal Care's price falls until it slightly undercuts Old English's price, in an effort to sustain market share. When Global Personal Care reduces its prices, there are two effects. The first effect is to attract more bar soap users into liquid soap, which expands the liquid soap market as a whole. The second effect is to reverse the flow of customers switching from Creamy Liquid Soaps to Antibacterial Liquid Soaps.

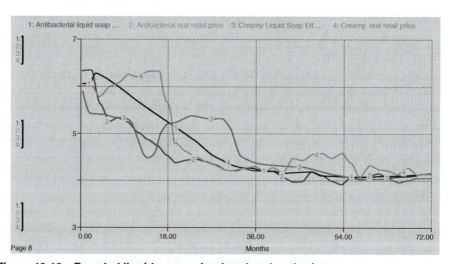

Figure 10.18 Branded liquid soaps simulated and real prices
Source: From *Supporting Strategy: Frameworks, Methods and Models*, Edited by Frances O'Brien and Robert Dyson, 2007, © John Wiley & Sons Limited. Reproduced with permission.

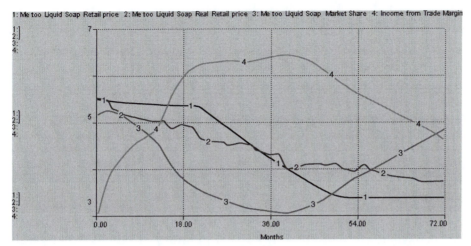

Figure 10.19 Me Too Liquid Soap: Simulated and real price; simulated market share and income from trade margin

Source: From *Supporting Strategy: Frameworks, Methods and Models*, Edited by Frances O'Brien and Robert Dyson, 2007, © John Wiley & Sons Limited. Reproduced with permission.

Supermarkets also reduce their prices as lines 1 and 2 (simulated and real price) in Figure 10.19 show. Even though supermarkets are obtaining more income from trade margin (line 4) due to growth in branded liquid soap sales, the retailers' desire to maintain market share (line 3) is reducing supermarkets' prices. When supermarkets' market share increases, prices stabilise.

The base case simulations explain the development of the liquid soap segment and the credibility of this explanation is reinforced by the visual fit with historical data. Two particular features stand out. First, an equilibrium price for Antibacterial and Creamy Liquid Soaps is established once both firms satisfy their evolving market performance goals. Supermarkets also achieve an equilibrium price once they acquire adequate bargaining power (represented here as a market share goal). Second, Old English's volume in the new product segment reaches a plateau after about four years, suggesting that growth potential is less than management had expected. This plateau is partly due to the high equilibrium price of liquid soap that reduces its attractiveness to more price-sensitive bar soap users. In addition, Global Personal Care stops losing customers to Old English when it matches Old English's price. Meanwhile, supermarkets' liquid soap volume grows strongly in the last two years of the simulation, which can be inferred from the steady rise in market share (line 3 in Figure 10.19). This growth in sales is driven by the simulated price gap between branded and Me Too products, which can be seen by comparing the price trajectories in Figures 10.18 and 10.19. However, close inspection of the time series data shows the real price gap is smaller than the simulated price gap, suggesting the need to revise the pricing formulation for Me Too liquid soap. As the price gap is made smaller, then supermarkets' sales volume and market share will reach a plateau and the liquid soap market will settle into an equilibrium similar to the mature bar soap market.

Tests of Learning from Simulation

Simulations can achieve more than mimicking history. Like Papert's gears of childhood, a simulator is a transitional object to improve understanding through testing and reflection. With a simulator it is possible to conduct a wide range of experiments to better interpret past behaviour (as in the base case above), to explain surprise behaviour, to learn about future behaviour, to test pet theories and hypotheses and to correct faulty expectations. Whenever a model provides useful new insight (to the client or to the modeller) then it passes the test of learning from simulation. Some of the most common learning tests are described below.

Comparing Simulations with Expectations and Interpreting Surprise Behaviour

How will the future unfold if no changes are made to the conduct of the business? Managers have their own views and opinions on this question against which to compare simulations and invite discussion. The soap industry model was run five years into the future with the same parameters as in the base case to reflect the assumption that the firm's decision-making processes continue unchanged. This business-as-usual projection led to several insights deemed worthy of discussion. It showed that the retail price of bar soap will rise in the future. At first glance, this result is surprising because the bar soap business is price sensitive and highly competitive. On reflection there is a good explanation. The price rise is a response to increased manufacturing cost caused by falling sales volume and reduced scale economies in traditional bar soap production. The simulation also showed that growth in sales volume of liquid soap will be limited by three factors. First, the diminishing pool of bar soap users means that, as the new market becomes saturated, it will be more difficult to sustain the same conversion rate to liquid soap as in the previous five years. Second, the reaction of competitors, especially supermarkets, starts to attract price-sensitive consumers to liquid soap. Third, stabilising the new product's price in the aftermath of initial successful growth establishes a price difference in favour of supermarkets' products that, in the medium to long term, will erode the client company's market volume.

Partial Model Simulations to Examine Pet Theories and Misconceptions

Pet theories and overly optimistic expectations often stem from idealised mental models that overlook real world constraints. One way to illustrate such misconceptions is to deliberately simplify a model, by switching off complete sectors or eliminating feedback loops, to show that a partial model can simulate an outcome that people were expecting. The correspondence between expected and simulated outcome frequently shows the rationale for pet theories (albeit flawed), which is reassuring to model users and helps to engage their interest. Partial model simulations provide an alternative way to build confidence in the model, much different than time series fit, by showing the circumstances in which simulation matches intuition. From this basis of agreement the modeller then overlays the extra feedback structure contained in the full model to show its confounding effect on dynamics.

In the soap industry project, lack of awareness of the effect of supermarkets on the development of the liquid soap business was a particularly important strategic misconception.[7] To highlight this misconception, a comparison of three runs was made, as shown in Figure 10.20. The first run shows what would happen if no competitors were able to copy the liquid soap innovation: an optimistic belief in first-mover advantage that was widely shared among the management team. This partial model test was conducted by setting to zero all the flow rates in the new product sector of the market model except the Antibacterial Liquid Soap adoption rate.

---

[7]Perhaps the single most important contribution of the modelling project to new product strategy development at Old English was to clarify the powerful role that supermarkets now play in exploiting the commercial benefits of successful new grocery products. Branded manufacturers invest heavily in developing such new products, tooling up to manufacture them, and then advertising to win customers. Meanwhile, supermarkets watch and wait like predators. As soon as there is tangible evidence from shelf sales that a new product is becoming popular then supermarkets move swiftly to offer an equivalent own-label product, without all the development costs and risks incurred by branded manufacturers. Retailers' own-labels can be priced low and still be profitable. Moreover, since supermarkets control shelf space, they can ensure consumer visibility for their own-label products and simultaneously manage the trade margins they receive from branded manufacturers who initiate product innovations. The refined conceptual model in Figure 10.8 reveals supermarkets as the potent rivals they have now become. Simulations such as those in Figure 10.20 demonstrate just how effective Me Too products can be. These findings constituted an important shift in Old English's perception of competition and rivalry in fast-moving consumer goods, a shift that is captured in the differences between Figure 10.7 (the management team's first conceptual model of the soap market) and Figure 10.8 (the refined conceptual model). Interestingly, the insights from the project are consistent with marketing literature that recognises a new competitive reality in the retail industry stemming from growth in private labels. The strategic marketing implications for branded manufacturers in general are documented and analysed by Nirmalya Kumar and Jan-Benedict Steenkamp (2007).

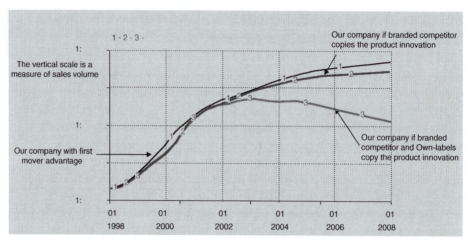

Figure 10.20 Partial model experiments: alternative trajectories for sales volume of liquid soap as imagined first-mover advantage fades and rivals imitate the new product

Source: From Supporting Strategy: Frameworks, Methods and Models, Edited by Frances O'Brien and Robert Dyson, 2007, © John Wiley & Sons Limited. Reproduced with permission.

Sales volume of liquid soap (line 1) expands swiftly in the historical period to 2004 and then settles into a pattern of sustained slow growth. Continuous growth was exactly what managers were expecting and hoping for. The second run showed the company's sales as if the other branded competitor were the only rival able to imitate the new product: a recognition that imitation is possible, but still an optimistic view since the branded competitor is the least disruptive rival (due to its similar cost structure and pricing policies). This partial model test was conducted by setting to zero the adoption rate and switch rates for Me Too liquid soap. Sales volume of Old English's liquid soap (line 2) is slightly lower than before and again seems to confirm the assumption of first-mover advantage. The third and final run showed the company's sales if both the branded competitor and supermarkets were able to quickly imitate liquid soap. This test was conducted with the complete model. Sales volume of liquid soap (line 3) expands for four years but then declines as supermarkets capture new customers from the branded manufacturers by pushing price down.

Family Member Tests

A model developed for a specific situation can often be generalised to other comparable situations. In other words, it is a member of a family of models. For example, the soap industry model, developed for the UK market, was used to test the introduction of liquid soaps in other countries such as France and

Germany by changing the initial conditions and by adjusting selected parameters. The recalibration process and, later on, simulations helped members of the project team to appreciate country differences in the growth of the new product and the performance of the traditional bar soap business.

Policy Implication Tests

A particularly powerful test for building confidence in a model is when simulations correctly predict the results of policy change in situations where the policy has been tried. A good example comes from a modelling project with the Harley-Davidson motorcycle company (mentioned in Chapter 4), whose purpose was to investigate Harley's dwindling market share in service parts and, if possible, reverse it. A policy recommendation based on model simulations was for management to invest in a large inventory of finished motorbikes in order to alleviate internal competition for capacity between bikes and service parts. A specific prediction from the model was that bikes produced for inventory under this policy would end up in the dealer network rather than in the factory – a result that was not intuitively obvious. Moreover, the model provided a plausible explanation of this phenomenon. Hence, when the policy was implemented in the real world and the dealers snapped up the extra bikes, then the model's credibility in the eyes of management was greatly enhanced.

Understanding Competitive Dynamics in Fast-moving Consumer Goods

The management team extracted a number of general insights from the soap industry model and simulations that clarified their understanding of competitive dynamics in the industry. The causal loop diagram in Figure 10.21 provides an example. The figure concentrates on bar soap, but similar processes are at work for liquid soap. The interaction between price and capacity is important. Sales volume drives manufacturing capacity. If manufacturing capacity rises then cost of goods sold declines due to economies of scale (and vice versa). Lower cost leads to lower price. Low price increases the value for money of the product thereby attracting more customers and more sales volume. Once established, success breeds success around the reinforcing loop R1 (market dominance dynamics) leading to a gradual demise of rivals unable to compete due to their higher costs. An effective way for competitors to halt this reinforcing process is to reduce the attractiveness of leader's products as soon as possible, either by launching similar products or by reducing prices, as occurred in liquid soap.

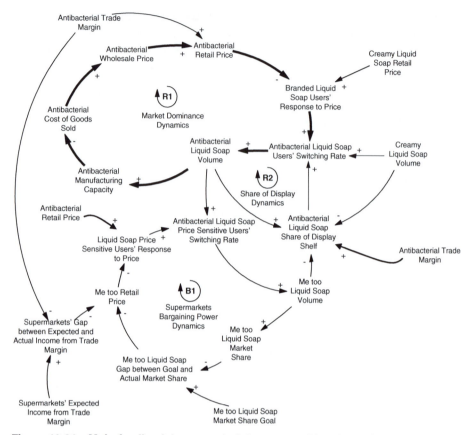

Figure 10.21 Main feedback loops underlying competitive dynamics in the FMCG industry

Source: From *Supporting Strategy: Frameworks, Methods and Models*, Edited by Frances O'Brien and Robert Dyson, 2007, © John Wiley & Sons Limited. Reproduced with permission.

An additional effect is the power of retailers to control the allocation of shelf space. As mentioned, display shelf is a fiercely contested resource in fast-moving consumer goods and has a major influence on the effectiveness of price promotions and advertising. Companies in the industry use trade margin to negotiate their share of display shelf with retailers. Higher sales volume and market share normally command greater share of display shelf because of the additional income for the retailer. Additional shelf space attracts more customers and higher sales volume and these relationships form reinforcing loop R2 (share of display dynamics).

However, there is more to the allocation of shelf space than sales volume alone. Retailers can use the display shelf for their own private label products and use this threat to negotiate attractive trade margins. Competitors with low market share may buy display shelf by offering a better trade margin to retailers, providing they are willing to accept a compensating reduction of gross margin in order to remain price competitive. Private label products therefore enable retailers to control the strength of the two reinforcing loops R1 and R2.

Summary of Confidence Building Tests

This chapter has introduced a variety of tests that can help build confidence in models. The tests fall into the three broad categories shown in Figure 10.22. There are tests of behaviour, tests of structure and tests of learning. None of these tests proves that a model is valid in the sense of being the best possible representation of the problem situation. But taken in combination, they demonstrate to modellers and clients that a given model is fit for purpose and of adequate quality.

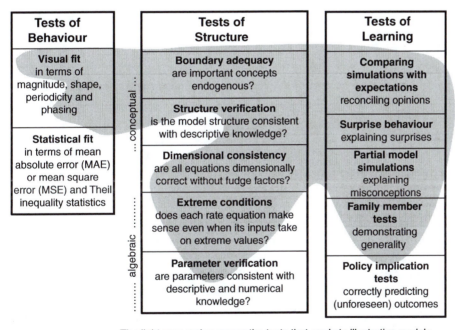

The light grey region covers the tests that apply to illustrative models

Figure 10.22   Opportunities for building confidence in models

Tests of behaviour include the visual fit between simulated and actual data in terms of the magnitude, shape, periodicity and phasing of trajectories. Good visual fit is a common and effective way to build confidence in a model because it is a criterion people readily understand, even if they are not modellers. Statistical fit is a similar but more formal test where goodness-of-fit is measured numerically in terms of mean absolute error (MAE), mean square error (MSE) and the Theil inequality statistics. Of course, fit alone does not prove a model is 'correct', it simply shows the model is capable of replicating behaviour from the real world.

Tests of structure evaluate the quality of a model according to criteria that experienced modellers recognise and follow. The tests are like those a craftsman might apply to a piece of furniture or a musical instrument. Is the device well designed and carefully constructed with good materials? Design is a property mainly of the conceptual model, and two tests apply. Boundary adequacy is a test of whether important concepts are endogenous and if the model has a clear closed-loop feedback structure. This is an important criterion for system dynamics models because, in a well-conceptualised model, the dynamic behaviour of interest should arise endogenously from interacting feedback loops (Meadows, 1980). Structure verification is another test of design that requires that the assumptions underlying model structure are consistent with descriptive knowledge. Quality of construction is a property mainly of the algebraic model, and three tests apply. The most widely used is dimensional consistency to check that equations are dimensionally correct, so the units on the left of the equation balance the units on the right without the use of fudge factors. Extreme condition tests investigate whether each rate equation makes sense and delivers a plausible output when its inputs take on extreme values. This is a powerful test that brings to bear common-sense checks on the formulation of individual equations. For example, in a fisheries model, if the fish population were to fall to zero then logically the catch rate should also fall to zero – no matter how large the fleet size that normally determines the catch when fish are plentiful. Parameter verification provides yet another test of quality of construction. Are parameters consistent with descriptive and numerical knowledge?

Tests of learning differ fundamentally from tests of behaviour or structure because they apply to the interaction between the formal model and people's mental models rather than to the fidelity or quality of the formal model itself. There are five tests listed. The most common test of learning is to compare simulations with expectations as a means of reconciling, through dialogue, conflicting opinions about likely outcomes. Notice this comparison is not the same as visual or statistical fit to data, since the comparator is people's expectations (from their mental models) rather than time series (from the real world). Surprise behaviour is a test often applied by modellers themselves who form their own expectations about likely model behaviour (Mass, 1991). Every so often, a model produces totally unexpected behaviour for reasons that, on close inspection, turn out to be entirely plausible. In such cases, both the modeller and the project team learn something new from the simulator.

Next on the list of tests of learning are partial model simulations that help to explain people's misconceptions about dynamic behaviour. They build confidence in the model by simulating a deliberately simplified feedback structure whose behaviour often coincides with outcomes people were expecting. Complex or counterintuitive behaviour of the full model is more understandable if it can be shown to arise, step-by-step, from partial model behaviour that is intuitively obvious.

Two more tests of learning complete the list. Family member tests demonstrate the generality of a given model by showing that its structure and feedback loops, when parameterised differently, can be applied to a broad class of related situations. Finally, policy implication tests are simulations that correctly predict the outcome of policy changes prior to implementation. They are a good way to build confidence in models because they clearly demonstrate that modelling improves foresight, particularly if a correctly predicted policy outcome was unforeseen by those responsible for the policy.

Modellers do not apply all the tests exhaustively. Instead, they use just enough tests to convince the client (and themselves) that the model is adequate for its purpose and provides a reliable basis for understanding and action. Some tests such as statistical fit or parameter verification best apply to relatively detailed and calibrated models such as the soap industry model. Other tests such as boundary adequacy, dimensional consistency and extreme conditions apply to models of all sizes. Tests of learning such as comparing simulations with expectations or surprise behaviour also apply to all models but are particularly useful for small illustrative models such as the market growth model in Chapter 7 or the simple factory model in Chapter 5 for which objective comparisons of simulations with time series data are impossible (due to the generic nature of the model formulations).

A guide to the applicability of tests is depicted by shading in Figure 10.22. The light grey region covers the tests most appropriate for illustrative models whose purpose is to capture the essence of feedback structure without necessarily being accurately calibrated to a particular case situation. For example, tests of behaviour on the simple factory model in Chapter 5 are confined to visual fit in terms of shape, periodicity and phasing. Statistical fit is meaningless for such a model and so is visual fit in terms of magnitude since the model's scaling is arbitrary. The most appropriate tests of structure on illustrative models are boundary adequacy, dimensional consistency and extreme conditions. Only a limited amount of structure and parameter verification is possible since there are few opportunities to compare the assumptions of an illustrative model with descriptive and numerical knowledge from the real world. Tests of learning apply particularly well to illustrative models because they are small and transparent enough to promote improved understanding, which is at the heart of learning. By design, illustrative models pass the family member test as their feedback structure is intended to be generalisable. Illustrative models also lend themselves to tests that explain surprises and misconceptions.

Conclusion – Model Fidelity and Usefulness

The reasons why different models present different opportunities for confidence building brings us full circle to the philosophical issue of model fidelity and usefulness that began the chapter. What is the value of a deliberately simplified model or representation of business or society? This question lies at the heart of the art and science of modelling and provides an appropriate conclusion for the book as well as an opportunity to review the various models we have covered along the way.

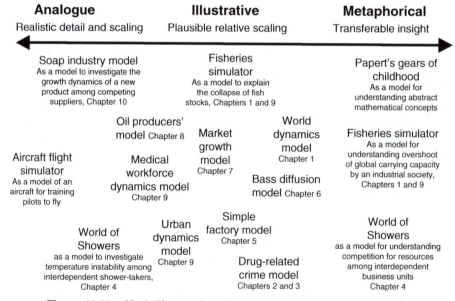

Figure 10.23   Modelling and realism – a spectrum of model fidelity

Models range in size from large and detailed to elegantly small and general. The spectrum is illustrated in Figure 10.23. On the left are analogue models, in the middle are illustrative models and on the right are metaphorical models. To appreciate the distinctions along this axis of fidelity compare the dictionary definitions of analogy and metaphor. According to Webster's Dictionary, analogy is derived from the Greek word analogia meaning proportion and equality of ratios. More specifically an analogy is an explaining of something by comparing it point-by-point with something else. For example, one might liken the atom to a miniature solar system (as the physicist Rutherford originally did) in which planet-like electrons circle around a sun-like nucleus. On the other hand, metaphor comes from the Greek word metaphora, a transferring to one word the sense of another. A metaphor is a figure of speech in which one thing is likened to another different thing by being spoken of as if it were that other. Consider for example the description in the following sentence. 'The tram, arriving with a tap-tapping of overhead wires, was a giant yellow grasshopper rubbing its steel legs together' (Miller, 2001).

Both analogies and metaphors can help us make sense of the world, but their usefulness for this purpose should be judged differently. An analogy derives its usefulness in large part from the fidelity of the point-by-point comparison and the implications that can be drawn from the comparison. So Rutherford's atom as a miniature solar system was a big step forward from previous analogies that compared atoms to ball bearings or incompressible plum puddings. In that relative sense it was a useful analogy.[8] By contrast, metaphors are looser. They do not purport to fit the situation point-by-point. Instead, they evoke vivid images in the minds of readers that help them to better envisage the situation, to examine more closely the imagined similarities, and thereby learn something new about their world. The usefulness of the metaphor is not so much in its fidelity but rather in its ability to stimulate reflection and learning. Hence, the comparison of a tram with a grasshopper mentioned above helps one to visualise the tram scene better. Whether or not the metaphor turns out to be completely accurate is not the main point. It simply needs to be plausible and vivid enough to fire the imagination.

Analogue models portray problem situations with close attention to realistic detail and accurate scaling. Examples shown in Figure 10.23 are the soap industry model, World of Showers in Chapter 4 (as a model to investigate temperature instability among interdependent shower-takers) and, at the extreme of fidelity, an aircraft flight simulator. By contrast, illustrative models portray problem situations in terms of realistic feedback loops, but with less attention to detail and scaling. Examples are the market growth model in Chapter 7, the simple factory model in Chapter 5 and the fisheries simulators in Chapters 1 and 9.

---

[8]However, viewing the atom as a miniature solar system later turned out to be a flawed analogy (though still useful) because it did not predict the stability and longevity of atoms. If one took seriously the point-by-point comparison of planetary electrons orbiting a miniature solar nucleus then the electrons should lose energy through radiation and spiral inwards to the centre, which they don't. This paradox was subsequently fixed with the quantum mechanical atom.

Between analogue and illustrative lie the urban dynamics and medical workforce dynamics models in Chapter 9. They are each of moderate size and complexity (50 to 100 equations). Both models include realistic detail about the institutions they represent (city or hospital) and are scaled with real-world data. The medical workforce model draws its terminology, parameters and structure from the personal mental database of an experienced doctor and from numerous medical journal articles. The urban dynamics model, though quite abstract and dynamically complex, draws its structure and parameters from the collective mental database of city experts. The oil producers' model in Chapter 8 also lies between analogue and illustrative with its structure and parameters drawn from oil industry experts.

Metaphorical models portray feedback structure or inner workings in one domain to aid understanding of a problem situation in an entirely different domain. Examples are World of Showers in Chapter 4 (if used as a model for understanding competition for resources among interdependent business units), or the fisheries simulator in Chapters 1 and 9 (if used as a model for understanding overshoot of global carrying capacity by an industrial society).

Despite the appeal of illustrative and metaphorical models, fidelity of representation is surely important too. Common sense demands that a useful model bears some resemblance to the situation at hand. Simulators of fantasy worlds do exist (such as Tomb Raider featuring Lara Croft), but intense interaction with a fantasy world does not enhance understanding of practical policy and strategy. Nevertheless, where to draw the line on realism is an interesting question, particularly in models of complex and poorly understood systems.

Consider again the two different uses of the World of Showers simulator indicated in Figure 10.23. In Chapter 4, it was presented as an analogue model representing hotel showers whose occupants unwittingly share a fixed supply of hot water. The comfort-seeking shower-takers become locked into an escalating battle for hot water. The result is wild and persistent temperature fluctuations and deep frustration because neither shower-taker achieves a comfortable temperature – just like the real world. However, the same model is also a good metaphorical model to understand the puzzling dynamics of resource allocation among infighting departments of a firm. Internal competition for resources is common among departments that share manufacturing capacity or skilled salesforce. The resulting cyclical behaviour is often dysfunctional, as the shared resource moves back and forth between departments. The shower simulator is a vivid metaphor for this expensive tug-of-war that sparks lively debate among experienced business people about how best to control cyclicality and infighting through improved communication and greater tolerance of temporary performance shortfalls.

The hotel shower model is obviously not a realistic model of a multi-department firm. Yet it stimulates thinking about organisational dynamics because insights from shower simulations are transferable to the firm. A passage by Herbert Simon (1999: 18), about 'simulation as a source of new knowledge' helps to explain why:

> This brings me to the crucial question about simulation: how can a simulation ever tell us anything we do not already know? The usual implication of the question is that it can't ... There are two related ways in which simulation can provide new knowledge – one of them obvious, the other perhaps a bit subtle. The obvious point is that, even when we have correct premises, it may be very difficult to discover what they imply. All correct reasoning is a grand system of tautologies, but only God can make direct use of that fact. The rest of us must painstakingly and fallibly tease out the consequences of our assumptions ... The more interesting and subtle question is whether simulation can be of any help to us when we do not know very much initially about the natural laws that govern the behavior of the inner system ... Artificial systems and adaptive systems ... have properties that make them particularly susceptible to simulation via simplified models ... Resemblance in behavior of systems without identity of the inner systems is particularly feasible if the aspects in which we are interested arise out of the organization of the parts, independently of all but a few properties of the individual components.

The idea that artificial and adaptive systems display behaviour arising from the organisation of their parts is entirely consistent with the core structural philosophy of system dynamics. It is another way of saying that 'structure gives rise to dynamic behaviour' ... regardless of context. Hence, a hotel shower simulator is a useful model for managers interested in dysfunctional dynamics of organisational resource sharing because it captures (in a vivid and amusing way) the feedback structure of interdependent and competing goal-seeking processes.

It is no coincidence that some of the smallest models are also the most insightful. Influential models such as World Dynamics, the market growth model and the Bass diffusion model have achieved their influence because they capture the essential structure and underlying regularities that underpin important dynamic phenomena and are accessible enough that people can test, reflect and learn from them. They are powerful transitional objects for better understanding our complex business and social world.

Endnote: The Loops of Feedback

Some years ago an edited book was published in tribute to Barry Richmond, a leader and pioneer thinker in system dynamics. The book (*Tracing Connections* by J. Richmond, *et al.*, 2010) shares stories from experienced modellers about systems thinking and the importance of its use in a world of growing interdependence. In a chapter about metaphorical models I wrote some verses entitled *The Loops of Feedback*, inspired by the theme of the edited book. They evoke the special contribution that system dynamics makes to the social sciences.[9] The words were penned to fit the melody of a famous song, called *The Streets of London*, composed by British folk singer Ralph McTell. Incidentally, the verse about the 'coiled-up slinky' refers to a vivid teaching demonstration, devised by Barry, to show the relationship between structure and behaviour over time.

Have you seen the asset stocks in the multi-looped beer game?
Amplifying orders when consumers drink more beer
The factory's working overtime and still the stocks are in decline
Feast then turns to famine but the reason is unclear.

Refrain (to be sung after each verse)

So how can you tell me that life's optimal?
Don't say we're rational all the time
Let me take you by the hand
I'll lead you through the loops of feedback
I'll show you something that will make you change your mind.

In the Fish Banks model, at the fish rate formulations
There are non-linear functions confounding fishermen's lives
Their ships return empty when once there was plenty
The sudden collapsed fishery is yesterday's surprise.

Have you glimpsed intangibles within the airline simulator?
Determining the destiny of People Express
Declining motivation and service degradation
Feed back to undermine the firm's growth and success.

Have you seen the coiled-up slinky's fascinating oscillations?
Showing that in structure dynamic patterns lie
There's no need for forcing factors only nature's spring-mass strictures
Plus the covert force of gravity's steady tie.

Reminder of refrain (to be sung after each verse)

So how can you tell me that life's optimal?
Don't say we're rational all the time

---

[9]The song and its refrain question the view of policy advisers who assume that the objective rationality of market mechanisms will prevail and help us to solve the problems faced by society. However, there are many real-world situations where markets are imperfect or non-existent. Moreover, even where reliable markets and pricing institutions exist, experimental studies show that, at best, they moderate but do not eliminate misperceptions of feedback in dynamic decision tasks (Kampmann and Sterman, 2014). We also need 'loops of feedback' and simulation to make sense of our complex and interdependent world – plus the ability and patience to communicate the merits of a feedback systems view to others (Repenning, 2003).

Let me take you by the hand
I'll lead you through the loops of feedback
I'll show you something that will make you change your mind.

Have you heard of misperceptions, turning into paradoxes
In the way that systems behave over time?
Information overrun and localised rules of thumb
Cause not only cycles but stagnation and decline.

In all problem situations, there are hidden feedback loops
Shaping how events unfold within our times
Despite complex society there's no need for anxiety
Just design better policies and we'll all lead better lives.

Ending Refrain (slightly modified)

So even though life is not optimal
And we're not truly rational in our minds
Let me take you by the hand
I'll lead you through the loops of feedback
Together we'll find something that will lead to better times.

(from *Tracing Connections: Voices of Systems Thinkers*, edited by Joy Richmond, Lees Stuntz, Kathy Richmond and Joanne Egner, copyright 2010 isee systems, inc. and The Creative Learning Exchange, reproduced with permission)

References

Forrester, J.W. (1975) Counterintuitive behavior of social systems. In *Collected Papers of Jay W. Forrester*. Waltham, MA: Productivity Press.

Forrester, J.W. (1994) Policies, decisions and information sources for modelling. In Morecroft, J.D.W. and Sterman, J.D. (eds), *Modeling for Learning Organizations*. Portland, OR: Productivity Press.

Forrester, J.W. and Senge, P. (1980) Tests for building confidence in system dynamics models. In Legasto, A., Forrester, J. and Lyneis, J. (eds), *System Dynamics TIMS Studies in the Management Sciences*, vol 14. New York: North Holland, pp. 209–228.

Kampmann, C.E. and Sterman, J.D. (2014) Do markets mitigate misperceptions of feedback? *System Dynamics Review*, 30(3): 123–160.

Kumar, N. and Steenkamp, J.B. (2007) *Private Labels: Competing with and against Store Brands*. Boston, MA: Harvard Business School Press.

Kunc, M. (2005) Dynamics of Competitive Industries: A Micro Behavioural Framework. PhD thesis, London Business School.

Kunc, M. and Morecroft, J.D.W. (2007) System dynamics modelling for strategic development. In O'Brien, F. and Dyson, R. (eds), *Supporting Strategy*. Chichester: John Wiley & Sons.

Mass, N.J. (1991) Diagnosing surprise model behaviour: A tool for evolving behavioural and policy insights. *System Dynamics Review*, 7(1): 68–86.

Meadows, D.H. (1980) The unavoidable a priori. In Randers, J. (ed.), *Elements of the System Dynamics Method*. Available from the System Dynamics Society www.systemdynamics.org, originally published by MIT Press, Cambridge, MA.

Meyer, R. and Johnson, E.J. (1995) Empirical generalizations in the modelling of consumer choice. *Marketing Science*, 14(3): G180–G189.

Miller, A. (2001) *Oxygen*. London: Sceptre.

Morecroft, J.D.W. (2004) Mental models and learning in system dynamics practice. In Pidd, M. (Ed.), *Systems Modelling – Theory and Practice*. Chichester: John Wiley & Sons.

Papert, S. (1980) *Mindstorms: Children, Computers and Powerful Ideas*. New York: Basic Books.

Pidd, M. (ed.) (2004) *Systems Modelling – Theory and Practice*. Chichester: John Wiley & Sons.

Rahmandad, H., Oliva, R. and Osgood, N. (eds) (2015) *Analytical Methods for Dynamic Modelers*, Cambridge MA: MIT Press. See in particular Section 1 on Calibration and Estimation.

Repenning, N. (2003) Selling system dynamics to other social scientists. *System Dynamics Review*, 19(4): 303–327.

Richmond, J., Stuntz, L., Richmond, K. and Egner, J. (eds) (2010) *Tracing Connections: Voices of Systems Thinkers*. An edited volume in tribute to Barry Richmond, isee systems publications, Lebanon NH and The Creative Learning Exchange, Acton MA.

Simon, H.A. (1999) *The Sciences of the Artificial* (3rd edn). Cambridge, MA: MIT Press.

Sterman, J.D. (1984) Appropriate summary statistics for evaluating the historical fit of system dynamics models. *Dynamica*, 10: 51–66.

Sterman, J.D. (2000) *Business Dynamics: Systems Thinking and Modeling for a Complex World*. Boston, MA: Irwin McGraw-Hill.

Theil, H. (1966) *Applied Economic Forecasting*. Amsterdam: North Holland.

About the Website Resources

To get the most out of *Strategic Modelling and Business Dynamics* it is important to develop a good intuitive feel for 'dynamics' – how and why things change through time.

The **Learners' website** holds chapter-by-chapter learning support folders, which contain models and gaming simulators that will allow you to run simulations for themselves and to reproduce the time charts and dynamics described in the book.

To access, go to www.wiley.com/go/strategicmodelling2e and locate the link to the **Learners' website** – you will be prompted to enter your email address and the password, which is '11884468'.

There are also additional resources available for instructors, hosted on the **Instructors' website**, which include PowerPoint slides with notes to accompany the book, as well as workshops, assignments, reports and video lectures.

To access, go to www.wiley.com/go/strategicmodelling2e and locate the link to the **Instructors' website.**

Index

Printed and bound by CPI Group (UK) Ltd, Croydon, CR0 4YY